The Street I Know

The Street I Know

The Autobiography of the Last of the Bohemians

HAROLD E. STEARNS

M. EVANS
Lanham • Boulder • New York • Toronto • Plymouth, UK

Published by M. Evans
An imprint of Rowman & Littlefield
4501 Forbes Boulevard, Suite 200, Lanham, Maryland 20706
www.rowman.com

10 Thornbury Road, Plymouth PL6 7PP, United Kingdom

Distributed by National Book Network

First paperback edition 2014

British Library Cataloguing in Publication Information Available

Library of Congress Cataloging-in-Publication Data

Library of Congress Control Number: 2014947807

ISBN: 978-1-59077-489-2 (pbk. : alk. paper)
ISBN: 978-1-59077-490-8 (electronic)

∞™ The paper used in this publication meets the minimum requirements of American National Standard for Information Sciences—Permanence of Paper for Printed Library Materials, ANSI/NISO Z39.48-1992.

Printed in the United States of America

"The wind blows cold down every street,
But coldest down the street I know."

C. D.—*Paris, 1920*

CONTENTS

The Street I Know

I. ACCIDENTALLY I GET BORN

"WHY," one of my alert classmates at Harvard once asked me, "do all the old autobiographies begin with the statement, 'I was born, at so-and-so on such-and-such a date, of poor but honest parents'?"

I shrugged my shoulders to indicate that I didn't know. He enlarged upon his question, his tone becoming mock-indignant.

"Why *'but'?* Would it not be more correct to say, 'I was born, at so-and-so on such-and-such a date, of poor *and'*—therefore or consequently being understood—'honest parents'? Why the opposition expressed by *'but'?"*

My classmate snorted.

"For God's sake," he said with great weariness, "if ever you come to write *your* autobiography—a fate I wouldn't wish my worst enemy—please, at least, begin it with this sentence: 'Born of poor, and consequently honest and decent parents, I reluctantly saw the light of day at——"

* * *

At Barre, Massachusetts, on May 7, 1891.

Or so I was told later—and have every reason to believe. Certainly my earliest recollection is of running after a "horse and wagon"—in which was a boy I knew—along a country road near Wakefield, Massachusetts; and I couldn't have been much more than three or four, because I didn't go to school until later. And going to school, in the Massachusetts of those days, as now, meant being five years old. Somehow, too, the words "eighteen ninety-five" have always been associated with that, my first clear memory of anything—words spoken by somebody in answer to a question propounded by a little girl, with a pigtail down her back and in bare feet, whose picture is almost as clear in my mind as that of the horse and wagon. And it was summer, too (I can remember *that* now); my May birthday must have gone by; I was a little over four years old.

It was only a few weeks or so later, for it was still near Wakefield, still the same summer, when I first became aware that I was different, that I had no father. For then I don't think I should have known what was meant, when you said anybody was dead. Like all young animals, I ran away from death emotionally as well as physically, whenever I saw it in the form of a still bird blown down from the nest by the wind, or a cat, which, I still remember hearing somebody say, "had gone into a dark corner to die." Also I can recall my mother telling me "Your father is in Heaven," which I thought was a place to which one might really travel—when one was a bit older and could do what one wanted.

The real facts of the matter, as I subsequently found out, were simply that I was a posthumous child. My father had died three months before I was born—suddenly, from heart disease, something that, during my early teens, I thought I had "inherited." His death—in Brockton, Massachusetts, where he had been in the retail jewelry business, owning a little store of his own, and where he had always planned to build a house, the blue-print plans of which my mother used to show me later on (and those plans I can remember to this day)—his death, I repeat, had so upset her, my mother told me, that she had temporarily lost her mind. As a result, she had not only forfeited all claims to what little property he had intended to leave her but didn't (dying intestate), but also she had had to be confined for a few months in a sanitarium in or near Barre, where I was born. She had recovered her reason shortly after I came into the world, but God had left her "a penniless widow with two children to support." The accuracy of this I cannot, of course, vouch for, but certainly my mother lived up to all those claims she imposed upon herself—which would have naturally resulted, *had* the story been true. (And for all I know, substantially it was true; though my brother, later on, for no good reason I ever was able to discover, gratuitously made my childhood miserable with—whenever I thought of them—dark hints that I did not "know the whole story.") In any case, my mother fought a valiant and surprisingly successful battle to keep her children and to keep up a home. Not many women would have had her courage. As a boy, I was supersensitive to her small faults; as a man, I now want to pay tribute to her indomitable spirit.

Only flashes of memory illuminate those early years. There were rides in the old-fashioned street-cars through Boston and many of the small suburbs; there was a month or so in a "home," where there were the clatter of small children in a yard—and all the children dressed alike in a kind of grey-blue suit, almost like a prison uniform—and the tasteless breakfasts with thin milk and not enough sugar for the oatmeal. But there are some visual images which still keep a certain vividness, and many of them, especially those of natural beauties like the ocean, marshes, frozen little brooks through the winter woods, hills, and country meadows under a broiling July and August sun, give me a kind of clue to what was, when all is said and done, a rather solitary and unhappy young boyhood.

Cliftondale near Swampscott and Lynn and Malden—then a little town—is for me the most enduring of those visual memories. I lived there with "Pa" and "Aunt" Gallup, some friends of my mother's. "Pa" ran a grocery store, with a Bon Ami sign hung up in the back (I remember that sign, which I used to pronounce "Bon-Am-I," with its chicken and its slogan, "Hasn't Scratched Yet!"), the cracker barrels—

which were literally just that—of the epoch, the sweet and pungent spices, the candy counter for children of my age with its two-for-a-penny licorice sticks, the soft, glue-like fly-paper, the bars and bars of neatly wrapped, clean-smelling soap. Pa Gallup had a bad limp—acquired during the Civil War—and had to hobble around the store with a big cane. Once in a while, when business was slack, he would tell me stories: I like to think now that he was fond of me—as I know I was of him. Occasionally I would run errands for him, and I was particularly proud when I was entrusted with some big order, which involved a half dozen packages.

From atop the little hill, only a short distance from Pa Gallup's store, one might see across the marshes to the ocean, with the blur of industrial Lynn in the hazy distance to the left. There were sailboats a-plenty, and now and then a steamer with its smoke trailing lazily behind it. When I got tired of looking at the sea and the boats, I would lie on my back in the soft, warm grass and watch the clouds drifting by, building magic castles in the air and day-dreaming all kinds of wonderful and pleasant things—just as do all children of that age. On other days I would take the two or three mile walk down to "the marshes" with a boy who lived in the house across the street from Pa's store. There was a salt-water swimming pool there, when you had been taught the secret of how to find it, but I had not yet learned to swim and could only paddle in the brackish seven or eight square yards of water. Other days my friend and I would go to the pine woods, atop another small hill which we passed on our way down to the marsh swimming-pool. My friend was three or four years older than I, and he delighted in telling me all kinds of fantastic yarns (whether he believed them or not I don't know), many of which I did not understand—particularly the sexual stories, for he was at just that age when he "knew all about it."

Fortunately, most of these stories didn't register very deeply; my mind and imagination were always on other things. I lived in a world of phantasy of my own. But I would break through that protective shell of my own dreaming now and then—often enough, I now remember, to become aware that what my friend was telling me about the mysteries of life did two things, rather contradictory: they shocked, yet at the same time attracted me. Alternately I felt a curious youthful shame (or perhaps it was just a vague fear of punishment, for I had been taught these things were "naughty") and a strange new excitement. But as I have said, I would soon go back into my shell. And this withdrawal was only partly due to my temperament; in a strange way it was also due to my experience, that is, my knowledge that I had nobody with whom to talk over these things. (I had tried Pa Gallup once or twice, but he had, I noticed even then, quickly changed the subject.) If only I had had a father! My friend's talks made me a little bitter —"there's nobody *I* can talk with," I used to say to myself. And I would feel strange and lonely.

The summer before I entered school—that is, the summer of 1896—when I was five years old (over a year had gone by since I had seen that girl with the pig-tail down her back near Wakefield!), my mother had some sort of temporary good fortune which permitted her to send me for my vacation (of course all my life, in one sense, had been nothing else up to that time) to the country town of my birth, Barre, Massachusetts. I think some of the early Singer Sewing Machine factories were there then, but the town was still predominantly rural—and the train that took me out from the North Station in Boston seemed to go on and on forever, though it was in fact only a question of two or three hours. I felt very "set up" at being able to take such a long and perilous journey by myself.

Barre meant little to me because it was my birthplace, but a great deal because of the country round about, the river which flowed through it, and the blacksmith shop I used to haunt in the hopes (now and then fulfilled) of getting a ride in a buggy.

I soon made friends with three or four boys of about my own age—and my lore in all things increased by leaps and bounds. I learned, for instance, that if a needle was put through the ear of a pigeon "just right," the said pigeon would ever after that, when he walked, stagger like a drunken man. I learned why certain horses needed certain kinds of shoes—and I was chagrined, the day before I left town to go back to my mother, when the blacksmith told me I had got it all wrong. Like most boys of that time, and I fancy of all times, I chased butterflies, pinning them on a big board and trying to obtain a collection that in color and size would outshine the collection of any boy in town. As the summer days came to their close, there were blueberries and wild blackberries to be picked—and when the market was not glutted by too many other industrious little boys, you might sell the result of all an afternoon's labor for perhaps three, or even four, whole nickels. (And each nickel meant a regular soda—two nickels an ice cream soda!) There was a more direct and closer relation between work and its reward here than most of us ever experience later on in life.

It was in Barre, during this summer vacation, that I performed one of the really heroic acts of my life. Some old town character—of the kind Eugene O'Neill later on put in one or two of his plays—had committed suicide by walking out into the river until the water swirled over his head. He had left his hat and coat—oddly enough, his shoes too—on a stump near the bank of the river, and it was thought that his body was caught in the roots of a tree. Somebody dived down and confirmed this suspicion. Then arose the question of how the body was to be released. Volunteers were called for, and though I couldn't swim, I said I would wade out and "duck down." I did—and just the sight of that old grey bloated face (he had been missing for a day) so frightened me that I had all I could do to keep from weeping. Finally, the boy who really could swim and dive went down again and released the body, which was pulled in to the bank—but by this time I was several hundred yards down the road, with a queer sickish feeling in the pit of my stomach. I had looked upon death too closely.

What I loved most and remember best were the long summer sunsets, and when dusk was coming down, the croaking of frogs in a little pond near the house where I was staying—a monotonous musical croaking that contrasted sharply with the otherwise soft hush of that New England summer twilight. And when it grew really dark, the fireflies were everywhere. Buildings and streets and the town square—all prosaic enough in the noonday glare—now, after dark, became mysterious and full of suggestion. Moths and mosquitoes would buzzingly hurl themselves against the protective glass which enclosed the few bluish street lights, whose arcs sputtered quite noisily at times. Sometimes I would walk out as far as half a mile away from the nearest house on the country road—filled with a sort of brave terror of the dark shadowy landscape, lit up only by the pale moon. The vague flickering shadows of the trees would waver across the road when a gust of wind agitated their branches. I thought of ghosts, sometimes hoping—but not too firmly—to "see" one, and at other times half imagining that I did. The sound of a horse and team coming down the road was very reassuring—I would always bandy a word or two with the driver. And though I wouldn't then have admitted it for worlds, I was always greatly relieved when he offered to give me a lift back to town.

The fact that I remember some things and not others makes me believe, as I try now to recollect that long-lost period of my boyhod, that I was a pretty normal sort of youngster. For what were those particular, specific things? Well, my lively "mut" dog, Murphy, with his ever-wagging tail, his intense interest in things he pretended to see but weren't there, as we would walk through the woods, and his agility at skidding around a corner when he was off pell-mell after a cat. That is one clear memory. Even his black and white markings, if I were an artist, I could paint correctly today. Murphy was an amiable and a smart dog; I felt not a little honored that he attached himself so definitely to me. None of the other boys had a better dog, I was convinced of that, although Heaven knows almost every one of them had one with a somewhat more definite blood strain than Murphy, who was just "dog" and little else. But it was great fun to go tramping through the woods with Murphy, who managed to convert a simple walk into a series of discoveries and alarums and excursions that always called for frantic barking. His appetite was another great source of wonder to me, for Murphy would eat, as far as I could see, any time and all the time, if he had a chance. Probably he never really had got enough in his whole canine existence, for he was not shamelessly fat, like the bitch, Mascot, whom I knew so well later on in life at Collioure, in France—in fact, he was lean and very fast on his four feet, as most of the cats in town could testify. I know that it broke my heart, as I solemnly told my mother afterwards, when I had to leave Murphy behind at the end of the summer.

I remember, too, the fight with one of the town bullies, from which I emerged slightly damaged physically but greatly improved morally, for I had shown—what every boy has to show sooner or later, if he is to live an un-nagged life among his age-equals—that I was not afraid to fight. As a matter of fact, I am very peaceable by temperament and hate all forms of violence, just as I do all forms of ostentation, and the real truth is, I was dreadfully afraid. But I was even more afraid of boyhood's public opinion and of what the other fellows would say about me, if I showed the white feather. It was my first experience with mass public opinion—I didn't then realize, of course, that it was, in embryonic form, the same impulse that sends the man who is "afraid to go home in the dark" to the recruiting office first, when war breaks out. I was still to learn the truth of the paradox that it is fear, not courage, which makes heroes of us—physical heroes, at all events. Hence, though I exhibited a black eye for quite a few days, it was a decoration which I carried about almost jauntily.

Even free and careless and adventurous boyhood summer days come finally to an end—though I then didn't see why they should—and I had to leave Barre. That meant leaving my dog Murphy, my blacksmith shop, my boy friends, the long walks in the woods, the summer twilights (which I thought could never be the same anywhere else), the berry-picking rewarded with sodas—all the great life which, of course, faded from memory and disappeared almost completely in less than a week after I got back home.

That year my home, if it could be called such, was to be in Brockton, and it was there I went through the ceremony of going into first grade. I can remember that my mother came with me the first day—and I felt ashamed of that, though I don't know why, for most of the other little boys had their mothers with them, too—to make sure that I got in properly, and there was a short whispered conversation between my mother and the teacher, which made me very self-conscious, though I couldn't hear a word of it. And after my mother had gone back home, I know I "tried" the desk to which I was assigned, and was a bit disturbed because my small feet didn't quite touch the floor. But the embarrassment of that was as nothing compared with my tremors of apprehension—mingled with considerable interest, too—at all the little girls in the big room, the prettiest of whom, a rapid survey and appraisal showed me, was seated beside me. (Her name was Mildred—I can still remember that.)

But for the life of me I can't remember much about the routine of learning my three R's. There was a lot of work at the blackboard, many repetitions of the alphabet—and then, bit by bit and in some mysterious manner, the First Reader, with its big type and graphic illustrations on almost every page, changed from a dead to a living thing. Almost before you could say Jack Robinson, I was learning to read simple sentences like "Mary had a cat" or "a little lamb"—why is it always Mary? I used to wonder—and to write my name. It seemed to me quite wonderful that for such little effort you could learn to do these two important feats. But arithmetic—with its "two times two makes four" and its "three times three makes nine" and so on interminably—at first seemed somewhat dull. My interest in it picked up rapidly when we came to the first simple problem: "If Mary"—always Mary, observe—"pays 5 cents for two oranges, how much will a half-dozen cost her?" Here, I felt, was knowledge that was highly valuable. I really worked hard at my arithmetic, and I learned the multiplication table well and precisely, so that I could rattle it off before and faster than almost any of the others.

For among my older friends of that period was a youngster named Doyle, tall and active for his age, who had a newspaper route, i. e., who delivered the—I think the name was—Brockton *Enterprise* every evening to about 60 or 70 regular customers, and "going the route" was particularly important on Saturday nights, when he collected for the week and had to be sure to give the right change for quarters and half dollars, when his customers did not hand him the exact 12 cents due. I liked to go with him over his route, and I can still remember—though this was three years later, but all those years I kept Doyle as a friend—the excitement of July 4th, 1898, which was not only a holiday, of course, but the day when the news was confirmed that at Santiago Dewey, with 11 ships, had sunk the Spanish fleet of 6 ships, under the command of Cervera. When we went the route on July 5th we didn't have half enough newspapers to supply the demand, though we took double the usual number needed for the "regulars." Santiago—and ice-cream sodas! How curiously history is recorded in the mind of a boy!

My memories of those first school years are rather blurred, but there were a few high spots—one of them being my first "licking," for which, I must confess, I was amply prepared in the fashion of that day, having very carefully rubbed rosin on my hands before the teacher—saying "this hurts me worse than it does you, Harold," the hypocrite!—slapped down the rattan the approved number of times for punishment, a full dozen times, with an extra thirteenth thwack for good luck, I remember with bitterness. There was pain, of course, but there was some dignity in these "lickings," whereas there was no dignity whatsoever in being forced to stand in the corner, with your face to the wall (sometimes a full period of twenty minutes), for having committed some breach of discipline.

It was not long—I think it was in the third grade—before we were introduced to Geography. All children of my time welcomed this for one reason—the books. I do not mean, of course, primarily what was in the books, but the size of them. You could prop them up on your desk, and they were big enough to hide your small head. Hence, while pretending to learn that the United States was bounded on the North by Canada and on the West by the Pacific Ocean, you could spend your time looking at the pictures illustrating foreign countries (those of China particularly, I suppose because it was so far away) and dream. Or pass "notes," as soon as you could put down in your bold childish scrawl, "I love Mary," "Teacher is an old fool," or something equally noble and public-spirited. It was an early point of honor with all of us, I recall, not to "peach" on anybody, when a note was discovered by the teacher, and a stern voice would ask, "Who wrote this?" as the incriminating document was held aloft. There were other points of honor, too, which seemed to arise spontaneously, without anybody telling us about them—contempt for the "sissy," contempt for the "fraidy cat," contempt (the points seemed to be chiefly negative) for that pariah of childhood, "teacher's pet."

Occasionally, during my third and fourth grades, I was invited to birthday parties—to all of which invitations I responded with alacrity. For each one of them meant, on the low physical plane, the birthday cake, with its frosting, and lemonade, while on the higher spiritual plane each one meant the thrill of innocent games, such as Post Office and Drop The Handkerchief, where, if you were lucky, you might legitimately bestow a kiss upon, or have one bestowed by, the pretty Marguerite, or Helen, or Gwendolyn, whose golden or raven locks and peaches-and-cream complexion you had admired in school but had hitherto been powerless to do anything about. (What agonies of jealousy you went through, too, when Helen—just the one *you* wanted—was called out, in the Post Office game, by Johnny Belwin, whom you didn't like anyway! Plain murder would have been much too good for him.)

And speaking of lemonade, was there any New England boy of my generation who didn't run a home-made lemonade stand at one time or another? This was a regular feature of my childhood summers, whether I remained at home or went away. With what care the big stone crock was selected, the lemons and sugar purchased, the ice procured from the morning delivery wagon, the mixture made (with generous "testings" by yourself to see that it was just right, not too sour nor too sweet), the location of the stand—usually a grocery box—determined upon (under a pleasant tree and at the corner of two streets, when you could), and, at last, the white cloth spread over the top of the box and the tumblers your mother had reluctantly loaned you put carefully in a neat row! Every step in this process was fraught with peril. Usually the price for a glass was two pennies (on bad days—meaning chilly or windy days, when nobody wanted a drink—I had to cut the charge down to a penny, thus obtaining my first vivid lesson in the law of supply and demand), and your profit consisted of what was left after a simple process of subtraction—that is, subtracting from what you had taken in in pennies the original cost of the lemons and the ice (the sugar was sometimes a gift from your mother, even if a somewhat forced gift). Once in a while, on particularly hot days, I have known this profit to reach the dizzy heights of 35 or 40 cents. And most often, when your commercial success was greatest, a thunder shower would come up late in the afternoon, and how you would scurry to get everything off the box and into the house before the downpour came. You could enjoy the fruits of your labor later on, when the storm had passed, for it seemed that there was a sort of rule of nature that nobody drank lemonade *right after* a summer thunderstorm. You were free, the seven or eight nickels jangling in your pocket, to walk past the corner drug store, To go in and have a soda (for you had already forgotten the lemonade you had drunk yourself; boys' capacities in that direction are marvellous) whenever you liked, which is to say, as long as your nickels lasted. Once or twice I even had a burst of great generosity and treated the fair Mildred to a soda, though I resented just a little my having to "cough up" another nickel for her, for in my boyish mind love and nobility were one thing, while buying a soda was quite something else again.

Winter memories, too, are not colorless during those tender years from five to eight. For in those days, generally speaking, the winters were still severe, and the picture of the Pilgrim Fathers bringing home the turkey for Thanksgiving through piles of snow did not seem so peculiar as it does today, when there may be no more than six or seven weeks of real winter. And if it wasn't a "White Christmas," there simply was no justice in this world nor in the next—but usually it was. Long before the snow became deep enough to drift, however, there was often enough ice upon the pond to make skating relatively safe. I can't remember exactly—though it was unusually early —when I learned to skate, but I know I felt it was a tremendous emancipation, for hitherto I had been confined to the innocent joys of sledding. Before deep snow had come—or sometimes, when strong winds would blow the snow clear from the pond—I went through the usual experiences of landing too hard upon my back, as my feet went skyrocketing in spite of all I could do. Nevertheless I stuck to it, as do most children, out of pride. It was grown-up to skate, *ergo,* I had to learn how. For whatever grown-ups did was divinely and mysteriously right then. Parents, I want to say again as I have elsewhere in this book, ought never to forget this grave responsibility which childish faith imposes upon them, whether they want it or not. (Indeed, I am certain that many a man has been saved from doing something foolish, solely because he did not want to betray the trust of his children.)

Though I took my degree in philosophy at Harvard—which, in my case, meant in fact much more work in psychology than in metaphysics—I have never pretended to be versed in that peculiar subject known as "educational psychology." But I can now remember enough of my own boyhood to distrust its adult bias. The only correct way to deal with a child is to start with the realization that he or she is, however amiable, sweet, or cunning, at heart nothing but a little savage, with all the blind cruelties and the blind unreason of a savage. If they were in fact fully human, the instinctive attitude of children towards whatever is weak, crippled, or deformed would be not merely shocking but deeply discouraging. (That is why Plato is so profoundly right when he says children should be taught, not things as they are—which, I want to interject, they will discover for themselves soon enough anyway, if they are normal—but things as they ought to be, so that they may have some standards of excellence.) I know—though now I shiver with shame when I think of it—that I, just like the other sweet little things I was associated with, made it always a point to jeer at the neighborhood cripple, to taunt the Jewish rag-collector (when we ourselves were not trying to get a few pennies for the old clothes, bottles, or newspapers) on his long beard, and to make uproarious fun of any child dressed strikingly different from what we were accustomed to.

And the clannishness of my little group! "Exclusive" clubs, as we come to know them in later years, are institutions expressing the free spirit of democracy, compared with the taboos children erect around themselves and the few they are associated with. I belonged to the "gang" that had, as a kind of unofficial meeting place, Old Riley's abandoned barn—and if I had betrayed our hiding place—if, above all, I had allowed any "outsider" in on any of our portentous secrets (today I should give a good deal to remember one or two of them, just as a clue to the child mind)—why then, I was told and firmly believed myself, the earth would open and swallow me up as the very least of my punishments. Even if my mother spanked me for not telling—and of course I was always casually letting fall mysterious hints, just to provoke her curiosity; children like to play with fire that way—I must, even at the cost of this great physical suffering, keep the sacred secrets inviolate. I would go out from our meetings feeling very important, looking slyly now and then at people I passed in the street to see if they detected on my countenance the sign of the great restraint under which I was laboring. I was so certain of my powers of keeping a secret that even had Mildred promised to give me a kiss if I "told," I should have repudiated her with a great histrionic show of my fortitude. (But yet when I thought of her, I must admit, I felt a little weak in the knees; almost I wanted to be tempted.)

But belonging to a gang did not satisfy completely my growing spirit of adventure. At that period the one final point of happiness for me would have been to own a pony—and to have ridden him triumphantly around the rather dingy empty lot in front of our house. For that was the period, in our social history, when Frank Merriwell and Diamond Dick and the others of the Nickel Series for boys were the real heroes of the younger generation. The movies had not come in, of course, and although once or twice a month during the winter we might be taken to some thrilling "show" at the local theatre, when lots of "firing" was our criterion of excellence and dramatic insight, these trips were too infrequent adequately to feed our eager imaginations. So it was the protagonists of the Nickel Series with whom we identified our own heroic—though slightly thwarted—selves. And I can remember to this very hour one insufferable little "snot," (I was reproved sharply by my mother for "using that bad word") who had the good luck to have rich and indulgent parents, who actually did buy him a pony, which he flaunted before us whenever he could. We were always looking for a chance to pick a fight with that young aristocrat, but he was too shrewd for us, and he escaped the just punishment of boyhood for being more fortunate than the rest of us.

I think the gnawing bitterness of envy for that boy might have turned all our heads finally, except for one thing: The circus. When that came to town, even the rich boy and his pony faded into insignificance. How we schemed to carry the water for the elephants (failing which, we made a careful study of the tent to see where we might slip under)! And how we thrilled to the music of the steam calliope when the parade came down the street! Although the much touted tigers and lions were usually tired and indifferent, old and lazy and fat, we saw in them cruel menaces to humanity (thinking how we would rescue our Mildred—always happily there to be rescued—if one of them ever broke loose). The clowns, of course, were the last word in comedy; the lady on the flying trapeze the last word in beauty. No, the rich boy could have—and keep—his darn old pony. We wanted none of it—we were going to the circus, and with two nickels extra for peanuts with which to annoy, as much as to feed, the monkeys. I suppose life, later on, holds no greater thrill than those early trips to the circus. Yes, there were two others—The Night Before Christmas and The Night Before The Fourth.

At no time later in our mature grown-up and conventional existence do we experience quite those vague but deep, those fearsome yet attractive anticipations and emotional flurries that we experience in our early boyhood. But I do know, too, that when I try—as I have tried here in imagination and memory—to recapture them, I walk the streets with a queer, new tolerance for the boys I see, at nine or even nine-thirty at night, huddled in a doorway near my New York home "telling stories," "boasting," exchanging those curious confidences and impressions of boyhood. I don't laugh at them; I walk with discreet speed past them, for I don't want them to think for even a minute that I am trying to eavesdrop on their tremendous secrets; sometimes, even, I feel a twinge of envy for them, and wish I had it all to do over again.

But *then,* of course, I envied people of my now age—or rather, I envied the assurance of them, the wealth they might have, the knowledge they did not share with me. I never thought *then* that the day would ever come, when as a man I might wish I were a boy again. And I would have considered any man who did so wish to recapture some of his youth somebody who was dangerously weak-minded, if not just a plain liar. Men, I thought, should keep their dignity—and their distance.

II. GROWING UP IN MASSACHUSETTS

MY first detailed memory is of the night of December 31, 1899. On that night I went with my mother to the Congregational Church in Rockland, Massachusetts, a couple of hours or so before midnight. It was for an historic occasion: To hear the New—the Twentieth—Century rung in. At that time I was just eight years and seven months old.

There was prayer; there was a young lady in a white robe, with a very long trumpet, which she blew vociferously when the church bell began to strike the momentous hour of twelve. Best of all, there was cake served before the ceremony—but not much more than cake, for Christmas, remember, was only a week past, and there was still a touch of the Puritan and the Spartan in the people of Massachusetts of that time (I mean a touch of it for public display). Then, too, there was the chance to stay up late, something boys of my then age consider a great privilege—as also at that time (something all New Englanders will remember) the night before Christmas, when you had to go to bed early, was far surpassed in thrills by the adventurous "night before the Fourth," when you could sneak out of the house (with your parents' strict admonition not to do so, but with their tacit consent nevertheless) and join "the gang" and start bonfires and set off firecrackers or shoot pistols. (I got a bad injury to my left hand one of those "Nights Before The Fourth," when a cheap toy pistol exploded prematurely; I carry a scar to this day.) So I was thrilled: Another chance to stay up late!

On that historic last evening of 1899 and the late Victorian Nineteenth Century, I had already been going to school for three years and a half—in those days you entered primary school in the September following your fifth birthday. And mine, of course, had been May 7, 1896. Those three school years were split between Rockland and Brockton. It is the school life in Brockton which I remember the better, though some details of my vacation life in Rockland are still vivid. Rockland always meant holiday in those early days. When I go back and see that New England industrial shoe town today I have to smile, for then it meant "the country" to me—and I can still remember one of my regular routes through the woods, where I hoped vaguely for Indians and bears and adventure. And today that romantic route of my childhood is only an industrial path of factories for all kinds of shoes, cheap and dear, turned out in mass production. Sometimes I wonder if *their* idyllic childhood spots have not been similarly transformed for many other Americans of my age, and if it doesn't sadden them a bit that there is really no old place to which to go back. With almost every tree that falls, when the woods are cleared for a new suburban development, a dream of childhood is also destroyed and made a waste-land. Where I had dreamed of friendly or—when demanded—heroic encounters with Redskins of the kind I was beginning to learn about in tales read to me from James Fenimore Cooper, is now a filling-station; where the brook led on to a mysterious thicket, is now a slag-pile. The world is too crowded, too filled-up. When I was a boy, there were great tracts of the world still unexplored—and "the West" did not mean Hollywood, or an attractive lady everywhere known as Mae. It meant cowboys and Indians—we used to play a game of that double name—and the green forest primeval.

It is the droning, warm quiet of the class-room (with little snickers when you "got" Herbert with a spit-ball, shot from behind your geography book, which you were pretending to read with great diligence); the clatter and shouts in the play-yard at recess; the walk home through the maple-lined streets when you boasted to your fellows and they, as solemnly, boasted to you (until, inevitably, there was a fight, a black eye, pride in your triumph when you slammed the other fellow, or shame in your disgrace when you were licked, and a scolding from your mother in either case, when you got back to the house); the pretty teacher and the disagreeable old-maidish one; the insanity of the English system of weights and measures, where so many gills made a pint (and you didn't care, or see why anybody else should) and so many pints a quart; the shrill high tremulo singing of "My Country 'Tis Of Thee" after the principal had read some incomprehensible thing from the Bible with which to begin the day's session:—these are the *real* things you still remember. That is, they are if you went to what we continue to term, despite English snobbery, "public school."

But my school memories from my childhood in Brockton are not the most vivid. I remember having my photograph taken, with the family cat, by flashlight. (I still have that picture and I marvel at the sweet innocence of my expression; I must have been a kind of New England hypocrite even then, for I can recall that just when that angelic likeness was taken, I was hatching some low deviltry in my mind.) There was coasting in the back yard that winter. When the spring came and the snow had gone, a workman came to lay a pipe, and I watched him dig, somehow fascinated—thinking that if only one could dig deep enough (remembering the globe in school) one would come through to China on the other side. He told me awful stories about people being buried alive, and for days I avoided going anywhere near the local cemetery. In the autumn there was the Brockton Fair—with its death-defying balloon ascension and parachute jump, its old-fashioned trotting races, its prize fruits, its side shows, its pop-corn and other delicacies designed to ruin young stomachs. Those were red-letter days. And oddly enough, the day the old Catholic priest, who had been in Brockton for years, lay in state in his church, and everybody filed past to view the body—why that remains so vivid a picture I don't know. Perhaps it was because it was the first time I had ever really seen death dressed up and formal.

My own church—that is to say, my mother's—was the Methodist Episcopal Church, which at that time certainly had little of the Episcopal about it. It was in Brockton—in a newly built stone church dedicated to that happy faith—that I was baptized and formally inducted, like so many good Americans of that day, into Protestant Christianity. My only real emotion was a little jealousy of the Baptists, and I regretted that my mother had not shown more dramatic sense in her choice of a creed—for, while I dreaded, I should have liked the thrill of the ceremony of total immersion. Of course, too, I went to Sunday School, where I strove for good marks solely with a secret eye upon the possible presents that were handed out to the prize pupils the Sundays before Christmas, but my duplicity here did not receive its just reward, for all I got was a Bible, of which, frankly, I had already seen too much. I liked the organ music when I went to the morning service with my mother before Sunday School, but even with the music, the long sermon, the collection, and the prayers were all too austere to be attractive. For a youngster, I think, the Catholic Church puts on a much more thrilling performance.

To many people at that time, when you mentioned Taunton, Massachusetts, only the picture of the State Hospital for the Insane came before their eyes. But to me Taunton was the rainbow end of a marvellous trolley trip from Brockton. And when my mother decided again to move—and to Taunton—for once I thought highly of the project. How my mother's work was going as a trained nurse, which was her profession she would proudly tell you, I never knew accurately. I know that at times she had good patients, by which I take it she meant patients who paid for her services the standard rate then of $3.00 a day and paid her promptly and without question. Also I know she meant agreeable and amusing patients. She was pleased when a patient recovered—that meant perhaps a week or so more of nursing. She didn't like to have her patients die, but I think she was a bit thrilled at her constant comaraderie with death—for at that time people did not usually hire trained nurses unless the case was already pretty desperate. And she would recount the full histories of serious operations and how Mr. So-and-So "looked on his death-bed" and what were his "last words" (she seemed always to be there to hear them), so that at times I had something of the feeling of a boy who is the son of an executioner.

When cases were not frequent, she would supplement her uncertain income by running a registry—something that became more and more important to her as she grew older, and, also, as the telephone came into more general use. She sent nurses out on cases, charging them a small fee. Always determined to keep a roof over our heads, in her expression, she had rather grandiose ideas about what was a proper home. But when she took a house or a flat she really couldn't afford, she compromised with reality by taking in roomers, to help her pay the rent. In Taunton, I recall, one of our roomers was an instructor in the local High School and another was a pretty young nurse, just graduated from a Boston Hospital. My mother would hint darkly that all was not as it should be between the two roomers, but just what she meant by that cryptic remark I didn't then know.

Nor did I much care anyway. I had a happy year at Taunton. The grammar school work was interesting then, and I played quarterback on a school "scrub" team with considerable success, or so I flattered myself. But I can remember the tang of the autumn air, the fun of passing the ball on the quick play, and those good old-fashioned line scrimmages where weight and ability to hit out with your legs (and not be caught doing it by the umpire) were the main requirements. Also I was introduced to world current events for the first time, for we took a "news" weekly at the school and were required to give a summary of what was going on in the world every morning. Manual training—which then meant carpentry and little more—was an extra flourish of that school curriculum. I remember I had a curious feeling that I was growing up fast—a feeling confirmed by haunting the Carnegie Free Public Library and reading magazines and books, many of which I didn't understand.

Then came another flight—this time to Cambridgeport. And there was no home here, only a double room. This didn't matter much to me then, I recall, for I was old enough now to take notice of things, and I enjoyed the grammar school work. I enjoyed being in—or rather, next door to—Boston, which for some reason seemed to me my natural home. I liked the walks around the Back Bay, over the bridge to Cambridge (there were trolleys, of course, but no subway, as now, between Cambridge and Boston). Being in Boston also meant going out to the beach from Rowes' Wharf—either to popular Revere Beach, or, on those happy occasions when I had almost a whole magic dollar in my pocket, a trip down to Nantasket by steamer or third-rail cars. Even Salem "Willows" was a place I intended always to visit—but somehow I never seemed to get there, though I visited Salem itself often enough. And there was, for me then, plenty of interest in Boston alone, especially around the old market and along the Atlantic Avenue section by the harbor. Even South Boston, incredible as it may seem to those who know it, was an exciting place; above all, I liked to see the many yachts.

And the father of one of my schoolmates was the chef in a stylish Harvard club, from which exalted position he made enough to own a small boat of his liking—though he called it, with a smile, a cat boat—and to keep it in South Boston harbor. Sailing trips on holidays and Sundays with him and his son were great adventures, for often we would go far enough out to feel the authentic roll of the ocean. And the food! Early in life I learned to love Cape Cod cooking, the kind you get at the old-fashioned clam bakes. Even today, if anyone wants to bribe me, they do not have to offer gold and diamonds—they have only to say that they are serving steamed clams for dinner.

In addition to these local Boston harbor trips, I spent one summer vacation with my school friend and his father in a tiny town near East Dennis, which rambled along a flat, sandy shore, where but a half mile inland from the sea blueberries grew in abundance. I slept upstairs in a big room, ordinarily a store-room, which could be transformed into a guest room simply by putting a cot-bed into it. The bare timber beams and boards of the side of the house were uncovered; when it had been hot, the fresh wood gave off a pleasant acrid odor. I can still remember how eagerly I sniffed that. (The house was newly built; my school-friend's father also prided himself on being something of a carpenter.) At night I could hear the roar of the surf on the long sandy beach a hundred yards away:—snug in my blanket, I listened to the deep, familiar sound of the sea and fell asleep dreaming of travel and sailing ships. I thought happiness could be no greater.

When the tide was out, we would stalk sand-pipers, with a rifle filled with tiny bird-shot, sometimes killing or maiming, so that they were helpless, as many as eight or nine at a time. (Even then I felt this to be a foolish and wicked thing, though I didn't know why. I suppose it was because the killing was so wanton—after all, the birds were not edible, like fish; we killed for the fun of killing.) When the tide was in, we would do our swimming, diving from a small abandoned wharf into about ten feet of water. There was enough of undertow to give one a thrill fighting the way back to a ledge of the wharf; the water was bracing and salty, but not too cold, and there was a ruffle on it—to remind you that on windy, angry days there was a real surf. Fresh water swimming has for me never had the "kick" to it that I get from the sea—and when, a little later on in our social history, we used the expression, "a fresh-water college," this always described for me an institution of learning a bit beneath the serious consideration of hardy sons of the bounding main—like myself, of course. And there was a popular song of that summer—as popular as the ancient classic, "In The Good Old Summer Time"—the title of which I cannot recall, but it went in part like this:

> "There's lots of fish down in the sea,
> All you need is a hook, and a line, and a bait, and a flea,
> But isn't it funny,
> When you're looking for money,
> All you get is Seem . . . Pathy."

The song was of the now ancient vintage of 1903 or 1904—I have, by experience later on, confirmed in full the sound Yankee doctrine there expressed—but it ought to have had, I should have thought, a certain heart-felt revival during the depression years.

During those Cambridgeport days—on Saturday and Sunday mornings, particularly, when there was no school—I liked to walk, first, up to "Old Cambridge," which meant Harvard Square for me then, and, second, up Brattle Street as far as the Longfellow House—and then back home along the river. There were some pleasant houses on Brattle Street then, and I was determined to own one of them—or one just like them—some day. My determination was firm: I had read in some fad book of the time that breakfasts were the cause of all evil. "Go without them," that damn book had said. And so I did—for a few weeks. I was almost proud of the faintness of my empty stomach, and firmly believed that subduing—or ignoring—the natural hunger pangs of a growing boy was certain proof of my superior will-power. Going without breakfast meant a strong character; a strong character meant eventual great riches; great riches meant the ability to purchase (or build, for I had ideas on that, too) a house on Brattle Street: The syllogism was perfect. I suffered; but, like a good Yankee, it was not suffering for its own sake (as with the more naive Puritans) but suffering for a high purpose—that I might possess, and hence enjoy, the more. There was nothing really disinterested about this self-abnegation, though of course I then thought there was, and fancied myself extremely noble.

Just why, I don't know—perhaps it was the imaginative awakening that comes with adolescence—but the richest and most colorful of all the dreams of my boyhood still seem to me those I had when I lived in Cambridgeport. So intensely was I in another world of my heart's desire, dramatizing myself and events, that sometimes I would go along the street oblivious of other people, talking or singing—or even declaiming—to myself, but out loud: At least out loud sufficiently for other people to hear me. Even now I can feel how my cheeks burned with shame, when one afternoon I came to myself with a start and looked up to find a man laughing at me. I felt humiliated, but I felt angry, too—why should he make fun of my dreams? Why did he do it? What did he know about them? Why couldn't he mind his own business? I think now that that was the beginning of my almost passionate hatred of interference of any kind, especially gratuitous interference. But being a boy, I didn't of course reflect in this fashion; much more simply, I then took refuge in grandiose plans for revenge—I dreamed how some day I should be powerful and humiliate *him* before all the world. I remember that I made up my mind to be firm, that I would *not* pardon him, no, not even if his mother came to plead before me, or his beautiful sister . . . but here I began to weaken a bit.

For it was now 1904; I was thirteen years old; sex was beginning to rear its lovely, if somewhat distorted head. By what mysterious process of instruction I had learned that children were not born in any of the fantastic ways I had at one time or another imagined I don't know. Older boys had given me a lot of imaginative and incorrect information—and once, way back among my earliest memories, was the recollection of playing "house" with two or three children of my own tender years, one of them a little girl, and in the game a "doctor" called, making it necessary for the little girl to take off her clothes for an "examination." I remembered that fantastic scene now; I remembered that girls were not "made" the same way as boys. It was all a confused, but an engrossing subject. Unfortunately for me in one sense, my mother, though a nurse by profession, was also something of an old-fashioned New Englander; certain things she would not discuss with children. "When you are old enough," she would say to me, "you will learn all about it." And she would turn to some other topic with evident relief. It was not exactly a liberal sex education, but at least I wasn't told a lot of gush about the birds and the flowers. It was quite natural, however, that this aloof attitude—coupled with the fact that I had neither a father nor an older brother, since the latter was at that time so often away, to give me any information—should have forced me to eat of the tree of knowledge where I could find it: Among older boys, in the streets, in whispered and mysterious hints. Now and then I was given the privilege of looking at a "dirty" book, which the older boys passed around among themselves with knowing winks—and for a fine, insidious, evil effect, I recommend this lavatory literature which flourished in such abundance in the New England I knew.

What impresses me as odd, even today, is that the *romantic* side of sex—dreaming of kissing the pretty girl; rescuing Hilda, her pigtails and all, from the burning house—had, during those early years, very little relation to the sensuous aspect of sex. Indeed, not only had the two no relation, in a subtle way I did not understand, but which really was a part of the old-fashioned Puritan moral atmosphere in which I lived without knowing it, the two were opposed. Very early in my New England boyhood I was made to feel that love was one thing, and sex another—and never should the twain meet, if the "right" and the "respectable" and the "decent" people I was taught to admire had anything to say about it.

As of course I regarded myself as by birth and right among these admired people, I was puzzled by the insistence of my sensuous interest. I concluded that I was especially—and, of course, distinguishedly—wicked, as other children have before me; with only a very little turn in the direction of fate, I should have gloried in the most anti-social acts—all in the name of my difference. What older people forget (even experts in education) is that during these difficult years youngsters want to be preeminent and to be looked up to; they want positive adulation, not negative restraint. The whole problem is to make children feel naturally that the moral life is not merely the barren and dull good life, but the kind of life which will be admired by their "gang" and by all the neighbors and all the girls—goodness for its *own* sake simply means nothing whatever to a normal child. He thinks (I shall not say rightly) that somebody is lying.

Like many youngsters of that period, I kept a diary. Sometimes I have wished I had it now, while I have been writing this book—even if only to amuse me. But at other times I have realized that, fundamentally, it would have done me little good—in fact might easily have tricked me into putting many a false emphasis upon how I then felt. For in that diary I put down things, not as they were, but as I wanted them to be. I was writing for the invisible public of all children, and I had to be careful to appear radiant in all the virtues. I do remember that there were long descriptive passages about the new places and scenes, liberally interspersed with bursts of criticism, which in reality were only suppressed desires.

What I needed at that time was—not of course the companionship—but the friendly acquaintanceship of older men:

I needed older brothers, uncles who had seen the world, the kind of tales a child in a seafaring village comes by naturally when he talks to the superannuated sailors mending nets and puttering around the boats. I believe there is a natural affinity, when it is not spoiled by adolescent sophistication, between boys and men in their first and, as we say, their second childhoods. Every boy, too, ought to have at least one short sailing trip with some "old timer;" he ought to have a grandfather who can answer his questions about the electrical theories underlying radio; and he will be the most fortunate of youngsters, if he has an uncle who has done a bit of exploring in South America or Africa. Boys are natural hero-worshippers; if they can't idealize one type of adventurer, they will another. They will try to emulate Edison or Stanley as easily as they will dream of being a super-gunman—provided they are given the chance. I know I should rather have been a Captain Nemo, such as Jules Verne depicted, than the most flamboyant Jesse James that ever flourished a gun on the plains. Besides, I had already begun to read my Sherlock Holmes, and I was determined, above all other things, to be the "silent, strong" man—almost volubly determined.

Don't all boys, at one time or another, go around with what they fondly imagine are intense and concentrated faces? Parents should not be unduly exercised over this phenomenon, nor attribute it to some mysterious malady:—It is simply the "masterful" period of boyhood, the time when every boy in imagination pictures himself the great leader, the matchless mind, the heroic adventurer, and the Sir Galahad of chivalry towards women and the weak, who are usually strangely confused in a boy's instinctive notion of things.

Because of my practically non-existent home life and because of my being continuously shuffled about from one town to another I missed one experience of boyhood—belonging to a "gang." Of course I had had brief flings at it (above all, when I played quarterback on the scrub football team in

Taunton), but I had not been a member of any one of the typical boys' organizations of that time (remember the Boy Scout movement came after my day), such as the "Hiawatha Athletics," or the "Fernley River Rowing Club," or the "Park Hill Social," or the "Secret Wanderers of Framingham," or the "Brockton Junior Baseball Club." I never remained long enough in one place to get in with the right crowd—indeed, seldom long enough to get in with any crowd. But I did not then like my enforced rôle of Lone Wolf; in fact, I hated it and tried to change it.

Boys of my then age, however, are terribly suspicious of outsiders who come from another town, especially outsiders who have no father and regular family status in the community. If they are accepted at all, they will be accepted on sufferance, or rather, perhaps I should say, out of defiance of their parents' wishes—for it is the gossip and suspicion they hear their parents express concerning "the Stearns widow and boy, who have just moved in" which they partly believe, though—sometimes—would like boldly to defy. Naturally, this tends to make "the Stearns boy" self-conscious; it also tends to make him a sort of silent partner in any scheme the youngsters are plotting against the paternal discipline. Inevitably the result is that he becomes the black sheep of the gang—and eventually is repudiated by it. After two or three such experiences, the "Stearns boy" is almost aggressively on his guard against joining a "gang." He learns to pick one or two intimates—disinherited or under suspicion, like himself—and to spend most of his time with these, who also are playing a more or less lone hand in the peculiar social heirarchy of boyhood. And with the even more peculiar moral alchemy of adolescence he transforms necessity into a virtue by finally pretending that, after all, he doesn't like clubs anyway. But it is a difficult pose to keep up—and he will leap with alacrity at the first chance to join something with the other boys, no matter what his isolation principles.

Cambridgeport was then a loose and rambling sort of place;

there was no town square, as in an ordinary New England village. I did join the local Y. M. C. A.—and I can remember the exercises on the handle-bars and the flying rings and pushing a huge handball around, joining the ping-pong tournament, and even playing basketball a bit. Also, I learned to swim, but not in any indoor pool—it was in the Charles River at a little beach of those days not far from Cambridgeport, and the courage it took to jump in over my depth was greater than I had ever been called upon to exercise before. But I did learn, and when, on hot days later on, I was permitted to go down to Revere Beach, hire my own suit and little room in the State Bath House, and swim boldly out to the raft, I felt very superior to the weaklings who only splashed in the surf.

I loved Revere then; I loved the salt smell of the sea itself (I am sorry for Middle Western children who do not experience this) above everything else; I could sniff the ocean long before we came in sight of it. But I loved also the odors of potato chips, of clam chowder served in the shore dinners, the melted butter for pop-corn (blown so enticingly by the hot wind), of the blistered tangy wood of the board-walk and cottages. All these nasal stimuli combined to put me in a pitch of ecstasy which great poetry, later on in life, only dimly rivalled. Those sensuous, mouth-watering desires of childhood!

But I was to be torn away from the sea again—for the old *Wanderlust* was impelling my mother on once more. This time it was back to Attleboro—I say "back," since Attleboro was not far from Taunton, which was not far from Brockton, which in turn was not far even from Rockland. Hence Attleboro presented no emotional difficulties of fundamental strangeness. It was too far from Boston and the ocean—that was the only hostile prejudice I brought to it. For as a town, when we landed there, I rather liked it. I liked the old grade crossings, the Congregational Church, the Opera House, the High School, and —quite far out of town on a plain—the baseball field, where I was later to shine, even if not brilliantly.

This time my mother rented a whole house—how she did it was, and still is, a mystery. It was a kind of cottage, belonging to and adjoining the much more pretentious house and grounds of one of the big manufacturers of cheap Attleboro jewelry. (I can see him yet—a distinguished, white-moustached Yankee—who later on used to give me "ten cents an hour, and good pay, too," for mowing his lawn.) And that summer—the summer before my last year in a grammar school—I worked for the railroad, which was erecting cement bridges over the dangerous grade crossings that went through the town. I was only a humble water boy, but the men were kindly, with the rough, and sometimes bawdy humor of semi-skilled laborers of that epoch, and I didn't mind the work. I used to look forward to the passage of the fast through trains, especially the Bay State and the Knickerbocker Limiteds, and I know now that then was born in me (as I saw the beautiful ladies languidly looking down at me from the platforms of the observation cars, or the handsome business men eating lunch in the dining-cars) the determination to travel myself. Some day I, too, would sit on the platform of that observation car and see Attleboro go by. (And, eventually, I did.) Some day I, too, would be famous. But these were short reflections; the summer was soon over; I had to go to my last year in grammar school.

Like many a man of my age, I have pretty well forgotten my studies that last year, but I can remember quite vividly (and I think this, too, many men in middle age will find true of themselves) some of the surrounding features of the graduation exercises in June (*my* June was that of 1905). There was the stiffness of getting dressed up and the self-consciousness; a blurred picture of the rows of parents in the hot auditorium of the Opera House, where the exercises were held; the singing and declamation, as it was called; the solemn (but you then thought it profound) nonsense about the great opportunities and the new world you were entering, by some local politician anxious not to be forgotten as a speaker; the handing out of the be-ribboned diplomas, and the little thrill that went up and down your spine when your own name was called out; the final singing of "My Country 'Tis Of Thee," and the conclusion of the whole business with a prayer by a local clergyman who recommended us all warmly—I thought even then a bit too warmly—to the tender mercies of a Divine Providence, which had the fate and happiness of every one of us as his special concern. And after the hot and uncomfortable afternoon exercises, there was the evening garden party of the class—with the Chinese lanterns, the strange little local pre-radio band, the refreshments, and the swearing of eternal loyalty to the pretty Agnes or Martha or Genevieve (I am ashamed to admit it, but I cannot recall the right name now; but had you asked me *then,* if I should ever forget, I most indignantly should have battled you to the death, in the approved chivalric manner.)

But chivalry and romance shrivelled up rather rapidly that summer. My mother was in money and rent difficulties again; I knew that in a short time (and I was right, it was in September, just before High School opened) she would move still once more. Meanwhile, whether I went to High School or not, there was to be no vacation for me that particular summer. I had to go to work. Thus far in my fourteen years of life I had gone on without doing anything more serious than odd jobs, selling newspapers, pestering housewives to buy soap so that I might have a Larkin desk, and the water-carrying exploit of the previous summer. Now I was to get a little taste of the horrors of industrialism—I think just enough to make me hate the monotony and stupidity of piece work on machines with an intensity that more or less altered the emotional direction of my whole life.

The job I obtained was not in itself so bad—it was not comparable to the exploitation of child labor in mill and cotton towns, but God knows it was bad enough. It was, simply, a job as a "puncher" in a small, cheap jewelry factory. That is, I punched holes in the holders, on which so-called gold chains of minus karat quality were eventually hung, in each of the four corners. Through the cardboard and gaudy tissue paper wrapped tightly around it, I forced a weighted knife arrangement which was attached to a lever. The bar of the arm of this lever I pushed with my right foot, shoving the cardboard and tissue paper neatly into a triangular corner, down upon which the cutting apparatus fell. If I put my finger even a fraction of an inch inside the corner, it would be efficiently shorn off by the sharp falling blade—and, in fact, accidents of this kind were quite common. Your attention could not relax for a moment, no matter how you tried to mechanize (or Taylorize, one might say today) the different motions required. Yet even with the visual and muscular demands upon you, you would strive to make the whole process routine-like—so that your mind could be free to dream. But just as you thought you were free, your physical attention would be demanded—either by a new pile of material to punch, or by the need of making some trivial adjustment in the machine. Even your imagination was chained and crippled.

Noboby since has ever had to lecture to me about the evils of industrialism, untempered by human consideration for the worker. That job was only a little thing in itself, but it was for me a vivid symbol of our whole mechanical era. I was at an impressionable age, too, remember, and I was young enough in any case to resent working like that at a bench so stupidly, so blindly, so unimaginatively. It was then, I think, that I made one of the few resolutions I have adhered to all my life since—that, come what might, I would rather die than ever again work in a factory. I am glad I went through that summer, if only because of that resolution. Any partisan of some new method of taking the monotony out of factory toil—by any system of dividing up work or anything else—has always, ever since, had my sympathetic attention. I don't wonder that factory workers are the typical historical material that starts revolutions—or at least an occasional riot. I don't blame them; almost I applaud them. It is the closest thing to de-humanization I know. And when the whistle blows in an industrial town, even today, I can still feel a sort of shudder of despair. It is to me a sign that the crippling of life still goes on.

Of course there were other interests that summer—and what was more, I was sure, with that strange conviction of youth, that somehow, though I didn't know how, I was going to High School when the autumn came. My ultimate intention being thus clear and firm, I consequently enjoyed my Saturday afternoons off, for I could go to the local baseball game or just loaf at home and read. Even Sundays had finally lost most of their early boyhood dullness; now they were the bright days of the week, and for the first time I realized how important they were for the ordinary man who worked. Sometimes I would go swimming or take a walk; sometimes—and always, when the weather was bad—I would stay quietly at home and read.

Like most growing boys, I had previously rather resented Sundays, without exactly understanding why: It was a profound change to find myself looking forward to them. Now that I was working, I felt I was under no obligation to go to Sunday School—and evidently my mother, though once in a while she would ask me to go with her to afternoon prayer meeting and though I would actually do so (partly out of a sincere desire to please her, partly out of my own wish to see people), thought my working entitled me to choose whether or not I should go to church. Sometimes I would go to the evening meetings, too—more, however, for social than other reasons. But the question of Sunday School was by tacit consent not raised; and that was the end, on my part, of any formal religious education.

Those social Sunday evenings at church were chiefly visual and auditory. I liked the music, and once in a month or so the short sermon itself would interest me. But I enjoyed the feeling of being in a crowd; also I was glad of the chance to survey the pretty girls. This appraisal, however, never turned into active admiration. It might have, I don't know; but neither my mother nor myself—I noticed with that preternatural sensitiveness of youth—was invited often to dinners or to the neighbors. And the few times we were, as it happened, there were no girls in the family. So I was forced back to my books, my walks, and my baseball exploits; and, of course, I began to take pride in what I had, pretending to be scornful of the boys who were always "running after the Chickens," as we said in those days, just as, a little later, we spoke with contempt—mingled with envy—of the enterprising young man who was always "after a skirt." And, because I didn't have my girl, I wouldn't have any. In which I was not entirely unlike certain more famous misogynists whose works I was to study in college later on.

The summer of 1905!—thirty years ago. Is it only a delusion on our side, or is it a fact, that not merely our America, but the whole world of which it is now such an important part, have both changed more than has at any time previously in two whole centuries a single country, even some small and isolated country of intelligent and progressive people, like Greece at the height of its glory? Beginning with the industrial revolution around 1850, the whole Western World, of course, began to change with great speed—a speed that has been increasing to a point where now, it sometimes seems, yesterday's ideals are only tomorrow's historical quaintnesses. We live in a world where you are out of "style" almost as soon as you have been able to formulate what the "style" is. But human nature—as we are certain to be reminded—changes very slowly. True enough; yet human nature has in it more capacities for good and evil than hitherto even the theologians and the philosophers had given it credit for. All it has needed has been the stimuli to arouse these hidden capacities—and it is in the invention and creation of these stimuli, rather than with the development of a social structure fitted to absorb and channelize these newly aroused capacities, that we have been primarily engaged during this last generation.

We have built the fast train, as it were—and now we don't know where to go, nor what to do when we get there. Recrudescent barbarism—like war, racial pogroms, and some of the nauseating "isms" of our day—have emerged, simply because something has had to emerge as we have changed the face of the world and made so many of the old faiths meaningless to the modern man and woman. Human nature, too, abhors a vacuum.

Reflections like these, some critics may say, are not relevant in an autobiography. I think they are; at least that they are in mine. For today I am able to put down in words something of this change. Then, as a boy, I had a kind of dim prescience that great changes were in the air—it was not only the purely instinctive attraction of novelty, which all youngsters possess, it was something deeper, even if vaguer. I didn't then know what it was, or what it was going to be—but I was sensitive to it. I felt that the world was going to change its whole aspect; I wanted to take part in that change—perhaps, even, help to direct it, since even then I was aware it would be a change made by men with their conscious intelligence and with their new power over nature.

Of course I didn't then realize that this profound change was in knowledge, not in will—a change in technics, not in ethics. I didn't comprehend how stubborn and perverse is the heart of man—how we can know the better, yet follow the worse path. I thought that merely to see and know the good and the beautiful and the true must also mean to embrace them gladly. I was not yet really aware that there was the problem of evil.

I was still a child.

III. BEFORE COLLEGE

WHY it never occurred to me, now graduated from grammar school, that I might "quit" the process of learning any more formal academic subjects and "go to work," as it used brutally to be phrased, I can only explain on the ground of inherent New England stubbornness. Even at that dangerous emerging adolescent age of 14 it never really crossed my mind that I was not going to have all the "advantages" of higher education: First I was going to High School, and after that, to college.

But how was I to do it. Even if I continued on my job—my job as a "puncher" in the small factory that made the cards on which cheap Attleboro jewelry was hung for display—I was earning from it only sufficient on which to live during that summer. How could I continue on this all-day job and go to High School at the same time? (There were no Night Schools in those days in small towns like Attleboro.)

Obviously I couldn't. I had to get some other kind of job—an old problem for youngsters in my economic situation at that time in our social history. However, Attleboro was a manufacturing and railroad shipping town, which was lucky for me. Lucky, because I might get a job assisting a regular Express Company carrier, one of the men who had to do fast and concentrated work collecting the packages of this cheap jewelry (every evening around four o'clock, when the products of the day's labor were put in boxes and stamped with impressive-looking red sealing-wax), then rushing them to the Express Office, where they were inventoried, checked, and weighed, and, finally, speeding these packages to the evening train—which in its turn took these blessings of an early 20th century industrialism to the far corners of our noble land. (Sometimes I shudder, when I think of the amount of trash, made in exquisite bad taste, which I helped deliver to a country seemingly eager to receive it.)

Such a job I did get—with hours from four to eight in the late afternoon and early evening. To that job I attribute my strong and lasting love of horses, for the auto-truck was still more or less in the experimental stage, and we had a faithful and fast Old Dobbin, who had more brains than later I was ever to see displayed by stylish thoroughbreds on the race-course. He knew the "rounds" perfectly, would stop at the right entrance doors to the different factories, and even knew when to "speed it up," if we were delayed by some slow packer. And when we got back to the office, and the rush to get all the packages down to the station in time for the train began, he would "step on it" without any demand on our part, seemingly loving the game. The last package would be thrown in; my partner, on the seat, would tell Dobbin to "let her rip," and I would bolt to the street-door of the Office, swinging onto the team in front (grabbing the shaft with my left hand one edge of the seat with my right), as the flying chariot came out of the alley-way from the loading station in back. In sober truth, when today I recall those perilous jumps onto that seat, I sometimes get a queer little sinking feeling in the pit of my stomach. It is a tribute to my youthful agility and fearlessness that I did this stunt regularly night after night—and never once missed.

Three things coincided for me that late September of 1905—first, my new and exciting job; second, my formal entrance into High School and the beginning of my study of Latin and Algebra, both of which subjects delighted me; third, my mother's leaving town to go again to Boston to find nursing work. Our "home" life in Attleboro, as everywhere else, had been pretty brief, and once more my poor mother had had to give up the little house that she had, in her usual manner, so grandiloquently and irresponsibly rented. As a consequence of her going, I had taken a small room, for which the weekly rent was almost nothing, in a house beside that of my "partner" of the Express Company team. Some of my meals I had where he boarded next door; others I "picked up" in little lunch rooms of the period. Directly after my work with the Express Company carrier, I had a light supper, came home, and went to bed. I was up early at five—and without any breakfast, either, for I still kept a strange, superstitious belief in the folly of heavy breakfasts, a belief I had acquired reading some faddist book of that period, way back when I was in my early grammar school days in Cambridge. I compromised on coffee, and at the eleven o'clock fifteen-minute "recess" at High School I ate a sandwich or a cream-puff or a bit of candy—anything to "stay my stomach" until lunch after school.

When spring came round that school year of 1906, I even tried to make the baseball team as catcher. But in the one and only game in which I was allowed to play with the regular team I was, after a single inning behind the plate, hastily transferred to the outfield for the rest of the game; my only exploits at bat were a weak grounder to short, so that I was nipped yards off first, and the dumb feat of being called out on strikes, when the count was three-and-two, without even swinging my bat—to this very day, I think that ball was much too low, that I should have "walked," and that I got a raw deal from the umpire. (It is one of those little things that give "kids" a vivid and early sense of life's injustices.) In my grammar school days I had once, at Taunton, been quarterback on the football team, but I did not go out for the school team the fall I entered Attleboro High simply because I couldn't afford a sweater and football trousers. (That fact, too, was bitterness in my soul.)

The exercise I think I enjoyed the most, however, was skating; late winter afternoons I would skim up the frozen brooks leading to the pond—at times it was like skating through a sort of twisted tunnel, the bare trees were so close together. And I liked it, too, when twilight came over the woods and the pond, and images turned indistinct, with the voices of the skaters coming through the sharp air out of the dark. I used to hum to myself, dreaming great dreams. What those dreams were about I can't remember now, but I recall that "Hans Brinker And The Silver Skates" was almost as great a favorite at that time as Jules Verne's "Twenty Thousand Leagues Under The Sea." In most of these dreams, of course, all sorts of heroic exploits dramatized me in the most shamelessly prominent way, until I glowed with the cold and the exercise —and my own imagined nobility. For I was always forgiving of my enemies in those dreams, generous with the money I had in such fancied abundance, shrewd in detecting and severe in punishing all evil-doers.

I kept up my Express Company work through the summer vacation, aided along by any other odd jobs I could find. Preliminary Latin was over now—and I was going to read Caesar under the direction of Gilpatrick, the principal of the school. Also my first course in physics looked promising—for it was to be given by a young college graduate, who was also our baseball coach. In addition I had made the acquaintance of Bill Macdonald, who introduced me to the mysteries of Elbert Hubbard, the Roycrofters, and "Little Journeys." (I think it is something of a testimonial to my "tough-mindedness" that, even at that impressionistic—and impressionable—age, I did not fall for that stuff particularly.) But Bill also induced me to read Stevenson as a pleasure rather than as a task—and for the first time, I think, I began to be highly self-conscious about what was meant by "style" in writing, as distinguished from sheer narrative. I now looked with superior scorn upon all those who read the Frank Merriwell series of exploits; even Henty and Kipling (excepting "Captains Courageous") was beneath me; and while I still secretly read and enjoyed the adventures of both Sherlock Holmes and those depicted by H. Rider Haggard in "She" and "King Solomon's Mines," I was too full of youthful literary pretense to admit it. Fortunately, I had started to read Dickens fairly early, beginning with the "Sketches By Boz," and I went on from one to the other of his great books with ever-increasing pleasure. And, of course, Mark Twain—is there any American of my generation who was not, so to speak, brought up on "Huckleberry Finn" and "Tom Sawyer" and "Roughing It"? For some reason or other, Thackeray never came into my orbit, though I wish now that he had.

But the strange mixture I have described in the paragraph above gives a fair idea of what was forming my imaginative and conceptual life at that time—as I think it also does that of many Americans now of my age. For although I used the adjective "strange" without reflection—and so, today, such a mixture *does* in fact seem—it really was then, in many ways, almost conventional. Notice that poetry hardly enters into it, though the usual New England poets—above all Longfellow, Whittier, Bryant, Holmes, and two or three of the shorter things by Emerson—were familiar. Of course Emerson's prose essays were likewise part of the conventional "inspirational literature" of that time—and almost as New England as the Cape Cod clam, even if the appeal was on a somewhat higher plane. "Self Reliance" was the bible of those times; the counterpart, almost, to a later generation's sophisticated plunges into the turbulent waters of Nietzche.

And oddly enough I actually enjoyed studying Caesar; I remember I was very proud indeed when Gilpatrick said to me in front of the class, "Why, Mr. Stearns, you read that passage almost as a Roman would do it." But I wish there had been a closer connection between history and my first Latin reading

—as it was, it was an exercise in abstractions. (Remember Van Loon's "The Story Of Mankind," and Wells's "Outline Of History"—these great popularizations of knowledge in a broad sense, such as we have several of today—did not then exist; history was one thing, Latin was another—only rarely did it come to you in a sort of flash that the people whose words you were reading were also the people who had made history.) However, I enjoyed these abstractions, and I got some sense of the rhythm of classical tongues. Also, of their logic, which I regard as important: call me old-fashioned, I still do today. I noticed that the boys who were good in Latin were usually good in Algebra, and even then I had a sort of intuition of the reason—that your *logical* apparatus, or whatever one wanted to call it, was involved in both scholastic disciplines.

Hence I went at my Algebra with natural zest—and I was good at it, too, for four years later, when I took my mathematical examination for entrance to Harvard, I passed both the Algebra and Geometry (study of that came a bit later in my third year at Malden High) tests very creditably. And the course in physics, that second year at Attleboro High, likewise had the natural appeal it might be expected to have for any normal, curious youngster—enhanced by the fact that it was given by our baseball coach. (Wireless telegraphy—let alone telephony, or the radio, as we call it now—was then only in its infancy; today, I should imagine all growing boys want, on their own account and without much urging, quite genuinely and sincerely to know all about the theories of the radio, of aero-dynamics, of television, and of the rest of our modern miracles.)

My first course in a modern language—elementary German, as it happened, instead of French—came that second year, too. I was not perturbed by the grammar, either, for after Latin, it seemed absurdly simple; also I enjoyed reading in the old script, as German was then taught. In some mysterious way I thought that being able to read in this script gave me a special distinction. (I suppose this was a racial hangover from our earlier days of symbol and voodoo worship.) I know that the course excited in me the desire to travel—most of my courses did. For I wanted to go where this language was actually spoken by living people; after all, Latin was a classical (which then meant distinction in my mind) language, but a "dead" one. People spoke German in everyday life; I knew that, but I wanted confirmation—or, perhaps more simply, the natural desire of all boys to "see the world" was being sublimated in my eagerness to learn. (And later, in my Malden High days, when I took "advanced" German, how I thrilled to that romantic book of travel, called *"Aus Dem Leben Eines Taugenichts"!*)

Shortly after the completion of the June examinations for the year, my mother sent for me again—this time to come and live in Malden, a suburb of Boston. She had met a Mr. Newhall, to whom she had become engaged; about the time I came on to live with her again in Malden they were married, and he became my stepfather. He was a curiously silent man—almost stone deaf, too, which partly explained it, I suppose—who was skilled in the rather unusual craft of goldbeating, with an old-fashioned craftsman's shop in Medford. Evidently the tradition of good old Medford rum had not been unknown to him either, for he tippled occasionally—rather to my chagrin, for at that time (odd as this may seem to my friends today; it was not until the second half of my Freshman year at Harvard that I took my first drink) I was still a convinced teetotaler, and would probably have joined any White Ribbon group of those times, had I ever happened to come in contact with one. But we got along all right without much friction on either side at any time, for I was quite glad that my mother, after years of polite gypsy nursing life—and for some time before my brother grew up (at the time of which I am writing he was, I believe, in the Navy), a polite gypsy nursing life that also involved "looking after" two sons, at least as well as she could—that my mother, to repeat, after years of this thankless task was at last really to have a home of her own.

And that home of her own, even if it involved no luxury, at least involved a home for me—and the chance to continue with my school career at Malden High School, where, I want to put in right now in defense of the Old Bay State's educational system at that time, any boy with the slightest bit of ambition could receive as good a "preparatory" training for college as at the most expensive private schools in the country. (In fact, I am now sorry I didn't take Greek, when I had the opportunity.) I continued with my Latin, reading mostly Cicero and some of Virgil; I continued with mathematics, being initiated into the mysteries of plane geometry. Chemistry followed on after physics, and, fortunately, we had a good laboratory, with decent equipment, and a competent instructor. History I still avoided—or perhaps I could not find time for it on my crowded schedule; I can't remember now. Anyway, I only took one elementary course in either ancient or modern history "formally," thought I passed my entrance examinations to Harvard in both—partly a tribute to my own reading and native intelligence, I like to flatter myself; partly to the intense "cramming" of my friend Spear, of which I speak later on.

But I still remember vividly our instructor in English—a man turned prematurely old and grey, but not sour or embittered. He was a quiet man, who liked reading and the scholastic life; he was happy in his job, through bored at times by the repetition. And any new talent of even the feeblest sort pleased him. He liked my compositions—what flights of youthful fancy some of them were, when they were not the bitterest and most self-assured of criticisms!—and encouraged me, as well as taught me soundly about fundamentals. He was proud of me, my last year in High School, when I reviewed books and plays for the Boston *Transcript*—and, I suppose, as I look back on it now, I must have been in a minor respect something of a youthful phenomenon, though I myself took it as the most natural thing in the world—and, I want to add hastily, in case I may give the impression of having been something of a "sissy," which I wasn't, I likewise enjoyed athletics. The only reason I didn't go out for the school teams was because I didn't have the time, and felt embarrassed at what I considered my slightly inferior social position. (It was partly this feeling of inferiority, I think now, which made me decide to go to Harvard, for I knew there was no laughing *that* off—and I was determined, if I couldn't be distinguished in one way, to be so in another.)

It is not easy, in middle age, to recapture some of the phantasies of our youth. But I recall two from that time in Malden High: I wanted to be a hypnotist (I read all the ten-cent pseudo-scientific books I could lay my hands on, and pestered everybody I might into being a "subject," with not much success, of course) ; I wanted also to be a great dramatist. Somehow I had been introduced to the plays of Ibsen, which I didn't understand, though naturally I thought I did—perfectly. And I remember trying to write a play, chock full of the richest kind of symbolism, called "The White Cat." I think I actually got two acts of this preposterous bit of modern stagecraft completed—before my youthful enthusiasm found other channels of expression.

These two ambitions were not unmixed; I wanted also to be a traveler. Those summer vacation days, in Attleboro of my grammar school period, when I had worked as a "relief boy," carrying water to the men who were making the concrete bridges over level tracks—designed to eliminate "grade crossings," those early deathtraps in some New England towns, where the "through" trains went speeding at sixty to seventy miles an hour—I had each day watched the "Bay State Limited" and the "Knickerbocker Limited," both all-parlor-car trains, with envy in my heart for the passengers. *They* were men of the great world; some day I should do that, too. (My first trip to New York, in the winter vacation of my Freshman year at Harvard, was consequently like a dream come true—even if we did, then, land at the old, dingy Grand Central, which in those days could not compare with the Boston South Station for impressiveness. But it *was* New York—really New York, of the kind, way back in Attleboro High School, when at the basketball games the boys and girls used to sing "Take Me Back To New York Town, New York Town—That's Where I Want To Be," I had always fondly fancied in imagination.) But I would travel—as a great hypnotist, acclaimed by all the world, or as an even greater dramatist—in ease and luxury, and always, it goes without saying, to my own immense personal distinction. For of such stuff are one's first adolescent dreams made!

Those dreams took a practical turn sooner than normally might have been expected. Not daunted by my own youth or lack of experience, I went to E. F. Edgett, the literary editor of the Boston *Evening Transcript,* and asked him boldly if I might review some books. I was just over sixteen years old (Booth Tarkington, I suppose, has made that the classic age for a boy's adolescence); I had just put on long trousers—I can remember my self-consciousness at my first pair, exactly as I can remember my eagerness to find some justification for shaving. I was at that age when I badly wanted to look and act "grown up"—as, of course, I felt I was in fact. Luckily, I was not brash or forward in manner—of course, I was rather self-conscious and, as a person really shy (especially a young person) often is, assertive and enormously opinionated, as a sort of embarrassed screen. (I didn't know this; I had no properly corrective home environment, which was abnormal to begin with—I suffered, as do most boys, who have never had the confidence and guidance of a father.)

Edgett gave me one or two rather unimportant, but—for that period—pretentious travel books on which to try my hand. I went at them with great diligence, looking up references in the library, trying, quite naturally, to write in a style which combined the distinctive characteristics of the other critics writing on the paper, tempered by the style of the writers to whom this "outside" reference reading introduced me. Like all youngsters, the two things I most dreaded were to reveal either how inexperienced I was as a writer—or how uninformed I was on the subjects about which I was writing, whether an exploring trip through the African jungles, or a summer jaunt in the French chateau country. Hence, to avoid these two humiliations, I put on the stylistic manners of my elders (and I was at the age, remember, when imitation and any native impulse of one's own tend to blend so closely one cannot honestly discriminate between them), and also looked up, in encyclopedias and reference books, all the information on the subject I could find. This was usually a lot more than I could assimilate, try as diligently as I might to do so. Of course, I realize now, I must have had a certain definite, even if a small, natural aptitude for writing—or I should not have done so well as I did.

From the travel sketches I was promoted to more serious books—now and then to some new novel, regarded as of moment at that period. (I can't remember the name of one of them today; before writing this paragraph I ransacked my memory for just a *single* title—but they are all shadowy and unreal now.) What was even more important, in this curious literary development, was my introduction to H. T. Parker, the dramatic critic of the paper. (Parker died only a week or so before I started to write this chapter; I read the account with a sharp sense of personal loss, though I had not seen him for years.) He allowed me to review some of the regular weekly change-of-program old dramtic standbys, performed by the excellent stock company at the Castle Square Theatre, including the regular Shakespearian favorites—an excellent training in the theatre, and in writing, too. Parker's own style was rather involved, and at times highly colored with adjectives and nuanced with sonorous phrases, but his instincts were sound and his knowledge of the drama (and of music as well) was really extensive—as extensive as his knowledge of life was varied and wide. Furthermore, he never encouraged me to try to imitate him; if anything, he discouraged it, though, I cheerfully admit, I couldn't help a certain amount of hero worship—and hence a certain amount of imitation. Then, too, I had the natural florid tendency of all too-youthful writers; this tendency I then firmly believed was only my native profundity of thought. Besides, it was not so much what you said that counted, it was how you said it—I had just begun to read Charles Lamb and DeQuincey, and I was determined not to appear "amateurish" compared with them. (I smile at that today, but just the same I am glad it was Lamb and DeQuincey rather than Hemingway or Joyce or any of the self-consciously "modern" writers of the 1930 decade.)

Restlessness was my mother's weakness—though I suppose anybody, who had led her roaming type of life, would have become restless by habit. Even her marriage hadn't cured her of her old desire to wander. In that single school year of Malden (my third High School year) we lived in two houses—first in one quite near the High School, the one from which she had married my step-father; then in another a bit further away from the school and the centre of the town, which somehow I remember more vividly—perhaps it was because in this house, through a window from my bedroom on the second story (we had the whole house), I saw the most vicious dog-fight, to the death, I had ever seen.

We had a roomer, I remember too, who remained with us only a short time—a male "nurse." He related to me my first stories of feminine weakness. Sex had begun to intrigue me, of course, and I admired one or two of the girls in my classes in High School with more than disinterested curiosity and warmth. But nothing had come of these co-educational encounters; the closest to any direct experience was an afternoon's boating trip, near Auburndale on the river, with an attractive French nurse, a friend of my mother's. An innocent trip, too, though a year or two later on I realized with chagrin that there had been no good reason why it should have been. I was still shy in that respect, inexperienced, and completely not so much un- as misinformed.

Had I, I suppose, joined the school "fraternity," to which I was invited after a certain amount of hocus-pocus, I should have learned to dance, gone to "parties," and obtained my first experience of sex in the conventional way of that time. But for some reason—similiar in nature to the one that kept me from "going out" for school athletics—I refused to go through with the initiation required; in fact, I had an instinctive dislike of secret societies, a dislike which increased as I grew older. It might have been, if you want to be cynical, an anticipatory fear of "not making the grade," and hence a way of avoiding the humiliation of being "turned down"—by not even trying. There was something of that in it, naturally; but it was very far from being the whole thing. All my life I have hated secrecy, pretense, rank, what we call nowadays "the stuffed shirt." In that respect I am almost frenetically democratic, that is to say, democratic as the French construe the term: I have always been strong for social equality. Quite aside from any envy of financial freedom, I have always despised "society," because its pretenses seem to me based only on fortuitous, lucky wealth—and when, later, I spent some time with the Long Island squirearchy (as I mention further in this book), I found no good reason for changing my opinion. Curiously enough, even at that adolescent age, I felt that anybody who yearned for this kind of "society" distinction did so only because of some personal timidity or feeling of weakness—without knowing it, I was an early believer in the Freudian doctrine of compensation. Had I been brought up in England, I sometimes believe that the social and caste system there would have made me either a snob or a rebel, depending on the station in life to which I had been born.

But I was an American—and I think now, as I thought

then without, however, then being able to express it, that our impalpable social filaments are different, that the backdrop to our social scene is one of rebellion and independence rather than one of conformity and tradition. (I still think so, too, despite the valiant proselyting to the contrary of so many self-consciously "patriotic" organizations during and right after the war—organizations that didn't appear to know the first syllable of the first word of what the American tradition really was.)

Much as I wanted to stay in Malden, when that third year was over, to complete my High School work with a fourth and final year, my mother's "moving" passion again got the better of her—and right after the close of the school year we changed our home to Dorchester. But I was not to be balked this time: My English teacher was a good friend, and he had little difficulty in persuading the school authorities to allow me, as a favor, to continue for my fourth year, and thus finish my course, at Malden High, even though I lived in Dorchester. Secondly, in order that I might have a little money for the trip over and back by trolley, as well as for lunch, that final school year, he sent me to a merchant in Boston, whom he had known for some time, with a strong recommendation to give me $100 for that purpose—which, rather to my astonishment, the said merchant quite cheerfully did. (Those were the days when people still had a pioneering sort of faith in the magic efficacy of education; some business men I know today would give a youngster $100 just as a reward for *not* finishing up with a lot of "useless" knowledge.)

Thus my last year at Malden High found me living in Dorchester and travelling every morning by trolley and elevated to Malden, taking first the trolley to Dudley Street Terminal, then the elevated to Sullivan Square in Charlestown, and from there to Malden again by trolley—employing the hour thus demanded in studying French conjugations and German inflections and grammar. From Sullivian Square out to the school I was going against the morning traffic coming into Boston, and I could work at my leisure. Also, I must add, I worked hard at home, for the entrance examinations to Harvard were only the following June away.

Naturally, I also kept up my work both for Edgett and Parker, dividing my literary and dramatic criticisms about equally—and though it got me no money, it did permit me to have a lot of the new books and to go to the new plays. Even now, over twenty years later, I can still see those "request" notes of Parker's, enclosed in a *Transcript* envelope, with the blue printed caption on the upper left-hand corner, addressed either to the manager of the Hollis, the Majestic, the Colonial, or one of the other Boston theatres of those days. When I had a play to review, I used to come home right after the show was over, make a few notes on my programme, and go to bed. But I was up at four o'clock in the morning to start work on the "review," which I wrote out in what I thought was a distinctive long-hand, carefully aligning my copy and leaving generous margins. On those mornings, after breakfast, I would break my trip over to Malden High, getting off the "Elevated"—which I put in quotations, because the "L" at that point, through the heart of Boston, ran underground and was in paradoxical reality a subway—near the *Transcript's* office on Washington Street. I would leave my copy on Parker's desk, and continue on my way to school.

A strange routine for a youngster, I suppose—but it made a newspaperman out of me early in life. And by "newspaperman" I here mean somebody who has, above almost every other form of conscience, a feeling that copy must be "in" by a certain time. Though the world is coming to an end tomorrow, the paper must go to press at a definite hour, and one simply has to get one's "stuff" down to the composing room with enough margin of time to permit its being set up. All diversions, all other ends in life have to wait on that great turning point of the day—when the paper is "put to bed."

By the end of May, 1909, my thoughts were already far less on what dubious honor was to accrue to me for being graduated from Malden High School than worry about my entrance examinations to Harvard—and how I was going to go to college anyway, even if I passed them. I had confidence, almost as touching as that of Mr. Micawber's least justified hopes, that something would "turn up." But I had no idea of what it would be. Meanwhile, I had to keep hard at it, for in those days getting through High School, even creditably, and passing the stiff entrance examinations to Harvard—the College Board form of entrance examinations was only just coming into existence—was quite another. Furthermore I intended to enroll for a Bachelor of Arts degree, which meant taking elementary *and* advanced Latin examinations. (How I regretted I had not studied Greek!) And I was nervous about my "advanced" Latin—I had had but three years of it, instead of the usual four; I was weak on Virgil especially, and I didn't know how to scan Latin verse. That examination was a nightmare of terror to me, which was probably a good thing, for it encouraged in me a certain much needed degree of humility. Even the fact that I was Class Orator—for some reason I selected a passage of Stevenson for my efforts—at the graduation exercises at the High School did not give me the assurance ordinarily it might, for, when all was said and done, I *had* to pass those Harvard examinations, somehow.

The worst of them—I mean, specifically, those in Ancient History, on which I was weak, since I had never taken an official course in the subject; in Advanced Latin; Physics, which I had forgotten since my Attleboro days; and Algebra, about which I was much more terrified than I had any cause to be, had I known it—came in June, the very month of graduation; the remainder, like those in English, French, and German, came in September, just before entering. A Jewish boy, named Spear, who had been something of a friend of mine during my last year at Malden High, kindly offered to tutor me in the advanced Latin and Ancient History, as well as to give me what he called a "brush up" in Algebra and Geometry. He did an excellent job, too—I passed both the History and Algebra with high marks; the Geometry was not quite so good, but even there I did considerably better than just "get by." What I particularly remember about his tutoring was the manner in which he taught me to scan Latin verse—even when I had never read it before. I think it was my proficiency in that, rather than any charm or accuracy of my translations, which allowed me to ease by that particular entrance examination. (That I wanted, however, to study Latin seriously was proved, I think, by the fact that I took a full course in it my Freshman year at Harvard, when I might have taken one of twenty to thirty other courses.) And it gave me confidence in my knowledge of Latin—not entirely, even if partly, misplaced.

So much confidence that when a Camp Director of that era asked me, on someone's recommendation, to come up to his Maine camp for boys solely for the purpose of tutoring a young Mr. Schwab in Latin, so that he, too, might "pass" his Harvard examinations in September I accepted with an untroubled conscience, for it gave me a vacation, a little unexpected money, and a chance to improve my own knowledge of Latin—as well as to study for the remaining examinations I myself had to take in the autumn. The camp was inland, on a pleasant lake—not far from Bangor, though the name of the nearest little town escapes me now. That year I learned to love the Maine woods and lakes in the summer, and I still today would leap at the chance to spend a vacation there.

But we took excursions—by horse and wagon in those days—to other lakes than our "own," the purpose of these expeditions being to teach us the gentle art of woodcraft and how to sleep out in the open in trick bags. (Though I somehow learned to do it, those nights were a horror to me, and I was always delighted to get back to our regular camp, my own tent, and my own cot-bed. I think it was those nights which have caused me ever since to hate roughing it.) Fortunately, the excursions were few and far between; yet I was glad we had them, because I always enjoyed getting back to the home camp so much after them.

I loved the swimming in the cool lake in the early mornings before breakfast; I learned to paddle passably well, too; I liked to take long solitary walks in the woods, which were so fresh and unspoiled, and like they were when Indians had roamed through them—something of my childhood Fenimore Cooper days came back pleasantly and strongly. Later on, in France, when I went on a long trip over the whole country, I looked for woods like them—but they were not there; everything was too old and too civilized.

As far as my pupil went, I can only say in self-defense that I tutored him, after my peculiar fashion, effectively enough for him actually to pass his Latin entrance examinations that ensuing autumn—though I am damned, even to this day if I know how I did it. Probably the simplest explanation is the true one: I was also studying myself, and studying seriously; my example had something to do with it. And perhaps the best way to teach even Latin is to be learning it yourself at the same time. Also, I was continuing on my English—I remember I wrote an article for Edgett on Charles Lamb, which he used in a Literary Supplement of the *Transcript,* and for which I received a check of $7.00—money that I have earned of which I still continue to be the proudest, for it was my "first check." No, it was very far from being an unhappy summer—perhaps one of the happiest of my late adolescence.

On my return to Boston—and my strange home in Dorchester—I continued my own work for the examinations I still had left to take. I felt fairly confident of passing them, too, even if at the last moment the "Advanced" German examination, for some reason or other which now escapes me, rather intimidated me. But I still had no notion of how I was going to pay the $90 installment on the tuition fee for the year's total $150 fee at Harvard, which was then the academic year's requirement. And in cold fact I might not have been able to enter college at all, had not the father of the boy I had tutored during the summer generously come forward and given me the money. He was pleased with what I had done for his son, he said, and—again like so many people of that period, when "going to college" was a laudable instead of a dubious ambition—he wanted to help. The help was contingent, of course, on my passing the last examinations still before me. I had worked up in camp; now in Dorchester I worked as I never had before—and very seldom have done since. And, speedily enough, the three days of trips over the Cambridge—with the silent, strained hours of writing in the quiet rooms, hoping and trying to remember accurately, and wondering if you had put down "the right thing"—came, and were gone. There was nothing left to do, for two or three days, but wait.

After all these years it is difficult to recall, let alone to recapture, that peculiar and special feeling of youthful elation which came over me, when I opened the letter that formally announced that I had passed "without conditions" and that I was eligible for enrollment for a degree of Bachelor of Arts in the class of 1913 of Harvard College. In all our lives some special things are to us landmarks—and the letter was one for me. Instinctively I felt that I had, as the phrase goes, "been welcomed into the company of educated men"—or rather, into the company of those who were to become such. I know it sounds a trifle naïve now—but there are many things I would gladly sacrifice to feel as I felt the hour of that morning, when I opened that letter. Though she didn't quite seem to comprehend what it was all about, mother shared in my elation, too. And when I went in town to Boston to see the father of the boy I had tutored, he gave me the promised check for $90—which, while he looked on smiling and obviously pleased, I proudly endorsed, "Pay To The Order Of The Bursar Of Harvard College—Harold E. Stearns."

And the days that followed, before I had physically to go over to Cambridge and "register," were something in the nature of dream days for me. I recall I went down to Marblehead, the Sunday before I had to go to Cambridge. I went out across the little inner harbor to the outer rocks, where later as a Sophomore and a Junior at Harvard I was to spend many Sunday afternoons dreaming the great dreams of youth. I had no way of guessing what Harvard was going to mean to me —I knew that I couldn't actually live in Cambridge, that I would have to live at home, at least for the present. But that didn't seem to trouble me much then. I was certain I should make good, get plenty of scholarship, be "a big man" in my class. Coming back on the little local train to Boston, I wondered why people who looked at me didn't realize how lucky I was, how (though I wouldn't have said this to anybody else) important I was—what a great name for myself I was soon to make in college. Nor was it a dream of athletic prowess, or of being the great football hero who carried the ball over Yale's line in the last few minutes of desperate play. After all, I was a bit more sophisticated than that—though, if I am honest, even that dream was not wholly absent. (Had I not been a good quarterback, when I was a youngster? Had I not once played on the Attleboro High baseball team? Who could tell?) I think I should have broken through even my native New England reserve and spoken to somebody on that train, if also another sort of pride had not come in—the pride of being "a man of the world." How silly, we say now, for a college Freshman to think anything like that.

But we are the silly ones; we are the ones that have forgotten what our sensitive and imaginative and dreaming years between 15 and 18 were really like. *We* are the tired and supposedly sophisticated people—just as we laugh at "cub" love, and wonder how youngsters can be such fools over ridiculous and immature girls. We have even forgotten that once we passionately wanted to be dignified.

IV. THREE YEARS—AND A COUPLE OF SUMMERS—AT HARVARD

FINALLY, the great day came—and I went over to Cambridge.

When I had completed the formalities of registration, which included also the little detail of paying the first "Term Bill" for tuition (and I made a little flourish with my check, for I had never before engaged in any transaction that involved so much money at once), I walked back through the Yard to the Harvard Union. I sat down in an easy-chair in the big Main Hall, and tried to look nonchalantly at a newspaper—that is, I wanted to appear very blasé and worldly, in case anybody took the trouble to look at me, as in my heart I hoped somebody would.

But I don't think I read that paper with much attention, for a song was going through my heart, or rather, the refrain of a song never written—"I'm A Harvard Man Now." I was proud and glad; the pride had a little justification, for I had entered with a clean record of having passed satisfactorily—in one or two cases even exceptionally well—all the required subjects, not forgetting Advanced Latin, which had so terrified me. Unlike so many, even of my own classmates, I had no conditions to work off. I was free to take any course I wanted—I could concentrate on one subject, or I could wander gaily from history to economics or to mediaeval literature, as I chose. For my degree of Bachelor of Arts I had only to pass sixteen "full" courses.

For though I had, of course, no way then of knowing it, my class—the class of 1913—was to have two important distinctions: It was to be the last class to benefit—or not to benefit, according to how you looked at it—from being under the "Free Elective" system of President Eliot. Lowell's scheme for concentrated work was not to go into effect, even in its first more or less tentative form, until the class following mine, that of 1914. Secondly, we were to be the last class of the Victorian era—that is, the last class before the World War.

But what a Victorian era! William James had retired, but he was still connected with the university. Santayana had not fled to England and the Continent—in fact, he was to be my greatest teacher. Royce was still expounding logic and symbolic logic, wherein parallel lines not only meet but crisscross; E. B. Holt was to anticipate and criticize the Freudian psychology long before it became the private property of Greenwich Village. Taussig still taught "Economics I"—an elementary course in common sense among other things, a course which might do many flashy expounders of economic miracles a great deal of good even today. Irving Babbitt was thundering out those amusing denunciations of Rousseau and the whole Romantic tribe. In the writing of English, if you were bold and clever, you might first be exposed to the sarcasms of "Copey" and later on, if you were extra clever and not quite so bold, you might receive very tempered praise from Dean Briggs—though in any case, you had the privilege of hearing him read Browning, as nobody else ever had done. You had Kittredge to make Shakespeare alive, and Neilson, who could actually come near to performing the same thing with Milton. You had Barrett Wendell to remind you not to be ashamed of, nor so ignorant as to be negligent of, your own American literature, and—to make you feel close to the soil—he would occasionally tell a witty smutty story that would have delighted any Pullman smoking car of those days. You had Bliss Perry to envelope even so tough a customer as Carlyle in sweetness and light. You had Ralph Barton Perry to make ethics so deadly a game that you found yourself going after Hobbes and Locke like a dog after birds. You had Yerkes—who later, when the war came, proved at least to his own satisfaction that the general intelligence level of young men in this country was so low that one would blush to think on it—to reveal to you how the internal psychological life of such lowly creatures as dancing mice and ants could be as exciting as Eugene O'Neill's later five-act plays; you had, besides, the whole range of science and history and religion and anthropology and art and music.

If you didn't want to become an educated man, it was nobody's business but your own. The college gave you the chance: You could just get by doing the minimum of work, or you could work for a degree with distinction, as it was called —"that very moderate degree of praise," sardonically "Copey" would sometimes describe it. For not merely was there a degree with distinction—that was a matter of a certain minimum number of "A" 's and "B" 's in your work; there was likewise a degree with distinction in a particular subject, say philosophy, history, Greek, English literature, Romance Languages. To obtain the second kind of degree with distinction naturally involved a certain concentration on the subject chosen, a grouping of your other courses around this subject, a thesis, and a general examination (quite outside the specific examinations in each subject) by the heads of the department in which you took your degree—an oral, grilling, nerve-destroying examination lasting sometimes as long as four hours. Just because I didn't like "Copey's" flippant remark—thus are we educated! —I determined early in my Sophomore year to try, as we were always politely reminded to put it, for a degree with distinction in philosophy. For "Copey's" observation might have been greeted with the superior worldly contempt of all things, so affected by Sophomores, had it not been for other experiences.

These concern my Freshman year.

Incredible as it seems to me now, I had a strong urge for scholarship—or thought I did. And like a sensible person, since I didn't have to take even "English A," but was free from the first to take what I wanted, I decided to improve my knowledge of what I thought was the key to all knowledge—language. So I actually took a full course in "advanced" Latin, another in "advanced" French, and still another in "advanced" German. The only concession I made to anything of a general nature was to take two half courses on the history of philosophy—the first one on ancient philosophy under Palmer (a course I suppose almost everybody of my own and earlier generations took); the second on modern philosophy under Santayana. I can't remember much about these courses now, naturally—though I still do remember that I learned to love and admire Horace. And while I didn't understand much about the philosophy courses, despite the elaborate historical charts of the variations of opinion (charts I made myself), I got enough from them to have my curiosity piqued. I said to myself that if I were to concentrate in anything, it would be philosophy.

Here again the influence of my Freshman experiences was deciding. Or rather, the last two-thirds of my Freshman experiences. During the first third of that school year I lived at home, coming over by trolley each day. The last two thirds I lived in Hollis Hall, with G. L. Harding as my room-mate. His own room-mate's father had died unexpectedly a month or two after college opened, and this room-mate (Miller by name) had decided not to come back, even to get his degree. It may have been finances as well as family troubles, I can't remember. Anyhow, Harding was left with this room in Hollis. So it was arranged that I finish out the school year with him there. And thus it came about that I knew the men of the class of 1910—men who were Seniors, when I was a Freshman, men like John Reed, Eddie Hunt, R. S. Holmes—much better, at least during those first early impressionable months, than I did the men of my own class. Even today, when sometimes I think of Harvard, I think of sitting before the fire in Holmes's room—he lived a flight above Harding and myself—while he smoked his pipe and laid down the law to me, incidentally remarking every now and then that I was probably as big a fool as it had ever been his bad luck to encounter in a year's travels—an opinion he probably holds to this day, for he was an obstinate man.

As old graduates can tell you, an unfortunate internal fight between "the Street," as Mount Auburn Street was called (where the expensive private dormitories were located), and the "Yard" (which stood not only for the Senior Dormitories in the Yard itself, but symbolically for all the poorer, less exclusive, less club-memberized, and hence supposedly more democratic men of the class)—this unhappy conflict had split the class of 1910 into two factions and had brought about a degree of bitterness that inevitably came to a head that last half of the Senior year, when Class Officers were to be elected for Commencement Day. Schemes, counter-schemes, plots, political intrigue—I saw it all in Hollis, for being a Freshman, and hence without any authority or interest of my own in the quarrel, both sides talked freely in my presence. It was an introduction to class and personal politics, to pettinesses, absurdities, and loyalties, too, of human nature, which was a better education than even an apprenticeship in a local Tammany organization in New York City would have given me.

Later on the little squabbles in my own class, which began with my Sophomore year, seemed mild and insipid compared with the Homeric battle waged in the class of '10. But the battle of the Seniors, waged right around me and even in my own room, gave me a sophisticated introduction to Harvard life. It helped to confirm me in my determination to be a decent scholar. Holmes helped in that, too, for he was an honor man himself—and a first-class thinker and philosopher on his own account, as his record in the Law School the three following years fully proved. I hadn't much social ambition anyway, and what little I had was pretty effectively squelched by watching the strife in the class of '10. Besides that, I was worried—as all my life, except for brief, happy, strange interludes—about money, and at Harvard as elsewhere social ambitions have little glamour if you are "broke."

Determined to have some kind of a margin for the next college year, I took a job—perhaps it would be more accurate to say that I pulled all the wires I could and obtained one—as a conductor on the old-fashioned trolley cars of the Boston system. My runs were from the Dudley Street elevated terminal back to the Dorchester barn, and I think I can today cross my heart and solemnly swear that I absconded, on the average, fewer nickels a day than did the "regulars." I simply played the game as I saw others playing it, easing my conscience with the reflection that it was for a noble cause—education. What spare time I had off I spent in studying and reading books like Irving Babbitt's "The New Laocoön," and I made up my mind to take his course on The Romantic Movement and Rousseau on my return to college.

As I think back now over the years, I believe that college year—from October, 1910, to June, 1911—was the happiest of all my years at Harvard. I went to live in Weld Hall with a classmate named Duggan—Irish as his name, and opinionated, too, but a good fellow nevertheless. There were also classmates of my own in the same building, including our class president, who had the neutral name of Smith, and who came, if I remember rightly, from Denver. Holmes was in his first year at the Law School and working hard, but I used to go over and visit him occasionally on Brattle Street, where he had a room. We had "beer nights" in the common room downstairs, for while many heart-aches were experienced by those who had the wish to "make" certain clubs, the men of my own class in Weld were pretty congenial and for the most part had no vaulting social ambitions. Besides, we had the class president with us, which was all the social prestige we wanted.

At least on the comaraderie side, it was a happy year. Most of us had our meals at the same tables in the enormous dining room of Memorial Hall; we went to the football games in the fall and the baseball games in the spring together; some of us even "went out" for athletics; we took many courses, such as "Economics I" together; when we were "flush," we would go in town to Boston and see a show. (Even to this day I can remember Elsie Janis, when she sang "I'm So Tired Of Violets, Take Them All Away," and Hazel Dawn, in "The Pink Lady," when she sang that lovely bit, "Flow, River, Flow—Down To The Sea.") Sometimes we would look upon the wine when it was crimson a bit too intently, for there were few teetotalers in the class. On Sundays, when the weather was good, we might go down to Revere Beach and pick up a pretty girl—though most of these encounters, while we all boasted furiously of our prowess on our return to Cambridge, were in cold fact quite harmless.

Yet for the most part it was our college life—our studies, our activities (I mean writing for "The Crimson" and "The Harvard Monthly" and "The Harvard Advocate"—or trying to—and organizing things like the Dramatic Club, the Debating Societies, and even the Anarchist and Socialist Clubs, for we all thought we were politically-minded, our "trying" for different athletic teams and our attendance at the big games)—which absorbed us. And I put in that list "studies" first, simply because that was true. I don't know what the classes of '12, '13, and '14 were like at any other college, though of course I had met many Princeton and Dartmouth and Yale men; I simply know that at Harvard they were pretty serious-minded and fairly hard workers. The "flaming youth" generation must have been after that—in fact, was not "This Side of Paradise" definitely of a later vintage?

As I had planned, that college year I took a full course on Rousseau and The Romantic Movement, given by that stalwart old mediator between extremes, Irving Babbitt. Like almost everybody else, I took economics under Taussig, as I have said. But unlike everybody else—for there was always a certain amount of palavering and persuasion involved—I took "Copey's" course on English composition. I can recall how in what I flattered myself was a noble flight of fancy, he said coldly to me, "Mr. Stearns, there are far too many unnecessary and pretentious adjectives in this story—it is fly-specked with them." It was an enjoyable course, but I then didn't realize that I was to learn more about writing English from Santayana the next year than I had ever learned from anybody before—or have since. I remember likewise a half course on Carlyle, given by Bliss Perry. It made me read Carlyle for myself, that is the highest praise I can give it. Also a course on Milton by Professor Neilson (now President of Smith, I believe). Again I want to record to the honor of my former teacher that I acquired a love for—and I hope an understanding of—Milton I should never have come to by myself, except through happy accident.

Also there was an introductory half-course in psychology, and one of the strangest courses (given by Ralph Barton Perry) I took during my whole career, one on the History of English Ethics, as it was called, where I read—and I must say, too, learned to admire—Hobbes and Locke and John Stuart Mill and Bishop Berkeley. At all events, I was sticking close enough to philosophy and allied subjects to allow me to concentrate for a degree with distinction in philosophy, if I decided so to do the next year.

But though I studied hard, and though I came through creditably enough on my scholastic record, I think it was on the social side the happiest year—and that because I was with men of my own age, and to a greater extent than my youthful pride then permitted me clearly to see, men of approximately the same natural intelligence and ability. Once the class elections were over—and the selections for the more exclusive clubs—there was not much point any longer in being "up stage." One began to make friends naturally, and without thinking too much of the possible social consequences to your college career. College opinion, as it is understood in most other schools, had never been terribly strong and compulsive at Harvard anyway—there was a tradition of irreconcilability, as William James has so finely written in one of his essays for teachers. Even in such little things as the kind of clothes to wear, jokes to make, and sophistications to pretend to—all those ridiculous social filaments that seems so all-important to youngsters—there was considerable freedom. And above all, most important of all, there was a tradition of respect and admiration for scholarship and sound knowledge—I think the most valuable thing I got out of Harvard.

Luckily, early in that summer of 1911, I got a job as a "cub" reporter on the Boston *Herald,* where I met Henry Longan Stuart, who was to be one of my life-long friends. Stuart and I took rooms on Willow Street in Boston—on Beacon Hill—for the balance of the summer, and I can remember how, after work, we used to go to a pleasant all-night cafeteria on Washington Street, where Stuart would tell me tales of his adventures in England, where he was born; how he had written "Weeping Cross," a novel about Catholics and Puritans in early New England (reprinted only a few years ago by my classmate, Lincoln MacVeagh) ; how he had worked and lived in Paris (he decided me to see Paris for myself some day, how strongly decided me I did not then suspect) ; how he came to America on a chance and had always found some sort of newspaper work to keep him going (his last job, incidentally, was on the New York *Times,* where I think he was—he must have been—well loved by all who knew him) ; how he admired "The City Of Dreadful Night" by James Thomson, long passages of which he could quote from memory—and how, finally, he proved that not all really good phantasy in verse was the prerogative of the then emerging "columnists," quoting sometimes, abundantly to illustrate his point, those absurd lines from the Ingoldsby Legends beginning with:

> "Then appeared the maid and the man with one candle,
> Which gave to unpleasant surmises–some handle."

There wasn't, in Stuart, a mean or ungenerous or unintelligent thought—which, when you come right down to it, is pretty high praise. He was a Catholic—perhaps my first experience (though it was not to be my last) with a highly intellectual and sensitive man who professed that faith seriously. When, almost ten years later, we met again in New York, I was engaged in editing "Civilization In The United States," and I asked him to do the essay in that book called "As An Englishman Sees It." He consented—and I think anybody who reads that criticism of America will say that it is one of the most perceptive and penetrating analyses of a fundamental weakness—our lack of proportion and measure—which has ever been written. And at the same time, oddly enough, one of the most friendly, for all its intense, almost passionate Englishness. Stuart is one friend I have had of whom I can say that, whatever I might have been had I not known him, it would have been something definitely poorer and meaner than I am now.

How much I learned about "straight" reporting during those summer weeks on the Boston *Herald* it is difficult for me to say now—though it must have been something, for once or twice I was given a really important local story to cover. At least, I did definitely one thing, for which I have never since ceased to be thankful: I learned to "touch" typewrite—which frees one from the bondage of the particular kind of fatigue, resulting from writing by hand, that probably as much as anything else has been responsible for a great deal of "sloppy," inaccurate, and merely impressionistic writing. In fact, I find today that to write by hand—say at night late, when you don't want to annoy sleeping neighbors even with the slight clatter of relatively noiseless modern machines—is a painful process, which makes me (and hence the style of what I write) self-conscious and almost stilted. To be at my ease, I have to work directly on a machine—at the keyboard of which, incidentally, I very seldom look. When a sentence or paragraph is completed, I may glance down at the paper, half to remind myself of what I have just said, half to suggest what I intend further to say—but at the keyboard itself, practically never. This may seem an unimportant matter; for a writer, however, I don't think it is. And I am certain that this use of the machine, instead of writing by hand, has at least two salutary and disciplinary consequences—it makes for clarity, while at the same time it leaves the mind free to play around the subject and to catch all the penumbrae of feeling, the overtones of thought, so to speak, which might otherwise escape because attention was at least partly on the physical process of writing.

That summer passed quickly, almost gaily. Aided by a small scholarship, by what I had saved from my job as a reporter, and by help from a distant relative (I never had seen him before; I never saw him then; I haven't seen him since—the whole thing was arranged by several of my classmates, who wanted to be sure I came back to get my degree) I returned for my third—my last year. For I knew that by taking as many courses as allowed, and adding to that a half-course, which I could take during the summer school term following, I could complete the full 16 courses necessary for a degree—meaning that by September, 1912, I should have done all the work required, thus saving that collegiate Senior year for starting my "outside" career. Of course I intended to—and as a matter of fact I did—return for a few days in June, 1913, formally to take my degree with my own class.

But I had signified my intention to try for a degree with "distinction." That meant not merely taking, during that final year, the five full courses, which were as many as the college then allowed, it meant also the writing of a thesis and the haunting terror of that stiff oral examination before the board, when all was over. Still, I intended to go through with it. The loyalty of my classmates had moved me more than I wanted to show—and I determined to justify it, if I could.

That final year, when I really worked at intellectual problems as I certainly had never done before and have only rarely done since, I passed in Divinity Hall, living alone. It was only five minutes walk from the Yard, but it was just sufficient isolation for my work. There was a "Common Room" there, too, where some of the graduate students of divinity played chess or checkers and read magazines, but I practically never went into it. A brilliant Jewish scholar, named Wolfson, lived next to me, and I found him quiet and interesting—and devastatingly well informed on almost any subject I brought up, except the subject of girls, or, indeed, of sex life in general, about which he appeared to be as innocent as a babe unborn. Yet I learned thoroughness in scholarly details from him—learned to be careful and to be sure of my authorities when I cited them, that is, to cite them in the sense *they* intended rather than to cite them by a random quotation which might temporarily, taken alone and without the context, appear to support my argument. I learned to cast all forms of "bluff" far from me—unless, of course, I was doing some frankly impressionistic thing.

Yet though I concentrated on my subject that year, as I had to, I still contrived to take a full course in English composition under Dean Briggs, though why I did, I don't know. Robert Benchley was in that class with me, and once in a while Dean Briggs would read one of his pieces, much to my own and everyone else's enjoyment. They helped considerably to lighten the burden of things. But now, years past, I think the one course I remember best was a half course on the Philosophy of Art given by Santayana.

Yet, strangely enough, I am not quite certain, now, whether I took this in my second or third year; I know it was the first half or autumn half of the year. Nevertheless, I remember the course itself vividly: The sunlight streaming in through the left-hand windows of a pleasantly small lecture room of Emerson Hall, sometimes lighting up Santayana's face with an intense glow, as he would say such things as: "The great substance in Leibnitz is not the truth or falsity of his views, but the sweep of a triumphant imagination," or "Emerson's thoughts are like the stars in the sky, each one of them cold, almost feeble, always distant—yet taken altogether they constitute a wonderful firmament."

This was a luxury course in a way, but it permitted Santayana to be one of the examining board, when I came up for a degree with distinction. He was not a member of that board, however, for he had gone home to Spain and England and Europe—never (at least up to now) to return. Later on I met Santayana again twice in Paris, when I remember his telling me he thought "Civilization In The United States" one of the most interesting books he had read from America in years. But I speak of those encounters further on in this book.

Just out of the arrogance of youth, I suppose, I submitted *two* theses, instead of the required single one, for my bid for a degree with distinction—and they were about as diverse as one might well imagine. One was on the concept of sympathy in the 18th and 19th centuries in France and England; the other was on the social life of ants, wherein, somehow, I got in all I knew about dancing mice, for I realized that this would please Yerkes, my professor in animal psychology. The essay on Sympathy was aimed squarely at dear old Irving Babbitt who I knew would be on the examining board. It was full of gentle irony about the confusion that resulted when you let even the most pellucid head be swayed by even the most generous heart, and I rang the chimes on that tune quite merrily.

Naturally, there was little, even a few months later, that remained in my mind about the kind of social life I lead that final year at Harvard. I simply didn't have a minute—the best

I could do was possibly once a fortnight to go "in town" (at Cambridge that always meant to Boston) and have a few drinks, and with luck take in a show. I think only twice that spring of 1912 on fair Sundays did I find time to take my favorite trip out to Marblehead, where I could look out from the high rocks over the sea. All the courses I was taking were exacting—and always, in the back of my head, was the terror of the original theses I had to do, for I early made up my mind that they would not be the conventional kind (I suppose all youngsters do the same, if they are serious). As for girls, well, that was just too bad.

What could I do—even if I had a girl? I had no time. Probably, of course, had actually I had one, I should by some form of casuistry found time to see her occasionally. But in any case I didn't, and I am inclined to think now it was just as well. The goal I had set myself, with all the hard and grinding work involved, really made the need of a girl very remote—though I refuse to draw any moral from that observation. Heaven knows, I made up for my asceticism later on, and at compound interest.

I tried to do some general reading, of course, and I kept up with current news better than the average youngster—chiefly because of my experiences as a reporter, I now believe, though I have always, both at home and later on in Europe, been something of a newspaper addict. Even in my Freshman year Holmes had made me feel that a purely literary view towards life, such as I was then naturally inclined towards, both because of my age and because of my experiences as a prodigy book reviewer on the Boston *Transcript,* was feminine and inferior and dull. I had partly for that reason turned to philosophy rather than to so-called pure literature—and I had contracted the habit of watching the newspapers and forming my "own" opinion on politics as well as on other topics. Ironically, as it seemed to me later on, I was an ardent Wilson booster in the campaign of 1912, and even in 1916 I swallowed him again on the slogan (though it seems difficult to believe now)—"He kept us out of war."

I shared the disinherited man's natural instinct in the America of that day to go Democratic, and, moreover, though I had only a lofty feeling of superiority towards Bryan, I was convinced that the Democratic Party was profoundly right on two points: A low tariff (Taussig had taught us the charms of Free Trade very persuasively), and State's Rights. But I think in my heart it was the underdog instinct which drew me towards the Democratic Party—had I come from a wealthy family, somehow I should have found an excuse to be a Republican. For I had an aristocratic impulse, too—what youngster hasn't? Luckily for me, I tried to express that impulse intellectually rather than socially. As I was "free, white, and twenty-one," a New Englander and a Harvard man to boot, I suffered no early feeling of racial or even family inferiority—sketchy as my actual family life had been. And I am glad I didn't; I have seen that sort of thing poison too many men's lives.

Finally, somehow, the year drew to its end—June was only a week or so off. My theses had been submitted, and on both I had received the flattering mark of "A." It was the day for me to go through my three-hour oral ordeal before the board—I remember I smoked cigarettes nervously and fast, one after the other, as I walked over to Emerson Hall for the examination that, when all my pretence and seeming indifference were alone with nobody to see them, really in my heart meant so much to me. Yerkes was there, Babbitt was there, for some strange reason Kittredge was there, all the others I had expected were there. I tried to act as if the examination were the most natural thing in the world, a sort of formality we were anxious to get through with on both sides as fast as possible and as amiably as possible. Probably scores of other nervous youngsters in the same boat had tried to put on the same mask scores of times before me—I remember hoping that I would be able to be a little arrogant and to return to the barrage of questions at least one or two amusing and "flip" answers.

As a matter of fact, the ordeal proved far less painful than my anxious imagination had painted it in the anticipation. There were, to be sure, a few searching and specific questions, involving facts, dates, names, where you either knew the correct answer or you didn't—and when I didn't, I said so. As for example, when I was asked "What was the smuttiest play of the Restoration," I remembered what I had been told by a member of the class of 1910 (I think his name was Lehman), and, stealing some of his thunder, I replied indifferently that the implication was that I had read *all* the smutty plays of the Restoration, which I had not and had no intention of doing, but that in my opinion Congreve's "The Way Of The World" would stand up with—"or against," I flippantly added—most of them. And when Babbitt asked me what was the idea of "sympathy" in Europe in the 17th century, I replied almost with defiance that he, of all people, ought to know that there was *no* concept of sympathy before Rousseau, who invented it, according to him, and that Rousseau was, after all, 18th century. Yerkes would ease the strain every now and then by asking me direct questions on laboratory method in animal psychology—for he knew perfectly well I knew the answers, as I had worked with him on method. And I think it impressed some of the other professors, who, I am sure, knew next to nothing about animal psychology, and who certainly cared even less. Then, too, the strain was eased in another way—somebody would suggest a general topic, like, say, the problem of consciousness and the different ways this problem had been approached, and ask me to give my own exposition of the problem and my own idea of where, probably, the correct solution lay. This would allow me to give a little lecture of my own, an opportunity I took full advantage of, embellishing what I had to say with dragged-in bits of carefully secreted and saved-up-for-the-occasion wit. Anyway, it allowed me to talk—and I was a pretty fast talker in those days and much surer of myself than I am today. I was willing to give them a talk on any subject they wanted, whether I really knew much about it or whether I didn't. And, after all, I did in fact know considerable about the topic on which I was being examined—philosophy. When the session came to an end (and it had gone much more quickly than I thought possible), I think it was Babbitt who pulled out an enormous cigar from his pocket and handed it to me, saying, "That will be all, Mr. Stearns."

Had I but known it then, that gesture was a practical hint that he thought I had "passed" and had nothing more to worry about. But I didn't know it, and I had that curious, awful "let down" feeling that practically everybody has who has gone through that kind of important examination as to whether or not you are, to be, as the phrase runs, welcomed into the company of educated men. I remember I walked back to Divinity Hall, wondering what I should do with myself—it would be days before I received official notification. And, suddenly, there seemed no more reason for doing anything. Why try to go home and read now? Even if I did, what good would it do me so far as this test was concerned? I had to wait and compose my soul in patience.

Of course I did nothing of the kind. Instead, I went in to Boston—to the old Marliave restaurant, I think it was—and tried to drink up all the strong liquor in the place. Had I had a home to go to, had I even had friends available (Stuart had left; all my college friends had, days before, gone speeding away on their vacations), I should have gone there, or to them. But I was alone—as so often at really critical moments in my life I have been. I went "in town"—and the memory of that evening is a sort of tired blur.

The next day I realized that, however well or ill my oral examination for distinction might turn out, I still, technically, had a half course "to go" to meet the requirements for a degree.

There was nothing to do but to take that half course in Summer School, after all. For some reason—probably because I had liked the way he had taught me to read Milton—I decided to take Neilson's short summer course on Shakespeare. That would be a welcome relief from philosophy. Besides, I had always wanted to read *all* the plays of Shakespeare chronologically, and here was as good an opportunity as I should ever have. Consequently, I enrolled for the course—and the College graciously allowed me to stay on in Divinity Hall the few weeks necessary for finishing it. In that respect, I always in my day found the authorities eager to help a serious student—in fact, I don't know why I wrote "in that respect," for they did in all respects.

Shortly after the course started, I received official word that my oral examination and theses were satisfactory, and that I was eligible to a degree with distinction as soon as I had "made up" the half course still lacking. In other words, I was in the rather curious position of having obtained honors before really I had fully earned them, for after all I *did* have to complete that half course. But I never entered on any course with a lighter heart—nor, I think, did I ever work more conscientiously.

If you worked—that is to say, if you really read through all the plays of Shakespeare carefully and intelligently—it kept you busy, of course, but it was the kind of industry which was delightful to me, after the strain I had been under during the previous few weeks. Neilson was almost as acute and helpful a commentator on Shakespeare as I had known him to be before on Milton, though he did not go in for the philological pyrotechnics that Kittredge occasionally indulged in. After all, it *was* a Summer School course, patronized by eager High School teachers from the Middle West, who sacrificed their vacations for this privilege, many of them, and he had to make much of his comment almost elementary. Yet I thought then, and I think now, that every one of those teachers was a better teacher

—and a wiser person—for having attended that course. As for myself, I know I should have read Shakespeare anyway in that fashion very soon, but I was pleased at the opportunity to ask questions about verbal and other interpretations, when those questions arose naturally from my reading—and to have them, I ought to add, always brilliantly answered.

I remember, towards the end of the course, I one day asked myself, "Why have I been such a fool? Why did I put off reading Shakespeare until this late day?" For I found for myself, as every English-speaking person must find, verbal felicities, bits of pure poetry, marvellous imagery, humor and drama, bursts of anger—is there any greater than that of Cleopatra, when she begins, "Shall they hoist me up and show me to the shouting varletry of censorous Rome?"—that ought to be as much a part of a writer's natural background as the way he hears words in the street.

Those few weeks passed all too briskly for me, since I rather dreaded going out into the world. Yet when I received my postcard, the course and the examination over, marked very plainly "A," of course I felt pleased. But once again I felt bewildered and almost frightened. I had done it! I had been graduated (that is, I would actually take my degree, with my class, next June in 1913, but the required work for it was over) from Harvard with honor, even if it was, as "Copey" might call it—as he would of course—that "very moderate degree of praise," a degree *cum laude in philosophia.* I was an educated man, or so I had been led to believe. That was very fine, of course, but what did educated men—especially young men just turned 22 years of age—do for a living? How did they get a start in life?

I reflected on the fact that already I had done considerable work—book and theatre reviews for the Boston *Transcript,* and then "straight" reportorial work for the Boston *Herald.* Surely, a young man of my talents would have no difficulty finding a place for himself in New York. Instinctively, I wanted to get to New York, though even to this day I do not understand what inner compulsion it was. I know that at the time it never occurred to me to stay on in Boston. I was distressed at the precarious way in which my mother lived, and I wanted to help, but I knew—or perhaps the wish was father to the thought—that I could be of little assistance staying on in Boston, even if I got a good job, which was doubtful. I felt that New York was the only place for me—it was the magnet, as I suppose it still is to all young writers and newspaper men in other cities, just as Paris is the magnet for all Frenchmen (and was later to prove an irresistible magnet to me, too). That I might not get a job, if I came to New York, never for an instant occurred to me—this was long before the depression days, remember. It might be terribly hard sledding for a while, but I was young and could stand it. And I was bound to succeed in time; all I needed was the opportunity. Well, I should find that.

Thus my mind was made up—I suppose by forces that none of us can quite accurately analyze when we try, after the fact, to do so. But I do know that I was as unflinchingly determined to get to New York, as a little over three years before I had been determined to go to Harvard. I recall walking through the Yard, of a late hot August day, and saying to myself, almost like one of the mythical Horatio Alger heroes, "Well, I succeeded here and got what I wanted, when it looked as if I didn't have a dog's chance. Why can't I do exactly the same thing in New York? Besides, I'm young—a little adventure won't, can't hurt me. Damn it, I'll go anyway."

I thought, it goes without saying, that if New York proved too tough a proposition to me, I could without any particular loss on my side return to my home town of Boston. Little did I realize then, as I got on the train for New York one bright morning, that I was leaving Boston forever—that never again should I see it but as a visitor and as a legal and voting citizen of another city. I didn't then realize that not only were my college days over for good, but so also were my Boston days. Henceforth I was to be a New Englander—if that means anything, and I think it does—only in origin and name. I was to be an alien and an outsider to the special spot of the earth that had given me birth and—what we could only hope—an education. Even my mother I was to see again but once in Boston, for after that our few meetings were to be in New York.

In fact, as I write this chapter in the early months of 1935, it occurs to me that although I have now been back in America, my own country, for just three years, somehow or other I have only been once in Boston–and that a single afternoon *en passant* from a trotting meet in New Hampshire back to New York. I have planned a real visit to Boston; several times I have started to go. Somehow, I can't seem to make it. I don't exactly know how to express it clearly; perhaps in my real old age, in a few years, some irresistible force will draw me back to the scenes of my childhood and early manhood—it sounds silly, when transportation is so easy and simple and cheap nowadays, doubly silly, since I should think nothing of crossing the ocean to Paris for a mere fortnight and then returning to New York. Yet getting up to Boston always presents ridiculous and insuperable problems. I think of it as a place I came from, I even have a curious patriotic feeling about it. But sometimes I think, and it makes me a trifle fearful and uncertain, that the New Englander in me has died.

Perhaps it is because I had no genuine "roots" up there, in the sense of a steady home, a town, a street, a crowd I grew up with. Perhaps it is because I am just naturally one of those unfortunate people who really are homeless and spiritual vagabonds. I like to think that that isn't so. But the older I become, the more I am convinced that there is nothing so conducive for happiness in middle age—other things being equal, naturally—as having a home town—who knows? with luck, even perhaps a home. But these are reflections which properly belong to a later chapter. I was going to a thrilling two years—the two years in New York just before the war. They were gay and colorful, and on the whole fairly happy years—is it really possible to be unhappy at 22?

V. NEW YORK BEFORE THE WAR

WHAT fledgling college graduates do today, if they are set upon coming to New York, I don't know. I suppose the more adventurous simply come, as I did, and take a chance, though to break into the newspaper game in New York today must be a heart-searing experience for a youngster who has no connections nor friends—unless, of course, he is lucky. I don't know—I have no means of judging—whether I was lucky or not. But I do know I had not been in New York more than a fortnight before I had my first job—on the old *Evening Sun*. And, if you please, not as a reporter or city man either, but as a feature writer on the editorial page. Sometimes it would be an interview with a politician or a writer (I recall that the paper sent me to Cambridge to interview the popular German philosopher of those days, Rudolph Eucken, who was an Exchange Professor at Harvard) ; sometimes it would be a semi-humorous account of an art exhibition; again, I would be told to see the men behind some new project, and to get them to talk; interviewing Mayor Gaynor was a sort of standing assignment, when you could get near him on those occasions he did not have a battle going on with what he was pleased to call "the corrupt press."

The hours were easy—from about half-past nine until the paper went to press for the Home edition, about noon, as I recall it now. That is, those were easy enough hours as far as the actual writing or "being in the office" were concerned.

Sometimes, naturally, a story would take all your afternoon time to obtain; again it was doing something for the theatrical page, when it usually meant that the evening was gone, for you had to attend the "show" out of courtesy. But I didn't get enough theatrical assignments anyway.

I was pretty naïve in those days, though of course I didn't know it. Don Marquis had a desk in the office near mine, and I used to marvel how, six days out of seven, he got out the "Sun Dial"—all the more, as he was then inventing Archy, the famous cockroach, and Mehitabel, the even more famous feline. He was also writing "Sonnets To A Red-Haired Lady," and a little later, "The Old Soak," and "The Almost Perfect State." I lived on West 86th Street, near Broadway, in a little room for which I paid, I think, $4.00 a week rent. My salary was $15.00 a week, hence with the carfare and a few pennies for newspapers and cigarettes, I didn't have much of a margin.

Indeed, so little of a margin was it that when after a couple of months of this general feature writing, the old *Dramatic Mirror* offered me a job at $18.00 a week—with the added inducement of plenty of free passes to the theatres—I thought I was already making fast strides forward in the world. Yet if I had my life to live over again, with the benefit of the newspaper experience I was later to have, I believe I would have remained on the *Sun*. But in those days the romantic, "roaming" type of newspaper man was still enough of a tradition to make it eminently respectable to skip light-heartedly from one newspaper or magazine to another—sometimes, indeed, even back again. Besides, that $18.00 and the free tickets looked awfully good. Perhaps, too, as for most young men, especially of a New England background, there was a glamour about the stage and the theatre—a touch of hectic adventure. Curiously, I didn't myself have any play-writing ambitions, as so many people seem to have—and even had I, I now think my two years of more or less close contact with New York playwrights, producers, and the actor world would pretty effectively have put an end to them. Outside the natural attraction of "Big" money from a success—intensified today, I suppose, by the chances of selling the movie rights—I had no particular desire to be a playwright. I *did* want to write; I didn't know exactly what I wanted to write, but I knew in a general way that it wasn't something for the stage. I wish now I had disciplined myself by doing—or trying to do—fiction, for I think it is still one of the best methods of training oneself for straight exposition. But a man ought to be a natural story-teller, too, I think—and I am not. I am an expository writer, and often now I believe I should have been much happier had I gone in frankly for an academic and college career. It is, however, impossible for us to analyze ourselves in this way with any degree of accuracy—most all of us, after forty, tend to think we would have been a great deal better off, had we done something else than what in fact we did.

At that time, in any case, for a young man not yet 23 years old, there seemed to be considerable fun and excitement in the New York theatrical world—I mean, I hasten to explain, as a commentator on that world, to be in it rather than of it. Inevitably, one saw a few excellent shows, as one was bound to meet interesting people and pretty and talented actresses. It was then, as I suppose it is now, a sort of special world—almost with its own patois of speech, as certainly with its own standards of good fellowship, sexual morals, and intellectual brilliance. I remember interviewing, for instance, Gaby Deslys in the Plaza Hotel, overlooking the Park, and congratulating myself on what a lucky thing it was I spoke French—though as I look back on it now, she must have had great patience or great perception, or both, to have followed what I was saying. I wrote a powerful piece on Fritzi Scheff; I went to see the popular composers of those days (they were less articulate than they seem to be today) and could explain to you the reasons for the popularity of Viennese waltzes, whether you cared to know about them or not. I interviewed David Belasco, of course, and gave a vivid account of his methods of work—though I didn't in cold fact know anything about them. When Doris Keane became the talk of the town in Edward Sheldon's "Romance," I felt it necessary to inform the readers of the *Mirror* about her theories of acting. Even interpreting Mrs. Fiske's peculiar repressed methods of underscoring her emotional points on the stage was not for me then a difficult assignment.

The winter and spring of 1913 thus passed quite happily. When the middle of June came around, it was easy to obtain a week's full vacation and thus be able to go up to Cambridge to obtain my degree with my class. I had met Martha—my first affair, at least my first real affair—during the winter months, and she had introduced me to the beautiful Florence. Perhaps as a sort of defiance, but now I believe more because I wanted to prove to Boston how I had captured the wit and beauty of New York, I invited *both* of them to come up to Cambridge, when I was going up to obtain my degree. And for some reason or other they accepted. How superior, how much a man of the world (and the really fascinating world), I thought myself to be; and I remember I even felt a little sorry for my classmates, who had had to put in that final fourth year at Cambridge, while I had been seeing the great sights and the great people in New York.

In one sense I enjoyed my graduation celebration more than many of the others in the class—I *had* a job; I was sure of myself. But in another sense, it made me feel like a waif, that same awful, *déraciné* homeless feeling I so often have had since, for, though it *was* my class, I had no room in the Yard of my own, where I could welcome my family (of which, anyway, I had nobody) and friends (of which I had only very few). I was out of touch with even those of my classmates that I formerly knew—I had missed the best year of all with them, i. e., my Senior year. Of course I visited some of them, but that almost made me feel worse. I was glad, finally, that I had not come up alone—and that Martha and Florence were with me. Glad, too, of the fact that it was June, when it really is not easy for any young person to be down-hearted for longer than two hours in succession.

Yet just the same I was also glad to get back to New York—back to my job on the *Dramatic Mirror. That* had at least some reason to it. Besides, there were the boys I knew with whom to play Kelly pool, the routine of the office, even the trip at night up home in the subway. And there were quite a few friends in the theatrical game, too, even though it was the "off" season. Furthermore, Martha had not yet gone on the road, as she did in some play in the early autumn, while Florence, too, proved friendly. It was a quiet, pleasant summer in New York, the last I was ever to know there until 20 years later—the summer of 1933. And as I write that sentence, suddenly I am aware that it was also the last, quiet, pleasant summer, that summer of 1913, for many people all over the world, the last before the great change, the great disillusion, the great deceit. How historical and far away it seems already—as, in 1954, this "New Deal" era will seem old-fashioned, too, with people wondering why so much fuss was then made about naïve people such as Gertrude Stein and E. E. Cummings, and with the *New Yorker* of that day referring to our 1935 jokes as smacking almost of the early pre-television days—as nowadays we refer to the late General Grant or Victorian eras. People will speak naturally of the old-fashioned, hide-bound technocrats a generation "behind the times;" the average citizen, riding in "stream-line" railroad cars will look at pictures in the New York *Times* of our present-day Pullmans, and wonder how we could be so backward; only invalids or old romantic fogies, who love the sea for poetic reasons, will think of going to Europe in anything but the 30-hour regular stratosphere planes—too bad we haven't our American H. G. Wells to speculate for us.

Some time during that summer of 1913 I met Carl Van

Vechten, which was hardly surprising, as he was then the dramatic critic for the old New York *Press*. And around Labor Day, or a little before—then the conventional date for the opening of the fall and winter theatrical season—Van Vechten asked me to come over, as a Sunday theatrical feature writer, to his paper. And at a salary, which I then regarded as princely (and could, in fact, live on today in New York, if I watched my pennies), that is, $25.00 a week. Yes, there was no doubt about it, I thought—I was coming up in the world. Had I not started at $15.00 on the *Sun?* jumped to $18.00 on the *Dramatic Mirror?* and now was going to $25.00 on the *Press?* There was progress for you—and all in the course of a year, since I had left Cambridge. I went over quite cheerfully.

And I can truthfully say that in many ways it was one of the pleasantest years I ever had. Carl was amusing, an easy and tolerant "boss," who never bothered me and was always full of suggestions for an interview or story of some sort, when inspiration on the one eternal topic of the theatre showed signs of running dry. He would get me all the tickets I wanted, though I had little trouble in getting them for myself ordinarily; he would lend me books and suggest articles to read; occasionally, his comments on my own stories were not only witty but in the real and professional sense of the word, helpful. Outside the office, as a matter of fact, I saw rather less of him than I had when I was not working on the same paper—which often happens, when you have the certainty that anyway you are going to see somebody in the "office." Which is why, not infrequently, men will work together on the same paper for years and yet hardly know each other socially at all—yet the moment one of the two takes a job on *another* paper, he will always be ringing up his old side-kick, asking him to lunch, and accepting his invitations to come home for dinner and "meet the wife." Talk about prophets being without honor, save on their own newspaper!

I don't know exactly how to describe the old *Press* of those days, which—when I joined the staff under Van Vechten—either had just come under, or was about to come under, the control of one of the mythical figures of American newspaper ownership, Frank Munsey. But of the old *Press,* whose tradition at least we attempted to carry on, Van Vechten used to tell me, with a slightly cynical smile, that it was "edited by Irishmen, owned by Jews, and read by Niggers"—and certainly it had, for those days, a big circulation in the Harlem region. But whoever read the paper, there were some interesting people on it—Hamilton Owens, for example, who later became City Editor of the Baltimore *Evening Sun,* and two of the most interesting and brilliant girls I ever knew, lovely Mary Pyne, and the dynamic, talented, curiously handsome Djuna Barnes, who herself wrote some of the most amusing feature stories and interviews for the Sunday edition I have ever seen in an ordinary newspaper. I remember, as if it were yesterday, the City Room, and how, when I came in to do my work, I would always look around to see if either Mary or Djuna were there. Seeing either one would make my day brighter.

And I met most of the interesting people of the theatre, too, of that time, continuing in many cases, of course, friendships I had already made on *The Mirror* the season before. In particular, when I worked on the *Press,* I recall meeting Somerset Maugham several times, writing a long interview with and story about him, and going with him to the theatre to see George M. Cohan in one of his earlier plays, like "Forty-five Minutes From Broadway," though I am damned if I can remember just what it was now. Also I met Cohan himself, and Van Vechten so arranged it that I should have the seat next to him in a parlor car going down to Philadelphia, where he was appearing in one of his plays. It gave me a good hour's talk—and, if you please, we discussed Ibsen, or perhaps I should say, I inveigled him into making some "wise cracks" about Ibsen. Of course he made plenty anyway—in fact, that was a very amusing interview, one of the best I ever did. But I did bolder things in some of those interviews than, I think, would be permitted today. I never hesitated to say when I thought the person I was interviewing was, as we now put it, "dumb," but I usually phrased it in such a manner that the unfortunate victim didn't quite know whether I was praising him (or her)—or not. I am certain now that Van Vechten enjoyed these stories that had a touch of youthful malice in them, and I should hardly be surprised, if he in reality encouraged me to "go to it."

My munificent salary permitted me to move from up-town to nearer the heart of things—and I took a room in the thirties, just East of Fifth Avenue. At that time Martha came over to see me quite often, but she was trying to "get on" the stage, and every now and then would disappear on some mysterious road tour—which must have been short in those days, for the company was always being left stranded, with its members forced to find their own ingenious methods of getting back to New York, where, of course, the same thing would start all over again. Florence stayed on in New York—she was so beautiful that she never had much trouble in getting an engagement for some small part in a Broadway production, and over and above that, she had considerable talent as well as a fine native intelligence. Of my salad days she was deservedly one of the most popular and admired girls in New York, for she had that devastating combination of good looks and a good head. And, I ought to add, a generous heart. Often she would bring over a book, a bottle of whisky, some much needed clothing, like shirts, which I never buy unless I am forced to, or even new shoes—and invitations to dinner with her were more frequent than I had any right to expect, had I not been so young and sure of myself. For she could have dined in state with some wealthy and witty admirer any time she wished. Of course at the time I took this as quite natural on her part. I didn't realize then, as I do now, that Florence, Djuna, Mary, and Martha all were exceptional girls—girls exceptional at any time or in any city. Somehow it seemed to me then quite in the order of things that Florence should spend hours going about to second-hand bookshops all over lower New York in order to find for me a special edition of Laurence Sterne's "A Sentimental Journey" and "Tristan Shandy"—just because I had asked for them. I didn't think it unconventional, if Martha found out "inside" things connected with the theatrical intrigues of those by-gone days—merely because I wanted to tell them to Van Vechten and have a nice cynical laugh. I actually thought, as Strong later phrased it in my Paris days, that "the honor was all hers," if Djuna invited me out to her own home in the Long Island suburban wilderness to meet her mother; I considered it in no way or manner strange that Mary would break engagements of long standing to have lunch or dinner with me—merely because I asked her to do so. As I think back on it now, I marvel at my calm assurance, and I wish I could live those days over again, if only to reveal to them some of the affection I now know—and then was much too arrogant to admit—I had in my heart all the time. Perhaps they knew it anyway; I hope they did.

It is not too easy to recall the intellectual stage-setting of those days, for everything was shortly to undergo such a violent disorientation with the war that even to recapture that pre-1914 *mood* is an attempt full of unexpected pitfalls. It was still the era of optimism and hope, that is, hope in an orderly, democratic, peaceable, inevitable progress towards a richer civilization. Reform was almost as challenging a word then as is revolution a conventional one to the youngsters of today—go back and read something like Walter Lippmann's "Drift And Mastery," or Jane Addams's "The Spirit Of Youth And The City Streets" to feel only a hint of that early, naïve, assured confidence. Anyway, I shared the common feeling around me. I was sure that everything was for the best, despite temporary scandals or difficulties—that America (of course with a little clever help, such as I felt myself capable of giving) was really the hope of the world. The Old World was romance—but romance powerless to affect our lives. I thought of a general European war only as I might think of a comic opera war in the Balkans, perhaps accompanied by such gay music as we were then hearing, with Mitzi Hajos singing in "Sari." I didn't really give a damn about Europe then—I mean, of course, politically, not culturally—and sometimes I wish I had never been forced to do so.

For New York was really a gay town in that year of 1913-14, as it had been since 1911. Prohibition seemed far away from us then—and drinks were considerably cheaper and better. It was the year, incidentally, of the beginning, or perhaps culmination, of the dance craze—the fox-trot, to start with—and of the "X-ray skirt." And speaking of drinks, at "Ike's" on Sixth Avenue, not two blocks around the corner from the Harvard Club on 44th Street, Bronx cocktails were two for a quarter (and twice the size given today to bootleg-enfeebled customers), and Ike himself would always throw in another for good measure on the house—so that for a dollar you could have a cool dozen. Exactly what, I hasten to add, I often had. For another dollar, or even 75 or 60 cents in some places down near Washington Square, you could obtain as good a dinner as you will find served today almost anywhere for double or triple the price. What I think was even more important was that, although there was little of the senseless extravagance which characterized the later boom and high wage days following our entrance into the war and the year just before, most people had a job and most people had a little money to spend. The hang-over from the earlier Golden Age was still not felt as anything but the continuation of a great and glorious tradition of "easy come, easy go." Ostentatious display was not frowned upon then, as it is now; it was regarded with mild, slightly amused tolerance and very little envy. Only a few years before that, remember, Anna Held had been reputed to take baths in champagne, relieving the monotony every now and then by taking one in milk—and everybody smiled then, and thought it was fine. For then there was (or we thought there was) enough milk, even cream, to waste in such extravagance. At bottom, too, we still believed that if a man went without anything—particularly the necessities of life such as food and proper clothing—it was because he was perverse, simply because he didn't want to work. There was a living wage for everybody, even the dullest; for those above that level of intelligence, there was—well, almost anything you wanted to make it. Economically, so to speak, it was the firm conviction of most Americans that you wrote your own ticket. Happy days! Happy days!

"Ike's" was one of the gathering-places of newspaper men, composers, playwrights, the more literate actors, and book publishers. It was convenient and quiet and purely "Stag"—and a fondness for the security given men by that is something even my many years in Paris, with its so-to-speak bi-sexual bars, did not completely destroy. My cronies, of course, included besides the regular men from newspapers and magazines the people I had met in the old days on the *Dramatic Mirror*. Sid Lane, for instance, who assisted Russell in putting on the free concerts in Wanamaker's Auditorium for many years, was a regular patron, and many of his music-interested friends, like Dr. Glass, would show up at the fixed hour. The new type of high-powered publicity writers—they didn't call them public relations counsels in those days—were just then getting into their stride, and many are the early "slogans" I heard invented there, under the inspiration of gin and the hope of a generous bonus—slogans, I mean, of that absurd, pre-Ballyhoo era, when "Happiness In Every Box," "One Drop Of Water Like One Shock A Day" (the shock that resulted from *not* wearing, of course, the rubber-heels advertised), "Tiz For The Feet," "Not A Stocking But An Experience," and all the others, some of them skirting the borders of indecency, were the fore-runners of the kind of thing we sometimes inadvertently listen to today on the radio. But the stories were good—better than the boys seem to tell today, more Mark Twainish and native, as it were—and the conversation much higher in intelligence quotients than the youngsters of a generation later than mine have been hearing in the speakeasies while I have been in France. I know it is the inveterate habit of all of us to romanticize the past, but for once I don't believe I have put on the colors too thick, when I reminisce about "Ike's." It was all I say it was—and considerably more.

But the mood of that year that I should like to recapture the most, if only for a kind of strange moral lesson to be drawn, is a mood of goodnature, a mood of feeling secure, a mood of tolerance towards other countries, other people, and even other people's ideas—a mood that seemed to wither up under the fire of the bitterness unleashed by the war, and later by the depression. A mood (I like to think it is the old and traditional American mood) of willingness—as today it is rather the feeling of desperation before economic and social forces too swift and compulsive for us to control—to try experiments, even on occasion to welcome them. After all, there is all the difference in the world between limiting the hours of labor out of respect for a man's right to leisure and limiting the hours of labor so that work—what there is of it—may be shared and passed around—the difference between giving out of abundance, and splitting the loaf because there is only one. Doing the latter may be admirable enough (I should be the last to say it is not), but it is not the same thing. Those older extravagances of course had their absurd side, too, but I think all of us instinctively would prefer to see a man make a fool out of himself through too much generosity rather than see him prove himself wise through too great caution. For whatever adjective can be applied to the mood of those days, there is one that cannot—niggardly.

It was in this gay, if not especially glittering, atmosphere of "Mid-Town" Bohemian New York that I passed most of that year, when I was on the *Press*. I did other work, too, occasionally, like articles for the old *Harper's Weekly*, then under the editorship of Norman Hapgood. The previous year I had written "The Confessions Of A Harvard Man," in two longish installments, for Mitchell Kennerly, of the old *Forum*, but that was to be the end of strictly autobiographical writing—that is, until I came to write this book. The howl of rage that had gone up in several newspapers over these indiscreet, unfair, and malicious reminiscences—judging from the newspaper reaction to them—might have even frightened me off from ever writing anything of a purely personal nature thereafter, had it not been for the friendly letter regarding these articles, which I received shortly after their publication, from President Lowell of the college itself, a man, I ought to add, who when he said he believed in free speech, evidently did believe in just that and nothing else. I also remember that I did one or two small bits—receiving very high pay for them for those days—for the old *Collier's*, of which Mark Sullivan was then editor. However, the *Press* work kept me pretty busy—and pretty happy.

Occasionally, as I have hinted before, I made trips down to Greenwich Village, which was just about that time entering upon the period of its ill-starred publicity as the Bohemia of America. John Reed was down there when he was not reporting revolutions in Mexico or strikes of silk workers in Patterson or something of the sort, and somewhere among my archives is a copy of an hilarious poem he wrote on the yearners of those ancient days. Don Marquis, from a different point of view, poked fun at the yearners, too—the satire in "The Almost Perfect State" wouldn't read badly, even today, after all the turmoil and the many new States we have seen, perfect and otherwise. But I was really not to know much about the "Village" until I came back from my 1914 trip to Europe. The New York I knew then was Mid-town New York, what I think a columnist nowadays flippantly refers to as "The Main Stem." Essentially, it was the newspaper and stage New York of that now mythical period—and a more amusing or gayer New York has certainly not existed for a long time.

"New York Before The War"—such I have called this chapter. For me that is accurate enough. But as a matter of fact, I should have called it something else, possibly "The Vanishing New York," for I really was but seeing the end of a great tradition—that of from 1884 to 1914, to date it approximately —rather than something which represented a new period. What confused me, of course, was my own age, my youth; it is not too difficult for me even today not to fall into a kind of supercilious attitude towards the younger generation that never knew the heroic days before Volstead had even been heard of. But at least I did see the end of that great tradition, and I am willing to cast my vote affirmatively on the question of whether or not it merits the adjective "great." It was the era when H. L. Mencken was a "discovery" of the brighter and more flip part of the younger generation in school and college—surely that dates it for the many, who have learned to admire the Mencken of a much later, more serious, even post-*American Mercury* period, unfortunately we have to say now. If you are an artist, think back (provided always you are old enough) to the first highly publicized "Armory" show, when Cubism made its bow to this country, and hardly a newspaper in the city didn't have three or four humorous articles on "Nude Descending A Staircase." If you are a musician, can you remember when Debussy represented the very, very last word in modernity? For an engineer, I don't know just how to fix the period—perhaps if I say that such a Sybarite luxury as "air conditioning" had never been heard of, outside school buildings, I shall give a fair notion of what those happy, wide-brim, "Picture Hat" days were like. And, of course, this was long before the aeroplane and the radio had become conventional fixtures of our mechanical life. In "Only Yesterday" I think you will find as fair and graphic account, in a short space, of the general aspects of that period as anywhere else. But writing about it has made me feel how inadequate are our best powers of description, even when reinforced with old plates and photographs. All I can say now is that the New York I knew before the war was colorful, interesting, full of life and hope—a great place and time in which to be alive. And, in case you are interested in a footnote, the girls were good-looking, too, even if you might laugh at them, if you saw them walking down Fifth Avenue tomorrow afternoon, dressed in the "latest thing," as they used to call it then.

So that second winter in New York sped by, as had my first—and even more merrily and swiftly. There were always new faces, new interests, new excitements and enthusiasms. Before it seemed possible we were in the spring of 1914. It was to be the last spring of the old era, but I didn't know it. I just knew that it was wonderful to have spring again in New York, that I was very young and life full of fine and infinite possibilities for humor and beauty and love.

VI. THE SUMMER OF 1914

EARLY in the spring of 1914 my old longing to go to sea came over me—that is what it was, though I kept persuading myself it was merely a natural desire to go abroad. I remembered my days as a kid on Cape Cod, when I had looked out over the sea; later days in college, when a trip to Revere or Nantasket, or Winthrop, or Salem Willows—or to Provincetown, most thrilling trip of all, because the longest—was all I needed to make me happy. The Sunday afternoon excursions to Marblehead, where one could sit on the high rocks overlooking the ocean (after crossing the little inner harbor in a launch) and dream great dreams, had made my Freshman and Sophomore years in the springtime unbelievably romantic. Those were great trips, and I don't know that any we have later on in life can compare with them—for our vision becomes restricted; then it is not.

For me there was always romance, always the unknown, across the water. And on the water, too. I don't know what it is; I am really never happy unless I am near the sea, as in New York, though I may not actually look at it for weeks on end. But at night, or early in the morning, one can hear the toots of the harbor boats, and sometimes at noon, just as you are rushing uptown to a business lunch, will come the familiar roar of the whistle from the Hudson—a liner is going out. I always look at my newspaper to see whether it's the Ile de France, or the Berengaria, or the Manhattan, or some other ship I know. How can people be unhappy in such a town? I ask myself naïvely. Because they can always step over to West Fourteenth Street, to the river—and away to enchanted lands. I have walked over to the piers many and many a morning, when things were blackest here in New York—and I have said, "Some day, I *will* go again, happily, as I want to go, as I have always wanted to go. With my ticket back, with security—as a carefree traveler on a few months' holiday." I suppose even the toughest-minded of grownups have their day-dreams, too—to hear them talk, it would seem so—and I know for many people they seem to be what Jimmy Smith in his essay on "Advertising"—in my book of many authors, "Civilization In The United States"—called riding in cars of unsurpassed luxury and speed, with matchless feminine beauty beside one, to the chagrin of all dust-weary foot pilgrims. But my day-dreams have always been partly sea-dreams, too; I can't understand how anybody can be happy in Denver, Colorado. I have lived in Chicago, a whole six months, but the "Lake" never meant the same thing to me. Of course you will ask, "And how about Paris?" But the Gare Saint-Lazare is really very much like the docks here—you welcome your friends from America and England there, as they pile out of the boat-trains; it is there you tenderly kiss goodby the girl who has meant so much to you during the summer vacation months, who swears to write every week and weeps as the train pulls out, and whom, of course, you never see or hear of again; nine times out of ten, when an American steps into a train there labelled "Cherbourg" or "Le Havre" it is not because he is going to either of those towns to spend the week-end—he is going to America. And, usually, he is going out of your life forever—I don't wonder that the French, with almost sentimental irony, officially label the main waiting-room, "La Salle Des Pas Perdus." No, Paris is the one big inland city of the world, where one does not feel alienated from the sea—and to remind you, every day, every night, how close you are to it, there is the river, sometimes with boats gaily flying Norwegian, British, Danish, and (once in a blue moon) American flags. People in New Orleans, for instance, though they don't hear the roar of the tide in their ears, can't feel alienated from the sea. Curiously enough, London seems to me an exception, despite the Tilbury Docks—but London is an exception to everything. Anyway, I shouldn't want to live, if I couldn't see the ocean every so often—and feel it near me most of the time.

That tragic spring of 1914 wore on. But how few of us then knew that we should always afterwards think of it as tragic! The "dance craze" was then sweeping New York and London, with the fox-trot the great thing of the moment: we called that spring hectic—and were almost a little proud that it was. My determination to go abroad became almost an obsession. I had read so much about Europe, thought so much about England and London and Paris—and I was restless anyway. My great love affair had turned out to be nothing but an ordinary love affair—and besides that, it was over. My work permitted it, too. I could do some interviewing "ahead" and get a few weeks pay in advance; and I didn't care much about how I got back, if I got over. I remembered Henry Stuart's telling me, back in the days of that summer, when we lived together on Willow Street in Boston, "Whenever I want to go to a place badly enough, I go. You'll always find a job of some kind to keep you going." Besides, had I not been invited by friends to stay with them in London—if ever I came there? Maugham, in particular, had been very friendly, following my interview with him for the *Press,* and we had gone to the theatre together several times—particularly, I recall, to see George M. Cohan in the popular play of that period, need I add, the period just before that unhappy song, "The Yanks Are Coming—Over There?" Anyway, Holmes had talked so much about Europe in the old days in Hollis at Harvard that I had what nowadays we call an inferiority complex about it. I had to get abroad—I had to see Paris. It wasn't any particular historical interest;

it wasn't any lascivious dream of the easy ladies of Paris—how could they be any "easier" than the home variety? For London, I think, there were real literary fervors—I wanted very much to see the Temple and the Inner Temple, which Lamb had described; the tavern, where Dr. Johnson and Goldsmith had dined; Westminster Abbey, the Tower of London, Waterloo Bridge and Lambeth; hardly a street did not have associations with my reading. And just being in London—"Oh, to be in England, now that April's here" of Browning, kept humming in my head—was enough in itself.

However, it wasn't in April, but almost the last day of June, 1914, when I climbed aboard the old S. S. "St. Louis," of the American Line—a "One Class" boat, if ever there was one. It was very fast for those days, making the voyage in a bit under seven days. I had, of course, an inside stateroom, and I shared it with two fellow passengers. It was too hot to sleep much at night, but it was clean enough and comfortable. As I always, on a steamer, like to walk the decks at night and reflect on my own and human folly in general, most of my sleeping was in the form of "cat naps" during the day—but that would be just as true today, if I travelled in a thousand dollar private suite. The sea excites me; I love to be on it, especially crossing the North Atlantic route; if ever I become rich, I shall make a couple of crossings a year, just to be on the water—or rather, skimming over the water at between 20 and 25 knots an hour. Like so many people, I persist in believing that I should like to have been a sailor. I know, of course, that had I really become one, all my dreams would have been of finding ways to remain on land—though sometimes I am not so sure. As I have said, outside of Paris, I cannot stand any big city not near, or on, the ocean. And I definitely do know that the "Lake" of Chicago depresses me—it seems to get nowhere. River towns, I imagine, are different, too, but I have never lived in one—outside of Paris and London, both of which are exceptions to this rule, as to so many others.

To people a generation younger than I am it may seem incredible the easy-come, easy-go fashion in which people went abroad in those mythical pre-war days. No red-blooded American citizen ever bothered with such nonsense as a passport; that was for diplomats and big-wigs. Your face—and your pocketbook—were what constituted sufficient passport in any country. And usually, too, you didn't decide on what boat you were going—very often, indeed, *where* you were going—until the last minute. It was considered quite "chic," if you had a few hundred dollars in your pocket, or had a checkbook that really warranted that amount, to step into a taxicab in front of the bar where you had been garnering Dutch courage, and say to the driver, "Pier So-and-So," and to your admiring friends, "See you in Paris next month." College boys loved to do it, just as so many grownups, who ought to know better, love midnight sailings—when you can go to the theatre with friends, before you casually (Oh, so casually!) "pick up" a taxicab to take you to the pier. I didn't myself go to quite this extreme, but I recall I bought my ticket only a couple of days before the boat sailed, and arrived nonchalantly at the pier just ten minutes before sailing time. I made that compromise with the spirit of "flaming youth" of my generation.

The trip over was conventional, of course, but I loved every moment of it, and tried valiantly to discover witty and sophisticated travellers in the rather dull and commonplace people who shared my table. But the morning when we sighted land, I could hardly contain myself for excitement, though to my fellow-travellers I flattered myself that I appeared the soul of indifference and boredom. Yet I remember that on the landing stage at Southampton I kept mighty close to the acquaintances I had made on board—what undying friendships, what romances, are gained on shipboard, only to dissipate themselves in thin air after we reach shore!—and was glad there was somebody to talk to, as the queer little English train pulled out of the station for London. Yet, curiously enough, hardly had the train been fifteen minutes in motion before I no longer felt the need of anybody. I remember I kept looking out the window and saying to myself, "I'm in England now!" as if it were a sort of personal triumph. The passing landscape fascinated me—the houses, the people, the towns, villages, rivers, everything. I wanted the train to go more slowly, so that I could see every foot of it; I was alive to my fingertips. And when we finally reached London, I was almost hysterical with suppressed excitement. I checked my bag, and went out into the street—a dream come true! I was in London now. That first thrill was recaptured twice again—when first I saw the shores of Europe (it was gay Ostende, from a Channel boat), and when first I set foot outside the Gare du Nord in Paris. But just then I had no thought of the future; the immediate present was too all-absorbing.

I walked around in an aimless way, but observing everything and everybody, listening to this curious new English. I remember going into my first London pub, and being highly self-conscious as to which class I belonged, when I ordered a "Half and Half" because I heard somebody else do it. I knew vaguely, of course, that the class to which you belonged depended on the money you wished to pay for your drink, but I thought there might be other social ramifications, too. And like all first visitors, I wanted—wanted pathetically—to be polite and yet to do the "correct" thing. Even on that first day I was made to feel the great heirarchic scale of social "caste" in England; and it didn't offend me just then. I was too interested—as an explorer might be interested in the home life of cannibals. After a couple of drinks I went out into the Strand, and for lunch went into "Simpson's," where again everything fascinated me—and the chops seemed good, but the vegetables too heavy and too much boiled. (I was to find this last objection to English cooking only too often aroused later on.) Of course I bought two or three London newspapers—the *Morning Post* fascinated me with its superior tone and detached manner of speaking of the "European" Crisis. (It would have fascinated me considerably more, had I known what was going to happen in a few days. But I was in a state of "fascination" anyway, which is why I find myself spontaneously using that verb three times.) Also I wanted the main news from home—there was not a boat newspaper, with the latest wireless dispatches and financial reports, as nowadays—and even the skimpy dispatches in the London newspapers gave me that. Chiefly the news was from European correspondents, the City (which I discovered meant stocks and bonds), and the Court (and there seemed an interminable lot of that), and a few special articles of a kind that would never get by an American Sunday editor of those days. The book page interested me, too; it was damn well written, but the tone was so supercilious that it was difficult to determine very often what the book was about, if anything.

On a chance—for it was Saturday, and I thought everybody in London went out of town for the week-end in the summer—I rang up Somerset Maugham. To my surprise, he answered himself, and said, "Where are you staying?" I replied that I didn't know, as I had just got in that morning. "Well then," he said, "get your bags and come up here. I may be out when you come, and I may have to stay out for dinner, but the servant will attend to you. The address is so-and-so, Chesterfield Street, Mayfair West. In any event, I'll see you in the morning for breakfast."

This was my first introduction to English hospitality—to its casualness in tone and manner, yet its desire to make the visitor feel, as the French put it, *chez vous*. But it is the kind of unobtrusive, non-critical hospitality that I personally relish, and I wish we had more of it at home. Leisurely I walked back to the railroad station, got my modest bags, and took a taxicab to the address, arriving around five o'clock. The servant took my bags, asked at once if I wanted tea (I felt too nervous to accept), showed me to my room, and arranged a bath without my asking. (He assumed I wanted one, I suppose, since I had just got off a boat.) Then he inquired what I should like to have served for dinner. Trying not to appear too naïve, I replied politely that I left that entirely to the convenience of the housekeeper. I recall, too, that I had one moment of embarrassment when he asked me if I intended to go out in the evening and did I want my evening clothes "laid out." I said "No" quite simply, reflecting with some bitterness that I had no evening clothes—in fact, few clothes of any kind.

"So that is the way it is?" I asked myself. "I'll remember that next time."

It was a strange, solitary dinner in that charming house (incidentally, Maugham told me afterwards, the same house where the original of the heroine of Meredith's "Diana Of The Crossways" had once lived.) I didn't dare to exchange anything except the most obvious commonplaces about the weather and my trip, with the impassive servant. (Yet even then I had an instinctive feeling—oh, had it only been France!) It was an excellent dinner, but I was glad to come to the end of it. After a respectable time, the servant said, "I assume, Sir, you'll want to see something of the town. Leicester Square is amusing, Sir, of a Saturday night. There's a bit of life there." He gave me a key, and explained how I could get in by myself. "And if you want anything, Sir, just ring." (To tell the honest truth, only late that night, as I was falling asleep, did I realize that the long cord hanging beside the bed was really the bell.)

Anyway, I went out and went to Leicester Square, as the "man" had recommended. By that time it was too late to go to the theatre—and besides, I preferred, for my first night in London, to walk about and see the sights. I went into one or two of the more pretentious bars, where I was at first rather naïvely surprized at the ease with which you might talk to almost anybody, especially the girls, of whom there were an unusual number—most of them English or Irish or Scotch, of course, but a few of whom were French, or Belgian-French. German girls were conspicuous by their absence, though I may not have been in the right "quarter" for them. Though I had "a bit of money in my pocket," as the English express it, I contented myself with buying a few drinks and exchanging a few sallies of what, I fondly thought, was worldly-wise wit. (Don't most people, especially young people, feel worldly-wise after their first trip across the ocean?) But I recall I obtained no definite impression from that evening—it was blurred and confused. And, finally, around midnight, I was glad to walk back to Chesterfield Street. I fell asleep almost at once. The excitement had tired me out.

The "man" woke me at ten o'clock, brought up my breakfast and the newspapers (the size of the Sunday *Observer* took my breath away), asked me if I had had a pleasant evening, adding at the end—as if almost casually—that Mr. Maugham would be pleased if I had lunch with him rather early at one o'clock. I took my time about bathing and dressing, and dawdled over the stupendous *Observer*. And at noon, or a little after, I went downstairs. Maugham himself was in the drawing room, and greeted me for the first time in person.

"And did you have any thrilling adventures your first night in London?" he asked pleasantly.

I confessed, rather shamefacedly, that I hadn't. I had wandered around. That was all. I had not even taken in a show.

"Well, that's too bad," said Maugham. "You're a young man. This is your first trip to London. You ought to have adventures."

Then, after a pause, "How much money did you bring with you?"

I confessed the extremely modest truth.

Maugham smiled. "You'll need more than that. You need clothes, too, don't you—and London is the place to get men's clothes, as Paris is the place for women's. I tell you—tomorrow you go to my tailor's and order some things. While you're in London, you ought to take advantage of the fact. And I'll give you some money, too, which you can repay when fortune smiles later on."

"If it does smile, ever," I said, somewhat taken aback at this kind of hospitality.

"It smiles as easily with good clothes on your back as it does with poor ones."

At lunch Maugham told me that he had just finished, as he described it, "a long, portentous novel." "And," he added, "I don't know what to call it. I like prepositional titles. Can you think of any? But I suppose you ought at least to read it."

I did read it, later—I honestly think one of the great books of our time, as, from quite a different point of view, D. H. Lawrence's "Sons And Lovers" is one of the great books of our time. But the only suggestion I had was "Of Fleeting Things," which Maugham had thought of, too, but had rejected. (I gave this title to Strong in Paris years later for the general name for his column of comment in the American newspaper for which he used to write there.) Finally, he hit on the title that expressed what he wanted. Need I add what it was—"Of Human Bondage"?

The Ulster and Irish situation, like everything else that summer, was very bad. Everybody was nervous about the Sarajevo business, and Maugham said that day, I recall, that the outlook was very black. After lunch we took a trip out to Windsor in the car; it was a lovely summer day, and he kept repeating that a general European war was "unthinkable." I know now—and I somewhat dimly understood and felt even at the time—that he was saying that because he *wanted* it to be unthinkable. But he was afraid of it. It was an obsession with him—as, indeed, it was with every intelligent man in Europe during those first few weeks of July, 1914. I think now that everybody in their heart of hearts knew there was going to be war—how great, how calamitous, how terrific, no; but war of some kind, and probably a general European war—just because that was what everybody *didn't* want. It is not easy for me to convey my exact feeling about this now, years after the fact, especially as I was an American—and such a thing as our ever getting into it seemed then as preposterous as a new Civil war. In fact, even the idea of a general European war seemed more like an H. G. Wells fantasy than a sober possibility. But everybody was talking about it.

Maugham showed me about London, and, so to speak, "put me on my feet." When my weekend visit was over, I found myself a room near Victoria Station—a pleasant room in a house managed by pleasant people. Nothing could have induced me to go to Bloomsbury. Walter Lippmann had come to London shortly before me to write things for the then *Metropolitan Magazine,* and together we visited Graham Wallas at his suburban home, for I had always been keen to meet Wallas, being an admirer of his works, above all of "The Great Society," which he had just then finished. Wallas, too, was worried about the possibility of war—there is even a curiously prophetic anticipation of it in "The Great Society" in the first chapter, written months before the war was even dreamed of. All this talk about war made me nervous, and I decided to get to Paris before anything happened. Lippmann was going over to Germany, and we arranged to go together to Ostende for a few days.

We crossed the Channel on a little steamer—and I don't believe I shall ever forget my first glimpse of Europe, of which I had dreamed so long. It was the beach at Ostende. But the gaiety of the colors of the houses, hearing for the first time in my life the chatter of people all speaking naturally a language that was not my own, seeing the French and Belgian newspapers on the stands by the quay—it seemed like a fairy story come true. It is almost worth while keeping away from Europe until you have grown up, just to get that first thrill which comes when you put foot on the Old World. In spite of yourself, all the memories of your childhood reading, a blend of old history and romance, will buzz for a while in your head. It is worth while not travelling too much, I think—things are so magical when you do. It was sunset, when we arrived, and all the little town seemed golden to me. We had dinner at Lippmann's hotel, where I stopped also, and I could hardly eat anything for the first fifteen or twenty minutes—to his great amusement.

In the evening Walter had some work to do, while I wandered about the *estaminets* (or bars), as I think they were called. I walked along by the beach, too, and gazed, for the first time in my life, *Westward,* over the sea towards home. Little did I then think how many times later in life I was to do exactly the same thing, with a kind of unspoken longing (and often unadmitted, too) for familiar homely things. It seemed to me then quite easy to understand why the sea always challenged Europeans; I could understand Columbus for the first time—I knew then why he had been unable to resist the pull of the setting sun. (Or at least I thought I did—I had, as the French say, "emotion" about it.) Yet I was glad to be in Europe, as a visitor. I did not then realize how soon I was to be glad that I was *only* a visitor.

We stayed at Ostende for a couple of days. Walter made a few shrewd remarks about men being the one really modest sex—for the daring one-piece bathing suits on the beach were the closest thing to nudity I had ever before seen in public. I didn't mind them in the least, once I became accustomed to the shock. Neither, in my private opinion, does anybody else. The real trouble with nudity is not moral at all; it is vanity. Most of us look so damnably ugly with all our clothes off that, if they didn't exist, we should probably have to invent them. I noticed that the natives of the town paid not the slightest attention to these Venuses.

It is difficult for one of us, who afterwards has lived for a long time in Paris, to recall exactly one's first impression of the city, especially if we make its acquaintance when we have grown up. I suppose it is Sacré-Coeur, gleaming on the hill of Montmartre, if you come in, as I did, to the Gare du Nord rather than, as do most Americans on their first trip, to the Gare Saint-Lazare. But long before you reach Paris itself, or even its outskirts, you find yourself looking at everything with a kind of strange intensity—the houses, the orderly, square, neat fields with the trim unwinding ribbons of narrow white roads that are lined with the inevitable high poplars, the villages, always as if all their buildings were huddled together for sociability or protection around the church or small cathedral, the softly rolling green of the trees and woods—as you come through the Forest of Chantilly, only one more hour's run to Paris itself—and the curious, startling unexpectedness with which, after you swing on the main tracks at Saint-Denis, you are there. No suburbs, as we understand them; no long, interminable shanty-town preliminaries. People are reaching for their hats, are snapping firmly closed their bags. *C'est Paris!* It is one of the things you envy young people for—that first arrival in Paris. And perhaps, too, you remember Mark Twain's joke about all good Americans going to Paris when they die; you remember—and smile. For you are alive, and young, and it's really true.

I wanted to get out of the station at once—to walk around. And without being exactly certain, I guessed that *"Consigne"* meant, as we should call it, a baggage-room, where I could check my suit-case. I can't honestly recall what street I went down, or how I did it (probably it was the Rue Lafayette)—but within an hour, watching everybody, listening to people speaking French without, on their part, any apparent self-consciousness, I finally reached the centre of town, that is, the Place de l'Opéra.

There, about five o'clock of that hot July afternoon of 1914, I had my first drink in Paris—a vermouth-cassis, I recall, because it looked gay and because other people were having the same thing. I remember it tasted like a heavier, sweeter syrup than I used to get as a boy in the fairs of New England—and always since then it has had for me this sort of carnival aura.

But it was fairly cold and hence grateful—for the weather was terribly, sticky hot; people seemed to have only enough energy to get out of the sun. Yet the bustle and hum of traffic were, to me, deafening; and one of my first impressions of Paris—one I have never lost—was of its animation, its life and color and stridency. The bells on the buses have a gayer sound; the toots of the taxicabs are shriller and more cheerful, less menacing even if they ought to be more, considering the way Paris drivers dart their cars in and out of traffic; there is always an undertone of people walking, doors slamming, little bells ringing, laughter, bits of music from the cafés, saucers being slapped down on tables, as the faithful consumers pile up their drink reckoning—and, of course, bits of the French language itself, of French slang, of Paris accents, *Midi* accents, argot, God knows what, none of which are entirely unmusical in themselves, as we all know, theoretically, before we visit Paris yet cannot quite get over being a bit surprised at when first we do go there.

My conversational French was poor and halting—it was the conventional High School and year-of-college French of my day, which enabled one to read the language easily enough but was of very little help to me in speaking—and I made no attempt to enter into conversation with anybody. Besides, I wanted to read the newspapers, and I bought several, including of course *Le Temps*. Was there, after all, to be war? I couldn't understand many of the editorial arguments pro and con, but I was shocked at the tone of the comments—not at their violence, I mean to say, but at their gravity. It was obvious every editorial writer regarded war as inevitable—and the accent was ominous. But a European war! No, no, that was like one of the H. G. Wellsian fantasies of the future, which I had just been reading. "In our civilized era of 1914 a general European war is unthinkable." I kept saying that over and over to myself—and yet, somehow (perhaps it was a sort of telepathic nervousness in the air about me), I didn't believe what

I was saying either. I didn't know what to believe; I felt jumpy —and alien. Almost I wished I hadn't come to Europe at all. Yet that was not true, either; it really was wonderful to be in Paris of all places at such a time. Yet . . .

After reading the newspapers I wandered around a bit more, still curious, still eager to see. Finally I went inside a restaurant, which had the usual side-walk tables spread out on this hot night, and started to order my first meal in France. The waiter had just taken my order, when everybody was startled by a sharp, ominous crack, like a whip—yet not like a whip. I think everybody knew what it was instinctively. There was an immediate uproar, suddenly the street was crowded, and the police seemed to be everywhere. I had only seen a man topple over a table, then everything was confusion. Somebody had been murdered, I knew that. I wondered if it had anything to do with the war. I walked on for almost an hour, found a quiet little café, and sat down and had a delayed meal. But even then I noticed the quality of some of the dishes, which years later were to become as familiar to me as my own native codfish and baked beans. I should have noticed that quality even more critically, had my mind not been on that dramatic episode.

The newspapers seemed to be on the street everywhere at once. The shouts came from all sides—*"Jaurés est assassiné!"* And my heart stood still for a moment; I knew that was the spark which might kindle the whole arsenal of rebellion in Europe. Would the murder of such a man make it possible for the Socialists of the world to unite? Only they could stop the war. I knew that then instinctively. Would they do it?

I do know, no matter what the history books may tell you, that for a few hours in Paris that night it looked almost like an even-money bet. I walked down the Boulevards, arm in arm with people I had never seen and whose language then I knew but slightly, singing with them—and my heart was in it, too— of all songs in the world to sing on the streets of Paris in the summer of 1914, the great "Internationale." As long as I live the swing and pathos of those first words will be with me: "C'est la lutte finale."

An introduction to Paris of this kind is not the conventional one of prowling for cheap sex adventure. I think that is why always I have had a more serious feeling for the city than does the average American or English visitor. I know that when finally I got back to my little hotel and fell asleep that night—or early morning, rather—I was emotionally worn out. And I felt dazed and uncertain all day Friday. I went around, of course, taking in all the regular tourist sights, and I enjoyed them, too. But the newspapers made me jumpy again. There was an almost ominous hush over everything—and that is not romantic recollection of the past, either.

Saturday morning my nervousness increased. I thought I would go out to Saint-Cloud, though not to see the races—at that time I didn't know there were races at Saint-Cloud, and even had I known it, it would have meant nothing to me. I went out by street car, and took a walk in the park near the famous Sèvres pottery works. It was still hot—abnormally, terribly hot. So, after my walk, I came back by one of the little river-boats. I got off at the Concorde landing, and walked up the Rue Royale. It was about quarter past four in the afternoon.

I noticed a crowd gathered round what looked like a bulletin-board of a post-office. Everybody was reading it—quietly, intensely, tragically. It was the order for "General Mobilization Of The Forces Of The Land, The Sea, And The Air."

It was war!—Everybody knew it. I knew it. It was then I heard all about me the French expression, so difficult to translate, though meaning, more or less, it has happened at last: "ça y'est!"

And I can't remember very clearly how I spent that late summer afternoon. I know that there were crowds again on the Boulevards, this time singing patriotic songs, like "C'est

Alsace et la Lorraine, c'est Alsace qu'il nous faut," to the tune of "Under The Bridges Of Paris." Everywhere you saw men hurrying to railroad stations with bags; on almost every street-corner you saw women kissing their men goodby, as you saw sons kissing their fathers and brothers kissing brothers goodby; you saw tears and heartache. And you knew that all over France these same scenes were being enacted. Of those I saw myself that afternoon I have often wondered since how many came back and how many are alive today to enjoy, as this generation of French sometimes sarcastically puts it, the "fruits of victory." I should hate to know the real numbers—perhaps there isn't a single one.

Sunday afternoon I left Paris for London. On the train down to Dieppe you couldn't have put another person unless you had put him in the smokestack of the locomotive. Mostly the passengers were English, of course, anxious to get back home. At Dieppe the cross-Channel boat was slow in getting off, too, and I well remember that it was not until early Monday morning that we reached Newhaven, arriving back in London about noon. I went to a little rooming house on Palace Street, near Victoria Station, which had been recommended to me, took a bath and a rest. That evening I went to a show in which Elsie Janis was singing "You're Here, And I'm Here, So What Do We Care?" And the English loved it, just as I did, too. I made it a point not to look at a newspaper. I saved that for Tuesday morning, the 4th of August, 1914. Little did I know that it was to be one of the memorable dates in the history of England and the world.

And Tuesday morning I did go at the papers seriously. First, of course, the general news and the progress of the German army in the invasion—there could be no doubt they were walking through almost unmolested. Where did France and Belgium intend to make their stand? Secondly, the news about England. Was she, or was she not, going to "march," as the French expressed it? How about the pledge to safeguard

Belgium's neutrality? Did that mean nothing to England? In any case, were not her interests seriously at stake? Could she afford to see France crushed? Please remember—this was the morning of August 4th, 1914. I was not even in my own country. If anybody had told me that morning that we, too, were going to enter the war and that I should only a little while later on be eating "Liberty Cabbage" in New York, because the German word would not be used by patriots of the 100% variety, I think I should have regarded him very much as I should regard somebody who believed that Kansas next week was going to pass a law approving of polygamy.

The news about the ultimatum to Germany seemed authentic in any case. And there could be no doubt that there had, as yet, been no answer. I looked again. What were the terms? An answer by 11 o'clock that night of August 4th—that very night! Something told me that there would be no answer; I knew that at 11 o'clock England would be officially at war. I think everybody else did, too.

But they were very gay about it—madly, insanely gay, it seemed to me. Was joining a European war a holiday? All over in three months, eh? Was everybody out of his mind? This was not a quick war of the 1870 variety, unless by a very lucky accident. It would probably last at the least a year—I felt sure of that much, though had you asked me the reason for the boldness of my prophecy, I couldn't have told you. I had the feeling that vast, obscure forces were jamming and forcing men into situations. It was sort of fatalistic, hopeless—the kind of look I had seen on the faces of some of the men in the railroad stations in Paris, waiting to go off to their regiments. I suppose there were cheers and flowers somewhere—there must have been; I have seen the pictures. But all I knew, all I felt, was the sadness, the tragedy of the living going to death that I had seen in Paris.

When, finally, at eleven o'clock the bell of "Big Ben" boomed out, the mood of the crowd became almost hysterically gay. It was unbelievable—girls riding on tops of taxicabs, their skirts up high enough to reveal most of their legs, tipsy, drinking out of bottles, singing cheap little catch-penny songs of the moment, such as "Another Pill For Kaiser Bill!" Walter Lippmann told me later that he spent that evening in the National Liberal Club, and that the atmosphere of the place and the mood of everybody in it was sad and depressed. Perhaps it was; I suppose it was. But why didn't he look out the window? I am always more interested in how the dull and ordinary common man takes big historical events—after all, they are the goats, as we put it, and they ought to have some interest and some reaction. Possibly they do act like sensual fools. Well, why shouldn't they? They pay the bills every time—the "Kaiser Bill" that they were going to do such things to, just as our boys later on were going to hang him to a sour apple tree, was at last accounts doing very well in Holland, thank you. And only the vanishing memory of many of those boys who reeled about London that night remains with a few relatives. I hate hypocrisy; I am glad they did reel—damn it, I am glad they did get drunk, if they wanted to. At least they don't sleep any less securely in their graves than do the noble boys who believed all the war myths, never took a drop, never winked at a girl, and died for dear old Chelsea or cheaper Lambeth, which had never given them a decent thought.

Often I have been accused of being a pacifist. I doubt it myself. But I know that as a young man at that time I was not only glad to be an American—I was proud to be an American. *We* would never be dragged into any such mass-murder as this European war might well turn out to be. That was my belief then (just as it was the spontaneous attitude of most Americans at that time). And about the only genuine pacifist sentiment in me is this: As I look at the consequences of our getting actually into the war later on, I wish we never had gone into it. If you can show me any great economic, spiritual, or social byproduct of our entering the war that can be set in the balance-sheet against what we lost, I should be glad to know what that byproduct is.

I stayed on in London just a few more weeks. I wrote a few stories for my own paper, and I sold a few stories of my impressions to one or two news syndicates. But I never got any satisfaction out of writing anything connected with those days and the hysteria of those days in Europe (nor did I then guess what the hysteria was to be like in my own country later on). Even if I tried, I could never be a war correspondent; there is something ghoulish about it—a real war correspondent, I mean, not somebody who writes about war in the accent of and with the romantic mentality of, say, Richard Harding Davis. I remember a few quiet excursions around London after the exciting days. But, bit by bit, the war began to "get" me. And when, finally, I climbed on the boat-train for Liverpool, where I was to take back the same S. S. Saint-Louis on which I had come over, though we had landed at Southampton, I was quite happy at the thought of getting back home.

The critical days of the first Battle of the Marne took place while we were on the water. And by the time I landed in New York we all knew that the Germans had been held up, that their main objective—Paris—had failed. And I thought then, when I was 23, as I think now when I am 43, that I shall never live to see victorious German troops marching down the Boulevards of Paris. As a matter of fact, I am not particularly keen to see the victorious troops of any one nation marching down the streets of the capital of the nation it has defeated.

But the war was still a great sensation when I returned home. Newspapers were so violently pro-Allies, some of them, that headlines such as this really appeared: "French Withdraw At So-And-So . . . Hotly Pursued By The Cowardly Germans." Others were quite mildly pro-German, for the stories about Belgian atrocities had not yet reached any wide circulation. And in one respect at least almost all the American newspapers were pro-German—especially, as I looked up files for the weeks of the beginning of the war which I had missed, being in Europe and not seeing any American newspapers, before the Battle of the Marne. That is, they were all, or many of them, pro-German as long as the machine did work. There was a kind of ashamed admiration for the way in which the German army had moved across the miles of varied territory with almost the precision of clockwork. But when the machine blundered, when it miscalculated, when it came upon the unexpected reserve power and moral courage of the French in defending their own on their own ground—then the tone changed. There was little genuine admiration, in New York at least, for Germany after the debacle of the Marne. Later on, of course, there was a recrudescence of this admiration of efficiency—an admiration Americans seem unable to control—when the submarine campaign began to give such a high batting average of results. Anyway, during those first few months on my return the war in Europe was the whole thing.

One would have thought that the autumn of 1914 would have been a good time, consequently, to find a job on a newspaper in New York. But it wasn't—at least for me it wasn't. Of course I did some work for my "own" newspaper, the New York *Press,* and for a time I continued feature articles and interviews for the Sunday theatrical section. But that soon was cut down to something precariously infrequent; finally, to nothing at all.

And there I was, just turned twenty-three, with all kinds of capacity (or so I thought), a college graduate, a European traveller and man of the world (this I was surest of), and with no end of personal charm. If there was any doubt in your mind about the latter, you only had to ask me about it. But I didn't have a job; I didn't have any money; I didn't have a girl. What ought one to do in a melancholy situation like that? Something was demanded.

I decided to become a Bohemian. But the story of Greenwich Village is another chapter.

VII. WHEN GREENWICH VILLAGE WAS YOUTH

THOUGH it lasted almost four years—from just after the war started in Europe until eight months after we had entered it ourselves—my typical Bohemian existence of that time in Greenwich Village is not easy to recall either in detail or chronologically. For during all that period my nearest approach to a "regular" job was that of being a "salaried contributor" to the *New Republic,* and that job, furthermore, did not materialize until after I had already been back home a couple of years. Of course, for some time before I got that particular job I had been contributing quite regularly to the magazine, and I sold an occasional article to other magazines or newspaper syndicates.

In a word, it was the characteristic pot-boiling existence of the time—except that I had few of the proper ingredients to put in the pot, even when I could find it. What I could do best was too special, perhaps too intellectual, for the kind of helter-skelter life of an occasional article here, a little piece or interview for a newspaper there, a book review somewhere else. I never could—and I didn't then—make a go of it; for I am a person, naturally, of pretty regular habits (above all, regular habits of work). If those habits are broken, or if I am not allowed to form them, I am miserable and unhappy. Yet somehow I managed to survive.

For I was still young; I was still flexible and adaptable.

Occasionally I picked up the oddest kind of publicity jobs. I played poker well enough to make a profit on it with fair regularity—when there was any money in the crowd. Living was cheap, too—incredibly cheap, when compared with today's prices. There were days of hunger, it goes without saying, but there were windfalls, too. My girl—for I soon acquired one, of course—was a good fashion artist and made more than her share of what was needed to keep up the semblance of a ménage, though as a matter of fact she lived out of town and "commuted," hence her contribution to the ménage was more in the nature of a manager than a resident. She bought everything; she prepared some of my meals; she paid the bills and saw to it that I had new clothes when my old ones could not any longer be repaired—and all this, as if it were the most natural thing in the world. I made more than enough to cover my modest expenses, but there were occasional celebrations—at Polly's (the old one on West Fourth Street), and at the Brevoort. These celebrations my girl considered her share or, perhaps, her pleasure. I taught her French and history and English literature—so well, in fact, that later on she was able to edit trade magazines successfully and competently at really decent salaries. In fact, she can still do so today, and will almost proudly tell anybody, who might be so indiscreet as to ask her, that she was taught by me.

Many people have their own memory of Greenwich Village. Mine, at least, has the merit of being extensive. There was the old Boni bookshop on Macdougal Street, and there was the famous Liberal Club. There were the different corner saloons, especially the one at the corner of Sixth Avenue and Fourth Street (now an empty lot), where in the back room hung a photograph of a nude lady looking out through the blinds of the window of a darkened room. Eugene O'Neill and Art Young and Jack Reed (when he was in town) and Walter Franzen (whom we have lost) and Peggy Johns and Clara Tice and Thorne Smith and God knows how many of the others, some of them still living today (and some not), may even remember that picture. I hate to think of the number of drinks I have had at the table directly beneath it.

Polly's restaurant was then the real meeting-place, and some of the poker games that went on around the big table in the kitchen—after the restaurant was closed—still remain vivid in my memory. On occasion Barney Gallant would play, and I shall never forget how when—on a "bluff"—he was finally forced to call. "Well, what have you got?" asked Barney. "Aces," said his opponent. "How many?" demanded Barney. "One," confessed his opponent, starting to throw his hand away. Barney looked long and thoughtfully at his cards—"That wins," he said, and there was tragedy in his voice, though of course everybody else roared with delight. But it worked:—I mean, ever after that, whenever Barney *had* a good hand, nobody would believe it—and would pay high for the privilege of seeing himself beaten. Advertising pays, sometimes. "Sept" Wilson was really master of ceremonies at these poker games, and the way he would and could control the game—"Come on there, Shaky Bill," he would say, "make up your mind whether you've got a chance to fill that inside straight"—was an example of how far diplomacy could make invective agreeable.

Before I had acquired my girl, while the poker games were still going on—interspersed with contributions to the *New Republic,* the old *Seven Arts* magazine, reviews for the Boston *Transcript,* anything I could pick up—I lived for a time in an old rooming-house on Greenwich Avenue. Walter Franzen, whom I had known in Cambridge my last year at Harvard, was a roommate of mine there for a time. Those were the days when the game room of the Lafayette was popular with everybody in the Village, as were the bar and restaurant of the Brevoort. In some respects the game room was more popular, for it was purely an after-dinner place for coffee and liqueurs and games and conversation; you could sit there and talk with the Villagers, both the successful and the indigent young hopefuls, without it costing very much. And on your way home, usually, you might "look in" at the Brevoort to see who was there also and who, by some miracle of selling a story, a picture, or an "idea," was for the moment solvent. Walter and I were often at the Lafayette together in those days.

Walter was a tall, young, handsome lad with a slight scar across his face, which, rather than detracting from his appearance, set in relief his fine, delicate features. In addition, he had one of the best minds—a gift of God, if ever there was one—I have known; it was quick, analytic, perceptive, humorous. He had read a great deal—and in German and French as well as in English—but he always had retained consistently his own highly personal point of view. He had physical as well as intellectual courage, and he was not afraid of man or the devil, though in manner he was unassuming, almost self-deprecatory. Now as I look back on it, I do not wonder that he was so attractive to women; he combined genuine romantic qualities in a fashion to be encountered only once or twice in a lifetime.

Luckily, too, Walter was tolerant—he needed to be with me. The constant worry as to how to "get by" would be enough to make anyone jumpy and irascible, let alone one with a rather high-strung temperament, such as I was the unfortunate possessor of at that period. But Walter was merely amused when I got drunk one night, wandered out late onto Greenwich Avenue clad only in my underwear, and somehow found my way back to our room by climbing an old-fashioned fire-escape. If I had missed my footing, or—what was more likely—mistaken the window and gone into the wrong room (they all looked alike), the consequences might have been quite other than comic. However, what bothered conventional people never bothered Walter—but goodbye to his friendship with you, if you lied to him, or if you made either scholarly or intellectual pretenses that you couldn't justify.

It was while living with Walter on Greenwich Avenue that I first met Charles Ashleigh—an English Jew, who, in spite of his conversational cleverness and personal charm, always gave me a slightly uneasy feeling, especially when he talked about the wrongs of the exploited laborers of the world, for Charlie's interest in "labor" was obviously debonair and unreal, as it so often is with a certain type of romanticist. (I mean, simply, real laborers have few illusions about their work; for the most part, despise it, and invariably will quit it, when they get the opportunity.) But Charles had done considerable "bumming"; he knew "the Jungles," Bill Haywood, and all the I. W. W. jargon of that period. Over and above that, he had considerable native intellectual power, and could understand —and quite frankly admire—anybody clearly and dramatically his intellectual superior, like Walter. Later on, Charlie paid dearly for his espousal of the cause of the workers, as he would put it. He was sentenced to a Federal prison along with the others in that famous and disgraceful I. W. W. case, where ten or fifteen years was considered mild punishment. But when reason came back, after the war, and all of them were pardoned, he returned to London. (Bill Haywood, you may recall, went to Russia, where he ate his heart out for a time trying to understand the whole business in a strange land among people whose language he couldn't speak and whose habits he couldn't understand.) Years later I met Charlie in Paris, over on a holiday from London, where he was editing a Communist sheet and having a good time. The memories of Leavenworth had faded; now that something much more extreme than the old I. W. W. idea was functioning in Russia and really working, Charlie was mellow and assured. We talked of "the old days" on the sidewalk café of the Dôme that afternoon, but only once did we mention Walter—it was too painful for both of us that he was gone.

For in those early days on Greenwich Avenue Walter seemed too vital—too inevitably destined for great things instead of destined, as it turned out to be, for a mysterious death on the rocks below a cliff overlooking the sea in England. That he was adventurous and restless did not then seem at all strange to me. But if one wanted an indictment of modern education and modern civilization, I still believe that the fact that Walter Franzen was permitted to wander around New York, without finding any outlet for his great talents, would furnish a better indictment than all the Socialist orators have ever been able to draw up since before Debs. Sometimes, when discouraged at the difficulties always faced in this country by anybody trying to do honest and unbiased intellectual work, I think of Walter—and, if perhaps not all the bitterness, the discouragement goes. At least, I have been permitted to survive, though, perhaps, that is because I have not quite the same kind of courage he had. Or better luck.

Shortly after the spring had come in 1915 Walter was off again on one of his trips—this time to Canada and a lumber camp. And it was then I moved into a little room on Washington Place—the house is still there, but has been made over—only a few doors from where I was to be living later on that tragic January day when I received news of my wife's death. But I had not even met my future wife then, and the thought of marriage was far from my mind. Those were my Bohemian days—the truly Bohemian days. And even at this late date I find it impossible to look back upon them with anything like what many people might consider the proper degree of regret—I suppose they were wasted; I suppose I was "getting nowhere." But I'll be damned, if I am sorry for them. For in certain ways, due to that Bohemian experience I can never be "taken in" by conventional people in quite the same way as the average citizen, even if that involves, as Chesterton would inevitably point out, that you are often left out in the cold. Well, I have always preferred cold clearness to confused warmth—perhaps that is my one serious anti-social trait.

Before I could realize it, the summer of 1916 had swung into calendar reality—and it was then I had the strangest job of my whole career: The job of companion. Herbert Croly obtained it for me. I was to go out to Roslyn, Long Island, and more or less make myself somebody to talk to (and with) the elderly Mr. Bryce, the father of Mrs. Pinchot, now wife of the Governor of Pennsylvania. I was, of course, to live with and be one of the family—though I could come into town any time I liked. Croly advised me to go, saying that the social duties would not be onerous, which, in fact, they proved not to be. And rather to my surprise, Mr. Bryce, despite his age and obvious weakness, was intellectually quite alert—at least on certain subjects—and had a fund of reminiscences from his diplomatic career that were vastly entertaining and sometimes enlightening. At dinner, too, there were usually guests of political and social importance. Above all, it was the summer of 1916—the summer when the elder Roosevelt was denouncing Wilson as a pacifist—and with election coming on in the autumn, discussion was sometimes heated. "He kept us out of war" was a slogan that infuriated many who thought we ought to be in it, just as it pleased the fundamentally pacific American majority—indeed, as I look back on it now, I feel certain that that slogan re-elected Wilson, ironical as that may seem today. And doubly ironical, as it seemed after April, 1917, was the *then* popular song, "I Didn't Raise My Boy To Be A Soldier."

There were things I learned about the Long Island squirearchy during those summer months that I have never forgotten. One thing particularly impressed me—the democratic notion of social equality was all a sham with most of these people, especially when they didn't know it and talked loudest about their democratic sentiments. Another thing was their abysmal ignorance of American history and economic theory. Their whole life was anecdotal and really devoted to the serious task of avoiding being bored; and politics was just another form of diversion, as social service is often a form of diversion with other and less monetarily endowed people who have nothing to do with their time. A real aristocracy—I mean, a genuine one of blood—began to look terribly attractive to me after a few weeks on Long Island. Failing that, what we used to call "Bolshevism" with an accent of terror, seemed mighty good to me, too. In fact, anything looked good to me which was not like that pretentious and ignorant vulgarity, flattering itself with unctuous "liberal" sentiments. It was then I learned to be suspicious of all people who have not at some time been hungry and cold—hungry and cold in the midst of plenty, because they *have* to be, not merely as a social service thrill-teaser.

During that summer I kept up my tutorial work with my girl—let us call her Felicia—by correspondence. I saw her, of course, whenever I came into town, but I made her do her work in French by herself and submit the results in writing regularly. She was reading, at my suggestion, Romain Rolland's "Jean Christophe" in the original, and certain chapters I made her translate, with explanatory notes as to why she chose certain English expressions and substituted one tense for another, or, sometimes, deliberately altered the tense in order to obtain an *equivalent* effect in English. My object was threefold: To introduce her to an important and interesting book, to make her familiar with narrative and descriptive French prose, and, finally, to give her some sense of the immense resources of our mother tongue. Part of her work, in addition to this, was a reading of the newspapers and preparation of summaries on topics I might choose—much as we see in *Time* these later days. Only, remember, *she* had to do it—it was not done for her. I forbade her to read the *Literary Digest* or any periodical that summed up the news, even going so far as to tell her to "lay off" the editorials in the *New Republic* (an occasional one of which I might write myself) and read only the frankly reportorial articles. Book reviews, too, were forbidden. "If you are not a perfect fool," I used to say to her, "all you want are publishers' bare announcements. You can go into any bookstore and in ten minutes tell for yourself—after all, you live in New York, where bookstores are handy."

Towards the end of that summer, Mr. Bryce had a bad heart attack—and it was obvious that what he needed was a doctor and not a companion. During my curious sojourn in the rich pastures of Roslyn I had met a Mrs. Cram—a strange, friendly, fluttery little woman of enormous goodwill, who interested herself in "causes" very much like that famous caricature depicted by Don Marquis in "The Almost Perfect State." But when I said goodwill, I meant it: She hated war and she hated exploitation of labor. There was a strike going on in the iron-ore mines on the Mesaba Range, near Duluth, Minnesota, which the I. W. W. were exploiting for their own purposes, and, if I remember correctly, Elizabeth Gurly Flynn was one of the chief "agitators." Anyway, Mrs. Cram asked me to go out and investigate for her—and if I could, write an article on the strike for the *New Republic.* As my work with Mr. Bryce was finished and nothing else engaged me beyond my occasional book reviews for that paper, I accepted and went.

That trip left three indelible impressions on my mind—first, of the unspeakable dreariness of those little industrial iron-mine towns out in the wilds of Minnesota, only a few miles from the border of Canada, where there were green woods, game, lakes, and natural loveliness; second, of Chicago itself during a record-breaking "heat wave," and third, of what sensuality might mean—from an experience in Chicago with a pretty young woman I had known only by sight before at the old Liberal Club in New York.

Even today, when I want to remind myself of what industrialism can do—I mean, of course, industrialism untempered by anything more gracious than a desire for all the profits going—I think of those ugly, dreary, desolate blights on the "open-pit" scarred earth of those iron towns near Duluth. I remember saying to myself then, "If civilization, after several centuries, has been able to bring into existence anything as ugly, hopeless, and cheap as this town, then it would have been a thousand times better had we remained in the pastoral stage." I had seen ugly places in New England, like Lawrence and Lowell and Pawtucket and Brockton, but even at their worst, there was always something to redeem them—relatively speaking. But these iron towns near Duluth had nothing. The population, too, was something of a shock, for English was almost a foreign language among the people I encountered, that is to say, the strikers themselves or the workers, if you wish so to phrase it. I suppose it was something like the "Black Country" of industrial England—only I hadn't dreamed that it existed in my own country. The more dramatic iron-workers' slums of industrial Pittsburg were known to me, but at least they were alive. These towns, though they furnished the sinews of iron without which all our so-called gracious living would collapse, were not dramatic and—except for this temporary strike, which was lost—were dead. I am glad I went, though. I knew for the first time what Socialist orators meant when they talked about "exploitation."

Returning through Chicago, I had a chance for my first and only interview with big, one-eyed Bill Haywood, whom—I must say—I liked enormously. I understand his power over men after five minutes' conversation, and I learned, too, as I have said elsewhere, what sabotage really meant. What I hadn't seen for myself on the iron range he told me and I knew that when I arrived back in New York I should have quite enough material for an article.

Also, I had my first experience, as I have already hinted, with real sensuality. It left an impression, a purely sensuous impression, almost as vivid as those we read about with startled shame-faced recognition in later adolescent years in the confessions of Rousseau. And here again I find our whole moralistic approach to such things not so much true or false as quite beside the point, and, when you come to analyze it, irrelevant.

Morals, after all, are concerned with action in its social significance—they are not, or at least ought not to be, concerned with personal sensations that have no general implications. These are matters of psychological interest perhaps, as some people are more sensitive to music than are others. But I came back from Chicago a changed, in the deepest sense, a grown-up man. Intellectual, sensual, emotional naïvete was gone forever.

The *New Republic* liked my article on the strike and the conditions in the iron mines, and featured it. Whether Mrs. Cram liked it or not I cannot say, or whether she thought she got her money's worth. Probably she did, for later on she asked me to help her to do some publicity work against war—yes, that was almost the phrase she used—at the rather indelicate period just following our own declaration, and I wrote a booklet for her on the civilian rights that soldiers still retained, despite being soldiers, in a democracy—a booklet she had printed and distributed in draft camps, unless it was confiscated, which, had I been an officer, it certainly would have been, since it was subversive of any kind of discipline, although I seemed blissfully unaware of it just then—but that, after all, was a later period.

On my return from Chicago and the mines I took a little flat on Charles Street—not a stone's throw from the house in which I am living today. And in that house, until I again went to Chicago, this time to assume editorship of the *Dial,* I spent some of the happiest months of my life. The *New Republic* had at last put me on a regular salary, which, though small, enabled me to live modestly—together with the help of a few articles, here and there, for other magazines. Felicia took a small apartment in the same house, a floor above me, so that I had all the advantages, whatever they may be, of "living with" a girl, and at the same time of being independent and having a place of my own to which I could invite my friends occasionally for dinner. It was in that little Charles Street house that I brought up the famous cat, Madamoiselle Rabelaise, whom I had plucked out of the gutter at a tender age—an abandoned little pathetic dirty *mèauw*. But she developed into a famous cat with a personality so strong and definite that I feel safe in saying that many people, like Alvin Johnson and Alfred Kuttner and George Soule, will remember her even to this day.

It was while living in that house that the memorable "close" election of 1916 took place—and I might as well confess that I, too, voted for Wilson. I fell for the "He kept us out of war" stuff, just as did so many others, though I had my suspicions, even at the start. The work on the *New Republic* was interesting at that time. I remember with enjoyment many of those late afternoon walks from the office on West 21st Street over to Sixth Avenue with Francis Hackett, Philip Littell, Walter Lippmann, Alvin Johnson, George Soule, Charles Merz, and the others. Littell was always good-natured, always amusing, and he was forever teasing Francis Hackett on his complete ignorance of any literature, even including his own, that is to say, Irish literature. But Francis didn't care and always came back with a good one in reply—I had the impression then that there was considerable affection between them. Walter, of course, was a little more stuffy and bowed down with the cares of the world, but even he would unbend occasionally long enough to laugh at one of Alvin Johnson's wisecracks—for Alvin had a merciless tongue, when he wanted so to use it. I think all of them looked upon me at the time as something of the "bad boy" of the office, and they refused—sometimes with a casualness that drove me to furious anger—to take any of my opinions seriously, but I think they all were fond of me rather than the reverse. I know that once Felicia and I worked for two days planning and scheming to serve a good dinner to Alvin Johnson the night he came to my little Charles Street apartment on my invitation.

No, those were happy days in Greenwich Village—perhaps the happier because we were all under the uneasy shadow of the war and vaguely felt that at any time it might reach out and draw us in, too. Walter Franzen had come back from his last adventure tour and was a frequent visitor. It was "boom" time, and even those who weren't making much money were always on the verge of doing so—and prices had not gone soaring either. Prohibition had not yet arrived to trouble anybody, though that, too, was ominous and in the wings ready to do its preposterous song and dance act. John Reed was doing some of his best reportorial work on the war; the Washington Square Players were beginning to function; Max Eastman and Art Young and the others of the *Masses* crowd were busy lambasting the life out of the war profiteers and capitalism in general—of course at a time when nobody cared. And for me, too, that period remains vivid, when otherwise it might become dim in memory, when I think of Florence Deshon, who was still alive, still so beautiful; she, too, would come to see me once in a while. Randolph Bourne was doing some of his freshest and most penetrating work; Floyd Dell was in New York, too, at work on his first novel. Who of that crowd can forget those evening meetings in Alyce Gregory's little apartment in Patchin Place?—where some of the wittiest and shrewdest conversation and comment of our day was to be heard almost any time?

Though I knew all about it, I have not mentioned the more publicized and spectacular side of the Greenwich Village of those days—the Pagan Rout balls at Webster Hall, characterized by nudity, intoxication, and the envy of rich "uptowners;" the spectacular performances of "Doris, the Dope;" the Sunday breakfast carnivals at the Brevoort; the heart-burnings of the young painters and writers, many of whom have since become so famous that they actually repudiate their Bohemian days. Bobby Edwards was still singing "Way Down South In Greenwich Village;" Thorne Smith had not yet written a single one of his hilarious books; Jack Macgrath was seen by and known to everybody (what has happened to *him*, too?) ; Clara Tice was doing her line drawings for the "flossy" magazines and parading up the Avenue with her two famous greyhounds. I could go on indefinitely, but for those who remember the old Village at all this will be enough to summon up a picture and a recollection that they can themselves recreate. It has, to tell the truth, struck me as curious that nobody has already done it in a book, in spite of the fact that there have been several attempts.

I think it is because it is our lost youth, when the world was young and amusing—that strange world before we entered the war and became one of the great nations of the earth; the world when "isolation" for us was a reality, at least as far as our feelings and hopes and memories could go. Sometimes I wish it could come back.

VIII. WAR AND CHICAGO

THIS afternoon, if you are in New York, you can take a Fifth Avenue bus down town, alight at Eighth Street, go downstairs into the Hotel Brevoort by the new corner door, and in back—in exactly the same spot as years ago—you will find the bar. And the little table on the Eighth Street side, nearest the bar, is where, in the good old before-radio days, was a news ticker, which gave you not only the important stock and bond quotations of the day, but brief summaries of the news events. In case of an important political speech, say during a campaign, or a President's message, the words would be typed out reasonably clearly and rapidly, so that there was always some helpful person standing near the machine, when a phrase was completed, ready to guess the conclusion of the whole sentence—though, of course, you had to wait a few seconds, as the actual words came clicking down on the ribbon, to determine whether the guess was correct.

It was here, that fine spring evening of 1917, I partly heard recited by some excited member of the group surrounding the ticker and partly read for myself, the famous address of President Wilson to Congress, asking for a declaration of war against Germany, wherein occurred the phrase which was to kindle first enthusiasm, then irony, and finally contempt—"We must make the world safe for democracy." I myself had hoped for some specific declaration of aims and policy, such as we supposedly obtained later in the "Fourteen Points" address, but the one unescapable thing proposed was conscription of men. The "selective draft," it was politely termed—what ironical memories that description of it must awaken in many men of my age! Well moistened, as Rabelais might put it, with the juice of several Bronx cocktails, I made a few loud, irreverent remarks during the typing out of the speech. And I obtained my first taste of what the war hysteria was so soon to become, when a man, whom I knew on other grounds before to be a particularly stupid fellow, wanted to "knock my block off" for not showing a proper patriotic spirit and respect for our President.

For a few days after that speech one might have deluded oneself into thinking that Congress—which at that time, let historians say now what they wish, was essentially not keen to "get in"—would fail to vote the measures asked, but I didn't so delude myself. I knew that we were going in (or rather, that we were being dragged in, as I then thought of it bitterly, but I now believe correctly), and that all the unlovely phenomena of a democracy at war were on the cards. I didn't, of course, anticipate how unlovely some of them were to be, nor, I imagine, did anyone else—even the *Masses* crowd, who flattered themselves then that they knew the inward causes of the whole business, just as certain *New Republic* editors today flatter themselves they know the inward causes of the universe and all its social, literary, and economic works. If I had not been in Paris when the war came, and in London, too, when England entered, I think my reaction at the time would have been slightly different: It might have been a curious feeling that here was the biggest show on earth going on, and that at last, for better or worse, we, too, were going to be a part of it, actors ourselves in the drama rather than spectators in the audience, as we had been since that summer of 1914. But as it was, I was depressed; I felt that no good would come of it.

One thing more, I ought to add: The trumped-up notion that we were in any danger as a nation, submarines or no submarines struck me as slightly ridiculous. Just as today the notion of an invasion by the Japanese strikes me in exactly the same fashion, even with aeroplanes and possible "death rays" as highly developed as possible; since whatever improvements are to be made in the gentle art of killing our fellow men, these improvements sooner or later get spread around. If there are new mechanical, poison-gas, aircraft tricks, the United States will almost always be able to carry them to a higher point of technical perfection than any other nation. And with most of the necessary materials for their manufacture, too, just to rub it in. Hence the whole attempt then made by busy and ignorant maniacs to create a notion of fear aroused only disgust in me. I even thought it possible that a "hate" campaign, too, would shortly follow the fear one—and that that would be even more dangerous and contemptible. I had seen the start of the "Belgian atrocities" propaganda in England; I knew that when we put our minds to it, we could do a much better job, though unfortunately we had no Edith Cavell of our own handy at the time for the right emotional touch. But we did fairly well, even as it was—if you have the heart to remember the stories of crucified and mutilated children, calculated to instill into the "rookies" at Plattsburg the proper spirit for bayonet practice. We were all keyed up for an emotional debauch, after the strain of so long being on the sidelines, and the Liberty Loan drives, above everything else, gave many a frustrated female the vicarious revenge of her life for sexual neglect. The whole thing was not a pretty sight—but it is just as well to be reminded of it now and then.

One of the worst features of the war in England—the "White Feather" campaign, when industrious females pinned this inglorious emblem on the coat of any man in civilian clothes, who *looked* as if he were of age and physically fit for military service (though, of course, tragic mistakes were not uncommon)—was avoided in our own country by the prompt adoption of conscription. There could be no question of your being exempted, if you were not in uniform. But in due course we made up for that, too. Remember the "slacker raids"—those ignoble exhibitions of coercion and interference, when anybody in civilian clothes might be stopped on the streets and asked by the police, or in fact by any little popinjay in military uniform (even though we were supposedly under civilian rule), for his exemption card? I hope you don't remember them, but I do. Of course there couldn't be any "slacker raids" until the conscription machinery had had at least time to start functioning—until the big lottery wheel at Washington had been solemnly dipped into and the first numbers withdrawn; until the fantastic local draft boards, with their even more fantastic medical machinery for examination, had been established in all the fair communities of the land.

But it was remarkable, when I come to think back on it now, how rapidly the machinery began to work, considering that it was all brand new. Remarkable, this speed in being able to pick men for death and mutilation, when you contrast it with the slowness of State relief organizations of the different kinds we have seen during the depression—but in the latter case, naturally, men are only being picked for life and hope, and that is always a slow sentence. Or at least it always has been.

As I was not among the fortunate—yes, the newspapers were ghoulish enough to employ that very adjective—ones conscripted on the first draft, I had a little breathingspace and time during which I could reflect on what I *would* do, if actually I were called. I had solemnly registered, and had thus obeyed the law. And I knew one thing right off—that whatever happened, I would not be a conscientious objector. First of all, because it wasn't true—I didn't hold any firm religious, or even personal, belief against war in general—I only had a sharp and definite objection to this war in particular. I could conceive of plenty of wars, where, as far as I was concerned, I would have been one of the first to volunteer, even a war of plain adventure and buccaneering. But Wilson's war for democracy was just more than I could stomach. I decided for the time being to do nothing, that is, to trust to luck, hoping the whole thing would soon be over. Though some people didn't think so in those first glorious days of preparation, consolidation of public opinion (as mild a phrase as I can think of), and training for slaughter, I knew that the war wasn't going to last forever, even if the era of peace meant a terrible emotional let-down for the safe, editorial, arm-chair strategists.

For some time I continued to work for the *New Republic,* at my own request limiting my book reviewing to books *not* concerned immediately with the war (the worst flood of war books was to come about a year later) but to fiction, travel in Africa or Tibet, scientific monographs, philosophy—to anything, in fact, which had no immediate, contemporary implications. I even carried over this self-imposed attitude to the daily business of life, so that—though I couldn't help reading the newspapers, through long habit, probably more carefully than nineteen persons out of twenty—I would not engage in arguments about the war and would go to the extreme of trying to shift the conversation to something else. Despite what Herbert Croly, and Alvin Johnson, and Walter Lippmann evidently thought (Lippmann, indeed, specifically said so later on, when he reviewed my "Liberalism In America" months afterward), I did not fraternize or associate with people who were of the same opinion as myself, with the possible exception of Randolph Bourne, the genius-smitten cripple, whose brilliant comments on men and motives were about the only intelligent comments I heard during those horrible weeks of relapse to barbarism.

This curious, unreal, monastic life continued through the summer of 1917—the one way, as I now think of it, in which I could "carry on"—to use the English phrase we then affected —without becoming hysterical. I remember there was a musical show playing at the New Amsterdam theatre, and in the second act of it was sung a melodiously simple but effective refrain, beginning with the words, "Some day, waiting will end; some day, there will be peace." For me, even today, that song carries a sort of nostalgia of longing; it reawakens the mood of desire—that unspoken, passionate desire—for an end to the war, a return to something like sanity. People forget things too easily, when they are unpleasant, and I wish that I, too, could forget many things—but I am glad to be able to remember that song and the mood of that time, when it seemed as if the war would *never, never* end, as if it were going on for an eternity with madness and death and unreality.

All the external processes of life during those months from April to late November, 1917, went on automatically, as it were, with that kind of hush and withdrawal from immediate sensation which one feels just before taking an anaesthetic in a hospital. And all this time, remember, I never knew when the mechanism of the draft might reach out to me—I know that many times I wished it would do so. Anything seemed better than this indecision and waiting and impotence; I began to understand why the boys looked really cheerful, almost gay, when I saw them marching clumsily through the streets to the railroad stations to entrain for the draft camps—things had been settled for them; there was no longer any need to feel responsible; what would happen, would happen. Already theirs was that curious peacefulness—to borrow L. P. Jack's unforgettable phrase—of being at war.

Somehow the weeks and months went by. Then late in November Martyn Johnson, at that time director of the old *Dial,* which was still being published, as it had been published for 40 years, in Chicago, came to New York looking for an editor. George Donlin, the editor up to that time (under Johnson's control), had been forced to go West on account of tuberculosis. Somebody recommended me to Johnson, and I recall that we had several conferences at "Ike's" bar on Sixth

Avenue—the chief question, of course, being whether I might not be drafted, just as I got into my stride editing the paper; Johnson, however, passed up that difficulty very lightly, as it seemed then to me. But I was soon to learn, too, that Johnson took a curiously unreal attitude towards the war, as he did towards many things—he seemed to think that it was a mere temporary inconvenience, very much like the "flu" epidemic we were at that time experiencing. At all events he made me what seemed a flattering offer—remember I had not had a "regular" job since my days on the New York *Press* in 1914—for those times, $50.00 a week, and, of course, my ticket to Chicago. In my heart, despite what Johnson said, I was a bit afraid of Chicago and didn't want to go. On the other hand, I didn't want to refuse, for this salary would give me an opportunity to send some money regularly to my mother up in Boston—something I had long wanted to do, for I suspected that she was not in the happiest of circumstances. And Johnson was shrewder than I had thought in another respect—he pointed out, when I mentioned my mother to him, that by sending her money regularly I put myself in a position to claim exemption from the draft, if it ever really did get around to me. Therefore, he went on, not only for my own sake (he rang the changes on the "opportunity" the job would give me), but for her sake, too, I ought to accept. That clinched it—and I did.

At first the idea of going to Chicago rather stimulated me. I had always been an Easterner; I had only visited the city once for a couple of days and knew nothing of its social and political life, which I imagined ought to be interesting; and after all, it could not be hopeless even from a literary and intellectual point of view, for I, too, had read my Sherwood Anderson and Carl Sandburg. It would be an adventure—and really, I kept saying to myself, one ought after all to see a little of one's own country. Yet when the 20th Century actually began to move out of the Grand Central station that December day of 1917 I felt a wave of homesickness for New York surge over me that was startling and deep; I simply had not realized before how much New York had become my "home" town. I think now, after all these years, I can truthfully say that only in Paris do I not feel occasionally homesick for New York—and even in Paris, as I was to find out later, when you reach a real climax in your life, instinctively you turn towards New York. The associations of our early manhood are much more compelling than we believe—until we are forced to break them.

However, the first few weeks in Chicago were much too full and interesting for me to have any time to lament my exile from New York. Johnson was an indefatigable social mixer, the kind of person who would have been really unhappy, had his name not been in the Social Register, and he insisted upon introducing me to everybody of any consequence—or perhaps I should say, to everybody he thought of any consequence—in the city, even going to the absurd length of giving formal lunches in my honor at one or two of the smart clubs. At that time—I say *that,* because I have a suspicion things are not exactly the same nowadays—Chicagoans were self-conscious, articulate, and proud about their city and its artistic and literary pretensions, not to mention its scholastic dignity, with both Northwestern University and the University of Chicago in its own territory, so to speak. I suspected then, as I suspect now, that a good deal of this amiable blowing of their own horn was really prompted by an unspoken jealousy of New York's prestige—but I didn't say anything. When my opinion was asked directly on points of comparison between the two cities, I could always gracefully dodge the issue by pointing out that after all I was a Bostonian—and hence unfit to judge, since all the world knew that Bostonians regarded their own city as the "hub" of the universe.

Fortunately, the war was not too often mentioned, strange as that now seems, though I think the real explanation lay in the fact that the type of people I met were aware of Chicago's reputation throughout the country for being "pro-German" in sympathy, and the war was a sore point to their civic pride. However, when the subject did come up, as inevitably it had to now and then, I never disguised my own hope that the next day would see the end of it, even if it was a "peace without victory," though the actual phrase was to be coined a trifle later on. Subsequently in Chicago I made it a point not to mention the war, except to my intimates, for it was shortly after my arrival there that the last German great offensive on the Western Front began, the offensive which for a few weeks looked as if it might succeed, the offensive that *had* to succeed, before our own American forces got into extensive action—or the war was lost for Germany. It didn't take any great historical perception to be aware of that, and when that offensive failed to "click," I for one knew that the end must be only a question of a few more months, as, indeed, it so turned out.

In my next chapter I shall describe more at length the nature of the *Dial* of those last days of its publication in Chicago. Here I wish rather to describe the social background of my work at the time. Shortly after my arrival it became obvious that I had to have an assistant, if I was to devote the proper amount of attention to the many book reviews and articles of a literary interest, which were practically obligatory, since the paper's chief source of revenue was publishers' advertisements. Johnson was agreeable, for he both recognized the necessity and had also been lucky enough to raise some money in New York for financing the paper—as, in fact, he did again later on, when it was brought to New York for actual publication. And after some inquiries and the usual diplomatic manœuvres, I was able to persuade Clarence Britten, who had been teaching English at the University of Wisconsin, to throw up his academic career for a working literary one, and to come on the *Dial* as my assistant.

It was a happy selection. Clarence was endowed with a quick wit, good judgment—especially in literary matters,—

and a capacity to get the paper out, which is a sort of special faculty in itself, as anyone who has ever had to make a "deadline" for a regular publication can explain. He was a Harvard man, too, and that helped a lot, for it gave us a common background. But better than anything else, he had a sense of humor—even about the war. He had some dependents, as I had my mother, on whose account he could claim exemption, but I am sure he knew, just as I knew, that if the war continued more than another year, we both would have to go—or try to volunteer before then, something I was determined not to do. In any event, the common prayer in both our hearts was that the war would soon end. Clarence was civilized; he knew what each day of the war's continuance meant in actual human slaughter and suffering—and he didn't try to convince himself that any possible political or social or spiritual byproducts were worth that indecent price. Over our cocktails at the bar next to the office after work he would sometimes say shrewd and merciless things about the war psychosis and the "inferiority complex," as it was called then, of the average man.

And often I wished I could publish some of those remarks in the *Dial,* but rigorously I limited my anti-war contributions to the sly book reviews of Randolph Bourne and to the outspoken letters of Robert Dell, our Paris correspondent, whose letters came into the office plainly marked, "Opened By The Military Censor." For that reason, when one of the issues of the *Dial* was held up by the postal authorities—of course they acted weeks after the specific number in question had already been circulated to subscribers—because of Dell's remarks about the shelling of Paris with long-range guns (and I think the one which caused the trouble was that in which he said he had never been able to get more excited over a dozen civilians killed in a church by a bomb than over two dozen civilians in uniform killed in a trench at the front), and when, as a result of this, one of the snoopers of those days came to the office and began to ask me questions about the war, my own exemption, my attitude towards Germany, and all the other stock loyalty-testers of those days, I finally lost patience and pitched him out of the office. I thought there might be some repercussions from that, possibly some unpleasant ones, but as a matter of fact nothing seemingly came of it.

Though I saw intolerance and war hysteria all about me, and read of enough to sicken me for life at the very mention of the phrase, "One Hundred Percent American," that episode was about the closest I ever came during the war to personal contact with that intolerance and hysteria. But that was close enough—and always, after that episode, I felt tremendous sympathy for "the alien in our midst," even though he was, as we were solemnly informed by the editorial desk-warriors, "coiled within the flag." I think I might have gone a little out of my head and said or done something rash at that time, if every day there was not Clarence there—urbane and understanding—to prove to me that reason had not entirely forsaken the world. When I returned from France three years ago, one bit of news genuinely saddened me—that in some stupid automobile accident Clarence had been killed. In any event I am now glad—especially after my Chicago experience—that, a few months later on in New York, I was able to persuade Clarence to do the essay on "School And College Life" in my "Civilization In The United States." To me it reads almost as well today as it did then—a fine piece of work.

Although everybody with any sensitiveness at all lived under enervating inner emotional strain during those months, there were, for me, a few compensations in Chicago. Robert Morse Lovett was then a professor at the University of Chicago, and he introduced me to a few of the more liberal-minded and agreeable of the academic circle. I remember also that Janet Fairbank—who since, I believe, has distinguished herself by a brilliant book on the Middle West and Chicago—was, on the social side, not merely pleasant, but intelligent and perceptive: I remember her taking Waldo Frank and myself for a longish afternoon automobile drive and her giving that somewhat apocalyptic gentleman just as good as he gave, which was something of a verbal feat in those days, comparable today, say, to not permitting Gertrude Stein to be obscure when you talk with her. (And I flatter myself that I accomplished this feat myself later on in Paris, when Ernest Hemingway brought me down to the Presence.) There were many others, whose names now escape me, but all of them left an impression of hospitality, friendliness, and intellectual interest which I still keep with me, to his day.

Among the feats of which I am justly proud during my Chicago sojourn was a visit of several days to the University of Wisconsin, at Madison. It was the first time I had ever visited a typically mid-Western co-educational State college—and although, unfortunately, it was in the dead of winter, I could see clearly enough that in the spring and summer it must, physically, be a really lovely spot. I attended several of the classes to observe the methods of lecturing; I talked with several of the members of the faculty; I tried to fathom the mysteries of the social system that the students had built up. And, somehow, I came back to Chicago feeling miserable and depressed; I couldn't put my finger on it then and even less can I do it now in recollection. But I definitely felt that if what I had seen and heard was "education," it would be better for those youngsters, better for God and the country, had they never learned to read at all—except for technical and mechanical and engineering purposes. "An honest peasantry," I remember saying to myself, "would be better than this kind of predigested culture." Partly, I hasten to be frank in adding, this was due to my deep prejudice against co-education, which I suppose I had obtained at Harvard without fully knowing it—but still a prejudice I find quite easy, theoretically, to justify. Partly, also, it was due to the incredible *bleakness* of the place, so traditionless, so shiny new, and so dull. Partly,

I think I can add, it came from the purely temporary bitterness I felt towards any kind of a world—even the little amiable world of Madison—that could so blithely seem untouched by that devastation that was putting civilization back a century at that very moment in Europe—though today, paradoxically enough, I think I should rather thank God for it.

Late in the spring of that year my own classmate, Scofield Thayer, who subsequently was to buy the *Dial* himself and convert it into the rather spectacular literary monthly that people later knew it to be in New York (though he didn't suspect himself of quite such intentions at that time), came to Chicago for a visit of a fortnight or so—and it was here, rather than at Harvard, where I had seen him only a half dozen or so times, outside the few classes we went to together, that I got to know him fairly well. A New Englander like myself from Massachusetts, though unlike myself from a rich and successful family instead of no family at all, he was of an almost psychopathic nervousness, the outward characteristics of which were a high, shrill voice and an almost hysterical laugh. He had plenty of money and was not loath to spend it, either—a fact which, I was told later on, was mercilessly exploited by all kinds of quacks and charlatans. But in any event he led me a merry pace for a few days, though it was a relief to talk with him just the same, for, oddly enough, he appeared to know little, and didn't hesitate to say that he cared less, about the war—an attitude of indifference which was neither a pose nor a sham any more than had been, though for quite different reasons, the attitude of Walter Franzen. He wasn't, I believe, called for service, which was just as well, for he might have wrecked the discipline of any company to which he was assigned.

On the personal side, too, there were compensations. I met several attractive girls. Some moralist might say that I took advantage of the fact that so many men were off to the wars, which really in this particular case of mine in Chicago could not apply. And for a very good reason—Chicago was the nearest big city to the Great Lakes Naval Training Station, so that the town was full of young, fledgling naval officers. I remember their giving an amusing musical comedy, words and music by themselves, which was amply good enough to be performed in a public theatre and draw crowded, enthusiastic audiences. (One of their own songs was "Goodbye, America—How I Hate To See You Go," a very stirring chorus, too.) Also at that time, remember, young, unmarried gentlemen in apparently fine enough health to consume all the cocktails passed around were not looked upon with any too great favor by the girls, either, for whatever hysteria and nonsense there was in the social atmosphere, I didn't observe that the opposite sex was any more immune to them than my own.

But how fleeting and transitory all those affairs seemed, even at the time—for overhanging everybody, whether we tried to forget it or didn't try, was the war. It was like the false gaiety of an evening dance by army officers before battle. There was always something illusory and desperate about those affairs, almost a pathetic clinging to a little bit of happiness in the all-enveloping threat of final separation. War, I mean, may not bring men and women to their senses, but it certainly awakens them to their sensualities. Possibly that is the real reason it has so many secret supporters in people otherwise apparently normal. Deeper psychological levels are stirred by the fact of death than we like to realize in our ordinary, hum-drum, rather prosy existence—as we can see, on a lower level, in the imperishable popularity of murder and detective stories.

I am glad, now, that I had those months in Chicago, though I can honestly say, too, that nothing short of drawing and quartering would induce me to go back there to live permanently. For Chicago is the city without hills, the city of eternal prairie-like flatness, which even the vista of the lake does not relieve but only intensifies. You can drive for miles, North, South, and West, as I have, and not see a hill big enough even for a very small urchin to coast down. Flat and even, always flat and even, and interminable miles of it. I suppose that is all right, if you are born and brought up in the even rolling prairie country; I can't say, though it seems to me I detect a sort of nostalgia for that rolling interminable flatness in some of Glenway Wescott's novels. But for me a city is not a city unless it is built on hills and near a great river, with boats from all over the world on it, or near the ocean. Perhaps that only means I am a Bostonian, *malgré moi,* and cannot really get over the impressions and feelings of my early manhood. Perhaps it simply means that I didn't really care for Chicago—and perhaps that's it. I know that one of the few happy days of my life was the day I got on the train at the La Salle Street Station which was to take me back to New York.

Yet I was genuinely sorry to leave behind many of the friends I had made during my rather intensive residence of six months. Never anywhere before or since have I found people any more generous, any more hospitable, any more eager to learn. There are plenty of sordid sides to Chicago—we all know what they are, or at least think we do—but there is a kind of indomitable spirit in its people, despite political corruption, race prejudice and riots, ugly industries—a spirit I cannot help but admire, for it is still touched with something of the old pioneering spirit. Perhaps things have changed since my day, for the speed of sophistication of a certain kind is always amazing me in America—as it would amaze anyone who stopped to think about it. But I very much hope that in that respect they haven't—and what I hear of Chicago today confirms me in that belief.

I think, too, I have a right to that hope. When I went there, although very few people read it, Chicagoans were still inordinately proud of *The Dial.* It was almost like a civic accomplishment, a living refutation to the Eastern ill-wishers who said that Chicago cared only about meat-packing and making money. I was astonished at the number of people I met in Chicago who seldom—if ever—looked at the magazine, but who could nevertheless tell you its history and string off the names of some of its early famous contributors. And I think many good citizens got up one morning and read in their *Tribune* with surprised regret that *The Dial,* so long a Chicago institution, had fled to New York—as many New Yorkers, only a few months ago, must have been surprised and a little chagrined, to find that *Esquire* was published and edited in Chicago. Hence what *The Dial* was like in Chicago, when I edited it for its last six months there and how it came about that I brought it to New York—and how, in New York, it went through the transformations it did—all this is a valid and interesting footnote on American literary history. It is worth a chapter to itself.

IX. THE DIAL UNDER A DARK SKY

THE editorial offices of the old *Dial* in Chicago were in the Transportation Building, a conventional business office building, not far from the La Salle Street Railroad Station—about as unlikely a spot for the home of an essentially literary magazine as could be well imagined. Though relatively small, the two rooms were adequate for our needs. In the larger room, Clarence and I had an enormous double flat-top desk, with our chairs facing each other and plenty of dictionaries, reference books, and the books under consideration for review piled up between us. There were, too, several of the old-fashioned sliding glass-door bookcases, usually crammed with books that were to be sent out to the different reviewers we had on our list—and it was a long list—or to be kept for shorter notices, since we actually tried to "cover" all the books published by the more important houses. I had a small typewriter desk beside me, because, as usual, I never wrote anything by hand, but directly on the machine. Clarence usually wrote out his stuff first and then typed it, though when we were in a rush for some copy to fill up a column and close a page, he was extremely fast. His own longer, more pretentious reviews or articles he wrote out rather slowly, two or three days in advance: he was conscientious, almost—as I would twit him now and then—to the point of absurdity.

Naturally our morning mail was very heavy, since all our contributors, with the exception of less than half a dozen in

Chicago itself, were in New York, or Paris, or London, or Madison, Wisconsin, or even Dublin, from whence we occasionally received a few amusing articles of a literary rather than political kind. Some of these contributors, of course, were almost traditional with the paper, and I tried to send to them for review the type of books they had been in the habit of reviewing before my advent on the magazine. Others—like Alfred B. Kuttner, for instance, who wrote two fine pieces on what he called "A Study Of American Intolerance"—I was myself able to induce to write for us, through my previous acquaintance in New York with the many liberal writers known at that time by their pieces in the *New Republic.* Also, I like to flatter myself, I discovered a half dozen or so from among the many who had been doing occasional reviews for the magazine before; I encouraged them by friendly letters, and I tried in a measure to compensate, by editorial interest, for the low rates of remuneration the magazine necessarily was forced to give. Edward Shanks wrote us occasional letters from London at that time, and very good they were, too. Usually I reviewed one or two of the more important books myself in each issue, and there was also a longish column or two of general editorial comment, of which, I should say now, Clarence did about a third and I the rest. John Dewey contributed an occasional article; Horace Kallen wrote part of a series, which afterward was made into a book. I think now I can say honestly that in every issue there were at least two or three articles which an intelligent person would not care to miss.

There was one discovery I made during those months in Chicago editing the *Dial,* which I want to put down before I forget it—a saddening discovery to me, though I can remember Clarence every now and then gently mocking me for it. (Naturally, I told it to him, just as it dawned on me.) That was the discovery, which I suppose every responsible editor of a serious magazine made during that decade in America, of the incredibly low standard of literary appreciation and of critical ability prevalent in a country that so long had had the blessings of general education. I don't mean to say that the contributions I received from those scores of aspirants to a critical career were exactly unintelligent, either in their general viewpoint or approach—they were not. I don't even mean to say that they were illiterate, either in the sense of grammatical confusion, or just plain mis-spelling—they were not. Most of them were fairly competent, to employ a rather devastating adjective. The trouble, really, was much deeper. They simply had no life in them; they were conventional in the bad and timid sense of the word; the attempts made to avoid certain *clichés* were almost worse than the *clichés* themselves would have been. I don't know just how to put my finger on it—and, remember, that was almost a generation ago—now in recollection; I should say that their feelings, and hence their judgments, about books were derivative rather than direct; they often wrote as if they had not read the book in question at all, and, when the technique was unfamiliar, they invariably had recourse to broad generalizations, which seldom had any real or genuine applicability to the specific use of this new technique in the book under discussion. I know that not once, but dozens of times, I would say to Clarence, "I'll be damned, if I can tell from this review what the book sets out to do, and far less whether it has done it or not. The book may be unintelligible to this unfortunate reviewer, but certainly what he writes about it is more so."

Clarence, I remember vividly, would look at me with a sort of quizzical and tired smile, and would usually say, "Remember, my dear Harold, as our old Professor Irving Babbitt used to remind us at college, 'Truth comes out of error much more quickly than it does out of confusion.' These people haven't the dignity of being clearly wrong. They are merely in a fog. Let it go at that, and review the book yourself—if you think it's worth your attention."

In spite of all the difficulties, in spite of the war hysteria, in spite of the painfully limited budget for contributors, I think I kept the standard of the *Dial* quite high during those first six months of 1918, when every day—and day after day—the pressure of war sentiment seemed to be becoming stronger and stronger. Sometimes, after the stenographer and Clarence and the office boy had gone home, I would stay on in the office rather late, either reading some new book or finishing up a review, and when my work was done, I would sit back and frankly wonder how much longer this kind of unreal life could go on.

I had received my official exemption, but it was temporary—as, indeed, were all. The war seemed to be going on until the end of time; it was the Germans who were advancing now—as if to welcome our participation, I thought ironically. In my heart I didn't believe the advance would succeed; I was sure it wouldn't succeed. But when was the "break" going to come? Must it always be like this? Couldn't something happen to put an end to this nightmare? Time after time I struggled with myself *not* to go down and enlist—I don't mean my convictions had changed; I don't mean, either, that I wanted to leave my mother in the lurch without a penny a week to bless herself with, as I should infallibly have done. I mean merely the social atmosphere was becoming impossible. How could one work at intellectual things, when young men were dying in France? And I would end up my reflections by slamming closed the cover on the typewriter and going down to the Congress Hotel, or some other bar-room, and having drinks until I didn't care. It was inglorious, I suppose; it was indefensible. But it was human—and at least I didn't pretend.

When I accepted the editorship of the paper that evening at "Ike's" in New York, one of the attractive baits that Johnson had held out to me was the promise that my stay in Chicago was to be but temporary—he intended, he said, to bring the paper to New York. And that would be just as soon as he could raise a sufficient amount of money. Rather to my surprise, he wrote me early that spring of 1918 that he had accomplished the purpose he had set for himself, and that the *Dial* was to come to New York, bag, baggage, and traditions of 40 years, on the first of July. He had even acquired an office downtown, below 14th Street, in Greenwich Village—and a charming office it turned out to be, too—and we were to have a much more "ambitious" programme for the new New York *Dial* than had been the purely literary and rather thin one of the later Chicago years. He had "hooked up," he wrote me, Thorstein Veblen, and John Dewey, and Helen Marot, among others, and instinctively I feared that we might be put in the position of merely trying to imitate either the *New Republic* or the *Nation.* But also, he said, we were to continue our rather unusual schedule of bi-monthly publication. We were not to become "just another Liberal weekly." Anyway, to tell the truth, I didn't much care what the programme was; I wanted to get back to New York, and now, certainly, there would be no excuse for staying on in Chicago. Less than an excuse, indeed, for I was continued on with my old salary of $50.00 a week.

For me, anyway, there was a real thrill just in arriving back in New York, for I had not been gone long enough really to get out of touch with my many friends. In those days—as again today—downstairs at the Brevoort was generally the place to meet most people; my very first evening "back home" I had a rather gay dinner with Victor Herbert, whom I had known in the old days of my work for the *Dramatic Mirror,* and with Vyvyan, in whose house I had for a time lived during my salad days. Talk about the war was taboo, I ought to add, as I think it was in many social circles that summer of the decisive turn in the long stale-mate: one tried to hope; for a few hours, to forget. And with such good company forgetting about the unpleasant reality was not too difficult, though our gaiety was hectic—as, indeed, it was with most people those days, a sort of determined spirit of "Eat, drink, and be merry, for tomorrow. . . ."

But those first four months back in New York, from July to November—before peace actually came—were among the strangest I ever experienced. During the summer of my return, the last summer of the war, I lived in a fine apartment on Lafayette Street, just below Wanamakers. I sub-let it for that short period; I think wisely now, for it kept me out of mischief and out of talking too much about the war, which at last—obviously, it seemed to me—was drawing to a close. The Germans were definitely defeated, and could stick it out only a short time, abandoned as they were certain soon to be by their weak-sister Allies, Turkey and Austria. Unlike so many liberal bloodhounds of those days I did not concern myself with drawing up mythical treaties of peace, though I did write one rather bold and striking leading article called "Withdraw from Russia!"—Something of a risky thing in those anti-Bolshevik days, when, to read most of the newspapers, you would have thought that even a return to Czarism was preferable to confiscation of private property, and with the changes always being rung on the theme of how the Bolsheviks had "sold out" to German gold—it really seems quaint today, doesn't it, with our accredited Ambassador to the Soviets returning for instructions from Moscow to Washington, and a regular Russian Ambassador being officially welcomed at the White House? For at that time there were many otherwise estimable people ready to tell you that the world (at least, the "civilized," capitalistic world) would infallibly come to a disastrous end, if such a thing were tolerated.

Meanwhile, the new "Reconstruction" *Dial,* as Johnson liked to call it, was coming into existence—and actually creating for itself something of a reputation, which, I feel sure now, would have been even more wide-spread, if the excitement of war-time had not been so all-dominant. Clarence had come to New York with the magazine, and he and myself—just as in Chicago—practically got the paper out, though we had a curious "advisory" board of contributing editors, whom Johnson had persuaded to give their good offices to the magazine—Helen Marot, Thorstein Veblen, and John Dewey I remember in particular.

In those days of final hysteria, just before the "break" that was to result in at least an official peace, it was pleasant to have such intelligent and liberal-minded people to talk with as Randolph Bourne, who saw more clearly—it seemed to me then, as it still does today—the spiritual evils the war was spreading like poison gas than did almost any other pacifist (a word of contempt then) of that time; as Clarence, of course; as Albert Jay Nock, whom I was to know much better later on as editor of the *Freeman*. In passing, I want to say that the attitude of the *New Republic* at that time—particularly of Herbert Croly and Alvin Johnson, for by the autumn of 1918 Lippmann had left the magazine to go down to Washington (and later to Paris, if you please) to "assist" the Wilson Administration in the framing of a (God save the mark!) "liberal" peace—the *New Republic's* attitude, I repeat, at first amused, then depressed, and, finally, revolted me. This curious determination to pluck liberal flowers from the wastelands of violence and unreason seemed to me a new and particularly dangerous kind of casuistry; for I have always believed—and I think on good historical grounds—that it is the liberal *temper,* the liberal *attitude,* which are all-important, and that the inevitable effect of a recourse to violence is a destruction of that temper. I have never been able to overcome my mathematical prejudice to the effect that nothing added to nothing gives nothing—no matter how many times you do it, nor with what cheers and emotional overtones.

But during those crowded, final months of the great struggle the official liberals—in the teeth of the evidence, I thought then and still think now—were very optimistic, very sure of themselves. They seemed to think that the terrific forces they had helped to unloose could be controlled (and composed), when it came to the making of peace, with a few kind words—

that is, the mood of the world was going to change overnight from the long, strained, belligerent obscurantism to a clear, sweetly rational, cooperative spirit, without rancor, without revenge in even the hearts of the humiliated, without a memory of the months and months of life under the shadow of death. Emotionally they believed in a sort of social conversion, not unlike—except on a broader, social instead of individual scale—the kind of deeper conversions depicted in William James's "The Varieties Of Religious Experience." Preaching what they thought was a cold *Realpolitik,* they were in fact sentimental and gushing. Good-will, so they seemed to be saying, could be invoked by almost a wave of the hand—had they not themselves always invoked it?

Those final months of the war! What different things those months mean to all of us who are middle-aged today! To hundreds of thousands, of course, they still mean those months in France—those exciting, emotion-stirring months, for to many of those men then in arms everything, even today, has seemed a bit stale and flat since, when they are honest with their own feelings. Vaguely in the case of most and sharply and definitely in the case of a few, those days were the epic months of our time and generation, when the face of the world was being changed and history being written on an heroic scale. It was more difficult then than ever before or since to be filled with any deep conviction of your own importance: They were months which explain why in perhaps the most insensitive of the middle-aged today there is still a kind of humility—which may not be exactly Christian, but is nontheless real. Not merely humility, either, but in America at all events a quite unusual and new kind of tolerance—which is why the "flaming youth" of the post-war days was allowed to flame almost as much as it pleased, while all of us not in that generation smiled; whereas before 1917 (had we then possessed, I mean, the age we do now) we should have cajoled, threatened, and been frankly shocked. Because even the dullest, when all is said and done, could hardly fail, during the last months of the war, to be struck by the banality of an older generation telling those who were then going out to die or risk death to be circumspect, restrained, moral, cautious. It was too much like a caricature —too much like a Kansas mother telling her boy to be sure not to get his feet wet and catch cold, when he went into those ill-ventilated trenches she had read about in the newspapers. Or too much like some of the fantastic moralists of those days, who wanted to be sure—seemingly above everything else—that "our boys," even if thousands of them were going to their graves, were at least going to them clean, pure, untainted by any loose woman's caress. A good deal of the false and over-emphasized masculinity in the writing of a man like Hemingway—who after all was a young man then and *was* fighting himself—is in reality due to the feeling of disgust with this safe-at-home, civilian virtue-standards blindness of those who could still talk about correct and moral acts at the very moment the vilest and most immoral acts—the slaughter of the world's youth in a senseless war—were not merely being condoned but applauded. There is much more—and much subtler, because not quite fully conscious—criticism of war-mindedness in Hemingway's specious (yet seductive) enthusiasm for gore than a romantic critic might surmise. When Max Eastman writes of Hemingway—as he did, criticizing the latter's study in comic exposition, "Death In The Afternoon"—that he became "intoxicated" with gore, I do not say he is entirely wrong, I merely say that he is essentially obtuse. Sometimes, even for writers of this generation, the only way by which some things can be imaginatively expressed is by donning the comic mask.

With Russia revolting and turning both pacifist and Communist, with Europe visibly changing its whole social structure and historical traditions, with America assuming an entirely new and dramatic rôle as the deciding arbiter in the destinies of the Old World, with age-sanctified moral standards as well as young flesh being burned to death by the guns of the Argonne,

I cannot believe it is just an error of remembering but a plain fact that, during those months, there was slowly conceived and born a new awareness of the infinite possibilities of human, social and economic relationships, a vivid sense that, whether we liked it or not, whether or not we were trying to do anything intelligent about it in the way of fore-handedness, a new world was coming into being right before our eyes. For better or worse the 20th century was putting down its foundations.

The 19th century was dead not merely in years but in spirit; henceforth Victorianism was to seem no longer near, but archaic. And, of course, the purely mechanical and technical inventions—many speeded up by the demand of the different armies, which had to be up-to-date, if they were not to perish—intensified that feeling. New wonders were being given us almost every day, until we began to think that anything might be done—especially, if it had never been done before. One of the bitter ironies of that period, which I remember feeling myself, was that at just the time when the world, with the inventive people in it, was promising so many new and wonderful things, so many of the young men who would most have appreciated and enjoyed and let their imaginations play around these new modern miracles were being destroyed. It seemed monstrous to me then—it seems almost more monstrous to me today.

The intellectual temper—if there could be said to be any intellectual temper at that time—of those last few months of the war is not easy now to describe. My own intellectual temper, I know, was biased by my wish for an end to the nightmare: It may have been mere "wish fulfillment," but at least it was a coherent and clear wish, not incompatible with any former—or, indeed, subsequent—intellectual interest or conviction. But what astounded me then was the casual, easy-going way in which people who, up to that time, had made real pretences to some sort of intellectual integrity—had even boasted about it—with not the slightest hesitancy threw all intellectual interests overboard for a nice, warm, animal, instinctive bath in hate and belligerency and emotional whirling-dervish frenzies. They seemed delighted to be able to shed their intellectual harness and scamper and romp gaily in the green fields of emotion.

Sometimes, during those last months, it appeared to me that the only people with any dignity at all were the young soldiers who were about to go over-seas. They were at least quiet and reasonable. For it is hardly surprising that the closer you came to the Front Line, the more sense you were likely to exhibit. I had talked with soldiers in France, but I had never heard such nonsense as I heard from perfectly safe and secure older people—or perfectly safe and secure women—in a relatively safe and secure America. I haven't yet found time to read "They All Sang," hence I cannot tell you when was written that highly critical ballad, "They All Look Good, When They're Far Away." But that is what too many of the stay-at-homes were singing at the time, though, of course, one can explain it on the ground that secure people, in their hearts, are always a bit jealous of gamblers and those who take a chance, especially with life and death. Those risk-inviting people may not be safe—but they are not bored.

By the end of September it seemed to me that the jig was up—for Germany. The line of death and desolation was shifting fast towards the Central Powers, or, rather, it was cracking here and there so obviously that a shift towards the East was just a matter of day after tomorrow. And so it was, when the first autumn leaves of October turned golden and red in Washington Square—and the suggestion of that autumn was like the suggestion of the greatest springtime I was ever to know. I mean, simply, the end of the war.

It is not easy to recapture the mood of people of that now mythical month, yet at the time you could feel it everywhere below the surface, the mood of resurrection and new hope and new life; the feeling you have on a steamer that has been rolling dangerously all night in heavy seas, so that you cannot sleep but instead stumble and try to walk on deck—that feeling, when the light begins to flush the East, the sea calms down, and the boat becomes steady and even on her keel. So it was for millions of Americans that late October of 1918—there was the hush before sunrise, the knowledge that light was breaking across the water which we faced when we looked towards Europe.

X. PEACE AND MARRIAGE

NEW YORK really had two peace celebrations—the false Armistice just a few days before the actual one, and then, of course, the real thing. But in some respects the false one was the more interesting, as certainly it was the more spontaneous and dramatic. I had been up to visit and to go to an early lunch with my publisher friend, Horace Liveright, and we left his old office on 40th Street I should say around noon. We walked up Broadway towards 42nd Street, when, suddenly, all the whistles and sirens either on ships in the harbor or on the two rivers, as well as all the factory whistles in and around Manhattan Island, let loose a roar that must have thrilled every one of the millions of people—no need to ask about it, either. It was Peace.

Nothing else would call forth such a frenetic high roar from all the whistles in town and on the bay and the two rivers. And, almost as suddenly as the roar itself, from every doorway of every skyscraper and office building and department store and hotel people began to pour forth. In those days, the old Knickerbocker Hotel stood on the Southeast corner of 42nd Street and Broadway, and high up, from a small balcony that jutted out from his apartment, Enrico Caruso appeared with baskets of roses and other flowers, which he began throwing out over the crowd in what seemed to me, even that soon after the news, deliriously happy excitement. Horace and I, too, forgot all about our lunch for the moment, and by some sort of blind instinct—an instinct which seemed to animate everybody in New York that afternoon—we found our way over to Fifth Avenue, which in those few moments had become packed with people. From all the buildings came down intermittent showers of torn telephone books—as in Wall Street, ticker tape was the easiest and safest to throw out—blank typewriter paper, newspaper and magazine pages, even sheets pulled out of notebooks and memorandum stubs. And the noise of the now thoroughly aroused crowd of happy men and women—combined with the whistles and sirens, which were still keeping it up, for many boat engineers and factory workers simply tied down the cord and "let 'er go"—made a vast living tumult that anyone who then heard it will never forget. It was the paean of joy from the hearts of the people of the greatest city in the world.

It was more than merely impressive and moving. Early in the afternoon—I forget exactly when, but the first "Extra's" began coming out before Horace and I had finished our delayed lunch—the news was official that the report was, to put it mildly, premature. In brief, it was simply false, though I learned later on that the newspaper man who had the distinction of stopping the war a few days before the event, thus scooping the world in a rather historic fashion, sent his dispatch in good faith, through a misunderstanding about the time actually to be set for cessation of hostilities. But whatever the facts about that classic "break," those facts had little to do with the mood of New York for several hours that afternoon. As everybody who experienced both will tell you, I think, the false Armistice celebration was deeper in emotion than the real one, and as the afternoon turned into evening—when there was no longer any disguising the fact that the news was unfounded—that emotion became downright hysterical. I myself saw the the proprietor of a popular bar snatch an afternoon newspaper, its headlines screaming denial of the rumor, from the innocent newsboy who was selling it, then tear it in two, and finally throw the pieces in the astonished face of the newsboy, shouting, "God damn it! It must be true; it *must* be true, I tell you." It was almost terrifying, this exhibition of long suppressed desire for peace.

But for most people, by the time the denial had become established as a fact, that denial meant very little. First of all, everybody was drunk—from liquor, or excitement, or both. Secondly, the celebration had got out of bounds; it was more than a celebration of peace (which everybody knew, of course, even if this particular report were false, could not long be delayed; everybody for weeks before had been talking about the end of the war, beginning with the German spectacular retreat). It was a celebration of the end of what had come to be a nightmare of nervous strain and anxiety. It was a celebration of a return to normalcy in a sense that Warren Gamaliel Harding never could then have anticipated. It was a celebration of the end of blood and madness and spying and hate. Never at any Christmas celebration for hundreds of years had "Peace on earth, good-will to men" meant what it meant then, that day. As I myself remember it, the expressions of even the dullest and most sordid people's faces really changed; countenances lighted up with new hope, new assurance. There was a new look in everybody's eyes. It was the dawn of a new world—and everybody knew it, whether they were articulate or reticent. A great curse, a blight, a pestilence that had cost us all so much of our youth and happiness—it was passing, passing forever! We were moving out of the valley of the shadow of death, and the joy in everybody's heart could not be held back unexpressed.

For the few days following that dramatic false Armistice very few people in New York either did, or pretended to do, any serious work. We were all of us waiting—waiting for it to come true. And we had to wait only a few days. At the time I still lived in a little room over the Greenwich Village Inn—beside the room occupied by John Reed, where he had put together his documents and papers and written that first book on the Russian Revolution, "Ten Days That Shook The World," which Horace Liveright had published, and where we had many a time stayed up until the dawn came, John telling me about what he had seen in Russia, what kind of a person Lenin really was (how, I recall in particular, he was very fond of cats), and of his determination to go back. I can't remember just what hour it was, but it was early in the morning, and there were sirens and whistles blowing again, but not so vociferously as on the previous occasion. Across the courtyard back of the Inn, just under the windows of my room, I heard a girl's voice crying—and I *can* remember very clearly the curious thrill it gave me then, feel it again even today—"Mother, mother, wake up! The war is over!"

Of course that day, too, there was a tremendous celebration in New York, which, though it lacked the mad, hysterical quality of that first day, made up for it, nevertheless, by its sincerity and thankfulness. In Paris, friends told me later on, the celebration of the real Armistice rather resembled what we in New York had witnessed the day of our false one—and one could hardly blame Paris for what it did on such an occasion. But in New York I think the great and common feeling was one of sheer thankfulness that, at long last, waiting *had* ended. The worst side, so to speak, of an emotional outburst had been drained away by the hysteria of the previous day—and peace came, when really it did come, with something like dignity.

That was the night I asked Alice if she would be my wife—for though I think she knew perfectly well that I intended to ask her anyway, I was determined not to do it until peace formally arrived. I knew that, if the war was going to continue, I should sooner or later have to go myself. And I did not want to ask her—did not want, either on her side or mine, to exploit any possible feeling of sympathy—until I really *was* free to ask her, as one might in normal times—until, briefly, the war was over. She said, very simply, that she had known all along how I felt about it—that now, however, we were both free to act as people do in ordinary peace-time days, not depending on the mere emotional upsets and illusions of abnormal excitement—and that she would.

But not, of course, right away. There were things we both wanted to do—and I, she thought, might want to see what the new conditions would be like now that the war was over. She herself, too, wanted to keep on—at least for a time—with her editorial work as assistant and adviser to Liveright, for the job was an interesting one, especially just then. For instance, there was this amusing (and she thought highly talented) Dutchman, Hendrik Van Loon; she had liked his colored drawings and entertaining text in a little history book he had done for children years before, and if, as he hinted, he really would go on with "The Story of Mankind," which he was then planning to do, it ought to be very good as well as very popular. And she had helped persuade Liveright to have confidence in him, and she thought he would back him to finish the book, for of course it was a long, hard job and he would need an advance to keep going. But Liveright was a good gambler, even when he lost—and she was sure he would not lose with Van Loon. Then there was a posthumus book by Mark Twain, which ought to be edited (and in fact she did edit it herself later on) and brought out. And when there was nothing else to keep her busy, there was always "The Modern Library," with its constant need of new titles and the complications of old copyrights to untangle. And, finally, why did I not write a book myself? The war was over now; there would be no fear of censorship or interference. I could write what I liked at last—and it was at that moment I had the idea of doing what a few months later turned out to be my first book, "Liberalism In America."

Meanwhile, I was busy with my work on the new "Reconstruction" *Dial,* which now could boldly advertise itself as just that—and did. At that time, I suppose, everybody had a peace scheme of his own, and most everybody was quite willing to tell the whole world precisely what it was, and in detail, even though most of the complicated ethnographical, political, and economic perplexities of a war-weary Europe were in cold fact a complete mystery—except where feeling or racial passion entered in, as it so often did–to most, even intelligent, Americans. As I look back on it today, it seems to me that in the old New York *Dial* office others and myself must have re-arranged the whole map of Europe at least two or three dozen times—and at least a hundred different ways. And we were not alone. Every kind of "liberal" group—whether or not it had an organ of its own in which to publish its opinions and beliefs—and every kind of then "radical" group, too, not to mention all sorts of business and women's clubs, fraternal organizations, religious bodies, Heaven knows what—all these, not to neglect, either, the innumerable individuals, who had money enough to buy advertising space in the newspapers and definite notions at the same time of how everything ought to be "fixed up":—All these had "peace" schemes. It was heyday for international fixers, of which, I imagine, the earlier pathetic and slightly ridiculous Peace Ship of Henry Ford was the most grotesque symbol.

Nowadays, of course, it rather saddens one to think of this wasted flood of good-will. For the real business of making what afterwards came satirically to be known as peace was in fact being done in private, by bankers, politicians, and diplomats, just as it had always been done before. And, after all, the small and self-conscious, voluble groups I have mentioned had no—or very little—influence over public opinion, either at home or abroad. For the great majority of people were busy trying to make the readjustment back to a civilian life that had so changed while they were away to the wars that it was not easy to recognize it when they returned. Peace-making was the sport of the privileged few with the leisure and the taste for it, but for almost everybody else it was the more prosaic question of finding a job. The doughboys returning on our big ships knew little about the Polish Corridor, and cared not a tinker's curse who was given a mandate over Syria, provided they were given their old—or as good a—job back, when they at last reached their own home town. They dreamed also of bonuses and extra pay and a month or two of just enjoying themselves as civilians—and who wouldn't that had gone through all that they had?

It always seemed to me that those who talked about the selfishness of the ex-service man were talking a lot of hypocrisy—after all, if a man risks his life for something, it is hardly unreasonable for him to expect to receive some sort of compensation for it. Naturally, it is unfortunate that the ones who did the least amount of risking usually demand the largest amount of compensation, but what, in the name of common sense and the plain lessons of history, could people expect otherwise? Especially, I might add to give edge to the question, in a democracy such as ours, which, besides, had already given a fine lesson in creating dependency, and all that goes with it, following the Civil War?

Anyway, the men who in cold fighting fact had made the peace possible thought precious little about what kind of a peace it might turn out to be—we had won the war, and that was sufficient for them. But they thought a precious lot of how they were going to get back to work—and whether the girls they had left behind them still felt the same or had found a new beau (sometimes a new husband). People who do a good deal of writing and theorizing always tend to intellectualize the motives of ordinary men, when in fact those motives are often much more simple and direct than they ever imagined.

Though I myself was one of the theorizers and intellectualizers of those times, I think I can now honestly say for myself that I tried to understand the ordinary man's point of view. In any event, I *can* honestly say that I had a great deal more sympathy with it than I had with the elaborate verbal hocus-pocus of those who had never scratched a "cootie," got cold and wet feet in a filthy trench, or had a bullet-splintered knee-cap bandaged up in a field hospital. The war anyway—and Wilson, too, of course—had made me more and more suspicious of just verbal gymnastics, suspicious of the trick of drawing great social implications, like rabbits, out of the hat of theorizing and philosophical viewpoints—and all the rest of it. I did try to keep up some contact with a living reality that even an ordinary man could understand.

And during these months one of the things that helped me most to keep up a contact with living reality was the fact that I was seeing Alice more and more often. I never have known a person who was less taken in by what we used to call "the bunk"—and the simpler name for which, I suppose, is just plain sham. I have heard self-consciously opinionated males, enamoured of theory, declare in very solemn tones that women —above all, as contrasted with men—are lacking in a sense of humor. Perhaps, as a generalization, this is fair enough; I cannot say. I simply know it was not true of Alice, that, as Van Loon one time said to me, "with a single turn of wit and her laugh she can cleanse and illuminate the whole day." I know that during this period, when the peace programme of the *Dial* made more and more demands on my time and seemed also, in some respects, to become more and more preposterous, I could always be sure, by asking Alice to have dinner with me, that I should be restored to something like sanity. She had a knack of making you laugh at what people did rather than making you laugh at the kind of people they were, for there was no malice in her judgments—and she regarded, sometimes, even her own reactions to things as fit subjects for merriment. And one of those reactions, it goes without saying, was her fondness for me. She knew it was absurd; she even, on a few occasions, said so. But it didn't seem to make any difference. She realized that everybody has to have some weakness—and I was hers. Yet I know now, and dimly I realized then, that she expected me to do real and important work some day. Well, I ran away to France, when I lost her, but perhaps it is not too late for me to do some of those things even yet. And I know, too, that whatever I do, though it may not be superlatively good, will at least be measurably and distinctly better than it would have been, had I never known her.

I know that now—but at that time I was only finding it out. And there was some excuse for this obtuseness, too, I now believe. The reaction from the war, especially for the many of us who had felt it so strongly, both from an emotional and an intellectual point of view, was an intense one: Seriousness was the one thing we wanted as little to do with as possible—hadn't we had our tragic full measure of it for too long. We wanted to play, to indulge in the "butterfly loves" Santayana speaks of in his essay on "The Comic Mask." Bad as the unemployment situation then was, it was nothing at all like what we have known it since to be; there was a sort of instinctive confidence that everything was going to be all right. And, in fact, when you come right down to it, that mood was eventually so strong that, despite the temporary flurry in "war babies," as certain stocks used to be known, we were setting the stage for that curious post-war "boom," that almost spectacular prosperity of high wages, high prices, production at top speed, new gadgets, excitement, making money over night, when we would have scorned merely two chickens in every pot but instead demanded, expected, and got, three. They really were great days, if it is not too difficult a task to think back to that mythological era before the market "crashed."

In literature, too, the change in mood from the seriousness of war propaganda—one way or the other, it didn't matter, but it was always serious (almost as serious and humorless as "Nazi" propaganda is today)—the change in mood, I repeat, to flippancy and, as it were, Dorothy Parkeresque smartness and briskness, was dramatic in its suddenness. Scott Fitzgerald was finding his stride to the point where he was to become the historian of the post-war, fast money, early prohibition and heavy gin-drinking days of "The Great Gatsby," while Sinclair Lewis was polishing up his machine to start on the series of novels that were to end by not merely glorifying the American scene (despite the specious realism) but by justifying it to ourselves. It was the beginning of the movement that was to eventuate, as we can see it doing more and more today, in our breaking away, culturally as well as politically, from dependence upon (almost interest in, in some respects) Europe. A burned child proverbially dreads the fire, and not merely had we got our fingers burned in Europe, almost we had had our very trousers burned off. But those were great days, and happy days, too. It was difficult to feel afraid of almost anything.

Thus, partly because of the mood of the time, but chiefly because she wished to anyway, Alice finally yielded to my request—and we were married. I can remember, as if it were but yesterday, waiting for her to come down from Liveright's office by bus and meet me in front of the Hotel Brevoort. We had got the license down at that terrible marriage room in the City Hall which is almost enough to deter anyone from matrimony, but Alice flatly would not be married by a Justice of the Peace. We went to the Church of the Ascension, the minister put on his robes, summoned the two witnesses required by law, I believe, and we went through the simple but dignified ceremony before the altar in the Church itself. I am glad now we did; austerity has its places, I suppose, but I don't think the marriage ceremony is one of them.

It had been agreed that we should a bit later take a trip together—for some reason we both avoided the word "honeymoon"—and also for the time being, until both of us were more definite in our plans of future work, we should not attempt to live together. Alice was to keep her apartment, and I was to keep mine. We planned later on, if we could, to live in an entire house in some agreeable town not too far away on Long Island, for both of us were tired of single apartment life in New York.

Alice had a business dinner that evening; I had been invited up to play poker with Horace and T. R. Smith at the latter's house. So we kissed each other goodbye, our first marital kiss, in front of the Church on Fifth Avenue, agreeing to have our wedding dinner and celebration the next evening ourselves at the Hotel Brevoort where we had had so many jolly dinners before. Alice had not specifically said anything one way or the other, but I think she rather expected to keep the marriage secret for a few weeks. Her mother was ill in California at the time, and she didn't want any news to upset her. As for our New York friends, she appeared to be rather indifferent, observing that they would know soon enough anyway, and, besides, that she would send out formal cards in a few days, when she had the chance.

I don't know whether Alice told anyone that afternoon or evening—I don't think she did. But I know I wasn't more than twenty minutes in T. R.'s house—Horace had come up, too, as he said he would—before I was unable to keep the information to myself. And although it was a good and lively poker game, as I recall it now the announcement brought the game to a halt for at least the time it would have taken for a full round of hands, while congratulations were offered and healths drunk. I think everybody was a trifle surprised at the suddenness with which we had finally made up our minds and done it—for the fact that we were engaged had been known for some time—but everybody tried at least to appear to take it as the most natural thing in the world, for which—for some reason or other—I have always been grateful. I can't really tell now, whether I won or lost in that poker game; I remember it seemed unreal to me. Everything seemed unreal—and when, finally, I got back to my little room early in the morning, I remember looking in the mirror to see if there was any change in my expression or appearance because now I was a married man. I couldn't sleep, either, except cat-naps during the day. And that following evening after the poker game I remember I asked Thorne Smith to come and have dinner with us, so that I might realize it was true.

It was one of the gayest and most amusing and jolly of delayed wedding dinners, too, and Alice told, with the proper touch of absurdity, how everybody in Horace's office that day had looked at her inquiringly to see how she "betrayed" her "secret." Thorne mildly observed that he hoped there would be more and better weddings, for he never knew any country, or any historical period, where or when a marriage of friends was not considered a good excuse for tippling to the full, "Not"—he added slyly—"that I shall fail to find some other excuse just as good tomorrow evening. Somebody's always getting married. There's always an excuse for a celebration, even if it is only to celebrate how old Mother Nature successfully got through another day. That's one place where what little ingenuity I have rarely deserts me."

It was not until some weeks later that Alice and I were able to take our delayed honeymoon. We went up to Provincetown, first, because we liked the town then in those days, and secondly, to spend a few days with Mary Heaton Vorse, an old friend of Alice's and of myself. We walked over the dunes to the house on the shore, where Eugene O'Neill wrote some of his earlier plays; we dug clams on the beach; we explored by car the whole tip of the Cape; in fact, we didn't do a single thing that was important when you write it down. Yet to me, today as vividly as then, there is a longing, a curious unrest about the vistas of the Cape. I would turn to Alice and say, "This is part of my boyhood experience. It seems strange—and wonderful—to have you here with me, while I renew it once more."

"We'll come up here often in the summer months," she said quite simply.

And then she smiled.

"You must work, when we get back to New York. You know you want to do that book on liberalism, and that somebody ought to do it. It may not be so good as you hope it will be, but you must do it just the same. You must do something to distinguish yourself; I want you to."

"But I married you," I replied. "Isn't that distinction enough?"

"No," she came back quickly. "It certainly isn't. I admit that matrimony is the only definite traditional thing some men seem able to achieve. But if I had thought your marrying me was the most important thing you had to do—well, I never should have married you at all."

"That's it. That's modern 'love' for you. Something else always than what it is in its essence." I was almost angry.

"No," said Alice "that's just common sense."

We started to walk back home silently.

She had the final word: "And don't think common sense is incompatible with a love much deeper than the romantic novelists ever dreamed of."

XI. WHAT CAN A YOUNG MAN DO?

SHORTLY after we came back to New York Alice told me that she wanted—and was going to have—a baby. She said she believed, from what the doctor had told her—that it might be difficult, and that, in any event, if she ever was going to have one, she ought to have one as early as possible. And in order that she might have the kind of care which even all the money in the world couldn't buy, she was going out to California to be with her mother. If advisable, she would go to the St. Francis hospital in San Francisco for the actual delivery—and I didn't need to worry. By the time the baby was born—she expected around the Christmas and New Year holiday time—I ought to know better what plans I had and what I wanted to do. Also, my book ought to be finished, if I worked hard while she was away. We could plan our life for the future without haste and compulsion, even intelligently. It was lucky, too, that there was no occasion for me to worry about finances, at least for the time being, as she had a little income of her own, and insurance, too, in case . . . But she saw I didn't want her to say any more.

Her work at Liveright's might continue, she thought, when she came back, but at the beginning she would give her time to the baby and the home we planned to have on Long Island. I could only agree with her—or, perhaps, only comply with her wishes. I didn't want her to be so far away; I didn't want to be left alone in New York. But I said it would be all right.

There was nothing else for me to say. And, besides, I thought that everything really would be all right. I had no foreboding of disaster.

Thus one fine September afternoon I found myself on the platform in the Grand Central Station, beside the 20th Century; Alice was standing in the doorway of the Pullman, which had just been closed, and she was waving me goodbye through the thick windows of the vestibule door. She was smiling; but there were tears in her eyes, too. I waved to her, and turned before the train had quite got under way—for I wanted it to appear casual and everyday. I wanted that for her sake more than for my own. Yet I can see her even to this hour as she stood there, saying simply, "Goodbye, dear, goodbye. Don't worry—and I'll write you often. Keep working, dear. Goodbye."

I walked out through the gate—and through the big main hall into the street. Then I found myself on Fifth Avenue, instinctively turning South towards home.

Trying to pretend that I had some important business appointment, but really trying—and I summoned all my New England pride—not to weep, I remember I thought with a touch of bitterness of my traditional use of the word "home." For I had never really had a home, as it is ordinarily defined, either when I was a boy—or now, when I was grown up and a married man. A married man and a prospective father, too. Yet there I was, as always and forever except for brief happy interludes, alone again. Alice at least had her own family to which she was going—and somehow, strangely, that reflection comforted me. It was bad enough for one of us to be a spiritual orphan; thank God, both of us weren't. Well, I said finally to myself in that inner discussion, a few more months, just a few more months of patience and work and waiting and loneliness—then, once and forever, the life of an ordinary member of the community. A taxpayer, a citizen, a voter, a father. Vagabondia was over with; I could—and would—do what every man in his heart at some time or other believes he wants to do, that is, settle down. By the time I reached my room I had become, if not cheerful, at all events more composed. I had begun to think again of my work.

For I was now getting towards the end of my first book, "Liberalism In America," which—whatever its faults, and they were plenty—was really for a young man, who had had very little historical training and not much taste for historical research, quite an unusual book. The chapter I called "President Wilson: The Technique Of Liberal Failure" was a shrewd and intelligent analysis, which subsequent events proved to be also, in the main, a sound analysis, both from the political and the psychological point of view. Even if the accent was occasionally hysterical, the attack on the principle of conscription was really much more philosophically profound than at first sight it might appear to be. Likewise, my frankness before the Negro problem—I mean, my refusal to employ the old, meaningless *clichés*, and my attempt to get at the reality—was unusual. No, for a first book it was nothing for a young man to be ashamed of.

Meanwhile—at first from a few stopping places, like Banff, along the route West, and finally from Carmel itself—came letters every two or three days from Alice. They were amusing, keen in the judgment she displayed towards the new people she was meeting, encouraging always towards me and my work (she had read, before she went away, the two or three chapters I had more or less completed), and, best of all, they reflected considerable of her own sweet and tolerant personality. Now and then she would make some Rabelaisean reference to "this business of having a baby," and she was explicit in telling me that she had never felt physically better and that on that score, she was sure she would prove to be a model maternity patient, when her time came to go down to the hospital. Vividly I remember how these frequent letters would lift my spirit and give me new confidence in what I was doing.

Thus the weeks of that autumn went by with surprising

swiftness, and, at last, the final chapter of my book was completed and the manuscript delivered to the publisher, Christmas came, and with it a telegram of good wishes from Alice, who had now left Carmel and had gone to San Francisco to the hospital. In New York at that particular holiday time of 1919-1920 all the talk was about the coming of prohibition in January—and everywhere you went, conversation shifted around to the subject of a "cellar," of what to buy that would last longest, of bargains in this, that, and the other liquor. I myself managed to acquire a couple of cases of Scotch whisky, and—solely because it was at a "sacrifice" sale and the price was low—a case of all the liquors in the world which I really detest, apricot brandy. However, the general feeling then was (and I, of course, shared it) to get whatever you could and as much of it as you could. There was a long, dry spell ahead of us, and nobody at that time, whatever they may have said, honestly had any idea of what was going to happen. As a result, too, it was a time of as heavy general public and private drinking as I at least have ever seen in New York. Nobody reproached you, if you got "tight." Always there was the feeling that it might be the last time—for the speakeasy era was not then very accurately envisaged.

A few days after the holiday period, in early January, came the telegram for which I had been waiting so anxiously: "Boy—Alice very sick but in best of hands." I was worried by the phrase about Alice; it told me everything, yet it told me nothing. And, of course, I telegraphed back at once for further details, which were not forthcoming, except the single detail that the baby "had to be taken by an operation," which I at once suspected—and correctly—meant that a Caesarian had had to be performed. Alice herself had known that this was a possibility, even, perhaps, a probability, which is why she had been so firm in her determination to have her baby before it was too late for her safely to have any at all. Like all young fathers I had wanted to celebrate. Somehow I couldn't manage it; I was just too worried.

The next four or five days were as unreal as any I have ever gone through. I cursed myself at the time—I do still—that I had not, cost what it might, interrupt what plans it might, gone with Alice to California and been with her at the time. Reason and common sense tell me, naturally, that my going would not, could not, have made the slightest difference, and I suppose that is the fact—yet, somehow, it is a regret I shall never cease to feel almost as keenly as I then did. I even thought of going anyway, and had there been fast trans-Continental planes then, as there are today, nothing could have stopped me. But at that time even the fastest speed with which I could reach her would be a length of time sufficient to determine whether or not the crisis was really over and whether or not she was going to pull through. I had sense enough to know that—to know that I just had to wait. To wait, hour after hour and for days, for that telegram, which in my imagination I had always framed as saying "Alice out of all danger."

But that telegram never came, and the days were going by. My son, Philip (for so he had been named at Alice's request), was apparently normal and healthy in every way, but to me at that time he hardly seemed to come into my consciousness. If and when I wanted to blame anyone, it was always myself, and I would ask myself over and over again, as if ever there could be an answer to that kind of hypothetical question, "Why? oh why did I permit her to have a baby, if there was this danger?" The sense of almost personal guilt was growing in me, a feeling that I had been reckless and, what was worse, reckless about someone whom I loved better than anything I had known in life before. Those nights I would walk sometimes as far uptown as 125th Street and back through the Park, seeking the physical exhaustion that would allow me to sleep.

But after the first three days, which were the worst, my confidence began to grow. To be sure, the telegrams were somewhat contradictory; however, I regarded every twenty-four hours that passed safely as a great gain. And after a week had elapsed, I began to feel really safe.

I had invited an old friend of Thorne Smith's and of myself, McAlister Coleman, to come down, and we would go out to lunch together. I remember polishing up a couple of glasses, and when the bell rang Alfred Kuttner, who lived upstairs in the same house with me, was down in my room having a drink and was mildly "kidding" me, on the dubious joys of paternity. He answered the bell, and rather to my surprise nobody came back with him.

Instead, he held in his hand an open telegram, and he said, quite directly and simply, "Your wife is dead, Harold." Mechanically, I took the telegram which he had opened; mechanically I read to myself, "Alice passed away this morning. Final services Thursday. We wish care of Philip and Louise will write."

I put down the glass of whisky. I said nothing; I felt nothing. It was a lie—it couldn't be true. It *wasn't* true; there was a mistake. They had the wrong address.

Finally, all I could say was, "I'm going out for a walk. Stay here and tell Coleman I can't have lunch with him. He'll not be offended; he'll understand why."

"All right, Harold," said Alfred very gently. "Perhaps tonight you may feel like having dinner with Rita and myself. Don't be too much alone. Walk up and see Horace Liveright. After all, you ought to tell him first, not anybody else."

There are some walks we never forget—as I shall never forget that walk that afternoon up through the bright sunlit streets of New York. The tears wouldn't come; everything inside me seemed choked up. I kept looking at people in a dull kind of fashion, wondering vaguely, now and then, how it was possible for so many to be laughing and joking and gay. Was I, after all, the only person in this vast metropolis of New York that had any personal sorrow? And then, once in a while, I would find myself asking, as I had never asked myself before, what was the meaning of this event we call death? "What is man that Thou art mindful of him?"—I hadn't thought of that before since my adolescence; with all my heart, all my soul, I wanted an answer to that question. There was no faith for me, as for many people, to fall back upon in a crisis like this. There was just emptiness, blank, loss of all feeling. Loss, too, of all hope of a happy life—I simply couldn't think of life without Alice there to share it with me. I had not realized how much she had meant to me, how much she had represented all the things in my lonely, non-family life I had always missed—and now could nevermore find again.

Horace was deeply and sincerely grieved—he had worked with Alice long enough to like her for her good nature and good sense and good looks and to respect her for her literary judgment and tact, upon which (as he then said, almost startled, I think, to find it out) he had relied much more than he realized. He wanted, desperately, to say something to "cheer me up," hence he made an almost pathetic attempt to overstress the importance and urgency of questions concerned with my book, which was in fact already on the press. There was the question of advertising (Horace was naïve in some ways about advertising; he usually thought that he could make even a poor book a good one by saying it was good often enough and loudly enough); there was the question of calling up the different critics and seeing that it got proper attention; there were important people to whom it should be sent for the publicity value of what they might say. He was full of all kinds of plots to put the book over on the public, quite irrespective, seemingly, of whether the public cared about the book naturally or not. There was no duplicity in all this. Horace himself believed in the book (though I doubt if he ever read more than a third of it) and wanted it to have what he euphemistically called "a fair chance." And being a good gambler, he was willing to back up his choice with a sizeable appropriation bet. I remember I tried to simulate an interest in all this; tried for his sake and for mine. Everybody was as considerate as they could be, too—I mean, everybody in the office: the stock-room boy, the telephone girl, the stenographer. I was a bit surprised, I recall, for I was finding out that there is far more of common humanity in all of us than we ever bother to realize—until something happens. And that night, too, both Alfred and his wife at dinner kept the conversation on topics of European politics that—ordinarily—interested me a great deal, though I doubt if on that occasion I said anything very penetrating. Still, it was a way of helping one to realize that life goes on—or, rather, *must* go on, no matter how we feel about it.

Late that evening, only a few moments after Alfred and his wife had left, Felicia came in to ask, as she pretended, a favor. Madamoiselle Rabelaise's silly daughter, Ophelia, the cat with no teeth and less sense, had to be taken care of for that evening, as Felicia had to go out to New Jersey to her family. (Whether Felicia really had to go out or not, I don't know. It was a good excuse, anyway.) Would I be so nice as to look after the kitten? Felicia told me what to get for it and how to take care of it—and then left. She had said nothing about my grief, had asked no questions, though of course she knew. She had merely tried in her way to give me something to do for those first hours that are so impossible to endure.

And it worked, too. For Ophelia was exigeant; her food didn't suit her; the box I arranged for her to sleep in only excited her contempt; and the pieces of string and bits of paper I dangled before her eyes to amuse her seemed only to provoke a tired yawn. It took me three full hours to amuse, feed, tire out, and finally induce that kitten to go to sleep. And, somehow, as a man may be drugged from too much sleep, I finally dozed off, the lights still burning and my shoes not even removed. I suppose, if I had not been so damn New England, I could have really broken down and wept—it would have been healthier and more natural. But I couldn't do that; I couldn't do anything at all. Things had to happen, as they would happen. And I remember that my only dread and fear was of waking up again, when just the process of going on and living and planning and working and meeting people seemed so unutterably dreary—the process that I should, infallibly, have to face.

I tried to face that process with something that resembled at least the outward appearance of interest. Nevertheless, I question if any young author has ever been less interested—fundamentally and really less interested, I mean—in how his first book was received than I was in what people thought of "Liberalism In America." I worked myself into a false frenzy of rage at Walter Lippmann's long and sometimes not so flattering review in the *New Republic,* and I wrote notes to the country editors who had made references to the book, according to the clippings I received. That Mencken, on the other hand, quite frankly thought the book good and said so did not have the effect such a review ordinarily would have. I was furious with him—because he had made it impossible for me to have a long epistolary quarrel with him. Senator Borah thought the book good, too, which immediately convinced me that he must be a greater fool than I had ever thought possible. When a few of the critics gave me, what—a little later in our social history—was inelegantly termed "the raspberry," I could really have embraced them. And not, mind you, out of what Dr. Johnson once called that "oblique form of self-praise," namely, self-depreciation, but out of the fact that the harsh criticism would sometimes suggest a point of view I had not anticipated or tried to placate. To put it simply, I was grateful for any kind of criticism which took my mind off my own personal problems for even so brief a time as fifteen minutes.

And some things helped. Mr. Alexander Bing, the real estate man who had had something to do with labor adjustments and disputes during the war, had the reckless idea of writing a book on The War Labor Boards—that is, a sort of descriptive and historical record, tempered only by the facts. But he had never written a book before, and the mass of material he had seemed almost too great and too extensive for any kind of reasonable organization. He looked around for somebody to help him put his material in shape, and Horace suggested to him that I was his man. Whether I was or not, he did ask me to help him out, working only four days a week and then only three hours in the morning before lunch, and at a very decent salary. I was glad to do it, for just at that time I hated anything suggesting speculation. Bare and unadorned facts were my solace. And Mr. Bing had plenty.

As I look back on those weeks today sometimes I blush for shame. I was as close to impossible as it was for any normal-appearing man to be and yet to escape murder. I was trying to cure the distemper—have not men done it before?—by intoxication through strong drink, even though outwardly, in the ordinary way, I looked conventional and even dull. But the plain truth is I was drunk all the time, terrified only of being caught sober. My greatest problem, those tired mornings when I went up to assist Mr. Bing, was how to appear to talk to him directly, when questions about the book came up, and yet not permit him to be assaulted by my breath—a problem that most often I solved by pretending to be in deep thought, as I looked out over the city from the high apartment building, where we worked. Luckily for me, and perhaps for him, my reaction time to any question (when I could put my mind on it, or sometimes even hear it) was very quick, and my native ability to shape to recognizable form the most refractory material stood me in good stead. Judging only by external appearances, one might have thought I was the last person in the world to have given him any kind of help—but as a matter of fact, curiously enough, I was just the right person. I was so disinterested that I could be impartial. And that is what he wanted. Yes, even if he should read these lines today at this late date, I think he would agree with me now on that. Paradoxically, had I been better, I should have been far worse.

But I was becoming more and more impatient. I wanted to do something of some real importance—or at least what I thought was important. The new *Freeman* under Mr. Albert Jay Nock's editorship, intrigued me because of its tone and its superiority in some respects, intellectually and stylistically, to either the *New Republic* or the *Nation*. I knew Brooks and Mumford and many of the others, too. The office was over on a lower West Side street, like the old *Dial's* had been, and it seemed familiar. I met almost everybody that was interested in intellectual things–that is, outside the strictly academic circles. And, gradually and uncertainly at first, but then more and more specifically, came the idea of doing "Civilization In The United States." It was a book that had to be done.

And another thing, trivial in itself, but important in another, helped me to the decision. Felicia had taken an old house on Jones Street, and had asked me to come over there to live. Evelyn Scott, the author, occupied the top floor alone —almost barricaded, too, for she locked all the doors to her little apartment so tightly that I always thought with horror of what might happen, if the old house ever caught fire while she was asleep. Felicia, of course, had her different boy friends, one of them in particular an amusing and charming person. But Felicia would not then permit anybody to "live with her," employing a now ancient euphemism. There was not then, there never was later—despite cynical remarks by such gifted gentlemen as Mr. Ernest Boyd—any question of Felicia and myself "living together." But we both understood each other and could get along and manage things better than most such strange *ménage à deux* combinations. And it was a happy household, for we both had many friends in common.

Furthermore, the Jones Street house proved to be an ideal meeting place for all of us, when my idea of "Civilization In The United States" went beyond the idea of just a dream to something like a reality. There are many people who remember that old house on Jones Street—Mencken, DeKruif, Katherine Anthony, Hendrik Van Loon, Ernest Boyd, J. E. Spingarn, Van Wyck Brooks, Lewis Mumford, Thorne Smith, Clarence Britten (though both the two last named are no longer with us), John Macy (and he has left us, too), Deems Taylor, Louis Reid, Ring Lardner (I had almost forgotten, he seemed so vivid, but he has gone, too), and so many of the others.

Now, as I look back on it (literally, almost, for I live near Jones Street and go over there once in a while to see that the old house is still standing in the same spot, unchanged despite the big apartments on all sides), I am glad that I went through the Jones Street experience, and I am glad that I did the book, or, perhaps I should say with more modesty, organized the book and made it possible. It was a good job, and it needed doing at that time—and, as for my editorial capacity, I can only plead in self-defense that those of the writers I got together, if they were not known at that time, have since become almost nationally known. I didn't pick badly, nor make many mistakes—though I still resent the fact that I couldn't get any civilized person to do an article on religion. It seemed incredible to me then, but it was a fact, nevertheless.

And, as so often in my life, when some crisis arises, I found some work, some genuine work, to keep me busy and occupied and safe from the one thing of all things I dread and fear the most—being alone.

But the story of "Civilization" and my flight to Europe on its completion is really another chapter.

XII. THE FIRST OF THE SYMPOSIUMS

THUS the early months of 1921 found me living in the house on Jones Street, with Felicia as general manager. My work on the *Freeman* was going fairly well, but it was my idea of "Civilization" which really gave me an incentive for living. However, that idea was so unusual and involved my getting into contact with so many different and interesting people that I had no time, either intellectually or socially, to feel other than occupied and busy. And fully and intelligently busy, too—the best antidote for grief that I know. Or that anybody else knows.

I think it was Van Wyck Brooks with whom I talked first about my idea. And then with Lewis Mumford; next, with Clarence Britten. In a short time, in fact, I was talking about it with almost anybody who would listen. Mencken wrote that he was attracted by what he was pleased flippantly to term a "hoax." Hendrik Van Loon lived around the corner from me in those days. He would be excellent for the essay on "History," if he would do it—and he said he would. Thorne Smith was also a neighbor of mine—what better man for an amusing and accurate essay on advertising? (It is worth putting in the record that Thorne, at the time he did his essay, was himself working in a typical advertising agency downtown, hence knew whereof he spoke.) George Soule showed interest, too—radicalism was the topic he wanted to tackle. John Macy was a frequent visitor to Jones Street at that time, along with

Charlie Wood, who wanted to suggest—and finally did—someone to do a piece on engineering, much as, two or three years ago, one would feel compelled in a simliar book to include one on technocracy. Macy's interest lay in doing an article on newspapers, because in one way or another he had been connected with the game a long time, and he didn't think (nor did I) that Upton Sinclair had come within a mile of doing the job properly. For the very ticklish topic of medicine, Mencken told me that he had just the man in Paul DeKruif, who at that time was working with the Rockefeller Institute and had never written anything for general publication. Deems Taylor was my own idea for the article on music, the suggestion coming, however, from my old friend of the *Dramatic Mirror* days, Sid Lane, who knew Taylor from his contacts with the music world as director of the concerts and entertainment at Wanamaker's Auditorium. Sid's judgment on music—and on people, as long as they were of masculine persuasion—was discriminating and intelligent.

Fortunately, the three with whom I worked first—Brooks, Mumford, Britten—had each his own subject. Brooks wanted to do an article on "The Literary Life" (I had taken for my own topic, "The Intellectual Life," which gave me some latitude); Mumford wanted to do an article on "The City." Britten seemed to me—remembering that he had been an instructor at the University of Wisconsin—just the man to do one on "School And College Life," while Robert M. Lovett, on his side, appeared to me logically indicated for the more general one on "Education." But Lovett was away most of the time in Chicago, and it was not easy to obtain his promise to do the piece—but, finally, he did promise. So I put him down as number 13 on the list, as he was, chronologically in the order of accepting the task—but in this case, certainly, not an unlucky number 13.

As always, the question of the Negro, the Jew, and other racial minorities—not to mention the question of other aliens, recently arrived immigrants in particular—interested me, and I did not see how, without an adequate "coverage" of these two questions, any book on American civilization could be complete. Frederic C. Howe had been Commissioner for Immigration; he was an intelligent, liberal man—could I get him to do "The Alien"? I have forgotten how I persuaded him to do the task, but persuade him I did. And, for that terribly difficult subject, "Racial Minorities"—by which I meant specifically the Negro and the Indian—I luckily had a conscientious and able young man to call upon, G. T. Robinson, with whom I had worked, both on the old *Dial* and the newer *Freeman*. I breathed a sigh of relief when I obtained Robinson's consent to do one of the most exacting and thankless jobs of the entire book, in fact, perhaps the most exacting and thankless.

By this time there was quite a sizeable group—fifteen, to be precise—with whom to work out a scheme. The project was actually taking form. Could we make that form a reality? The time was propitious for it; I mean, the unlovely wave of intolerance, "Red" hysteria, and "spy" mania was having the natural consequence of bringing closer together all men and women of good-will.

"Women," I wrote almost without thinking in the above paragraph—and in just the same way I suddenly realized then that I had not, when I contemplated and dreamed about the book, thought of women at all, one way or the other. Yet sex had reared its lovely head just as surely and gracefully in these United States as elsewhere, and, although I had practically no family, and never had had, of my own, the family was an indubitable fact in American life. Lay it to my strictly male, old-fashioned Harvard education, if you like. Yet I was secretly somewhat shocked at my cavalierly waving aside these two vital subjects. I said nothing, but determined to have the subjects dealt with, and adequately, too—even if I had to call in women themselves to help me out.

In my distress I appealed to Charlie Merz, an old friend from *New Republic* days—who later was to do that gorgeous book, "The American Band Wagon"—to give me advice. And he did, too, sound advice. "If you can," he said, "persuade Mrs. Elsie Clews Parsons to write for the book. She is charming, intelligent, a student of anthropology, and a mother, too. What more do you want?" Here again luck was with me. Once Mrs. Parson had seen the list of names, had come down to Jones Street herself, and had read a few of the essays already finished, she consented. Only—rather to my surprise, I confess—she chose to write on the subject of sex in general instead of on the family specifically, as I had expected. But I wanted her in the book even at—almost—her own terms. (As a matter of fact, she did an excellent essay.)

Of course I was pleased that the subject of sex was settled, nevertheless there was the problem of obtaining some woman to do the essay on the family. I think the fact that I was having a married woman do the essay on sex suggested of itself—probably abetted by a few flippant remarks from Ernest Boyd—the seeming paradox of having a spinster do the essay on the family. The deciding thing, to be honest, was much simpler—I knew just the spinster I wanted, that is, brilliant Katherine Anthony. (I might add, to flatter my own perspicacity, that she was not at the time so generally known as when her important biographical studies began, later on, to appear.) Miss Anthony, too, was not difficult to persuade once the facts were laid before her. It would, perhaps, be impertinent for me to comment on her essay at this late date, though, as editor, I was enormously pleased with what she did. But I do want to observe that, quite aside from its brilliance and the soundness of its main contentions, the essay was compact with a sly wit that delighted as well as astonished me. I recall Mencken saying to me one afternoon he came down to Jones Street to read what essays had already been written (about six or seven then), "Why, damn it all, Stearns, both the gals are doing better than the men."

Mencken was so pleased, in fact, that when I pointed out that, up to that moment, I had been at a loss to find somebody to do the essay on the theatre, he said not to worry, for he would persuade George Jean Nathan to break the rule of a lifetime by contributing to an anthology. Mencken was as good as his word—and Nathan wrote the piece. It was a first-rate bit of work, too, as a re-reading of it today again convinces me. But, curiously enough, Nathan was one of the very few—especially of those who lived in or near New York—who never came down to Jones Street, though as a matter of fact I don't know what he was afraid of, and—had he come—he would have had a good time. Anyway, I saw him at his hotel up in the Forties, where, I remember, he served me very good cocktails—very much as Bob Benchley does today.

Because of my own family connections—I mean, simply, since my father-in-law, Dr. D. T. Macdougal, was a distinguished scientist himself—it was a point of pride with me to obtain a good man for the subject of science. Dr. Robert H. Lowie was at that time Curator, or something of the sort, at the American Museum of Natural History uptown; he had just finished a general book on his own topic of anthropology, which Horace had published. It was easy, therefore, for me to meet him, and, in fact, we became rather good friends. Furthermore, he had a European background and could see the American scene in some perspective. He was critical in the real and inclusive sense of the word—and he wrote a very good piece.

Fortunately—or unfortunately——I am not the kind of person who allows a personal quarrel to stand in the way of any intellectual end I may be pursuing—if I can help it. In that sense, perhaps, I am false to my New England ancestry. Anyway, though before leaving Washington Place, I had had a violent quarrel with Alfred Kuttner over what he was pleased to term my moral collapse, following Alice's death, I still knew that he was just the man to do the piece on "Nerves," for he was at that time one of the best students of psycho-pathology in the country. So I put my pride in my pocket, called him up, explained the situation about the book, and, after he had read what had been done and I had made clear my purpose, he consented to write the essay, called "Nerves." And a penetrating bit of work it was, too—just what I wanted.

My own rather lamentable indifference to art did not blind me to the importance of the subject. But I soon found myself in some difficulties—almost similar in nature to those I was to encounter (and insurmountably in the latter case) with the subject of religion a few weeks later on. I mean, there were any number of people I could obtain to write on the subject, but every blessed one of them, on examination, turned out to be some sort of a special pleader—somebody more interested in a particular aesthetic doctrine, or in disproving somebody else's, than in the relation of art to the American social scene. If Mumford had not already taken the subject of the city (which, incidentally, covered the vital topic of architecture), I think he might have done a quite adequate job. But I could hardly ask him to do two subjects; besides, it would look slightly absurd. After many heart-burnings, inquiries, trials of one person or another (I must have acquired at least a half dozen life-time enemies by asking these people to write a piece and then coldly turning it down, but I shall not now, years after, mention their names), and absurd suggestions, I finally got in touch with Walter Pach, who, from my point of view at least (and I had the final word by this time; the authority had been formally delegated to me by vote), could at least make an attempt to relate art to the whole of American civilization. From a stylistic point of view, I suppose, his essay was a trifle dull and the essential soundness of its aesthetic judgments I was not in a position to affirm or deny. But it did make an attempt—and I thought an intelligent attempt—to relate art to the whole of American life.

Possibly the idea of a little supplement to the main body of the book—"American Civilization From The Foreign Point Of View"—would not have occurred to me at all, had I not been keen to have, somehow, Ernest Boyd in the book, for I enjoyed his Irish wit and his way of laying down the literary and intellectual law. Mencken liked Boyd, too, and we both, so to speak, schemed to include him—and, finally, I hit on the simple and honest way, that is, the supplement. There is no need here for me to recapitulate that essay, "As An Irishman Sees It," but it makes amusing reading even today. In fact, I think it is one of the best bits Boyd ever did—and he did it, too, before he had been soured a trifle by later literary quarrels, for, like most Irishmen, Boyd was always looking for a fight.

But Boyd's writing "As An Irishman Sees It" made me, as editor, want to hold the scales of justice even, and I determined to find somebody to write "As An Englishman Sees It." And here I played in real luck. For just at that time my old friend, Henry L. Stuart, was working in New York on some newspaper job—afterwards, I was told on my return from Paris, he was on the staff of the New York *Times,* which is one of the things the *Times* can legitimately put down to its credit—and it was a pleasure, quite aside from obtaining his contribution, to renew my old friendship of the Boston days, for I can truly say of Stuart that he was one of the men I have known I really loved. Even today I can remember the look of pleased astonishment that came over the countenance of J. E. Spingarn, when I showed him this essay up in the old offices of Harcourt, Brace and Company. Boyd's essay amused him, but Stuart's genuinely moved him.

And it accomplished two things: First, it settled the difficult question of who was going to publish the book. Harcourt, with Spingarn's approval, gave me an attractive contract, which permitted me to have $50 paid in advance royalties to each contributor, on my statement that their essay was completed and accepted—so that those living on their work would not feel that they were working for nothing. And second, it persuaded Spingarn himself to contribute the essay on "Scholarship And Criticism," which I had wanted him to do anyway.

By now I had such a distinguished list of definite contributors to the volume that I had less hesitation than I might ordinarily have had in trying to obtain—and successfully—the man I had always wanted to have do the essay on the Law, namely, Zachariah Chafee, Jr., the distinguished member of the Harvard Law School. I wrote to him, asking him particularly that—before he reached a definite decision—he pay a visit to Jones Street, when he came to New York, and have a look at the essays for himself. If he was at all well disposed towards the idea, I knew that would settle it—and it did. Nor do I need to speak of the essay he finally wrote. How any serious student of American law, either its history, theory, or practice, can ignore that essay is simply not comprehensible to me. It should, as a matter of fact, be required reading for every American citizen. It has since been a legitimate source of pride to me that I was the editor of a book that could include it—perhaps a latent Harvard pride getting the better of me.

But no Harvard pride or vestigial Boston correctness prevented me from going after Ring Lardner hammer and tongs for the essay on Sport and Play—he was the man I wanted, and I wanted him badly. He could write in his "Americanese," if he wanted to. Why not? That was his natural style of writing anyway; he would be self-conscious, had he tried to do anything else. Besides, he was writing on sport, where such language had applicability—and where, I might add, he himself had enriched the language with expressions that were known by every baseball and football and prize-fight and racing and athletic and tennis fan from Coast to Coast. "You Know Me, Al" was an American folk classic of that time. I don't know, even to this day, exactly what Ring thought of being in such "high-brow" company, but I know how I felt—that he was doing us an honor, not we him. Anyway, I managed to persuade him finally, though I had to see him several times before he was quite convinced that the whole thing wasn't a hoax, which Mencken, of course, solemnly assured him it was.

Sport naturally suggested Humour. And here I was in a quandary, for I had no Benchley at that time to inveigle, as I might, with luck, have today. At the end, however, I contrived to convince Frank M. Colby to do the piece, which, although it was rather slight in substance and almost flippant in tone, was really a much subtler bit of work than too many hasty critics gave it credit for being. And if the reader was in any doubt as to what Mr. Colby meant by certain of his phrases, he had only to turn back to the essay immediately preceding, that is, Lardner's "Sport and Play," to have a rather vivid exemplification.

When I had asked Lewis Mumford to do his essay on "The City," I had kept a reservation in my mind—I mean, simply, that I was determined to obtain also an essay on "The Small Town," without some understanding of which the whole pattern of American life is inexplicable. On this subject I had my own ideas, especially of the man to do it—Louis Raymond Reid, who came from a small town up-State himself. I had known Louis well in the old days when I was on the *Dramatic Mirror* and I thought he would do a good job. In fact, he did an excellent one—in his criticism of the whole book, published some time later in the *Dial,* Santayana went out of his way to give this particular essay especial praise.

The mention of Santayana's name recalls to me how I labored—in vain, in this instance—to get him to do the article on "Philosophy," but when he cabled me from Paris that he was neither a philosopher nor an American, I could, perhaps, dispute one of his negations, but I was helpless. Due to my own academic training I felt the subject should be included, however, and after weeks of trying here, there, and everywhere obtained a fairly adequate essay from California, by Harold Chapman Brown. Brown, along with Conrad Aiken, are the two people in the volume whom I never saw—nor have I seen either of them since. I had had considerable difficulty in finding somebody to do the essay on "Poetry," and I think it was Clarence Britten who suggested Aiken, whom, if I remember correctly, he had known in college. At all events, Aiken did the piece, and it was duly included with the others—which I soon thereafter felt to be a mistake, for Aiken was in England and out of sympathy with the whole idea of the book, as he rather ungraciously took the trouble to state publicly later on. I should have got somebody like Witter Bynner or even Max Eastman to do it—but, after all, I couldn't think of everything.

Garet Garrett, who had been an editor of the old New York *Tribune* at one time, was suggested to me for the absolutely essential essay on Business, and, after some manoeuvering, I obtained not only his promise, but, finally, an interesting, critical, and sprightly essay. And, very late in the project, I obtained an excellent piece on "Economic Opinion" from Walton H. Hamilton, who had been recommended to me by several people whose judgment I knew I could trust.

During these last few weeks I was eating my heart out, as I explain briefly in my introduction to the book, in trying to persuade—and first to find—the right person to do an article on "Religion." I was successful three or four times in finding somebody who would do a good job (like James Harvey Robinson), but somehow I could never quite bring pressure enough to bear upon them actually to do it. And to my great regret—just as I was sorry I had not been able to find what I considered the right essay and the right person for that growing phenomenon in American life at that time, the moving-picture—the subjects had to be abandoned, at least as far as a specific essay on either of them went.

The plain truth is that my old restlessness was coming over me again. I felt I had done a good job, and I wanted to get away to Europe. The shadows of prohibition and intolerance, all the unlovely aftermath of the great Wilsonian crusade, were closing in on me too fast for my comfort. Europe was calling me again, or—and it came down to the same thing—what I thought was Europe. If Alice had lived, things might have been different; I am sure they would have been different. But as it was, I felt exhausted and tired and a little bitter. Mencken had said he could arrange for me to do some correspondence work for the Baltimore *Sun*—which he did—and that I could probably sell other stuff, too. And right at that time, what is more, George H. Doran Company offered to buy for cash a collection of several of my essays, which had already appeared in the old *Dial* or in the *Freeman,* and this gave me some ready money. Moreover, I had only envisaged a short summer trip to Europe; I did not realize, though I think I had a sort of dim, subconscious feeling that it was going to be longer than just a summer trip, that I was going to stay in France for almost thirteen years. I know it was with a feeling of elation that I wrote the introduction before dawn, dated it—and it was not a pretense, as some critics thought, but a fact—July the Fourth, and took a taxicab over to the Cunard Line piers, where I boarded the "Berengaria." Felicia promised to see to it that all the copy got up safely to Harcourt, which she did; as for my own essay on "The Intellectual Life," though I had done it early, I wanted to re-write it, and I told her to tell Harcourt that I should mail it from England on landing—which I did, also. For better or worse, "Civilization" was finished. As the boat pulled down the bay I did not think of the conventional things—I thought how lucky I was that for my final essay, the tailpiece, so to speak, I had that excellent and moving essay in the supplement, "As An Italian Sees It," by Rafaello Piccoli, and I blessed Spingarn in memory for having brought him down to Jones Street. It gave just the right note for the final word—critical, gracious, urbane, warm with real feeling. Who could resist a book like that? I recall asking myself as I fell asleep the first night out.

The trip over was very pleasant, for Thorne Smith and Celia, his wife, were on board, too, and we had a gay time. They got off at Cherbourg, because they were planning a Continental trip, while I stayed on and landed the next morning early at Southampton. When I reached London, I did not go to my old 1914 address on Palace Street, and Maugham, whom I had not seen since the war, was not then in London. I went out to Grosvenor Gardens and took a little studio, sharing it later on with Egmont Arens, who ran a bookshop in Greenwich Village and who had made the trip over to England rather spectacularly in a small sailing boat. But I couldn't seem to get much done in London, though I *did,* finally, put the finishing touches on my own essay and sent it back to Harcourt. The real writing of it, however, I had done on the boat.

Horace Liveright, before I left, had wanted me to do another cooperative book on American civilization—this time, all of it by foreigners. It was a good idea, even if slightly grandiose. I did make a few efforts in the direction of doing it, but when I received a saucy postcard from the great Shaw himself stating that my idea was insane (it has since been done, incidentally), I became quite angry and abandoned the project. Besides, I was doing my first articles for the Baltimore *Sun* at that time, and trying to "make good" as a correspondent. Evidently I did, because they continued to publish my "stuff" with great regularity from then on, and when I got to Paris, I was one of their special Paris correspondents for the entire five years that elapsed before I came back home again. But in London I didn't know what was ahead of me. I began to get restless.

Sinclair Lewis was living down in some old town in Surrey finishing up, if I am not mistaken, "Arrowsmith." He invited me down for a weekend. And a day or so before I went down Sherwood Anderson came around to see me. I remember his telling me with a curious earnestness that I was really "European"—and didn't know it. I think what he meant was that I was Bostonian; perhaps he meant simply that I seemed to adapt myself suspiciously easily to English life. If he thought the latter, he was mistaken—it was all on the surface. I never adapted myself to it, and I found out afterwards that I never could. French life? Yes, up to a certain point. But English life, English manners, the English viewpoint—never. Curiously enough, one of the things I always held against Santayana was that he spent the years he did at Oxford. How could he stand it! How could anybody stand England?

It may be my weakness, a curious Yankee lack of sympathy, I don't know. But although I have liked individual Englishmen—like Stuart—and have really admired English civilization in its best estate, I simply cannot endure the average Englishman. He makes me want to fight right away; I feel he must be destroyed. And I remember saying to Sherwood that afternoon, "Well, I don't mind much, if you call me European. But damn you to hell, if ever you dare to call me English." And Sherwood merely grinned.

Sinclair said he had been working hard. Before dinner we took a walk around the countryside—the train from London had got me down just in time for tea—and Sinclair kept on reiterating that he needed a bit of rest. "Fine," I said at length, "why don't you knock off for a few days and take me for a little trip with you over to Paris? I know the ropes; you'll have a good time. And I'll introduce you to some nice people. Probably it will do your work good, too."

Anyway, we did it—Sinclair providing me with a few extra clothes, for I had not brought down anything except overnight things from London. It was the first time he had ever been on the Continent, let alone to Paris, and he was as excited as a young man donning his first pair of long trousers. There was no sleeping either in the train down to the boat, on the boat, or on the French "rapide" that took us swiftly to Paris. Whenever and wherever we could lay hands on a brandy or a whiskey, we did so. We arrived so groggy and sleepy that there was nothing for us to do for the first few hours but to go to a hotel—I think it was the "Oxford et Cambridge," not far from the Rue Royale off the Rue de Rivoli—and get some rest. After a snooze and a cold shower, Sinclair was ready for any great adventure that Paris had to offer. I rang up Lewis Galantière, and asked him to come to my aid and help me pilot Sinclair around—which he graciously did. It was as hectic a five days and nights as I have ever put in; Sinclair was full of vitality. He wanted to go everywhere at once, to see everything, to visit every bar, explore the "Quarter"—and we cut quite a dash in Montparnasse those few nights, too. How much he saw, or remembered, of historical Paris that first visit might be put into a very small page of a very small notebook. But I saw nothing to object to in that. He was on vacation; and, after all, where can one better spend a vacation than in Paris?

Yet most things have to come to an end, and Sinclair's vitality was not inexhaustible, though sometimes it seemed so to me during those five days and nights, when even two hours of sleep was the exception. He had to get back to England and finish "Arrowsmith." But, he pointed out to me, why should I have to go back? He would lend me any money I needed, and I could write for my things and have them sent on or brought over from London. I said that would be great, for I had no desire to go back to London anyway. Arens was coming over to Paris himself in a few days; I could telegraph him to bring my typewriter and my other few effects. And so it was arranged.

And thus, what had begun as a simple weekend jaunt from London over to Paris and France ended in fact in my staying on in Paris over 250 weekends, that is to say, for five years. The story of those years is another chapter.

XIII. PARISIAN FLIMSY

OF COURSE Sinclair's money did not last me more than a month or so. And though I was writing occasionally for the Baltimore *Sun*—and getting paid for it, too, albeit the rate was pretty low—I did not at the time even know whether or not my articles were being accepted. The work I did on August 12th would be paid for on October 20th, unless there were lucky "breaks." That is a stretch between what one is doing and payment therefor of nine weeks—quite normal with a business house, but a good deal of a strain on anybody living on a close margin.

All that first autumn in Paris, though there were interludes, the worries of how just modestly "to make the grade" were all-compulsive. I had no idea when either "Civilization" or "America And The Young Intellectual" were going to appear, let alone whether they would sell at all and make me anything, though only the first really counted, for I had sold the second book for a flat sum. (Both books came out early in 1922.) As I say, Sinclair's money helped the first few weeks; Lewis Galantière was very nice, too; the newspaper boys, especially Sam Dashiel and dear old Roscoe Ashworth, were always buying me a meal, and, as they would say almost with embarrassment, "slipping" me a few francs now and then. Arens came over from England, as he intended, and he brought me my typewriter and clothes. With the arrival of these necessaries I left the down-town hotel in which I had been stopping and went up to the "Quarter"—that is, to Montparnasse—to live on the old Rue Delambre. It was cheaper all round, and there were people I knew up there, mostly Americans, either students, newspaper men, artists, or plain serious drinkers. But cheap as it was, I didn't even at that see how I was going to get by. I couldn't go back to America, had I had a job at home (which I hadn't), and had I, moreover, *wanted* to go back (which I frankly didn't).

Thus somehow the weeks and months dragged along. But "drag" is not the verb, for it was gay up in Montparnasse in those days, with a genuine gaiety, too. The tourist flocks had not yet swooped down on the place—to make it vivid to some, I'll merely say that *Le Dôme* was just an old-fashioned corner *"bistrot,"* with César still puttering around and never giving you the drinks you ordered; what is the "Select" today was an old furniture shop on the corner of the Rue Vavin; *La Coupole,* opposite, was an old coal-and-wood yard; *La Rotonde* was small and dirty and historical (Trotsky used to go there in the old days, when Paris was a place of refuge for Russian Revolutionists of the ancient school); the "Dingo" was a tiny workmen's *café; Le Vertige* and the others did not exist. Then, too, the art students of those days—I mean, of course, the American and English ones primarily—were pretty serious, and were not in France (as were so many later on) "doing" art just for the sake of an irresponsible sexual and alcoholic holiday. Nina Hamnett worked like a slave; so did Jack Green (who afterwards got a Guggenheim scholarship), while "Jo" Davidson, whom I had met with Doris Keane in New York in my salad *Dramatic Mirror* days, had a home of his own near the Quarter, and could even then tell us how the *"Bal des Quatz' Arts"* really was a show in the good old days before the war. People like George Biddle were working with an industry that would reflect credit on the wall mottoes of Kansas Y. M. C. A. yearners for better things. I think Man Ray had already begun his pioneer photographic work—in the days when Kiki was young and beautiful; though it was a trifle later on that I got to know him fairly well. Of course there were always a few who "came over" for but a month or two—usually in the summer—to acquire "atmosphere," as many people acquire a tan on their holidays; but they didn't count, except for incidental amusement.

Yes, the weeks and months "dragged" along—magically. And when a Frenchman says to me, "La vie passe comme une rêve à Paris," I know just what he means. Life really *can* go by like a dream in Paris—it so often has for me. It did then.

And then I was shaken out of my dream.

It was about two weeks before Christmas. I had gone to bed hungry and late—hungry, because I had no money with which to buy dinner; late, because I wanted to avoid seeing the proprietor of the hotel and having any quarrel over the rent I owed, at least until the next day, for I had in my pockets exactly four cigarettes and five sous (less than two cents). I got to sleep finally, when my nerves had quieted down—and it seemed only a moment, but it was ten o'clock in the morning: The proprietor was pounding on my door. "I'll be kicked out," I thought to myself. And then the humor of it made me smile in spite of myself—"My Paris Christmas present."

Then I opened the door.

The proprietor seemed in fair humor—I noticed that at once and with gratitude. "Some letters for you, Monsieur Stearns," he said amiably. "Two of them were registered, and I signed for you. That's all right, eh?"

I nodded, surprised that anybody should bother to send me a registered letter.

The registered letter was from a bank, stating that a money cable order to me had been received from my publishers, Harcourt, Brace and Company, and would I be so good as to call at the bank for the money, with proper identification. The second was from the New York *Herald* (Paris edition, of course), stating that there was a job for me there on the copy desk, if I would be sure to come in right after the holidays. (I blessed "Jo" Davidson for this—and correctly. I knew at once he had "sold" me to Larry Hills.) The third was from Jessica, the nice American girl I had met a week or so before, asking me to pass the *fête*—meaning the celebration the night before Christmas—with her, for although I had wanted to, I had not dared, being broke, to invite her.

And people say miracles do not happen! There I was, fearing eviction, without a penny or a friend, as I thought and had reason to believe. And holiday tomorrow! Yet all at once I had money, a girl, and a job—right out of the blue sky (though it was in fact grey and foggy, it was the most beautiful blue to me).

I turned to the proprietor and explained, and my joy must have been obvious. "Lend me a hundred francs until I get back from the bank—I want a half bottle of champagne right now, for breakfast."

He laughed—"Very well, Monsieur Stearns, here you are. But don't get drunk before you go down to the bank—today it closes at noon, remember—and come back here and pay your bill before you spend all your money." He gave me the hundred francs, then said, almost affectionately, "You Americans—you are all the same. Children, just children."

For once I was sensible, and although I had my little nip of champagne, I arrived at the bank a full half hour before it closed, did my business, and took a taxicab back to the Quarter and *Le Dôme,* where I went down to the comic telephone both next to the toilet and called Jessica. Luckily she had kept the evening free; she suggested *Le Rotonde* for our *fête,* because, she said, everybody we knew was going there. We could, of course, have preliminary drinks at *Le Dôme,* and she would meet me there at eleven. Unless I was keen on it, she was agreeable to passing up the midnight mass; anyway, the best music was at the church down in *Les Halles,* and it would be crowded to suffocation, even if we were lucky enough to get in.

I told her, honestly enough, that I was glad people went to mass on the holidays but that it meant nothing to me except as a spectacle.

I went to my hotel, paid the bill, and—except for three or four hundred francs which I kept out for the party—gave the rest of what I had to the proprietor to keep for me. Early in my career in France I had learned to do this, that is, when I had the chance. I dressed with some care, for I had bought a few clothes at a couple of those fantastic shops on the Rue de la Gaieté, opposite the snail shop. Getting dressed, together with the excitement of a bath and of donning clean fresh clothes, acted as the best "soberer" imaginable. For shortly after Jessica had come into the café, and we had promptly guzzled several *mandarins, Pernots,* and *vermouth-cassis,* she began to feel quite "high" and gay, while I, on the contrary, despite the fact that I had had no dinner, was unaffected—or seemingly so. (And I have noticed since that the general *social* situation in which you find yourself has almost as much to do with whether or not alcohol is or is not going to "take" as has any physical condition of tiredness or hunger—at least this has been true for me.) Anyway, Jessica was having a good time—she told me not once but a dozen times that I didn't need to go home the next morning, but could come and stay with her—and I felt content with all the world, just the same kind of feeling you have when you back a hopeless outsider at the track and it comes romping home first to fill your pockets with gold and bring confusion upon all the "wise boys." About one o'clock we scampered over to *La Rotonde* and to the table I had reserved upstairs—which was packed, as I had seldom seen it before. Sam and Marjorie and Anne and Roscoe and everybody else of that vintage was there, drinking merrily and starting in on the feast. There was dancing with a fair orchestra playing the popular tunes of that day—like "Avec Le Sourire" and "Ca C'est Une Chose"—and I encouraged Jessica to dance, for that keeps one sober to a certain extent and, more than that, it gave me a chance to ogle any good-looking gal that took my fancy as well as to imbibe a bit more than my share of the champagne. Sam in particular was in excellent form, and I recall his solemnly announcing that rain-checks would be passed out to everybody so that they could make sure they got home to bed with the right partners. Horace Liveright, my publisher, was making one of his brief, hectic trips to Paris at that time; I recall his looking in on the scene of gaiety and inviting everybody to breakfast at the Hotel Crillon. (About a hundred accepted his invitation and about a dozen actually showed up, but that was no criticism of Horace's hospitality. He didn't realize that hardly anybody would be in a condition to arise from bed and go downtown to the Crillon, even with the tempting bait of a stylish breakfast.) It was a happy *reveillon.*

In what moralists sometimes call "the cold, grey dawn of the morning after" (though in fact the light had that curious and beautiful "violet hour" quality, which anybody who has ever been to Paris—and has ever remained up all night—will at once recognize), I took Jessica home, returning happily to my own room, which was not five minutes' walk from hers, for she had promised to have Christmas lunch with me at the popular old Saint-Cecile's. We met there as agreed, wondering now and again how everybody had made out at Horace's elaborate breakfast—but not envious about them. We were content to be with each other and by ourselves—as we were to be again so often in the months that followed.

Good luck, like bad, seldom comes single. "Jo" Davidson was not content just to get me a job on the Paris *Herald.* He also knew the editor of *Town And Country*—the society, sporting, country-life magazine, that is, the type of magazine for which one would think I ought to be the last person in the world to be selected as correspondent. But as a matter of fact, I was something of a success on the job—for I didn't write about fashions, or society, or horses, or country châteaux, or any of the other things that Mr. Veblen used to cite as forms of conspicuous display. I wrote on politics, French wines and the prohibition question, the *"Quatz' Arts"* ball and morality, the French sense of humor, absurdities of the administrative system as especially shown in the passion for cards, receipts, stamps, and "papers" of all kinds—in fact, on almost all the subjects you might normally expect, in those days, to see discussed with preternatural seriousness in *The New Republic* or *The Nation.* Seemingly the readers of the magazine liked my stuff—and I was the regular Paris correspondent of that magazine until I returned to America on my first visit home some four years later. The work was fun; it was easy; and at the then rate of exchange it paid well.

That job, however, took only two or three days of hard work a month. It was the job on the Paris *Herald*—from eight o'clock at night to half past twelve in the morning ordinarily, unless something "big" broke, when I might have to stay until quarter past two in the morning—which took up my time, kept my habits regular, and continued my life-long series of newspaper experiences. And each week during all this time, remember, I was doing a column for the Baltimore *Sun,* which I contrived to mail for the fast steamers leaving Le Havre or Cherbourg on Saturdays, either by bringing the copy down Friday nights before seven o'clock to the Central Paris Post Office on the Rue du Louvre, next to the old *Herald* office, or "catching the boat train," as it was called, at the Gare Saint-Lazare on Saturday mornings and myself putting it in the mail pouches marked "S. S. Olympic" or "Paquebot Paris" or whatever was leaving.

How could one be bored or miserable? I had three jobs, a brilliant and amusing and pretty girl for company on my rare days "off," and a city to explore—a city, the fascination of which seemed never to grow less for me but always more. For I never got tired of walking around Paris; I was always diligently and delightedly trying to find some little corner or *place* or hidden back street that I had not seen before. And then I would read what I could find out about its history and the changes in its architecture—for the streets of Paris are the streets of romance, if ever streets were. Romance: and sometimes tragedy, because they are soaked in blood, too; you get a vivid feeling every now and then that the tolerance and the liberty you enjoy have all been fought for, have all cost a high price in human life. You get a feeling of heritage, much sharper than even I have in my own historical town of Boston, though there, too, one experiences something analogous. Analogous, but weaker. Paris is the student's city, if one has any historical imagination.

It is the lovers' city also—and especially in the spring, after the dreary and dark days, when the lights go on at four in the afternoon and have to be kept on sometimes until nine or ten o'clock in the morning. For the hours of daylight expand swiftly; the sun becomes much braver and more constant; the flowers are very gay—and they are everywhere. After the gloomy Paris winter, it is good to be alive—in Paris. And I was very happy with Jessica that spring; perhaps all the happier since she knew she would soon have to go back home, and we both knew, instinctively but surely, that that would be the end; and there was a kind of perverse joy in savoring to the full an experience which must so soon and so inevitably and finally end. It is sweet, said Goethe of his successive love affairs, to see the sun rise while the moon is still mildly shining, but it gives a touch of intensity to this emotion when no new sun has yet risen and you know that the light of that moon must infallibly go out forever. Parting is such sweet sorrow, the older poets sang—and they weren't so foolish as many imagine.

But I wasn't long left to lament and grieve after that day when I kissed Jessica goodbye as we stood on the platform of the Gare Saint-Lazare and as, a moment later, she waved to me through the windows of the Le Havre express that was taking her to the boat for America—and out of my life. For loneliness was not to be my lot, as it had been so many times before and has been so many times since. A few afternoons before her departure, an extremely pretty American friend had called on Jessica, while I happened to be still there, and I knew at once—don't ask me why, either; every man is entitled to one or two such intuitive insights—that she was attracted to me. Yet I was genuinely fond of Jessica, and out of just romantic decency, I made no attempt to see her pretty friend—that is, for a fortnight or so, while I enjoyed my despair at Jessica's departure. But after about that length of time the thrill of being desolated wore off—and besides, the *"Quatz' Arts"* Ball was coming again, and I was determined this time not to goad myself to restlessness, as did so many "onlookers," and as I had myself done the previous year, but to have my own girl with me. And thus I asked Agatha, Jessica's friend, if she would come with me, knowing in advance that she would protest that it was "indecent" and even dangerous—but that she would come just the same. Few women, whatever their morals or even their looks or age, would pass up an opportunity to witness a genuine *"Quatz' Arts"* Ball of the old vintage. And, of course, Agatha, saying she would n'er consent, consented.

If Agatha had neither the brains nor the artistic ability of Jessica—the latter had introduced me to the work of Dérain, for instance, and was no mean artist in her own right—she had attractive looks and great personal charm. Also she had what I had so often liked in women, a consequence of what Lee Simonson once told me was my "grandfather complex," that is, a desire to learn. In particular, she wanted to learn to write, and not fiction or anything pretentious, but how to write practically, for a newspaper, so that she could do fashion articles for home and add to her small divorcee's income. I promised to help her in this, and I scrupulously kept my promise—but that is a bit later.

Right then I wanted a vacation from the *Herald.* It was not that the hours were long, but I had begun to find the work rather boring. I mean, of course, the perpetual "re-write" of local stories, the obituaries of famous Americans, when the flash came that they had left for happier worlds (I spent one whole evening, I recall, getting out all the "stuff" on John Wanamaker, when he died), the petty personals and society gossip, the figuring out of the standings of the major baseball teams (the results of the games were always the last cable flashes), the eternal "playing up" of prohibition enforcement farces and tragedies (the boss, who was French, loved these stories; they gave him a feeling of civilized superiority), trying to put some sense into the interviews with American big-wigs who came to Paris and, instead of giving our local man any kind of an interesting story, usually spent their time hospitably attempting to give him a "good time" (with the result, naturally, that the local man often came in with more of a breath than an interview), the so-called book and play reviews which for the most part were mere publicity "puffs," and, finally, the local side of big "interpretative" stories, which the highly paid New York correspondent of the paper in Paris brought to the office for cabling. In substance, that was my desk job—and while it had its amusing side and while, I am glad also to report, the boss himself had an almost American sense of humor, it was the kind of work that, after a few months, made you scream for a vacation—for anything that would take you away from Paris and news of any description. I had started in the first few weeks with the *Herald,* to keep the record straight, doing "leg" work, as it used inelegantly to be called, that is, making the rounds of the hotels, the bars, the police courts, and other sources of misinformation, and although I had not been too bad at it despite my poor conversational French (which quickly improved under pressure of the necessity of being understood), before long I had pleaded to go "on the desk for re-write," a plea the boss had graciously granted. Notwithstanding all my experience, I simply do not like what is sometimes called "straight" reporting. But while my desk job pleased me more as regular routine, it was one that demanded a vacation every six months, if a man was to keep his sanity.

Why we went down to Saint-Malo in Brittany for that vacation I can't remember—probably Agatha decided it, for she had always wanted to go down. Anyway, it was summer and the seashore—and it gave us a chance to see Mont Saint-Michel at leisure, since it was only a short excursion run over there from Saint-Malo. (Incidentally, Chartres is about the only important cathedral—or other—town in France that I have not visited, the industrial North always excepted.) I enjoyed the little beach above the town, even the ridiculous *hôtel des voyageurs,* where we stopped. The food was good; there was plenty of wine; people were absurd and amusing; all about us were things of historical interest and present beauty (that trip across the bay back from Dinard to Saint-Malo, when the setting sun gilds all the high ramparts, is a visual experience for anyone); as at all French summer "resorts," even the smallest and least pretentious, there was always something "to do." And another thing, which I always enjoy—flocks of dogs, of all breeds, all colors, and all degrees of muttdom or canine aristocracy. When a French family goes out *en vacance,* little four-footed and trouble-finding Pierre, "le bool-dogg," or even more trouble-finding Rose-Marie, the vivacious "fox," invariably go with them, and Heaven help the hotel that does not treat them with proper respect and at least a show of affection. The pleasures were simple, yet seldom have I enjoyed a short vacation so thoroughly. And Agatha, too, had a good time, for in those days there was not a stylish Casino, *à la Deauville,* to awaken envy for the rich and well-dressed in her all-too-feminine heart.

Back in Paris after our somewhat brief vacation, the old grind started in once more. I say "grind," because it is a sort of newspaper convention to use that word for any kind of regular work, but the truth is, it was quite far from monotonous. Also, I had arranged with a newspaper back home to use Agatha's articles on Paris fashions once a week, which simply meant that, in addition to my own work, I had to teach her how to write simply and effectively on what was—for me, to boast of my masculinity for once—a particularly repugnant and uninteresting topic, namely, women's clothes. I avoided going to the dressmakers' "openings" pretty successfully, breaking down only when I knew the champagne would flow with abandon, but I cross-examined Agatha on every point, when it came to "doing" her articles, with the result that I learned more about women's clothes than a lifetime spent in a monastery would ever enable me to forget. (In passing, it has always seemed to me that a much better explanation of the traditional place of women in society might be furnished by a furbelow interpretation of history than by interminable discussions about the psychological and economic determinisms that were so popular only a few years ago.) My own work, too, was going fairly well—not merely my articles for the Baltimore *Sun* and for *Town And Country,* but also on the *Herald* night desk. And thus, before I realized it, my second Christmas in Paris had come—and gone.

And with it went my desk job on the *Herald.* Nor was I "fired," either. I merely walked out a few days before Christmas—and never went back. I was fed up; I could sing Mistinguette's song with a pious and honest heart, "J'en Ai Marre." After all, I still had my two correspondence jobs, and together they paid me twice what was my salary on the *Herald.* I thought I should do more and better writing, free from office routine—and, of course, in fact (Paris has its way of tempting you to let time slip by) I did less, and probably worse. Yet whatever other faults may be justly attributed to me, I never let down Agatha on her fashion job, always conscientiously rewriting her stuff, on each occasion hammering in the principles of clear exposition, and ending up, oftenest, by taking it down to the Central Post Office myself to see that it got off in time for the next day's boat.

The June of that year—1923—stands out clear in my recollection because of one episode, around which memories naturally cluster, the Grand Prix de Paris. Not merely was it my first Grand Prix—it was the first thoroughbred horse race I had ever seen, for I never had gone to the races in America, and my knowledge of the sport of kings was limited to childish memories of New England "fair" trotting races of the David Harum kind, particularly the Brockton (Massachusetts) fair. Agatha had been keen to go, of course, to see the fashion parade, though in fact the Prix de Diane at Chantilly and the Paris des Drags at Auteuil the early weeks in June (the Grand Prix is always run on the last Sunday of the month) are much better sporting events for that purpose. I hope Agatha got some ideas for her fashion notes; I know I had eyes for only one horse—and any follower of the turf will feel a bit more friendly towards me, when I say that the name of the horse was the name of M. Ranucci's famous grey, Filibert de Savoie. Like the boy hero in Ernest Hemingway's first (and one of his best) short stories, "My Old Man," I also can say, "I never saw such a horse." Ugly as sin in a way, with a long barrel body, high off the ground, spindly legs, a straggly grey rather than a pure one, and a head like a tack-hammer. But I liked the way he walked around the paddock; he had the "air," that talismanic something which stamps a horse at once, as the French say, *"de race."* I bet on him, and I persuaded Agatha to put all she had on him, too, though rather against her will, for she was skeptical.

But not after the race. In all my subsequent years of racing I never have seen a horse win a great race more authoritatively than did Filibert de Savoie win that Grand Prix de Paris of 1923. It was not merely the question of the number of lengths, which were plenty. It was the ease, the assurance, the uncoiling of great speed at the end, just when it counted the most, the way in which (though it cost him distance) he kept on the outside to be clear and free in his action. I have forgotten the exact price Filibert paid, but it was around 16 or 17 to 1—quite enough to give Agatha and myself an extra good Sunday dinner at a stylish restaurant in town and to allow us to purchase some of the things we had been longing for for weeks. And it "sold" me on the races, too, at least in France—the physical setting, the spectacle of the crowd, the beauty of the races themselves, the thrill of quick-action gambling, with the odds a matter of chance (it was in the days before the "unification" of the Pari-Mutuel) and sometimes preposterous, when your luck was "in," the horses walking around in the cool green of the paddock as the jockies jumped on their backs in their bright silks, the humor of the old-timers—I found all these things charming and parts of a new world, a world untroubled by politics and sexual disappointments and money worries (I mean money worries in the terms of our ordinary, hum-drum life, of course). But I did not realize then how much horses and races and the French turf were subsequently to mean in my life.

Though a formal vacation was more or less out of the question, Agatha and myself did manage one or two little trips that summer—one to the seacoast near Dieppe (four days that I didn't particularly enjoy, for small French beach resorts can sometimes be stuffy and dull), and another to the magic town of Provins (four days that I did enjoy). But these were only excursions: When I think of that summer today I think chiefly of how hot it can sometimes be in Paris during August and how empty the city can be during those weeks of almost universal *"vacances"*—empty of the people you know, for Paris is crowded with provincials (who in turn are on their vacation) and with Americans and English. August in my time was a month when Paris seemed to be turned over to serious American school teachers, who had come over on a small budget and who, though stylish shops were closed, though the races were at Deauville, though a true Parisian would rather be found guilty of forgery than be caught walking the streets of his city during that month (he had to get out of town; if it was financially impossible, he would barricade himself in his own home and pretend he wasn't there), still were convinced that they were seeing the *"vrai"* Paris, when in fact they were seeing only the tired—albeit beautiful—shell of a great city. Life flowed elsewhere during those weeks. Even the majority of the theatres and music-halls were closed tight.

Of all my many years in Paris the autumn of 1923 and the spring of 1924 seems the most nebulous period. I had drifted away from Agatha—though I continued to help her in her fashion work. And that Christmas I deliberately and with malice aforethought—to bring finally to an end an emotional bewilderment and uneasiness—went down to Lyons for the holidays with an American girl I had known in the old days back in Greenwich Village. As I look back on it now, I cannot for the life of me explain why I did it. I wasn't especially fond of the girl, and I am sure, though she was polite enough not to say so to me, she was not exactly enraptured of me. But she was lonely; I was, too—and loneliest of all when I was with Agatha, from whom finally, as I said, I broke away.

People will often do things when they are lonely for which they will afterwards give the most preposterous explanations, and the person who lives a normal life of family, friends, a job, a home town, and all the other things that make life in my opinion (rather experienced in the opposite) worth while cannot comprehend what compulsive power this loneliness has. The normal person sees only the external side of the actions of these disinherited people; it is only in rare imaginative flashes that he understands how they might possibly feel, for *he* has never felt this way, and thanks God for it—I believe with entire correctness. Even if it is only his stupidity and emotionally tough integument, the result is the same: He is better off. That is why, I suppose, poets envy the butcher, the baker, and the candlestick maker, as in fact they ought to. The latter get the better "break," even if they don't know it.

Anyway, when I returned to Paris from that particular gesture of despair—left alone, too, for my companion in the gesture sensibly returned to America—I was not, as might be expected, in Agatha's good graces. After that in fact, I seldom saw her, even casually on café *terrasses*. For by this time she had really learned to do her fashion articles by herself without my help, and I think I can say, without hypocrisy, that I really was glad of that for her sake. I hadn't given her much, but I had shown her a way to be independent—possibly the best gift of all.

It was in that spring of 1924 that I met Joan, a divorcee considerably older than myself, but attractive, intelligent, witty, and a good sport, if the world ever produced one. Joan was not exactly wealthy, but she had a nice apartment, her own car (she was an expert driver, for she had had cars ever since she was a young woman), and nothing to do with her time. Except look after me—a difficult task, I presume, but she did it so quietly and, as it were, offhandedly, that I hardly realized what had happened, until one day at the old Dôme M. Chambon said to me (and in a flash I realized it was true), "Monsieur Stearns—à vous, eh bien, Madame Joan a sauvé la vie." Whether true or not, Joan decided that one way to save my life was to take me out of Paris for a time—to give me a complete rest and a brief interlude from the worries that had been piling up on me for so long.

That was a summer holiday I can remember even to this writing. We explored all of Brittany at our leisure, stopping off for a day or two at any town that struck our fancy. We drank cider, and ate the oysters and omelettes and *moules* of the country—anybody who has passed a summer in Brittany will find his mouth watering at the mention of these succulent dishes. It was warm and sunny most of the time, too. And although I had a pang that last Sunday in June, because I should miss the Grand Prix de Paris (and a good thing I did, too, for it was won by the "impossible" outsider, Transvaal), we compensated for it by witnessing some amusing country races on the sands of a beach not far from Saint-Malo, where we were both delighted and astonished to see the village priest, in his robes, boldly walking up to the Pari-Mutuel and backing the horse of his choice. "That," I remember remarking to Joan, "is what I suppose the smart Parisians mean when they refer to Brittany being sunk in Catholic ignorance and intolerance." I recall writing a rather "different" kind of descriptive piece on that trip for *Town And Country*—years have gone by and I still recall it; I hope the readers enjoyed reading it as much as I did writing it, which, after all, one feels but occasionally about one's own descriptive pieces.

For me the trip was a great success—in fact, it would have been, had it only given me the friendship of Joan, who to me was—and, indeed, still is—my ideal of what a woman companion can be, but only so infrequently is. My health was better than I had known it to be for a long time, for after all, night work, irregular eating, and no exercise beyond that of glass-lifting are not designed to furnish a doctor's prescription for keeping fit. Psychologically, too, Joan was a sure exit from the psychopathic ward. A woman who had two grown-up daughters and a grown-up son naturally understood the essential childishness of most men and might not even be abashed at the particularly absurd form it took with me. I never had been very keen on the flapper type anyway; when I was not suspicious of the motives back of it—that is, where it was natural—I hated any form of naïveté in a woman, for it recalled my own painful "awkward" age. I wanted, as I found in Joan, a woman who was sure of herself, of her views of life, of her economic and social position, and of native and amusing intelligence. A large order, you say. Yes, I suppose it is. But Joan filled the bill to perfection; I wish I might find another like her.

That autumn of 1924 in France—the very early part of it in September, I mean, for later Joan and I took another trip this time all over the South of France, which I shall describe in my next chapter—was one of the high spots of my life. My correspondence work was going well, and at least for the necessities of existence I was independent. And Joan was always there to furnish the luxuries, to cap experience. We went to the early autumn races when we felt like it; we made a conscientious and diligent gastronomic tour of all the better but more obscure restaurants of Paris that we could discover; we saw the comedy of the Montparnasse of those days without becoming involved in any of its tragedies (for there *were* tragedies, even then, make no mistake about that); we went to the theatres, to art galleries, to literary teas even (though not often, for a little of that goes a terribly long way with me); we had many friends and we had them with us often. The newspaper crowd, particularly Sammy Dashiel and some of the boys I had known on the *Herald,* would frequently have lunch with us (lunch rather than dinner, for they worked at night)—and those lunches would often last until the cocktail hour before dinner. Everybody liked Joan—I don't know any greater pleasure for a man than to feel that the woman with whom he is associated is welcomed by his friends almost as much as he is, if, in fact, not a trifle more. It is a sort of perpetual soothing-syrup to his good taste, his intelligence—and, perhaps, his luck. For many a man's ego expands more generously at implied praise of his social irresistibility than at any justified praise of his intrinsic merit.

But a happy period of one's life, like a happy country, has no history. It was—that is all you can say. Yet even in this new happiness there was a curious undertone of restlessness in me, something I felt I had to do. Joan knew this intuitively, even knew what it was, though I didn't. And one day she put her finger squarely on it: "You want to go back to America—oh no, not to live there; I know that. You want to go back to see your son. That is what is troubling you. Isn't it?"

I nodded, amazed that she had guessed what even I myself

had been unable to formulate clearly.

Joan smiled.

"I'll stake you to a trip to California," she said quite simply, as if it were offering to buy me a new necktie. "You'll never be satisfied until you see Philip, your boy. He'll be five this coming January—just old enough to know you and, perhaps, remember you later on."

"And when ought I to go?"

"To get there for his birthday," said Joan. "But before you go we might take a trip around France, especially the South of France. You have always wanted to see it. We'll start tomorrow, if you like."

"And where's our first stop?"

"Oh, I don't know—Tours, I suppose, or perhaps Saumur. We'll lazy along as we did in Brittany this summer. But I do want to see Carcassonne and Biarritz and Lourdes and the country of Auvergne. Don't you?"

"Sure I do, sure I do," I said. "I've always wanted to see just those very places."

But as a matter of fact I hadn't really thought much one way or the other about them until that very moment—and I could see from the manner in which Joan looked at me that she knew that, too.

However, that didn't matter to her. Nor to me, either. We were going because we wanted to and because we could. That was enough. If only other things in life could sometimes be decided so simply!

XIV. AROUND FRANCE AND BACK HOME

MOST of us, I think, are enamoured of itineraries—for what person with normal curiosity can resist the maps and folders of the well-known travel agencies? As the $15.00 a week New York stenographer cannot forever heroically refuse to go "window shopping," with a tour of the swank and envy-creating shops of Fifth Avenue, so even the least imaginative of men has on occasion gone traveling in spirit—by looking at the alluring pictures of ocean liners of unrivalled luxury (always with beautiful and democratic women passengers), towns of unsurpassed quaintness and charm, and scenic wonders of penultimate grandeur. For more people than I like to think on, life would lose considerable of its savor, if these day-dreams were rigorously denied them. Hence I make no apology for presenting this chapter in the form I do. Only, if the reader wants fully to enjoy it, I urge that he provide himself with a large and detailed map of France.

The time of year, too, is important: It was—for the trip around France—from September 21st to October 24th, 1924. For the trip back home and the return to Paris (the trip over home by the Southern route), it was from December 1st, 1924, to the middle of February, 1925. I dodged the worst of the Paris winter that season, basking either on a sunny sea or on land in sunny climes. For the South of France, if you want to explore around at random, the month of October is almost the ideal one—the grapes have turned and it is harvesting time along the banks of the Gironde. There is not likely to be much rain; even the sudden summer showers have merged into the golden warm October haze that spells good wine and late fruits. As with us, too, the months with the "r" in them (consider the French, i. e., *Septembre, Octobre, Novembre, Décembre,* right through *Avril,* as against the four: *Mai, Juin, Juillet* and *Août*) are the "safe" months for eating oysters, so that the first crops of the aristocratic *Marennes* and the more humble *Portugaises* were on the menus. And later, as we got further South, the early game began to appear on the tables—partridges especially, thrushes or larks (*alouettes*), wood-cocks (*bécasses*), wild boar (*sanglier,* to be had near Carcassone in October), pheasants (*faisans*), jugged hare (*civet de lièvre*), rabbit (*rable de lapin*), and special forms of cured, smoked and clove-flavored hams. Chicken, turkey, and young turkey—the latter with chestnut stuffing—were, of course, common dishes, as were the marvellous mountain-stream trout (sometimes larger than a small salmon) near the Pyrenées. Like any tour of France, granted tourists of fair health and reasonable digestive powers, our tour turned out also to be a gastronomic adventure. And a mild vinous one, too, since obviously we had to drink the "wine of the country" wherever we went, if we wished to appreciate the full flavor and richness of the different dishes served us.

But now to get down to the important thing:

Sept. 21—Left Paris early. To Poitiers (lunch), Niort, La Rochelle —Sept. 21.
Sept. 22—Along coast and La Gironde to Rochefort, Marenne, Blaye —Sept. 22.
Sept. 23—To Biarritz by Bordeaux, the coast, Dax, and Bayonne —Sept. 23.
Sept. 26—To Lourdes, mountain side trip (two nights in Lourdes) —Sept. 26.
Sept. 28—Lourdes to Carcassonne, a long trip (ten

nights in Carcassonne) —Sept. 28.

With side trips to:

The "Black Mountain"

Limoux, Perpignan, Port Vendres, Port Bou, and Collioure

Oct. 8	—Carcassonne to Arles Arles, Les Baux, Aix-en-Provence (two nights)	—Oct. 8.
Oct. 10	—Aix to Marseilles (two nights)	—Oct. 10.
Oct. 12	—To Toulon (one night), Cannes, Digne (one night)	—Oct. 12.
Oct. 14	—Digne to Grenoble (two nights)	—Oct. 14.
Oct. 16	—To Valence and Puy-de-Dôme	—Oct. 16.
Oct. 17	—Auvergne (three nights), Figeac, Aurillac, Saint-Flour	—Oct. 17.
Oct. 20	—Clermond-Ferrand (two nights) .	—Oct. 20.
Oct. 22	—Bourges (one night), Montargis (one night)	—Oct. 22.
Oct. 24	—Back to Paris	—Oct. 24.

This was a magical journey—at the right time of the year, with the right sort of intelligent and amusing companionship, employing the right means of transportation in France, the automobile. And a Citroën at that—I put that in, not for advertising purposes (personally, I hope some day to own a Voisin), but simply because the Citroën, at that time at least, was the equivalent of our own Ford, and was the most satisfactory car for touring, when you meant to stop at small towns—if only because no town was too small not to have a garage with replaceable parts. Service stations for the Citroën were in the least significant villages, and in case of a blowout or anything going wrong with the motor or the carburetter, you had only to limp or be towed the few kilometers to get the proper repairs or even new parts. This may not seem important to an American of today:—in rural France of ten years ago it was of great importance.

But the automobile method of touring in France is important for another reason. The network of railroads (and canals—some day I want to make a water-ways trip around

France) reaches everywhere, of course, but it is not the same thing as seeing a town from the vistas of the long white road. Furthermore, there are many picturesque automobile roads in France, through charming and sometimes even thrilling country, which you miss entirely, if you go by railroad. That explains—quite aside from the question of expense—the popularity of 'bus tours in France, for many important spots, both scenically and historically, will be just too difficult and troublesome to get at, if you also have the problem of train connections, baggage, and hotel 'buses. There is a little 'bus tour from Arles, for instance, to Les Baux—but half the fun of seeing Les Baux is seeing it as you want, loitering and examining the remains of old walls and dreaming of the old days, as you look out over the vast plain of Provence. Or, when you reach Carcassonne (and, incidentally, do not fail to go to the Hôtel de la Cité in the historical town on the hill itself), it would be pretty exasperating to read your guide book and find out about all the fascinating places that were near you—if only you had an automobile to get to them. Of all countries in the world, for tourist purposes, France repays you with compound interest for the trouble involved in acquiring (or hiring) a car of your own.

Going out of Paris—headed South—early in the morning of a fine day in late September is a pleasant thrill of itself. It will be a trip of adventure. It is bound to be that; you know as much by intuition. And we hummed along briskly, in part out of sheer excitement and in part to get clear of traffic coming into town for the business day. Also, we were headed for Poitiers—about 150 miles South—and we wanted to make it for a late lunch.

As we went through the gate of the city I noticed it was just 7.30 o'clock, which meant Poitiers in six hours to arrive at 1.30 p.m., which, in turn, would not involve too great a strain on a French provincial restaurant, where *déjeuner* begins pretty promptly at noon and is over just about the time we had set ourselves to arrive. But we did better than that, even taking our time, and got into town about a quarter before one. I was emotionally so shaky from suppressed, nervous, high-strung interest—a trip around France had been one of the dreams of my life, and here it was coming true!—that I don't recall much about the town, except that it was colorful, perched high up overlooking a plain on all sides, and that there were some fine mediaeval streets and houses, and, of course, the inevitable cathedral. We had a good meal—I only recall two or three poor meals on the whole trip—and wine enough to make us a bit sleepy and lazy. But we got going promptly and, much too fast to see the country as we should have done, sped to Niort, where we took a look about and an *apéritif*—and then made the short and interesting trip over to La Rochelle, our first over-night stop of the trip. The shops in the colonnades, the bell tower, the tragic quai, where the poor devils sentenced to hard labor for life (and in the old days that often meant speedy death from disease and exposure) in French Guiana embark, one of the tragic boats itself (it was there then, when we were there, and was to leave in a few days), the restaurant where we had dinner and the hotel where we stopped the night—all had their provocative interest for me. (I thought then, and I still think—I could spend the rest of my life travelling, stopping when and where I liked, and yet never get bored—though after a few months of it I suppose I inevitably should.)

Yet for all its charm we left La Rochelle quite early, for I had discovered even during my salad days in France that, no matter how charming a spot may be, oftenest there is another just a bit more charming further down the road. We went along to Rochefort and then to Marenne, where I was glad it was time for lunch—because I wanted to try some "Marennes" (the famous and delicious thin, large, pinkish-colored oysters). But there weren't any such oysters; either it was not the season (an assertion which seemed incredible and, I concluded finally and correctly, false, since it was then late September) or else (and here I hit on the real reason) all the good oysters had been shipped to Paris for high prices. That is an aspect of modern large-scale selling and distribution which I hate—and, while it is not anywhere near so completely true in France as with us, it is still true enough. Try to get the best year and vintage of Burgundy wines—in Burgundy! Just as, if you want the best of the Lyons style of cooking, you will find it in a "specialty" restaurant in Paris. Of course, being still France, there really are three or four famous restaurants in Lyons itself, making a feature of the food and traditional cooking of the region: But I speak of a tendency, which even during the thirteen years I lived in France, showed a dishearteningly increasing momentum. (To be fair, I *did* eat the big Concarneau oysters at the town of that name in Brittany on my trip there; however, that was luck. Only at Prunier's—and by paying a ridiculously high price—will you get them in Paris. The bulk of the catch goes to England, where the gourmands justly smack their chops over them—probably at the same time they are reading of French instability and unreasonableness in their morning London *Express*.) Of course it comes with a bit of ill grace, you may say, to criticize the French for what we do ourselves—do not the children of the Wisconsin dairymen that ship the finest cream in the world to the cities have to content themselves with condensed milk? Yes, but it is precisely because I want France to be France—to be local, provincial, narrow-minded, split-up, heterogeneous—that I make my howl about this. After all, if I want standardization and uniformity and all the lovely by-products of large-scale production, coupled with "national" distribution, I can get them at home. I don't have to go to France for them.

There is a curious walled village near Marenne; you get to it on a road built across desolate marshes—and I can't think of its name. But it doesn't matter, anyway, if you remember to visit it when on a trip to this region, for you get a curious feeling of not being in the modern world at all—it is completely outside our century. Even the people seem unreal and a bit mad, and all the dogs gave us queer looks; I was glad to get out of the place. Probably that is why I can't remember the name, but I do recall it was reputed, in the middle ages, to be a sort of prison colony for all the people the King dared not openly execute. I can well believe it; the air of past tragedies hangs over it even today. Don't take a *"melancolique,"* as the French say, to it—ever. And Joan and myself were glad to get out and on the road again, South. We stopped for the night at Blaye, down on the Gironde.

Thus, coming in over the immense bridge spanning the river, we had a good morning look at Bordeaux, with its shipping and animation and color. All port towns interest me; we were almost tempted to stay in Bordeaux and explore it, but we had to get on South, if we were to make Biarritz before what was left of the summer had gone. All that morning and afternoon, with a brief stop for a bit of lunch, we "let her out" along the coast of *"Les Landes"* going through miles of lovely scrub-pine forest over the straightest road I have ever seen, even in France, the home of long straight roads. We turned in to Dax to get on the Route Nationale to Bayonne (a delightful old town, famous in modern France for, paradoxically enough, the excellent chocolates manufactured there), of which Biarritz is really a sort of stylish summer and autumn suburb. It was the end of the season, but not too cold for ocean bathing, and somehow we found ourselves staying on in Biarritz for three days—making morning dashes just over the border into Spain and often down to Saint-Jean-de-Luze to see the French tennis-playing set *en vacance.*

From luxurious, worldly, gay Biarritz we went on to Lourdes —not, I hasten to add, with any particular notion of dramatic contrast, but primarily because Lourdes was more or less on our way East to the Mediterranean. Yet it *was* a dramatic contrast. As long as I live, I shall remember that crippled girl, with the lovely, spiritual face, weeping so softly, so pathetically, as she stumbled down the steps of the long high stone stairway beside the cathedral to the main magnificent entrance gates below—had not her prayer been answered? Had God forsaken her and had her faith been of no avail? I shall never know—I know only that she clutched protectively yet shyly at her crutches, and somehow my heart was sick within me. Even the grotto of miracles was then spoiled for me; I couldn't see the relics, so-called. I saw only the twisted anguished countenance of the child weeping so softly, so pathetically.

Yet we spent two nights in Lourdes, for we made a couple of mountain-trips—in particular, up the Col de Tourmalet, where we got stopped by the mountain-snow that had already so early in autumn drifted on the road to make it impassible for any car—even with thick chains. (Before I die, I am going over that damn "Col.") Then we went round-about and back up North to Carcassonne, delaying our Mediterranean quest for the moment, for, after all, was there not a saying in France, "See Carcassonne before you die"? And in Carcassonne, where now I feel almost *chez moi,* we remained ten days—to the morning of October 6th.

But not idly. The Hôtel de la Cité, located in the old fortified city itself, which juts boldly up out of the plain, is one of the best hotels in France from every point of view—modern comforts, food, wine, service, beauty of natural location, combined with great historic interest. High praise, perhaps, but I mean every word of it. Because, in France, when something is bad, it is very, very bad—so, when it is good, it is likely to be superlatively good. The side trips were fine, too, especially to the Black Mountain, where we had a Gargantuan feast of game, and to Perpignan and the Vermillion Coast, where I had my first glimpse of beautiful Collioure, which I was to visit later on under somewhat less happy circumstances. It was harvest time, and I understand why the coast gets its name—for it justified it. All the vineyards on the sloping hillsides to the blue Mediterranean *are* vermilion, and bright, gay vermilion at that. We spent a night at Perpignan, visiting the famous round-the-clock café (a circular building, so arranged that by changing tables every two or three hours during the daytime, you can always be sitting in the sun), and on the way "home" to Carcassonne, saw two curious towns I shall always remember—Limoux and Montréal—I suppose French settlers originally gave this name to our Canadian city.

The morning of the 8th of October we made our break, taking our own time up to Arles, where I looked for the beautiful *Arlesiennes* of whom I had read and heard so much in story and song. But although I didn't see any, I did see the vastly impressive ruins of the old Roman amphitheatre (as I had seen the more pretentious one at Nimes, when earlier during my stay in France I had visited Avignon with Agatha). Arles, of itself, would be an interesting enough city for at least a week's visit, but as we had a car, we took advantage of being there to visit Les Baux, that curious and beautiful city in ruins atop the plain that stretches South to Aix-en-Provence and the Mediterranean. I shall only say here that all the descriptions you read about Les Baux, all the pictures, etchings, and paintings you may see of it, are inadequate to give even a faint suggestion of its haunting and somewhat sombre beauty—and its tragedy, too, for it is a shell now, a ruined sketch of what it had once so defiantly and proudly been.

After lunch at Les Baux—and I cannot think of any place in the world, where one feels more out of our own time and century—we drove down to the plain (a long, low, mosquito-infested stretch of country, where the laborers in the fields wear big protective nets over their heads and arms) and along it until, finally, we reached Aix-en-Provence, where the warm mineral waters gush up through artesian wells even in the open squares. We remained there overnight; the next morning we drove in a leisurely manner to Marseilles—every yard of that little journey has its own special pictorial charm, and, above all, as you get near the coast with ever-beckoning, ever-inviting glimpses of the Mediterranean.

I have never known a romanticist who has not, when I mention Marseilles, either asked me about Conrad or about the "Isolated Quarter," or both. We took a look at this famous dumping-ground of the nations that borders on this ancient sea, but we made no attempt to explore it—one would have to be tough-looking, pretty shabbily dressed, able to stand vile liquor, and with at least a cursory knowledge of the *argot*. And even then the police would try to keep you out, especially if you were touring it only for descriptive purposes. In Conrad's time, of course, this surveillance was not so rigid —and besides, Conrad knew the *argot*—as he knew many other things, including the art of writing in a language that was not his own. But we took our motto from Plato, who said that when you are travelling in a wild and savage country, it is not necessary to explore all the dark and concealed caves of that country—usually it is sufficient to know that they are there. In fact, far from being romantic about Marseilles, we took unashamed delight in again being in a big metropolitan city, with modern hotels, where we could indulge in the luxuries of a noble bathroom, a telephone, wireless, and efficient service. Of course we went over to the "Old Port," and the second day, just before starting out for Toulon, had lunch at the famous restaurant there. That was unfortunate for me, and I give this free advice to all journeying through—do not eat *palourdes* (a small shell-fish very similar to our smaller Little Neck clams, except in taste) in Marseilles. There are plenty of other things to eat; you will not be forced to go hungry. But the *palourdes* are dangerous. It is a lovely ride from Marseilles along the coast to Toulon, where we went that afternoon, but by the time we reached there I was in no condition to appreciate the beauties of the landscape—I had as pretty a case of near-ptomaine poisoning as you might wish on your worst enemy. Even the sight of sailors lined up outside a house of prostitution, awaiting their turns with numbered tickets, did not move me to astonishment at the simple sensuality of man, as ordinarily it would have done. I was so sick that I thought them very silly—how sensuality is conquered by a stomach-ache! But the hotel doctor gave me something which, followed by a hot bath, nearly killed me—only it worked, and though I was so weak I could hardly climb into the car the next day, I was cured. And by the time we reached Cannes, I was even able to make a stab, albeit a feeble one, at lunch.

That afternoon we took the thrilling trip from Cannes up through the Maritime Alps—stopping of course at Grasse (where the perfumes come from) for the wonderful view back over the sea—to Digne, a town seemingly almost as much Italian as French, at least as far as language went. The architecture, too, is distinctly Italian, and I should imagine of great interest to anyone long a student of that subject. (I remember wishing I had Lewis Mumford with me to explain what it all meant.) But an hour permits you to see about all there is to be seen at Digne—and then we were off to the university city of Grenoble, familiar to all American exchange students, as, during the war and for some time afterwards, it was familiar to our student soldiers. I thought it an indifferently dull, bourgeois, comfortable town, somewhat like my own Cambridge, Massachusetts—it had that peculiar college look about it, something, incidentally, you do not find at Montpellier. But the town is located in the shadows of the mountains to the East, and I fancy that on fair spring holidays the students make many a picturesque pilgrimage up their sides; I think, if I were young, I should not mind being a student at Grenoble. We stayed on two nights, for it was very comfortable there, and—as almost everywhere on our trip—the food and wines were excellent.

From Grenoble we went West and a bit South to Valence,

the junction of the Isere and the Rhône, where we had one of our typical lunches of two hours' duration, and then almost due West to Le Puy in the Haute Loire (a short trip in miles, but one of the most picturesque of our entire journey), where we landed after dark. And where, too, we had the devil's own time finding a place to sleep, for we arrived on the night before the annual horse fair, and the little town was jammed with farmers, small merchants, and breeders of those wonderful big Southern dray horses that are so powerful in body yet so gentle in spirit and affection. But we had already become used to "pot luck" in the country, and no matter how mean a little French provincial hotel may be, it is usually clean and there is usually something appetizing to eat, for, failing all else, there is always the omelette, which, I am convinced, only the French know how to make properly.

Up early for a look at the horses (and a finer lot of work-horses I have never seen), around ten o'clock we began our three day tour through what the residents of Auvergne sometimes dub their own country (with a sly wink, implying that the phrase might also apply to the heads of the inhabitants), *"le Massif Céntral."* We stopped the night at Figeac, making a side trip the next day to that remarkable town—Saint-Flour—built on a narrow high tongue of land jutting out high upon and above a low plain (how many of these ancient towns in France were built with a sharp eye to roving marauders!), returning for the second night to Figeac. Our third night was at Aurillac, and in the morning we determined to pay a visit to the family of M. Chambon (our old friend of the Dôme in Paris) at Saint-Christophe nearby. We did so, and were invited to a regal "home" lunch, before we set off once more on our journey—this time to Clermont, where we regaled ourselves for two nights at a hotel which the guidebook described with the modest adjective of "princely." It was, too; and so was the food, for the game season was now on in full force.

The morning of October 22nd we suddenly realized that

we had been away from Paris for just a month and a day. Joan had business and family matters to attend to in Paris. Although I had written and mailed my articles for the Baltimore *Sun* with fair regularity, I, too, had to return and settle down to some serious work. We had had our just share of holidaying, though I know that at the time I didn't think so. And both of us were becoming a bit homesick for Paris, perhaps a trifle impatient with each other, though even as I write that last, because it *seems* logical and almost inevitable now, I doubt it on reflection. We were as good a pair of travelling companions as I have ever seen.

So we set off without more ado, by speeding up making Bourges for the night stop. And we took a good look around the next day—take my word for it, Bourges is well worth it. Because of bad roads and tire trouble we only contrived to get into Montargis late the next evening—it was to be our last stop overnight together. For the next day we came back "home" to Paris—and I don't know why I put quotation marks about home, either: Paris has been as much of a home to me as has any other city, more of a home, I suppose, since I spent some of the best years of my life there. And—as always—it looked awfully good to us—Villon was right, when he penned, *"Il n'y aie bon bec que de Paris."*

For a fortnight or so after our return Joan and I revelled in being back in Paris. Although the flat races were drawing to a close for the season, we made a few sporting excursions to Maisons-Laffitte and Auteuil (even one trip out to Enghien, a track Joan had always hated)—and we had, on the whole, pretty good luck, though God knows we were as innocent of "form" and the other supposedly important technical points of horse racing as babes in the wood. That was a happy time for me, that November in Paris. I recall that at the annual frolic and dinner of the Anglo-American Press Association (of which I was a member by virtue of my correspondence work for the *Sun*) I performed in some sketch as Cupid, with Hudson Hawley, who played opposite me, cursing me *sotto voce* because I forgot my lines, and that I fell weepingly and demonstratively in love with Yvonne George, who had come to sing for us. (She was one of the finest of French *chanteuses* and *diseuses;* what a tragedy that we have lost her!) Joan came in her car after that dinner and took me home and put me to bed—still weeping out of strong emotion (and considerable liquor). But the dinner was a great success, nevertheless. Most of those annual dinners, in my time, were.

Joan was as good as her word in another respect—hardly had we returned to Paris before she began to make arrangements for my trip back home to America. I wrote to my father-in-law that I was coming—with the date set tentatively for that winter—to reach California in time for Philip's birthday on January 10th. Joan studied all the different ways of getting there, in the end, because it was winter, deciding on the Southern route. I could return (I often wondered afterwards, if she thought I really *would* return) by way of New York and the more convenient route of the North Atlantic crossing to Le Havre. For the French Line then ran an excellent Southern service from Saint-Nazaire to Spain, Cuba, Texas, and Tampico (Mexico). And, of course, that is the ideal way—always provided that other things, like food, service, and accommodations are equal—to cross the Atlantic in winter.

It did not occur to me that perhaps Joan wanted to be rid of me—vanity has more power over us, I believe, when we are dependent upon somebody than when we are free agents. Probably it is a compensatory satisfaction for our strategic weakness; then, more than ever, we must bolster up our pride. But I think, now, that my case was not quite so simple as that, though a strong element of impatience at least ought normally to have been expected on Joan's part—I mean, the relationship was in an important respect too one-sided. She was giving everything; I was giving nothing except the charm of my company. And I can't honestly pretend that, in my right mind, I consider that an eminently fair bargain. Yet I then naïvely thought it was—perhaps because, whatever my actual years, I was still pretty tender-minded about social things like that, gladly allowing the wish, as the saying is, to be father to the thought. That is not an unamiable aspect of youth—the sincere and hence often unspoken assumption that our company compensates for everything else. It is vanity, but unselfconscious vanity—hence very charming, when you are interested in a person, hence doubly exasperating, too, when that interest begins to flag.

Anyway, as I have said, Joan lived up to her promise—let us put it at that. She got me my passage to Texas, by way of Havana, and bought me travellers' checks sufficient to enable me at least to get from Havana to California without difficulty. From there on, I suppose, God was to be my guide; at least I should be with what I had of a family, on Alice's side—and Joan thought, in all likelihood, that I should be made welcome. I had my own doubts on that point, but I wanted to go anyway. Why not put it simply and honestly?—I wanted to see my own son, Philip; I wanted to meet Alice's mother, about whom she had often talked with accents of deep affection; I wanted to see Tucson and Carmel, where she had spent her early womanhood before college at Leland Stanford. There had always been a nostalgic accent in her voice when she had told me about Carmel and Del Monte—I wanted to see for myself what they were like. Perhaps it would clear up things for me, perhaps give me some hope and a suggestion . . .

It was a dark and gloomy December morning, with cold rain belying all the charm of the city, when I boarded that train for Saint-Nazaire, the coast town of lower Brittany, at the Gare de Lyon—the kind of day to make anyone glad to be going South. I was almost cheerful, I remember; even leaving Joan and Paris and the races and my newspaper friends didn't seem so bad—in a sort of intuitive reflection from a new mirror of reality I suddenly realized how fugitive and uprooted my life had been for so long. Perhaps, now that I was really going home, I might find a new America—perhaps, yet even then I doubted it, though I don't know exactly why. But I did know, even then, that I was not over with Paris for good; I knew, infallibly, that I should come back soon.

The landscape, as it flashed by the car window, was dreary and wet and cold—could it be in this same soggy country that Joan and I had spent two gay sunshiny months? I stayed on in the restaurant car most of the day, sipping at *café-au-rhums* between breakfast and lunch and again between lunch and dinner. A few of what I knew would be my fellow-passengers stayed in the restaurant car, too, playing cards and gossiping and laughing: I saw at once that there was going to be jolly company on board, and I hoped French would be spoken as much as Spanish, for it was obvious that English would not be heard from dawn until dusk, or afterwards either. (The vessel, incidentally, was the S. S. *Espagne.*) We reached Saint-Nazaire about eight o'clock in the evening, the train going through the town right to the dock, where the passport and ticket formalities were expedited with that seeming carelessness, which some people often mistakenly imagine is the "easy-goingness" of the French, but which really is not—as you speedily discover, if your papers are not in perfect order. Since the boat sailed at midnight, I had plenty of time to put my medium-sized suitcases and small portable typewriter (I like to travel "light") in my cabin, which turned out to be a pleasant outside room—and to have my last dinner on shore near the dock. For an hour or two we went along the ship canal, with lights and bells and people shouting *"Bon voyage"* along its sides, and then the open sea. We got into the harbor of Bilboa in the afternoon, and we had a chance to take dinner in the town, the boat leaving the harbor for the long run to Havana shortly after lunch. Already the weather had changed from the gloomy rain of France to the most dazzling of sunshine; it was even warm enough for the stewards to start the fans going in the salons and staterooms. White summer shirts made their appearance, too, and that first evening out from Coruna there was talk at table of a midnight dance the next evening—for nobody went to bed early on the *Espagne,* and the first meal really was lunch. Cocktails in the smoker with the Captain before lunch were almost a ritual for the male passengers. And after dinner, when there was not some special entertainment (at which the Spanish, especially, seemed to be quite inventive), the Captain gallantly had a few liqueurs with all of us, including one or two Cuban young ladies, who had that devastating attractiveness which made them the inevitable storm-centre of all the mild and amusing gossip that an ocean voyage seems to develop as naturally as the prow of the boat cuts its way through the waves. The Spanish like to dine late, and on this boat dinner was seldom finished before 9.30 or even 10.00 o'clock, and often this was followed by a midnight dance on deck. However, there were no flirtations, no *scandale*—there was plenty of fun, but it was all formal. Something, I have noticed, that the Latin peoples seem able to encompass without any affectation or lack of cordiality. The gift for having a good time without nurturing intrigue is a social blessing, and I wish we had more of it. All I can say of that voyage is that it ended far too soon, though it was a full ten days before we came to anchor in the hot, sweltering harbor of Havana.

I don't know how much Havana has changed in these last ten years, with all the political and social troubles that have followed the depression and the ruinous collapse in the price of sugar (now, I suppose, the repeal of prohibition will help the Bacardi and liquor industry), but at that time it seemed a very care-free sort of place indeed. And I have never had such a steady diet of gambling—matching for drinks before lunch; plunging on the races in the afternoon and at the Ja-Alai games in the evening, if you did not go to the Casino and do some really fancy high-and-low plunging; buying lottery tickets as you bought postage stamps. It was gay enough, and I enjoyed it for a few days (I went to the races on Christmas), but I was glad to get on my little S. S. *De La Salle,* and see the New Year in on the waters of the Gulf of Mexico. We still could have a drink—but as soon as we got within sight of the American shore the bar was closed and padlocked, though wine was served on our last lunch, as we slowly went up the Ship Canal of which Houston is so inordinately proud, and landed a fair taxi-ride distance outside the centre of the town.

Though I had never been in Texas before, I was not interested so much as shocked at what I saw—the interminable cheap "movie" houses, the clean yet somehow tawdry streets, the brash, unfinished quality of so much of the town. Yet the hotel I went to—the Rice Hotel, I believe, called "Houston's Welcome To The World," or something equally modest—put any French provincial hotel I had ever seen to shame for comfort, modernity, and efficient service. I couldn't get over the fact that the maid told me, if I would leave my soiled linen in a bag it would be delivered freshly laundered, the shirts and collars all ironed properly, the next morning. This was true, but I didn't quite believe her, for I still was accustomed to the cheerful French method of telling you that your laundry will be finished on Tuesday and actually getting it on Friday or Saturday—maybe. The elevators, "womanned" by the prettiest girls I had seen since my New England boyhood, were another surprise. And though I missed my wine, of course, there were excellent fish and meat dishes and fruits and salads on the extensive bill-of-fare. I also was surprised the next day, when a local reporter called and solemnly took down—and almost as solemnly had printed—a longish interview with me concerning every subject under the sun about which I was especially ignorant. He took me for a little tour of the town in a "flivver," showing me the buildings and grounds of the

Rice Institute, which unaccountably depressed me, though I can't remember why. And the next day he invited me to a tea, where a few instructors from the Institute, a couple of other newspapermen, and three local magnates' wives, who had been to Paris, gave an intellectual tone to the occasion. I thought them all nice and charming people, but still I felt depressed. Until, in a flash, I realized that I was, very simply, homesick for Paris—a homesickness which sometimes (but, I am glad to say, less frequently) comes over me even to this day, fight against it as I will. For an hour or so that afternoon in Houston, nevertheless, I should have given my right eye to have been back at Longchamp or the Rue Trudaine, or at the Namur, on the Boulevard Sebastopol.

The following morning I received a telegram from my father-in-law, stating that he would be on that evening's "Sunset Limited," which runs between New Orleans and Los Angeles, making a brief stop at Houston, and asking that I join him. Sometime between eleven o'clock and midnight the train came in; I boarded it, and, after learning that Dr. Macdougal was in pullman number so-and-so and had asked the porter to tell me to meet him for breakfast in the diner, went out to the observation-car rear platform and watched the flat plains of Texas roll past in the moonlight, wondering how often Alice had looked out over these same plains on her many trips back and forth across the Continent, wondering what life meant anyway and why I was there and if Philip, my son, would like me, wondering what my newspaper friends were talking and thinking about in Paris then . . . nothing, I concluded, since at that hour it was forenoon in Paris, and they were all still in bed asleep, while I was rolling over the plains of Texas.

In the morning my father-in-law greeted me cheerfully enough, and—just as always before—our talk at once took on a highly general and impersonal tone, our subjects ranging all the way from the latest discoveries in biochemistry to the political situation in England and the state of literature and poetry in the (then) newly discovered artistic centres of the South-West, the last subject not without a few amiable comments on Mary Austin and her search for what she later was to term "Earth Horizons." I told briefly what I knew of the general situation at the time in Europe, France in particular; we agreed that the debt business had sunk to political charlatanism on both sides. And—by indirection rather than any explicit details—I gathered that both Philip and Mrs. Macdougal (my mother-in-law, whom I had never seen) were in good health. We were to get off at Tucson, Arizona, for a day (Dr. Macdougal was the administrator of the important desert laboratory there), and then go on to Los Angeles and Carmel.

Tucson itself impressed me chiefly by its university (where I saw the girl co-eds riding horses, as in the East they drive cars), Dr. Macdougal's own highly efficient botanical laboratory and grounds (he had quite a staff there, as I recall it, working on different experiments connected with plant hydration and growth), its number of semi-hospital hotels housing tuberculosis patients—the air at Tucson is very dry because of the town's height above sea-level—and its long, paved automobile highway leading to the border and Mexico. We remained overnight, and in the evening I visited a teacher at the university (who had been a contributor to *The Dial* in the old days, when I was its editor) at whose house once again (as in Houston), I found that everybody "made their own" and that as an inciter to social drinking prohibition was proving a great success.

In the morning Dr. Macdougal showed me his own home, when he was in town (at that time, I believe, he spent about four months of the year at Tucson, seven at Carmel, in California, and another month travelling to and from New York and Washington, where the Carnegie Institute's offices were located). It interested me, for Alice had spent some of her girlhood there. And it made me eager to get on and see Carmel, too.

Hence I was pleased when we climbed into our pullman-sleeper that evening, and when—on the second morning from Houston—the train began going through orange-tree groves, of the kind I had read about in the earlier real estate "boom" literature. We stayed the whole day in that fantastic city of Los Angeles, Dr. Macdougal having some business that demanded his attention. I took advantage of my leisure to explore the city (avoiding Hollywood) and one of the nearer beaches, with its elaborately housed, artificial swimming-pool, built almost on the ocean's edge. (Proving, I suppose, that out-door, all-the-year-round bathing is just too common!) It was a brief impression, and it is difficult for me to analyze it now years later, but I want to go on record as saying that I should infinitely prefer, from what I saw, to live in hell itself than in that town. I never got on a train with more satisfaction than that evening, when we boarded the San Francisco coast express, which would land us at Carmel, en route, early in the morning.

Or rather, at Pacific Grove, a sort of twin-town to both Del Monte and Carmel, both of which places haughtily repudiate it, I believe, for Carmel prides itself on being a great literary and artistic colony, while Del Monte is famous for its view over the bay, its luxury hotel, and its world-renowned golf course. Indeed, the only thing of distinction I saw in Carmel itself, which resembled a sort of grown-up summer cottage colony, was Dr. Macdougal's own coastal laboratory, the pride of the village. But near Carmel, about five miles away on the rugged coast itself, was Carmel-Highlands-By-The-Sea, where Dr. Macdougal had built a permanent home and where millionaire estates, with elaborately big houses and garages and so on, had sprung up around him. His own home was modest, but charming and convenient—and for me romantic, because you could look out over the Pacific and at night hear the roar of the waves against the shore.

Philip, my son, was playing with some mechanical toy in front of the kitchen porch; Mrs. Macdougal, my mother-in-law, came to the door and kissed me without a word, as if I had always been an old relative—but away on a long visit. Dr. Macdougal said quietly, "Philip, this is Harold." (In a quick, low aside to me, explained. "He's still too young, I think, to try to explain the relationship. He knows you as Harold already; he has heard us talk about you as about ourselves—you are one of the family.") I shook hands with him, and it seemed to me I could see Alice again—here in a little gesture, there in a turn of his chin. His eyes, too, were like hers, more like hers than like mine. And he seemed curiously sturdy and robust, as Alice had always seemed, too. For my first few minutes of recognition I could hardly see Philip at all. Unwittingly he gave me the sharpest pain, the keenest sense of loss, I have ever experienced—and then, somehow, a feeling of warmth and comradeship and common adventure together in a lonely world. I don't know how other fathers feel; I know I felt a bond with him, that unspoken and perhaps not wholly understood bond of common solitariness before alien things—a bond that nothing might ever break.

The week of home-coming—for, whether I had a right to or not, I felt Carmel as at least one of my homes—was a week of discovering how much I had wanted the realities of life. Now that the dearest of them was gone, I could find no genuine impulse of ambition or desire; slowly the conviction in me grew that I had to get back to Paris once more—to a slight, a derivative, a fundamentally unsatisfactory reality, but still, the only one I knew. It was charming to watch Philip, to see how naturally quick and imaginative his mind was, how—like Alice—his impulses were generous, and how—like her, too—he saw the humor of the little things that for most boys just turned five (we celebrated his birthday a couple of days after my arrival) would be unimportant and probably would go unnoticed. I knew, however, that his education and upbringing would be guided by the best people in the world for him—his grandfather and grandmother. Indeed, to have taken him away from the second (or to have attempted to take him away) would have been to rob her life of what meaning it had had, or could have had, since Alice's death. In Philip she lived again—and Dr. Macdougal, too, despite his scientific work and his wide interests, was after all only human; Philip also meant everything to him. Besides, I was young; they were already past middle age. Later on, perhaps, Philip could turn to me, if he so wished; but right then, and at least until he was ready to go away to college (and, just about the time this book appears, he will be), it seemed better that he should stay with them. And, even had I wanted to, I do not believe that, under California law, I had a legal right to take him away, unless they approved. But such a thing anyway was out of the question—it was only my loneliness and my day-dreaming that made the idea haunt me. I knew that the miracle could not happen—that soon I should have to go, that it would be years before I saw him again, that perhaps I should never see him.

These unsolvable problems, so mixed up with deep instinctive racial desires, haunted me all the few hours of my journey up to San Francisco, where I was to take the Overland Limited for Chicago and the East. I tried to forget them there that night by walking all over the town, but I couldn't. My last morning on the Coast brought a certain relief, for it was the kind of gorgeous January weather that sometimes one gets on the Riviera—and here I was in my own country. All the afternoon (the train left Oakland, across the bay, at eleven o'clock), as we climbed up the slopes of the mountains to the "American Pass," where the train makes a brief stop so that everybody can have a glimpse of the unforgettable view, I was stimulated by the scenery and the strangeness of my emotional adventure—and yet full of confidence that somehow I should make an adjustment with the strange world in which I was forced to move and have my being. That mood of confidence lasted the days and nights across the great flat plain, East of the Rockies, that rolls on interminably until, at last, you are in Chicago.

Only a few of my old friends were there then, but I did call on young Schaffner, of the famous clothing firm, who had helped me in the old days, when I had had the idea of doing "Civilization In The United States." He was a Harvard man, after all; then he was full of plans and intellectual ambitions, and I have often, in later years, wondered how many of those plans and ambitions were realized. Just as it had done in my old days on *The Dial,* the city exasperated me by its monotonous flatness, and I was glad—though I enjoyed my brief visit with Schaffner—to get on the train for Washington.

Washington?—Yes, I wanted to see young Saxton, whom I had known in Paris and who had sent me some extra money for my trip—he was there. And I could stop off at Baltimore, on my way back to New York, to see Mencken and the *Sun* crowd—after all, I had been their Paris correspondent for five years. The trip was pleasant, especially in the morning, when we went through a cheerful, wooded section of Pennsylvania that made me realize how provincial (dominated by the idea of Pittsburgh, I suppose) had always been my notion of that State as purely industrial—and rather unpleasantly and aggressively industrial at that. It was then, I think, that I acquired the ambition (which I still have) to see my own country by the high-road and the automobile, even if I am forced to run into hundreds of the members of what Charles Merz termed his book, "The American Caravan." At Washington I stopped only a few hours—long enough to see all the familiar sights, though, somehow, this time they gave me no thrill, and went directly on to Baltimore.

The *Sun* crowd all seemed glad to see me. Duffy—now their famous cartoonist—and Anne took me to their home, and we talked over the "good old days" in Paris, when Montparnasse was young—just as, I suppose, every succeeding generation of

Frenchmen has done since the time of Rabelais. I stayed for the night, and Mencken kindly brought over one of his flagons, in defiance of what little prohibition law there was in a town almost fanatically "wet" in sympathy, to my hotel, where he regaled me with the latest literary, social, political, newspaper, sexual, intellectual, and other scandals and absurdities of the day. It was as good as a cocktail—and about equally confusing to one's judgment, for the opinions flowed with bewildering and paradoxical speed.

At six o'clock the next evening I arrived at the Pennsylvania Station, where Malcolm Cowley—and this certainly would not happen today—greeted me with a typical booster's "Welcome To Our City" banner. He invited me to his apartment, where Peggy, his wife, and he and myself had a dinner, washed down with a bit of the synthetic gin of the era. Anyway, it was jolly—and he took me down to Frances's house, where Thorne Smith and his wife and child lived on the floor above Frances, where the gas was not turned off that night and I was nearly suffocated, where liquor was plentiful and cats numerous (all of them, Frances solemnly assured me, were related in some strange manner to Mademoiselle Rabelaise), and where, to sum it all up, some of the ancient atmosphere of Jones Street of the old days was recaptured. So much of it, in fact, that for the last few days of the week I remained in New York before taking the S. S. "La France" back to Le Havre, I spent in the Lafayette Hotel. Yet it was fine to see everybody again.

Horace Liveright was as affable as usual. He had an attractive assistant editor, and she pleaded my cause so effectively that Horace decided to take my book on America—when, if, and as finished. (I made one or two ineffectual attempts to do it, after I got back to Paris, but I am convinced the only place in which to write a book on America is here in America. In a way, I have lived up to my promise to do that book for Horace—because it is written, even if not in quite the terms I then should have thought possible, and its name is "Rediscovering America.") In his usual manner, Horace went beyond merely accepting the book—he gave me a modest advance on it; and I am glad that debt is now repaid, even if it is too late for Horace to know it. But among other business matters I did contrive to sell him Ernest Hemingway's first book of short stories (indeed, first book of any kind), called "In Our time" —and I have often wondered since why he did not keep Hemingway as an author. Possibly Hemingway's caricature of Sherwood Anderson's style in "Torrents Of Spring" put Horace in some difficulties; I can well imagine it might. After all, it is a delicate problem for a publisher as to whether he ought to allow one author on his list to poke fun at another. But I was always sorry Horace lost Hemingway over that episode.

Before I sailed I sent for my mother, who came down from Boston to see me. People talk to me about "premonitions" very often—even ask me for those of my own that have come true. I have never had a one, as I understand the meaning of the word. Certainly I had none then that those brief few hours in a New York hotel were to be the last time I was ever to see my mother alive, for although I returned to New York for my present stay before she died, I failed to get up to Boston in time to see her—as I shall explain in a later chapter. But then I bade her goodbye with a light heart, assuring her that I should send for her to come over and visit me in Paris either that coming summer or the next—and I believed that, too, extraordinary as it seems to me now. How sanguine I was then! How sure of myself!

With all the confidence of a new-found youthful vitality, I looked over the rail of the liner, as we drew away from the shore. When the toot of the little pilot-boat, picking up our pilot, was answered by our own short roar, and the turbines began to churn and rotate with that steady, even sing-song so familiar to the ocean traveller, I thought with satisfaction of my trip. I should finish my book in Paris; I should add to my correspondence jobs; I should make lots of money and send for my mother to come over on a summer vacation. I should even, perhaps, very soon own a horse of my own and run it under my own colors at the French track. I thought a lot about those colors, imagining all kinds of combinations that would be modest yet striking, individual yet discreet. I even visualized my grey horse that was to win for me.

Day dreams—and sea dreams. Longings, restlessness, spiritual wandering in clouds of fancy. Vague regrets, forced anticipations of great days to come. I was dreaming and hoping. I had lost touch with life for a bit.

And I was going back to Paris—poor and alone, as always.

XV. PETER PICKEM ON THE PONIES

IT was a hectic trip over—and all my own fault, too. There was something exciting in the notion of going back to Paris in the off season. Obviously, the mere summer tourist class; the college boys on vacation; the rubber manufacturer from Akron, Ohio, who had always previously gone to the Canadian woods for fishing and camping "with the boys" on his July and August holidays, but who, at long last, had yielded to his wife's solicitations for a "cultural" trip to Europe; the High School teachers who had skimped for years to go to hear spoken, in the countries themselves, the German and French languages that they had so long been teaching, with dubious accents, to our youngsters; and the politicians taking advantage of legislative recesses—all these particular classes would not be on board. There would be the inevitable "buyers"—what boat is without them?—and perhaps a handful of financially independent followers of certain sporting events, like the Grand National. The rest of the passenger list would be made up—especially going East to Europe before the depression—of people, like myself, returning to England or to France, as one returns home to New York after a tour of what Mr. Mencken used to term "the Hinterland." But Bob Hallowell, who had given up managing the finances of the *New Republic* to go to Paris to indulge his old passion, painting, was on board; and though he was shocked at my never being found very far away from the bar, he gave me assurance of at least some human contact. And Vyvyan—my old friend from the early days in New York, whom I had not often seen since our dinner with Victor Herbert at the Brevoort that summer night in 1918—had come down to the boat to see me off, one of those unexpectedly nice and human things that people are so often doing to refute the cynics. That set me up, too. Finally, the young gentleman who makes (or rather, has control over) a nationally sold fountain pen was to prove a very amusing companion. No, it didn't promise to be a dull trip—and I made sure that it wasn't. I crossed the ocean that time at least wrapped in a high alcoholic dream.

For as I look back on it now, I realize how deep and strong was the emotional conflict within me—I felt I was running away from America, this time really without good and sufficient reason; and yet I couldn't help running away. "Home" was not home to me any longer. But Paris was not my home either. I was just an uprooted, aimless wanderer on the face of the earth. And a lonely one, too. I didn't like that; I hated it. And, since there was nothing else to do, I would go into the bar and take another drink—and try to forget. I was glad when the boat rolled, and the cocktail glasses would slide like bowling balls down along the slippery polished wood, so that you could make a bet as to whether or not you could catch it before it crashed. The bet would involve another drink, of course. That kind of thing is the worst form of moral disintegration: Instinctively I knew that, but I *pretended* not to care. I *pretended* it wasn't true.

All these fantasies vanished fast enough, when we reached Le Havre. I was so unfeignedly glad to get back to France—I remembered what a French woman had once said to me, "Il n'y a un plaisir dans le monde comme cela quand la France vous souhaite"—that I hardly knew what to do with myself. The special train from the dock beside the boat—for *one* advertisement really told the truth, the one of the French Line which used to say, "From Covered Pier to Covered Pier,"—stopped only for a moment at Rouen. It was jolly in the restaurant car, where many of us remained until we got as near as Maisons to Paris, singing and joking and making absurd comments on everything we saw through the car windows. That little train trip that day would have given Bob Benchley enough material for three *New Yorker* articles—I can still remember it with delight after all these years. And, mind you, I was landing in Paris almost completely broke and without a job or a friend or a woman to keep me. (I mention this last, for I saw three gentlemen who were being so supported among my fellow passengers—and at that time it didn't offend me morally; it merely made me jealous.) But I didn't mind. I took a taxicab straight from the station to Montparnasse and back to my old room, which miraculously had been kept for me. And all that evening, still a bit dizzy from the days of rocking on the boat (do other people have this too? I mean, this shakiness which comes *after* you have alighted from a boat, and of which you are not conscious while still on it?), I went from place to place in the Quarter—to make sure each one was still there.

The days the followed were not so thrilling as that first day of arrival. I had no money, no regular job, no girl. Of course I had still my Baltimore *Sun* and *Town And Country* correspondence work, though both were to go sooner than I thought —since misfortunes never seem to come singly. It was the end of February, and the races would be opening at the jumping and flat tracks soon. And, to make matters worse, a girl I had met in New York, who had surprising confidence in the book I proposed doing for Horace, was coming over for a vacation towards the end of May or the early part of June. I wrote her the sad truth of my situation, even—as I recall it —expressing the hope that she really wasn't coming, inasmuch as I preferred that she shouldn't see me "on my uppers" in Paris—especially after she had seen me self-confident and active and fairly successful during the brief week I had been, *en passant,* in New York. Her answer to that missive was friendly and humorous—and she even cabled me quite a bit of money at a Paris bank, but, ironically enough, I didn't know this until she arrived herself, as the bank got my name and address wrong and she herself had not mentioned her generosity in her letter. It was a fairly common irony of Paris during that period for an American to be walking the streets, like myself, literally wondering where his next meal was coming from—at precisely the time when a few hundred dollars were waiting for his call and demand at some bank downtown. This helps to explain the curious attitude of irresponsibility so many Americans in Paris developed during that period—for, quite literally, they seldom knew just where they were at. Everything was a matter of luck and of chance. Any day you might—or, of course, more probably might not—get a *pneumatique* from a bank, asking you to call to collect some money sent you by Aunt Emma in Iowa or Uncle Clifford, who had just made a "clean-up" in California or Florida real estate. And, even if nothing romantic did happen to *you,* it was always happening to one or the other of your friends. Emotionally that affected your sane judgment almost as much as if it had happened to you. As I remember that time, it seems I was always and forever celebrating somebody else's unexpected good fortune.

How I got through those weeks until, towards the end of May, Belinda arrived herself I don't know—except that Joan, who had been in Switzerland—where she had gone on a mountain-skiing expedition with Ernest Hemingway and his wife—came back to Paris a few weeks before Belinda was due. What Joan thought of the success or failure of my American trip, which after all had cost her a fair penny, she kept strictly to herself. But she proved once more that she was one of the best sports I have ever known. And when Belinda finally *did* land and went to a hotel in the Saint-Germain Quarter, Joan insisted on taking us both out to dinner, before that in the afternoon driving us herself around Paris and the Bois and showing Belinda some of the sights—at every new spot ready with a goodnatured bit of banter. And at the same time genuinely friendly towards Belinda, and interested in her, too: The whole thing made me marvel at the infinite adaptability of women—when they want to be adaptable.

Belinda did some shopping the next morning—she was, as she herself put it, in the language of those neo-speakeasy days, "lousy" with money—and in the afternoon I took her out to Longchamp to see the races, which, to my chagrin, appeared to bore her to death. That is, the races themselves and the horses did; she was interested enough in the people there, in who they were, and in what they wore. It was an object-lesson to me in learning that my enthusiasm for a horse-race is not shared by a considerable portion of the population, even of the feminine population, who I believe are naturally more of gamblers than are men. However, we had an extremely pleasant weekend at Fontainebleau, though it was somewhat spoiled for me by the ridiculously high cost of everything—I had lived too long in France not to be horrified at the manner in which some pretentious hotels gouge travellers, at that time, of course, American travellers above all. I couldn't help but contrast these prices with those Joan and myself had paid for far more amusing days on our trip through Southern France the year before. But I can remember some of the walks we took through and beside the forest; Belinda herself had come from a small town, and she was Jewish, too—it was the first time I had ever really heard the note of determination to succeed and get on, socially, in a hostile racial environment sounded with such sharpness. It almost frightened me.

Her visit to Paris came to an end all too soon. Do you wonder that I hate railroad stations? I kissed her goodbye on the train in the Gare Saint-Lazare. (And memories of how I had done precisely the same thing, with much the same emotions, when Jessica had left four years before, came over me in spite of myself; vaguer memories of the farewell in the Grand Central in New York; was I always doomed to be saying farewell?) I remember she actually had tears in her eyes—it seems incredible now. Since my return home I have seen her here in New York a couple of times, but only, as it were, accidentally. Sometimes it almost disheartens me, I must confess—that relationships, which seem so vital and so important at the time, can so easily be withered and destroyed. Is there nothing permanent? Must all our loves, as Santayana somewhere says, be only like the light caresses of butterflies, perhaps as charming but certainly as evanescent?

That summer and autumn of 1925 were the summer and autumn of my discontent in Paris. There seemed nothing to do—no reason for going on with anything. Belinda had left me enough money for a few weeks—weeks that went by, as had so many others before in Paris, in a kind of soft haze of pleasant unreality. I knew the dream couldn't go on forever, yet I couldn't see what the awakening would be. And I didn't care—Paris is like that. Only there, I think, is possible such a complete mood of each day and hour for itself, without regrets about the past or plans concerning the future—a sort of soft animal contentment at just being alive. It is a very dangerous nood for an American of my New England temperament, the strong and beguiling reaction from a tradition of purposefulness and accomplishment and moral integrity. Even as an experience I don't recommend it.

And on the practical side my troubles were beginning to pile up with a vengeance. I had had to give up my little apartment, and had moved to a cheap hotel near the new Café Select on the Rue Vavin. Cheap as it was, I was always worried about how to meet the bill—and my meals became less and less frequent, though, miraculously, I had about the same amount to drink as usual. (It is not any cheap cynicism on my part; it is an observation I make two or three times in this book, and in each case from practical experience: People will often buy you drinks, take you to the races, give you luxuries of different kinds, provided you don't ask for or appear to care about necessities. Moralists might pay more attention to this fact than they do.) The pressure was getting just about intolerable—when Adolphe Strong appeared on the scene.

It was not that Adolphe had much money, or could do much more than buy me a few meals now and then. But he was working on the Paris edition of the *Tribune,* and, what was more important, he was on good terms with the boss, Ragner. He said that the sporting editor—whom later we came to know as "The Once All Over," because of his column of comment, "The Once Over," which he finally produced in a kind of friendly competition with Sparrow Robertson's sporting gossip in the *Herald*—was too lazy to go to the races himself, and would welcome an assistant.

"That bird," said Adolphe, "comes from Texas, which means that he will welcome, embrace, and call brother any man that will help him unload from his own shoulders the burden of even the most trivial routine."

"But the boss himself?" I inquired.

"Keep your demand low—$20 a month, or 500 francs to start, as salary. Then get what you can on an expense account. It won't be much, but it may keep you from starving. And it *will* keep you out of the cafés during the day. Who knows? You may even make some money at the track, after you get to know the horses. It has, I understand, happened before. And if you aren't more intelligent than the average race-track tout, then I'll throw a grand piano from here to Boulogne."

How he persuaded the boss I don't know for sure, but I am convinced that "The Once All Over" pleaded my cause manfully—for the reason, I am certain, that Adolphe had anticipated. And the boss himself was weak and goodnatured, as I was to see only too pathetically later on, when I learned and watched how some of the boys "rode" him almost to death, coming in late with fantastic excuses, falling asleep on the job, getting plain facts wrong, mistranslating the French newspapers, and, in general, performing in a manner that, back home, would have caused any city editor to fire them after three days. But after all, the revelation of that particular psychopathic ward came considerably later—at the moment I was delighted to have a regular job again. It restored my morale, as it restores any man's morale. And all the details of going to the different racing societies, getting my pictures taken, and arranging for my racing card *de la presse*—details which, ordinarily, would have bored me to tears, proved delightful forms of a new activity.

"Peter Pickem" was the trade name of my paper's "expert" —it had been invented either by Floyd Gibbons or Dave Darrah, I was told, back in the early days of the paper, that is, when it was just a method of advertising and popularizing the home paper—outside of performing the real service of giving news from the States) with the men under our colors in Europe. For the *Tribune* (or "Le Shecargo," as the French would insist on calling it) was a "war" baby, if ever there was one—but a war baby which continued to thrive, long after the war was over. In fact, I now think that McCormick was jealous of the prestige of the *Herald,* and was determined to show Europeans that there was another and important city in the United States beside New York. (The Chicago World's Fair, naturally enough, has done a lot to slay this inferiority complex.) Also, just following the war, there was an unprecedented demand for news from Europe—the stories of the different peace conferences and stories of the new "line up" on the Continent were in demand everywhere. The Paris edition's office was likewise, consequently, the office for the European news service of the big syndicate of "feature" stories and special "spot" news items, all of which was controlled by the Chicago *Tribune.* In my time "Hank" Wales was the head of this service, as "Jimmie" James was the head of the New York *Times* European service in Paris; luckily there was no rivalry between the two—on the contrary, by special arrangement, the services used each other. One more thing: Although the local

(i. e., Paris) edition of the Chicago *Tribune* had the same address as the *Tribune's* foreign service, and in fact was on the same floor in the *Petit Journal* building, there was more than the partition and a glass door which separated the two. The foreign service boys were paid in dollars from Chicago—the boys on the local edition were paid in francs. Many a time, as "Hank" walked self-confidently back to his office to send some story by cable, I have seen one or two of the boys at the city-room desk of the local edition glance up at him enviously. And not out of admiration for his ability, either; they were thinking of how he was paid in good American dollars, while they were paid in francs that might be worth a nickel today and less than four cents tomorrow. Yet in spite of what ordinarily might have caused bitterness in an organization, there was pretty good feeling between the two offices, and this because, after all, we were Americans together in a foreign country. Whenever there was a showdown—whenever, because of some political row over the debt or something else, there was a scream of rage at Americans and all things American in the kept Parisian press—you could feel this. Our own petty rivalries disappeared; we were Americans together.

All this—and a great deal more—I learned bit by bit as the weeks went by. But during my first couple of months I was busy learning my own game, the racing game. I went religiously every day to the track, no matter what the weather, no matter how late I had remained up the night before, no matter how much I had had to drink. (My "rival" on the *Herald,* who was an old man, went only on the "big" days—and then only when the weather was fair. He always gave the logical—and usually popular—favorites, with the natural result that when his choices *did* win, their prices were very low. He practically never gave an outsider. And, though he gave a larger number of winners than did I, if you "followed" him—betting, say, $4.00—$2.00 to win and $2.00 to "place," which in France means betting on a horse to finish either first, second, *or* third, on each of his choices—you would have lost a lot of money.) I made it a special point to talk with my *confrères* in the press box at the tracks themselves and, where I could, to make friends with them. I am glad I did, too. I met some very amusingly cynical gentlemen. However, I think the fairest way to sum the whole thing up would simply be to say that I took my job seriously and went at it intelligently. With the consequence that I learned a great deal about racing—its charm and its boredom, its beauty and its dullness, its dishonesty and its fine sportsmanship on occasion. And, anyway, I learned to love a good horse, and to tell a thoroughbred when I saw one. What I did not know, though I learned that, too, in time were the technical aspects of racing, the different blood lines, the problems of breeding, the various training methods, the selection of the right race, at the right time of the year, for the right kind of horse.

But while these technical problems interested me—how can they fail to interest anybody, when money is involved? —I feel sure that it was the spectacle and the humors of the different types in the crowd that first aroused my interest. (An interest I have not, in fact, lost to this day.) For the spectacle involved not merely the race itself, but the incomparable stage on which it was set—lovely Chantilly; proud, magnificant Longchamp; bright little Le Tremblay; the high view over Paris from Saint-Cloud; the long straight beside the river at Maisons-Laffitte, set in the little wooded park; comic Enghien, with its double jumping and trotting tracks; gorgeous Auteuil in the Bois; the cold, bleak sweep of the wide plain at Vincennes. And on the human side, once you got to know your steady Parisian racing public, as I very soon did, there was plenty to entertain you. I could give a six page category of the different types to be seen at the different tracks. (As a *tour de force,* I once did precisely that for a French magazine.) And most of these "teeps," as the French themselves call them, were amazingly funny. Funny and pathetic and generous and petty—once in a while, when they thought they were being cheated just a bit too shamelessly, quite ugly and not incapable of tearing out the light sockets and burning down the whole show, as three riots I myself witnessed dramatically proved. But on the whole, it was a good-natured, sport-loving crowd. The majority didn't bet much more than about twice what they could afford to lose—which is seldom fatal. It was only in the *pésage* (or enclosure, as we call it) that the "big shots" crowded the Mutuel machines with last-minute 5,000 and 10,000 franc bets. (And for all their "wise" money, I am glad to inform you, usually lost.) And a much larger number of people than you would believe went out just to see the fun, for an excursion. On hot Saturday afternoons later on in the spring I used to see them stretched out, sleeping blissfully, on the warm, sweetly odorous grass in the fields way beyond the clamor and the betting booths at Enghien and Chantilly and Saint-Cloud. I never understood why these people went to the races or what particular attraction drew them there rather than to one of the many public parks. It was a kind of symbol —of the intense social gregariousness (coupled with high personal individualism) of the French.

And another thing beside the sheer physical attractiveness of the tracks was the constant *change* in this stage setting, as well as in the kind of racing witnessed (i. e., on the flat, over the jumps, the trots, or mixed, that is, where jumping and trotting were combined, as at Enghien, and, occasionally, at Vincennes, where a cross-country steeplechase for saddle horses sometimes gave a seventh race contrast to the afternoon of six steady trotting events). Outside the winter season—from the middle of November until the middle of February—and the brief August summer holiday period (nowadays with special trotting races at Enghien four days a week), there is racing every day of the week in what is called the Paris region, the big races taking place on Sundays and holidays. There is no let-up for a single day. (I used to wonder what the English racing experts did on Sundays, for England, like our own, being a Christian country, does not permit racing on the Lord's Day.)

But if there is no let-up, there is also no monotony. Except for the Saturday and Sunday double-day (i. e., the day before and the day itself) of the Grand Prix de Paris, in June, and the double-day of the Prix De L'Arc de Triomphe, in October, when the races are for two successive days held at the same track—do I need to explain that it is at Longchamp?—the scene of racing changes every day. A typical week might be like this: Sunday, Longchamp; Monday, Saint-Cloud; Tuesday, Maisons-Laffitte; Wednesday, Le Tremblay; Thursday, Enghien; Friday, Vincennes; Saturday, Auteuil–and the following Sunday, if it was in the early autumn or late spring, Chantilly.

The importance of this *daily* change in scene, together with the *daily* change in the type of racing to be witnessed, is not, I think, fully recognized. The first question people would always ask me, when I was taking my *apéritif* before lunch in *Le Select* or on the terrasse of *Le Dôme* was not, "Are you going to the races, today, Harold?" but, "*Where* are the races today?" Going racing was no fixed routine either of place or of kind; there were plenty of people who went to Longchamp but scorned Vincennes, as many foreigners imagine the only place to see a fine steeplechase in Paris is at Auteuil or think of Enghien only as a little town that has a tiny gambling Casino beside a toy lake. Hence there was no sense of routine, as it is ordinarily understood—each day furnished a new setting, new faces, new kinds of sport. You had little opportunity to become bored. Your interest *had* to be flexible, practically speaking, whether you wanted it to be or not. And in the end you always wanted it to be—you soon learned to enjoy the diversity in unity. For the unity was, of course, always there—love of horses, and love of the excitement of the races themselves, of the gambling, and of the crowds that go with both.

As the June of 1923 (when Filibert de Savoie won the

Grand Prix) was Agatha's, as the June of 1924 (when Transvaal, the long shot, won) was Joan's, and as the June of 1925 (when that marvellous filly, Reine Lumière, captured the prize) was Belinda's, so the June of 1926 was my own—and my first as an accredited Paris racing editor. To the public I was "Peter Pickem;" to a comparative few I was Filibert (I was dubbed that one summer at Deauville, because of my eloquence about and admiration for the 1923 winner; some people call me that to this day); to my French *confrères* I was "Monsieur Stearns de Chicago." With what pride, I recall, I dressed up in my best (which, even if none too good, was modestly passable) and enjoyed the spectacle of the crowd jamming the three big grandstands of the *pésage* and the *pavillon,* including the roofs to the last square foot, while I, unworried about finding a place to see the race, in the security of my special card to the press box, watched the jockeys mount, receive final special instructions from anxious trainers and owners, and slowly parade their horses out through the gate. Then, with great dignity, I mounted the stairs, took my place with my colleagues, and critically observed the horses in their traditional, slow *défilé* as well as (to be sure to distinguish them) the colors of the jockeys' silks gleaming bright in the afternoon June sun—followed by the galloping back to the starters, who were only about ten yards to the right of us, directly in front of the *pavillon.* (The finish was about twenty yards or so to the left, the horses thus making the entire circuit, and a little more, of the *grande piste* to complete the 3,000 meters of the race—or almost two miles.)

There was the usual fidgeting and nervousness at the start. (In those days only a slender tape was snapped, when at last the "Go!" signal came; late in my time, the Australian mechanical starting-tapes, which are "sprung," were used.) The crowd shouted advice, often seasoned with humorous and sharp comments on the jockeys, the starters, the owners, or anyone else that caught their imagination at the moment. But somehow, after what seemed hours of turning and wheeling, though in cold fact it was less than ten minutes, the signal was given, the bell rang, and the crowd roared—they were off! And not in a cloud of dust, either–since races are run on the springy, green turf in France—but in a compact, gaily-colored, fast-moving mass.

I wish I might say that I had, in the *Tribune,* given in advance the winner of that 1926 Grand Prix—but I hadn't, and neither had a single other one of the many Parisian journalistic "experts," despite the fact that the winner was guided home by the lucky jockey, "Parson" Jack Jennings, who, though English, was well liked by French turf followers. For the winner was none other than the colt with the name so easy to remember, Take My Tip, belonging to M. James Hennessy, the amiable French brandy-maker, whose own name—confirmed by his ruddy face and jolly manner—suggests a certain Irish lineage. Yet in spite of the jockey, and, perhaps even more oddly, in spite of the colt's suggestive name, which one might think would have tempted at least a few people to back him, Take My Tip paid the handsome odds of 66 to 1—so that the "triple" of wild outsiders (beginning with Transvaal in 1924, followed up by Reine Lumière in 1925—both at far better odds than 100 to 1,—and now underscored by Take my Tip) was duly confirmed. I mention this, because it is a tradition of the French track that luck—either good or bad—tends to run in series of three. At least 50,000 or 60,000 spectators thought of this that June Sunday afternoon in 1926—that is, just about ten minutes too late. Of course I *did* know two American lady tourists, out for their first horse race either in Europe or back home, who bet on Take My Tip solely because of his name—and even today, when I think of them, I can put on a pretty good imitation of wrathfully (and jealously) frothing at the mouth. Probably that race and those lucky bets made uncontrollable gamblers of them—in which case they undoubtedly lost everything in the stock market later on. With this flight of fancy I comfort myself—for whatever they may have lost theoretically later on, I in fact lost a week's pay on that race.

Following the Grand Prix de Paris, the season begins to taper off, but the races nevertheless keep up steadily until almost the last day in July. (On July 14th, the French national holiday, the Prix des Marechaux—a very important event for horses of both sexes, four years old or more—is put on at Saint-Cloud.) Then the important events shift their stage setting to Deauville, where the Grand Prix de Deauville, run on the last Sunday of the month of August, is the high point of the summer out-of-town races for thoroughbreds. And of course I wanted to go.

Because, beside the races themselves, there were also the important yearling sales at Tattersall's (the French branch of the famous English firm) and at Cheri's (the leading French agency for thoroughbreds) during the last week of the season. The sales themselves (at auction)—prospective buyers, of course, had inspected the horses long before the actual sales and had had hours of preliminary discussion with their trainers and breeders—were held the last week of the season, each day's recess following immediately upon the conclusion of the afternoon's races. The track was only three minutes walk from the picturesque "ring" and its surrounding box stalls (some of them with the names of horses, later become famous, sold from them, printed in big gilt letters on the door), almost across the way, and unless there happened to be a particularly exciting polo game on after the races (and on the days of the "big" sales, when the best blood came up, the polo games were not played), all of the money of the sporting families of Paris and of London and of South America and even of New York seemed to be represented. Reporting these yearling sales—though it involved sending complicated fast dispatches to the paper—interested me. Moreover, it gave me an extra reason for asking the paper to send me down. Finally—and reluctantly, because it meant extra expense—old man Ragner consented and one bright July morning in 1928 I was speeding down in the "Blue Train" (fortunately the paper had a free pass on this luxury affair, or I should have had to go down on a milk train) to the "Plage Fleurie," as it was grandiloquently—but quite correctly, I must admit—termed on the flamboyant advertising posters.

The station at the end of that line is called Deauville-Trouville, because it is at the mouth of a tiny river, which empties into the small yacht harbor, which, in turn, separates the older Trouville from the built-up, more stylish and modern, and much more expensive Deauville. Walk to the right, as you get out of the station, crossing the bridge, and you are along the *quais* of Trouville; walk to the left—by the row of cafés, crossing another and smaller bridge, where you can look at several magnificent steam pleasure yachts, belonging to world-famous millionaires, such as Solly Joel, the English diamond "king"—and you are on the main street of Deauville that leads up to the handsome Casino. But just before that street makes the final little turn is a square, Deauville's home market place, around which are clustered several cafés of the usual Normandy provincial type. And a step from the square, up this main street towards the Casino, is Harry's Bar (also a little hotel at that time), where I spent two summers. A later summer I spent opposite it—the summer that Jim came down—in a nice private house, but I was in Harry's almost as much as ever, though I took my meals at Luigi's—a branch of the famous Paris restaurant, right beside Harry's. (The Harry that ran the Deauville place was not the Harry of Harry's New York Bar in Paris, who then had a summer place of his own at Le Touquet and would come over to Deauville to see the Grand Prix; it was Harry Fink, an Englishman, with certain Cockney affiliations it seemed to me—a good fellow, a gambler himself, with a divine trust in his ability to beat the races, which he regarded as a test of wits rather than as a sport.)

It was one of the gayest summer vacations I have ever had —even my routine of sending a story by telephone or wire back to the *Tribune* office every day was not too irksome, for usually I had it finished by eight o'clock—and then the whole evening was free for whatever Deauville (or Trouville) had to offer. And in those days, what those two towns had to offer, in the way of wine, women, and the song of the chips and the cards, was plenty. Also real song and music, too, for Billy Arnold's American band, made up of twenty or more good players of collegiate age, was teaching the French what American dance "jazz" of that vintage was like, when presented with "pep." The boys of the band came down to Harry's for their drinks between the afternoon tea dances and the after-dinner music, which very often lasted until three in the morning. The gambling part of the Casino, in particular the *usine* of the big baccarat room, or *la salle privée* as it was called, where the big money was wagered, might keep open all night, its grey-faced, evening-clothed gentlemen and ladies making a strange spectacle in the morning sunlight that flooded the beach, as they cheerfully or resignedly made their way to one of the two big hotels on each side of the Casino. (In my time there were only two or three suicides, due to heavy losses; the crowd that then played at Deauville was a moneyed crowd, which, speaking generally, could afford bad luck.)

Sometimes I would watch them those mornings, either when I stayed up all night myself or got up early, for I liked to go down by the Casino to the beach to see the thoroughbreds get their morning salt-water splash in the sea—a splash only, for they never went higher than quarter way up to their knees. The grooms said it was good for their legs; I don't know about that, but it was beautiful to watch. Bright sunlight and a blue sea; tired, grey-faced gamblers in evening clothes; high-spirited colts and fillies splashing in the shallow water; the gulls wheeling and the sails of the early fishing boats coming from Le Havre, occasionally the low body and trailing smoke of an ocean liner far out; the bright flowers in the formal gardens in front of the hotels and along by the tennis courts and before the Casino; the receptive but pleasant sense of holiday and remoteness from all industrial grime and ugliness, almost an adumbration of money and wealth and leisure in the very air; a kind of sensuous vibrancy, too, made up of vague memories of the beauties seen in low-cut gowns at the Casino the night before and of the anticipation that they soon would be again lolling on the sands before the Beach Bar, unclad in even more revelatory one-piece bathing suits; and, when you listened, the sounds of a language that never quite, even with fishermen or workingmen, loses all its music.

Yes, it was very gay at Deauville that summer holiday—a kind of pre-depression gaiety, too, when many people still found it easy to have no feeling about the social consequences of too much money, when, I mean, there were still many people who possessed too much. Or, to put it brutally, when those who had a lot of money were not yet too seriously worried about how soon it was going to be taken away from them by the rising taxes and eventual confiscation of a new social order. There was then at Deauville something, I fancy, similar to the old champagne-caviar, big-money-changing-hands-over-night atmosphere of St. Petersburg in those now strangely remote days before the pains of parturition for a new world started in 1914. For the irresponsibly rich, Deauville was still in 1926 a happy little interlude—three weeks, when you could pretend that the hands of the clock of history had stood still.

Avery Hopwood, the writer of money-making farces, whom I had known in my old New York *Press* days, came down for a week that year—he was, to me, a kind of success symbol of the era. But somehow I was always fond of him, even when he did absurd things like invite all the "Dinges" (as he persisted in calling negroes in terms that antedated Carl Van Vechten) he could find in Paris to a formal "dress-up" breakfast at Claridge's—or come down to Deauville without once going near the Casino, or the race-track, or the bigger restaurants, or the tennis-courts or golf links or polo field, but just stay at Harry's drab little bar—and "kid" the boys and girls. Bill Ulmer, a stout and jolly gentleman from Pottsville, Pennsylvania—Diana Swift used to call him "the bright little boy from Culver Academy," both to his rage and his amusement—was also among those present: And I am glad I thought of him, for I sent a feature story about Bill having the Casino band play in the surf while he took his bath, their instruments raised high above the purling waves (for Bill was a mysterious Eastern potentate in my story). There were pictures to go with this fantastic yarn, or rather to confirm it, for the band boys loved a practical *blague* and posed willingly and solemnly—and that story was syndicated everywhere in America. I suppose it was just silly enough to go over.

Anyway, as a result of that story, I returned to Paris with journalistic colors flying that last Monday in August, following the Grand Prix de Deauville. (There was no Clairefontaine then—a new mixed jumping and flat track built near Deauville just to prolong the season a fortnight after the Grand Prix—as there was later, when I was on the *Daily Mail;* at that time, however, everybody cleared out of Deauville the moment the Grand Prix was over, fleeing usually to Baden-Baden or to Biarritz, at both of which resorts there was then an early autumn season; the Paris autumn season always begins formally with the Prix de L'Arc de Triomphe, run the first Sunday in October at Longchamp.)

And the first week or so of that return from hectic Deauville, until about the middle of September, I found always pleasant in Paris: The weather is fair, Indian-summer like; there are a few good weekday thoroughbred meetings on Thursdays and Tuesdays at Chantilly, when the leaves in the forest are just beginning to turn deep and rich; French people are starting to come back to town and the loud-mouthed college boy drunks of that period were being poured on liners in their liquor-spotted Brooks Brothers clothes, leaving Paris to its own inhabitants; and as the evenings began to give just a suggestion of the fast-approaching cool autumn, oysters appeared and you could almost anticipatorily smell the roasted chestnuts, which would soon emerge, as if by magic, on every Paris street-corner and before every Paris café. The cherry-vendors of the spring, and the *poireau*—what the French call "the asparagus of the poor"—merchants of the summer, became the chestnut-sellers of the autumn. What these seasonal merchants do in the winter (though they sell chestnuts up to the holiday time) I don't know; perhaps they hibernate, like the mysterious vagabonds that every April, when the Paris sun gets bold enough to stay out at least ten minutes, seem to spring up like dandelions along the *quais,* particularly near Notre Dame and the Isle Saint-Louis—you can see them any day in that feeble but gracious April sunshine washing their winter-battered left-overs and even, on occasion, showing enough energy to give their dogs a bath and themselves a shave. Perhaps for a few of the younger ones of this strange vagabondia there are even other and more ambitious thoughts and stirrings—perhaps then thoughts of love come also to the disinherited, as to the self-assured and the powerful. Paris and the spring—could it be otherwise?

However, I did not myself hibernate that late autumn and winter—because, when the regular thoroughbred races were ended for the year, the trotting races began at Vincennes. There were four meetings a week—Tuesdays, Thursdays, and the Saturday-Sunday double-day weekend: Just enough to keep you busy, but not too busy. Hence that winter of 1926-27 was my professional introduction to French trotting and to the French half-bred, or *"demi-sang"* (as we call our trotters "standard breds")—and to the greatest of them all; that is, to the big mounted trotter, Vassal, and to the small harnessed trotter, the beautiful and champion mare, Uranie. That winter was, I believe, more or less the swan-song of Vassal, then an old horse, and the beginning of the great days of Uranie—the days when she won the Prix d'Amerique, de Belgique, del'Europe, and d'Italie—to mention some of the better known so-called "International" trotting events in Paris. When, in those days, Uraine trotted at Vincennes, no further advertisement or announcement was needed—all sporting Paris went out, even people who ordinarily never went near a race track. For little Uranie captured the affection and the admiration of the thousands that saw her by her grace, her speed, her beauty, her courage, and—as we say in trotting—her "manners." She had everything. (Despite her retirement at a very late age, she was bred to The Great MacKenna, an American sire highly thought of by breeders, and her first-born will be trotting on the French track, I understand, about the time this book is published.)

Also—and this is important, when you try to visualize her performances—in France important trotting events are not run in heats—the winner capturing, as with us, the best two out of three—but in one long race, sometimes as much as two miles or more, with the faster horses penalized by actual distance. Hence little Uranie, on her record as the fastest, always started yards and yards back of her opponents, to give the semblance of a handicap, and sometimes—according to the conditions of the race—she was so far back at the start, all alone and small as she wheeled and wheeled and spurted again and again before all of them got off to a fair start, that from the grandstand it looked almost pathetic and cruel. Yet how quickly she would make up most of that handicap! Not all of it, of course, but she would go by enough horses early in the contest to put herself in the race by the time they had come once around. And then, after the last long climb up the hill opposite the stands and through the "little wood," she would come around into the short straight with only two or three antagonists ahead of her. Swinging wide (and losing distance, too) on the outside, to avoid any collision, she would "step on it" at the cluck of her driver, Capovilla, who loved her as he did one of his own children, and come tearing down that short little straight so fast that you couldn't see her feet separately but only as swiftly flowing lines. Her light mane would stand out, from the wind her own speed created, but the whole performance, nevertheless, had a deceptively effortless and inevitable quality about it—and before you had realized it, she had "nipped" her struggling opponents right at the finish line, sometimes by a head, sometimes by a neck, never by much, but always with just enough to win. (The French used to say that she "combed the hair" of her rivals at the finish.) It was as if she timed and calculated the whole thing herself. And the stands would roar and applaud and look happy, for nobody bet against her. If you couldn't bet on her, you didn't bet. And race after race, as a consequence, she paid 20 to 1 *on* to win—you bet $20.00 to $1.00 against there being an accident. It was a spectacle, not a gambling proposition. And you made your small or large bet on Uranie just "for the honor of it," for the pleasure of saying years later to your admiring offspring, "Yes, way back in 1926 *I* bet on Uranie to win."

Nevertheless, though I enjoyed the meetings at Vincennes, I, too, was glad—along with the vagabonds, the lovers, the foolish and wise, the young and old—when the spring of 1927 came to Paris. The *fêtes* of Christmas and the New Year had been pleasant, with the holiday crowds out in an expansive mood at the "Plateau de Gravelle" to see the trotters, and the weather, too, had been unexpectedly mild and sunny instead of the traditional Paris dark winter wet. Also that three month period from the middle of November to the middle of February, when the physical routine of going out to the races slackened to the four trips a week, was a sort of psychological breathing-space. Other interests had some chance—I even did a bit of writing then, and considerable serious reading. And to avoid any danger of becoming too academic, I spent more time with the boys on the paper, which was a cure-all for any kind of temptation towards superciliousness or feeling of superiority.

But it was good to see the thoroughbreds again—first at Enghien, over the jumps, and then at Saint-Cloud on the flat; later at Maisons-Laffitte, with a few early spring jumping meetings at Auteuil in the Bois; when the weather became a bit warmer, at Le Tremblay, where already the talk was of the forthcoming Prix de Diane and Prix de Jockey Club, both to be run, as always, at Chantilly; finally, on Easter Sunday, at Longchamp—and the full season was on. This was the yearly balance and contrast, the racing systole and diastole, leading up slowly to the *Grande Semaine* the last week of June, which that year of 1927 was won by the noble animal, Fiterari—more or less of a favorite, just for a bit of a change.

And again I went down to Deauville, on the *Tribune's* behalf, for the August season. But this year I went down in style, even with dress clothes and an admission fee to the *salles de jeu* of the Casino. For I had met Steve Green, a well-to-do and pleasant chap from Philadelphia, a Harvard man of the post-war generation, who staked me to enough money to buy a proper outfit (the *Tribune,* of course, had not increased my salary, except by just about enough to make it possible to buy an extra package of cigarettes a day) and to play a system at the races. (Because I, like everybody else, thought I had discovered a sure method of making money out of the French racetrack by playing always to "place" in a certain way—perhaps it would have worked, too, I can't really say; the plain truth is, I didn't have enough patience to stick to the system. I cared about certain horses too much, and every now and then I *had* to bet to win—which of course meant throwing the system out of the window.)

Again I went to Harry's and once more it was a jolly three weeks, this season with formal dress evenings at the Casino, where I wisely let baccarat very strictly alone, contenting myself with watching others lose—and a certain few, naturally, win. But I didn't envy these last (except spasmodically), for their winnings seemed to burn their pockets, and I noticed that most of them left Deauville "broke" just the same, since somehow the money they won, no matter how much, disappeared—a part of it at the track on horses I did *not* recommend and a larger part of it on pretty ladies whom nobody could recommend. Not to mention a certain amount on high living, which was almost compulsory at Deauville in those piping times, when a small whiskey and soda was $1.00, a hotel room $6.00 a day, and a good dinner for two at the Ambassadeurs or Ciro's (the summer Deauville branch near the Casino), with wine and tips, at least $14.00 or $15.00 the total. Of course there were the occasional miracles—one American college boy, who came to Europe *via* the cattle-boat system and landed in Deauville with 1,000 francs, left two days later with over $5,000—and the occasional near-tragedies, symbolized by new, expensive cars marked "For Sale, Cheap," the remnant of fortune of some unlucky plunger. Steve and Sophie came down for a day's visit and watched my system work successfully (the one, and almost only, day; it was only a week later that I was "cleaned"!) ; I remember a Scotch girl friend with her Philadelphia boy pal, who was what is delicately known as a trifle "queer"—both from Montparnasse and among the Quarter's most distinguished drinkers—also came down and made the night hideous with song at Harry's, for no amount of hard liquor would put either that Scotch girl or her hybrid sex friend under the table. Oh, it was a fine season—to employ Adolph's old expression, I wasn't making lots of money, but I was having a lot of fun.

When I returned to Paris, the fun continued. It was not an unhappy winter, that one of 1927-28 in Paris—and I can sum it up in a few words: Every day work at the office on my stories; four times a week Vincennes and the trotting races. Even Steve didn't seem to care that my system had gone up the chimney—and, as a sort of compensation, I began making quite a bit of extra money at the track, following my own tips in the paper; for by this time I had got to know French trotting races at least as well as any of the old harridans (whom the French call *rombières*) in the *pélouse*. At night, after a dinner over town with Adolph or one of the boys at "Flo's" or the "Namur," I would stay up at the *Select* until dawn crept through the windows, drinking champagne and watching the boys and girls do their vaudeville stunts. It was a useless, silly life—and I have missed it every day since. Diana was friendly, too, that year—and I recall meeting all kinds of pleasant and amusing people during my nightly vigil at the *Select*. The depression had not arrived; and the political situation, for a miracle, was fairly calm—everybody, I mean, was free to make just as big a fool of himself or herself as his or her own natural inclinations suggested—and the inclination seemed to be strong. (Read the first part of Hemingway's "The Sun Also Rises" to get a vivid picture of that era in Montparnasse.) I understand quite well how some people went morally to pieces during that time, and, if I was saved, as naturally I flatter myself I was, it was simply by my work and my regular, even if absurd, hours and habits. I was marking time; life was just going by, and again I could say with the French, *"La vie passe comme une rêve à Paris."*

That June of 1928 was the month when Cri de Guerre won the Grand Prix de Paris (another favorite, if you please) —and when July was past and it was time again to go to Deauville for the August racing, I skipped gaily down for third (and, as it was to turn out) and final year at Harry's. It was a modest season that time, for I had abandoned any attempt at a racing system—abandoned the attempt in fact, I mean, for I had no money with which to try one, but not the hope that one might be discovered. However, it was a happy season, for Diana came down for a few days that year, and Bill Ulmer was there (we used to make preposterous journeys over to Trouville in an open carriage, drawn by a tired and discouraged horse that Bill insisted on calling "Gladiator The

Twenty-third"), as well as many of the old members of the American "jazz" band. There were the ups and downs of fortune, of course, at the track—and I still had my dress clothes, so that I could, on occasion, go into the Casino in the evening and watch the gamblers at work. But on the whole, it was my quietest year at Deauville—and in some respects, my happiest.

Certainly that autumn, after my return from *lá plage fleurie,* and that winter of 1928-29 were to prove among the happiest of my life in Paris, for at one of the early autmn meetings at Saint-Cloud Jeanne—one of my lively sporting American girl acquaintances introduced me to Jim, who was to become one of my dearest friends. Jim was pretty constantly with me after that in my "off" hours, and also he became himself a fairly regular devotee of the races—except for Vincennes, to which we went a few times, but not too often, together. I would go up to his home for dinner after work at the *Tribune* office; Dolly, his young wife, became fond of me, too, and I was always welcome: It was the nearest thing to a home I had ever known.

Even Jim's first indifferences to the trotting events I contrived to transform into something near to enthusiasm—quite to his surprise. I recall his saying to me one day late that November of 1928, "Never did I think I should be going out to the trotting at Vincennes in a ridiculous little car like this of Bouboule's—and enjoying it." For lovable and fantastic Bouboule (and his even more fantastic dog) was regularly our racing chauffeur now, when Jim did not drive his own Talbot.

Jim had a comfortable income, was tall and blonde and very good-looking as well as charming and intelligent—I don't wonder the girls went after him. And the fact that he was married, and happily married at that, only acted as further provocation. At that time, however, Jim was more interested in fillies of the equine than the human kind; the girls were just out of luck. I recall our going out a December "off" day (i. e., when there was no racing) to visit Capovilla and to see the great Uranie at close quarters in her stall. Of course we saw all the other horses in his stable, and heard his very shrewd comments on the relative merits of the newcomers that would soon be racing—and a vivid sense, we felt, too, of his great love for the champion, Uranie. For which, I have to ald, I don't at all blame him. I have never seen a more beautiful horse than she.

Jim talked about our starting a little trotting stable ourselves, and from that, if it turned out to be fairly successful, we might branch out into the more pretentious and costly business of having a few thoroughbreds, including a good jumper or two—the last, I suppose, not to miss anything. We even had dreams of some day winning the Grand Prix de Paris—and I say "we," for Jim intended to make it a joint ownership affair, giving our stable rather than our individual names as the official entry on the card, as is sometimes done here in America. In brief, the winter passed happily and all too swiftly; everything was all right with the world.

And when, after the glorious spring days in Paris, the "classic" June period came—and you had then asked me what I had done with myself during this six or seven months (outside the regular routine of my job and going to the races, of course), I think I should have answered you almost blissfully, "Nothing." There were the amusing intrigues and scandals and fun of the *Tribune* office—about which I shall speak more at length in my next chapter—and the nights at the *Select* and in the Quarter. That was all. I made no attempt to read anything or to do any "extra" work; for once, I was content with the routine of living. Content? No, quite happy—I was busy, not lonely, and in good health; life was amusing and something not to be taken too seriously. I hoped—and then believed—that this might continue indefinitely. It was not the first time I was learning the truth of the French saying I have quoted elsewhere in this book, *"La vie passe comme une rêve à Paris."*

That June of 1929 was signalized in French racing history

as the year when Hotweed won the Grand Prix de Paris—again something of a favorite, both with the press and the public; were the days of the big outsiders coming to an end? But for me it was signalized by two other things—it was the last Grand Prix de Paris Jim was to see with me or anybody else; it was also my last summer on the *Tribune*.

But it was not my last summer at Deauville, though it was quite unlike my earlier summers there. Because this time I had enough money not to have to live at Harry's; I lived in a private house, almost directly opposite on the Rue Desiré-le-Hoc. My patronage for meals and drinks I divided among Luigi's, Harry's (for old times' sake), and (since I now had good dress clothes and some extra money, thanks to the successful turf ventures of Jim and myself) even, now and then, Ciro's and the expensive restaurant in the Casino itself. Jim, who was fond of Le Touquet as a summer watering place, shifted his allegiance to Deauville (to future turf proprietors Deauville was important on account of its early yearling sales, as well as on account of its being a racing center), and came down for the last three days of the season. The afternoon after the day of the big race—and a bottle of champagne with Strassburger at the Casino the night of it—we set out for Paris in the Talbot.

At least once, I thought to myself as we scurried through Normandy, I am going back to Paris in a style befitting one of my station in life.

SUPPLEMENT TO CHAPTER FIFTEEN

Two Tables:

Table A: Grand Prix De Paris, 1913-1935.

Table B: Winnings of Some Famous Horses, American and French.

GRAND PRIX DE PARIS

Year	*Horse*	*Owner*	*Myself At*
1913	Bruleur	E. de St. Alary	Harvard Commencement
1914	Sardanapale	Baron E. de Rothschild	New York
	(1915, '16, '17, '18—not run; the war)		
1919	Galloping Light	Baron E. de Rothschild	New York
1920	Comrade	E. de St. Alary	New York
1921	Lemonora (filly)	Joseph Watson	New York
1922	Kefalin	M. Ambatielos	Paris
1923	Filibert de Savoie	C. Ranucci	Paris
1924	Transvaal	L. Mantacheff	Brittany
1925	Reine Lumière (filly)	Baron J. A. de Rothschild	Paris
1926	Take My Tip	James Hennessy	(R) Paris
1927	Fiterari	M. P. Moulines	(R) Paris
1928	Cri de Guerre	Ogden Mills	(R) Paris
1929	Hotweed	N. Birkin	(R) Paris
1930	Commanderie (filly)	Ed. Henriquet	(R) Paris
1931	Barneveldt	M. de Rivaud	Paris
1932	Strip The Willow	A. J. Duggan	New York
1933	Cappiello	Lady Granard	New York
1934	Admiral Drake	Leon Volterra	New York
1935	Crudite	Baron E. de Rothschild	New York

Note:

Distance: 3,000 meters (1 mile, 7 furlongs).

(R) refers to years when I was racing reporter for first, the Chicago *Tribune* (1926, '27, '28, and '29), and second, the *Daily Mail* (1930).

WINNINGS OF SOME FAMOUS HORSES, AMERICAN AND FRENCH

American		*French*	
Sun Beau	$376,744	Ksar	$335,340
Phar Lap	332,250	Massine	241,559
Gallant Fox		Sardanapale	211,505
Zev		Filibert de Savoie	193,525
Mate			
Top Flight			
Blue Larkspur			
Equipoise			
Twenty Grand			
Display			
Victorian			
Exterminator			
Man o' War	249,465		

NOTE:

Purchase Price of Fiterari (French) was $205,000.

XVI. NEWSPAPERS, FOLLY, LITERATURE

IF THE specific events in this chapter are confined more or less to the brief three month period of September, October, and early November of 1929, it is only because they are used illustratively: The months were typical; indeed, with a few changes in names and episodes, what took place during this autumn of 1929 in the *Tribune* office on the Rue Trudaine was only a duplication—and, in some humorous respects, an intensification—of what had taken place there all my previous years on the paper, that is to say, during my entire fantastic career as "Peter Pickem" in 1926, '27, '28, and the period of '29 up to going to Deauville—from which garden spot I had just returned at the end of the last chapter. My next chapter, "Winning Days," is also of this period and of the two years just before—1928 and 1929 again—but to understand the mood of it, the newspaper background against which I moved and had my curious being must first be described. And it is this newspaper background, using these months of 1929 as a sample, which I shall attempt to picture here. I can do this the more readily, as my technical racing reporting work for the *Tribune* I have already sketched in the preceding chapter.

First of all, the hours of work. As a racing man, of course, I did not come into the office until I got back from the track —anywhere from quarter past five (when the races were, say, at convenient Auteuil) to half past six or even seven (when they were at distant Chantilly). On my way to the office I bought a Paris *Sport,* which had the technical results, with the prices, of that day's events—I marvelled at the speed with which this was printed and on the street, for even on the short trip in from Longchamp the newsboys would be crowding around your autobus or taxi to sell it to you when you reached the Place de l'Opéra, or even before at the gates of Paris; one activity, I might add, where the French really *were* efficient, as they often are when money and gambling are concerned. Paris *Sport* also had, of course, the official entries for the next day's events, with the weights, jockeys, and so on—invaluable for making your own prognostics, because, after all, there was not much point in writing a powerful piece on a horse that was wonderful—but wasn't going to run. At tracks like Maisons-Laffitte, where the entry lists were sometimes enormous, there were many over-night scratches; and my tips for these events had to be taken with a grain of salt, since very often the horse I had so painfully selected as the probable winner would not, at the last moment at the track itself, compete at all. (I knew one such horse to be entered officially seven times, paying forfeits, too, before finally he did appear on the track in the race itself—only to come in an ingnominious fourth.)

With Paris *Sport* to study, I would alight as near the office as possible, and over an *apéritif* make up my mind what horse *I* intended to give—for sometimes I would agree with the paper's recommendation (it was in fact an excellent and, on the whole, soundly conservative racing form sheet), and sometimes I would have an idea of my own. As soon as I had made my selections for the next day, I would go to the office across the street and type them out in duplicate, first sending down the programme of racing for the week and my tips, keeping duplicates for reference. Then I would write the story, beginning around quarter past seven and having an eye on the clock, for I wanted to get through at eight—the hour when the night staff came on duty and typewriters were at a premium; and also the hour when Diana Swift finished her "society" column, for often, when she had no other engagement, she would have dinner with me. The boys on the day staff, Adolph and Louis and the rest, were also supposed to be through work at that time—and, when they really were through and not finishing up some long yarn, they might come along and have dinner with me. I seldom dined alone when I worked on the *Tribune*—leaving out of account those nights, which sometimes happened, when I was too "broke" to dine at all. And on those nights it was not easy to borrow the price of a meal either, for by some diabolical turn of fate my nights that followed bad luck at the track were usually the nights just before payday. Most of us, however, had credit—at one time or another—at Gillotte's across the way from the office, and there never was a real necessity for going hungry, though I did in fact once in a while do so—as a sort of hair-shirt of discipline, perhaps a relic of New England conscience.

After dinner—which was usually over with around ten o'clock or eleven, depending upon whether it was a place like the restaurant Namur, which was expensive, or at one like Flo's, which was cheap, we would go up to Lipp's in the Saint-Germain Quarter and drink dark beer and gabble until half-past eleven or twelve in the morning. Several of "the boys" lived near there, and would discreetly "turn in." But I would walk up past Saint-Sulpice and the Luxembourg Gardens and the Rue Vavin to the Select—where *coupes* of champagne, gossip, Madame Select's account of the events of the day, Fernand's queries about the races, the antics of Bobby, the shame-faced dog, the spectacle of all that strange crowd of variegated nationalities and dubious sexes would entertain me until around three or even four in the morning. Then, perhaps, a fight would develop, or things would quiet down—usually the latter, and I would trundle off to bed.

To be awakened at noon sharp, take lunch—alone or with

friends, and, later on, of course, usually with Jim, when we went out to the track together—and then have faithful Bouboule meet me (or us) in his little car. Of course many days I went alone, either by train or bus or a shared taxi, but the routine in any case was about the same. And to be repeated over again each day—with no days off and no change, for (how many times have I repeated this!) there is racing *every* day in Paris. Much as I enjoyed what might be considered an irksome routine, I should sooner or later have found it impossible—had it not been for the entertainment I derived from the *Tribune*.

What a newspaper! And I use the exclamatory form half in amused wonderment that such a fourth-dimensional organization actually existed and, in some mysterious manner, functioned, and half in genuine affection for what has now become for me a vanished world. But comically unreal as that world seemed then, at least it was not nebulous—you knew certain things about it and could bank on them with something like assurance. You knew first that, whatever else happened, *somebody* would be certain *not* to show up for work because he was drunk, and that this extra burden would fall on the other members of the staff. (The "boss" would accept fantastic excuses for these absences simply because he had to; he had to reckon, as a steady performance, on two or three delinquencies a night, hence normally he was forced to keep the staff a trifle excessive, so to speak, if at the last moment there was to be no hitch in getting out the paper.) You knew, secondly, that *somebody* would be certain *to* show up because he was drunk. (Drunkenness affected "the boys" in one of two ways: First, either they were completely paralyzed and *had* to stay away, or they *wanted* to out of a kind of elementary shame; or, second, they were intoxicated just enough to be bold or defiant or stubborn in trying to do their work, when in reality they were helpless—sometimes they would go out to the toilet and fall asleep for hours.)

Hence a certain almost fixed proportion of the staff—about half of which proportion was useless to the "boss" because it was not there, and the other half because it *was*—were always a dead loss. Between those who were drunk in the office itself and those who were drunk, so to speak, in absente, the "boss" had a crippled staff with which to begin—and end. Sometimes, when the alcoholic wave was general—as it was the night of "The Great Fog" in Paris, for the boys seemed determined to be in one of their own that day—it was a sheer miracle that the paper came out at all.

Can you marvel—and I ought to add that the compositors, though intelligent enough, were *French,* hence often made innocent mistakes in following copy literally—that many errors, much more absurd than just typographical ones, often enlivened the pages of that noble sheet? To any shrewd American reader, the *Tribune* was his comic morning cocktail—and this, notwithstanding the fact, greatly to the credit of the home and London cable services, that we sometimes had scoops on news from the United States, and occasionally, too, a crackerjack local Paris story by one of the day boys, like Louis. (I modestly refrain from pointing out that my own racing stories not infrequently attracted "the favorable attention of our readers" —and certainly their general average of interest was much higher than those either in the *Herald* of the *Daily Mail.*) For you never knew your luck, when you picked up your morning *Tribune.* We had one charming story about the Prince of Wales battering out the brains of some schoolboy at a private institution in Saint-Cloud (this caused an awful—if temporary —scandal, and the two or three men responsible lost their jobs on account of it); we had stories that for sheer fantasy deserved a Pulitzer Prize for imaginative literature (the one about President Coolidge playing a trombone on the roof of the White House to welcome in the New Year was a "pip"); we had "suggestive" stories, obtained by leaving out—sometimes accidentally—important vowels (don't forget that the French compositors followed copy literally) in words like "Count" in describing what a man went down for in the eighth round, or by putting an unimportant consonant before a word like "hit," when speaking (otherwise calmly to all appearances) of a certain drama's appeal to the public. If my reader will let his own verbal imagination roam a bit—and if he will remember that our copy-reading was not too often double-checked, after French compositors had set up the stories—he will appreciate better what curious statements were sometimes boldly set down in black-and-white in the *Tribune.* Everybody who has ever worked on a newspaper knows how errors often, in the best regulated shops, creep into the first edition and are hastily rectified or taken out in the next or the final—but the *Tribune* had just one edition and one only. If a mistake got in, it remained in. As an other illustration, I remember a story from our correspondent in Cairo, informing us that Herr So-and-So (an important and well-known German industrialist) was stopping at a certain hotel, where he had taken an apartment with Madame So-and-So (the wife of a highly reputable French banker). This might seem like a new attempt at international amity, unless you looked closely at the original copy on "the stone"—and discovered that a whole line had been light-heartedly dropped out by the French compositors; the line that saved the honor of both parties.

But I think the best of our stories were those which were simply pure fabrications—hence innocent, for they harmed nobody, the names and places being fabricated as well as the stories themselves. Sometimes, out of sheer effrontery, it would almost seem, they were featured on the front page—to the great chagrin and confusion of our rival, the *Herald,* the editor of which never quite knew for certain whether these stories were "built up" out of a brief cable dispatch or simply made out of whole cloth. Such a story, for example, was one we put in a box—heavily leaded, too—on the front page. It began with a curious and imaginative date line—"Okokomino, Ind.,

Friday"—and the first sentence of this bit of "news" read as follows: "Mr. Lysander C. Chew, head of the local House of David, was today severely injured, when his beard was caught in the automatic wringer of a steam laundry, where he was working *incognito.*" For sheer and unadulterated absurdity that is an opening sentence difficult to beat.

If little flights of fancy like this were not enough to fill the front page of the paper at those critical times when news lagged and cables from home were scarce, we could fall back on several sources of supply: Paris local "opinion" stories on the political situation and French "reaction" towards American foreign policy, quoting mysteriously well informed but nameless "authorities," reinforced now and then by that Godsend to newspapermen, "The Man In The Street"; prohibition "repeats" of older stories on enforcement, simply bringing them up to date (the boys loved to write one of these and then rush down to Gillotte's for a strong drink); shameless Bull Dog stories (that is, stories cut out and pasted up from our many exchange newspapers, again changing places and dates to disguise the source); free translations—and how "free' they sometimes were!—of some interesting local murder or scandal from one of the many Paris newspapers; generous helpings from the big London dailies, without bothering to tell where these items came from; scientific discoveries, like a new cure for leprosy (for some mysterious reason this was a great favorite with the boys), culled from magazines or just plain invented; descriptive or travel bits cheerfully lifted out of folders and introduced with such casual flourishes as, "The inauguration of the new world-famous bridge here Thursday"—though of course no bridge had been opened, the city in question being miles away from any kind of water; but that was a minor detail—"gives special point to the statement of eminent scientists that more honey-bees are to be seen in this region than anywhere else in the temperate zone" (you think I exaggerate? you didn't know that paper); fancy-free accounts of the intelligent exploit of some dog or cat in a tiny village of Southern France, usually saving a whole family from death by fire or flood (to give the color of reality to these stories, it was usually solemnly stated at the end that the noble animal in question would undoubtedly be recommended for a medal to the French Humane Society); new "style notes," with semi-nudist implications; and, when all else failed, some story about the new regulations for drinking and café hours in the different quarters of Paris—a subject on which the boys were not only well informed but also highly critical and full of helpful suggestions. No, we never lacked for material for that front page—not while the imagination of man remained triumphant.

Remember, too, that we had standard features that were as good as (for they were identical with) those of the home paper—any smashing editorial we wanted (even if the boys, with fine tact, especially enjoyed reprinting the ones that slammed France); all the comics, particularly The Gumps, which we all loved; the sporting articles of Westbrook Pegler (a Heaven-sent gift to the not-too-active sports editor, "The Once All Over," as we insisted on calling him); first printing of society news, which was to be cabled to New York and Chicago, and of fashion-house openings, above all for women's wear; the long interpretive stories of the Foreign News Service, of which we had copies, of course; and, finally, any feature stories from our own home Sunday magazine edition.

Curiously enough, though, we had two features of our very Paris own, which in some ways were better than any we so cheerfully copied. (Again I omit my own racing stories, popular as they were, because they were a special, and, after all, a purely local, Paris thing.) And I am not speaking of the special Port and Steamship Editions, designed primarily to attract advertisers, nor of our own Sunday magazine features, of which we were inordinately proud—that is, the men who wrote the art, theatrical, and book special articles, such as they were, were proud of them (nobody else was). One of these two features was the sporting column, "The Once Over"—and this had faithful reporting of all the jokes, wisecracks just arrived from Broadway, gossip, and "dirt" of the bars where the sports and racing men (like myself, when I could afford it) assembled. The other was Adolph's Strong's column of highly general comment, on any subject he chose to write about, called—I gave him the name for it, remembering the title Maugham did *not* use for "Of Human Bondage"—that is, "Of Fleeting Things." That was a good title, and what is more, the column lived up to the title, for it covered any subject under the sun that attracted Mr. Strong's fantastic attention. But you didn't have to agree with Strong's general theses to enjoy the wit of some of these vindictive bits of satire or description—and, appropriately enough, the column stuck pretty rigorously to French subjects and French absurdities—and of the last Mr. Strong seemed to find plenty.

To put it bluntly, Strong's column was in one sense (even though its temper was quite in keeping with the high Never-Never-Land accent of that strangest of newspapers) much too good for the *Tribune*—and the best things in it were wasted on a wastrel Paris audience that to a melancholy extent had no deeper or keener intellectual interest than has anybody trying to recover from a hang-over. When a man of learning or perception chanced, now and then in just the normal turn of blind luck, to run across "Of Fleeting Things," his emotion was of pleased astonishment, coupled, as might be expected, with some curiosity about the author. So as another natural consequence, Strong was often meeting the really brilliant people who came to Paris—only, I regret to record, with the unhappy outcome of frequently offending them. For Strong, in addition to his brilliance and to a certain extent because of it and because of his consciousness that he possessed it, suffered from an acutely developed case of inferiority complex. His early social background in a small manufacturing town, where his people were not socially important and financially were on the ragged edge, his brilliant scholastic record at Harvard in the classics, and the experience every man, actually at the front as was Strong, had during the war—all nicely combined to give him a sort of feeling of conspiracy on the part of the world to thwart his power. Like all people so afflicted, he was seldom able to discriminate between those who were merely sodden, indifferent, or stupid and those who might, for one reason or another, have malice in their souls towards him. It was talismanic, his so often using the phrase, "an impartial and disinterested observer"—for an impartial and disinterested observer was precisely something which Strong was not. He was a brilliant, but a psychopathic, observer. Excellent and amusing as were sometimes his judgments, they were not the result of surveying the external evidence but of adroitly dressing up and prettifying and romanticizing internal compulsions. It was sometimes amazing—when you knew him as well as I did—to see how cleverly and how engagingly he could do just that. Always I found—and I think any sophisticated person would have found–his column remarkably attractive and interesting —I'll say this for it: Not in New York have I seen a better.

The physical setting of the paper was almost as remarkable and unusual as the paper itself. Both the *Herald*—then in its old building on the Rue du Louvre, near the Paris Central Post Office, and later, as today, in its new and much more pretentious building in the Champs-Elysées section on the Rue de Berri—and the *Daily Mail,* in its building on the Rue de Sentier, had their own "plants" and did their own printing. The *Tribune,* on the other hand, occupied part of a floor of the enormous building belonging to the *Petit Journal.* For the *Tribune* did not do its own printing, but made use of the printing plant of the *Petit Journal.* That is why the compositors were French, as I have said above—the proofreaders, of course, were American or English, but they were just like "the boys upstairs" (meaning the editorial staff), and would let stories get by with the same lack of any real feeling of responsibility which was displayed by those who wrote them.

Now the main entrance to the *Petit Journal* building was on the Rue Lafayette, just above Nôtre Dame De Lorette, and almost the entire lower floor was usually taken up with some sort of exposition or "fair" or even entertainment feature—only a small section being reserved for business purposes. (And there was a dance hall on the second floor, too, where readers of the paper gathered for *fêtes* of all kinds, which the paper was always organizing.) The small side entrance was on the Rue Trudaine, and *that* was the real entrance to the *Tribune* though sometimes the boys, when very late getting through, or when, as on Sundays, say, the outer door on the Rue Trudaine had been locked, would go through the downstairs offices of the *Petit Journal,* climb the back stairs past the *Petit Journal's* editorial and what we call city room, and go into the *Tribune* by the upper rear door.

This had the advantage for the boys of being a way to dodge creditors or girls—the lubricity of "The Once All Over" was famous, and often got him into trouble; one of his girls, a Corsican, came up with a dagger, for days at a time, determined to cut his heart out, while our brave sports editor crept timorously in and out the back way through the *Petit Journal*—creditors or girls, who might call and wait, of course in vain, in the small front office, which had its entrance on the Rue Trudaine. The paper was remarkable for members of the staff who did their work quite regularly, but who never (officially) were in the office—except to answer the telephone, as they would carefully say, "just before leaving."

Furthermore, some of the entertainment features, so called, on the ground floor of the *Petit Journal's* building had disastrous effects upon certain members of the staff—above all, the professional "faster" in a glass cage, who went through the stunt of consuming only water for I have forgotten how many incredible days (French people would come in and stand around the cage thoughtfully munching huge and succulent sandwiches); and the sea-lions, also in a glass cage, but this time filled with water, who so bestank the entire building that for days the only way to do any work in the *Tribune* office was by donning a gas mask. The moment the first "break" came—there was a more or less official one from 10.30 to 11.30 p. m., when for some reason cables usually lagged—the "boys" would dash over to Gillotte's and fortify themselves with *Calvados* or *fines*. Whenever they had to pass sea-lions, or a professional faster, or some other equally absurd show, they also had to take a few extra drinks to survive the shock—and to keep what they were pleased to call their minds on the job. The almost inevitable results may be imagined.

Beside the more or less "regular" members of the staff, whom I have already mentioned, there were many "in-and-out" stars. For example, there was Eugene Jolas (later well known for his magazine, *transition*); Elliot Paul (who also was on *transition* and had written two or three books; Paul was from Boston, like myself, but you would never have guessed it to look at him; Rosetti, a Rumanian by birth, but well known in Paris (our authority on foods, wines, and political intrigue); Kosputh, who knew Turkey well (in fact was married to a charming Turkish woman) and who did our "Embassy stuff" among other things; nor must I neglect Emily Craven—before Diana's day—our first society editor, who was likewise a real poetess, and, among other accomplishments, could set Mr. Strong's hard heart a-flutter. (Sometimes a trifle too disastrously, for when in his cups—that is to say, when he had gulped down 30 or 40 large glasses of Lipp's dark beer—Mr. Strong was not above giving the fair Emily a poke on the jaw.)

And then, too, there were the men on the Foreign News Service, like "Hank" Wales, "Robert" (our one valid French newspaperman), and Lansing Warren, who later was taken over by the New York *Times*. Occasionally our strange correspondents from Berlin and Rome—correspondents with whom the paper had varying degrees of luck—and our excellent one from

London would drop in to the office, when in Paris on a visit. And, of course, a celebration had to be organized at once. But "Hank"—who was affable and a good newspaperman, even if no intellectual giant—usually covered our big European news, outside of Paris: And for a naïve, charming, yet somehow revealing account of what Moscow was like then from a human point of view (his visit to Bill Haywood, the former I. W. W. leader, living then in a cold garret in Moscow, was a masterpiece of reporting), I recommend his stories of that trip, published in the Paris and the "home" paper, and, I believe, quite widely syndicated, though of the last statement I am not certain. They were *American* stories, too—I mean, they had the little revealing touches in them, which Duranty, who had a far better head on his shoulders, but who, after all, was English, simply could not get into his more formal and more comprehensive dispatches. In "Hank's" stories the natural questions of what people drank; how they amused themselves; mating and marriage (or lack of them) customs; whether you could really get warm or not; what prices actually meant in terms of American "jack"; the thoughts—if any—of streetcar conductors on Lenin; how the girls looked and the dresses they wore:—these were the burning questions he answered. Ask him about the Five-Year-Plan, and he would tell you what he got for breakfast and whether there was any warm water in the morning with which to shave. After the long and tiresome political stories from Russia, I know I for one welcomed "Hank's" home-spun descriptions of the little things that make life bearable—or not.

As if the ordinary routine of the office did not provide sufficient amusement (though routine is hardly the word; phantasmagoria would be a bit better), every year the boys organized a big dinner, beginning at three o'clock in the morning (so that everybody could come, with the paper safely and finally "put to bed"), at, usually, an ancient restaurant on the Left Bank near the river. But not in the restaurant itself—no, in a deep sub-cellar, huge in size which could only be reached by a long ladder. From this big sub-cellar tunnels led under the river, dating from the Middle Ages and before, to the Isle de la Cité and the Isle Saint-Louis. In the old days, it was the exit for all escaping from those two islands, when riots or murder or wars and alarums were afoot. How the food was ever served down that long ladder was as much a mystery as how the boys ever got up the ladder when the dinner was over. For those annual dinners were "stag," Anglo-Saxon debauches, of which every true American male has, at some time or other, dreamed. Dinners, I mean, where those dreams came true—all except any sexual side to them, I hasten to add, for they were strictly, entirely, and whole-heartedly alcoholic. Everybody got drunk sooner or later; several of the weaker-stomached "put their lunch" before the grey Paris morning came, and one lad had the happy notion of rolling and wallowing in it, like a Rabelaisian Gargantua in miniature; songs were sung and stories told that would have made even the liveliest and most highly-disapproved of passages of privy Homers appear tame and insipid; any pent-up repressions (difficult as such things may seem in Paris) came out joyously and happily. Amazingly, there were no fights—amazing, that is to say, when you consider that everybody was American, and that our tendency to fight when drunk is proverbial among the peoples of the earth. But I think the explanation was simple: Fights develop because people get drunk only up to a certain belligerent point; beyond that, give them a chance, and they wallow. We wallowed—and enjoyed it. Though I always marvelled, after these dinners, how there was anybody left to get out the paper the next day, somehow it did get out. But I know for myself, when, the next afternoons, I crawled to the races, once or twice I saw the horses flying over the grandstand like a flock of silly geese.

Dinners like these—and the farewell lunch to Mr. Strong, to give him a good send-off to Berlin, where, for a few weeks, he was our special (very special, I ought to add) correspondent

—emphasized the continued phantasy of the paper on what one might be pleased to term normal days. They made the more formal literary efforts of our staff seem a trifle inferior, in quality and excitement, to our own compositions (or rather, flights of unrestrained fancy) appearing day by day in the *Tribune* itself—routine pieces that had nothing of the routine characteristics about them, of course. But these more formal literary efforts—*transition,* in particular—were much better publicized, so to speak, back home in America. Both Jolas and Paul knew all the French Sur-realistes and their hangers-on of that time; both knew Joyce well (it may be recalled by some that his "Work In Progress" was first published in *transition*); no writer with any faint umbilical dissatisfactions—which he often mistook for philosophic protest against something or other—was turned away without a little dole of sympathy, not to mention an occasional 200 or 300 francs. Some of Mr. Strong's "Of Fleeting Things" columns were re-printed back in the home paper in Chicago, too—so that there, at least, the real flavor of the Paris Edition was partly recaptured. Yet I think, to have had an adequate idea of what that flavor was like, you had to spend at least a few months in Paris itself, and meet the "boys"—if you had the constitution and rugged individualism to stand it.

Like all newspapers, it is worth pointing out as well, we had plenty of men on the staff—by plenty, naturally, I refer rather, since we had a sort of elastic-band staff which expanded in good days and contracted in bad, to the constant comings and goings than to actual numbers—with literary ambitions, men whose hearts were really set on "making" the magazines back home. But if their hearts were set on it, their wills were often feeble and their abilities hardly of a kind to justify their hopes. All newspaper offices are to a certain extent the graveyards of vaulting literary ambitions that have o'erleaped themselves, but at least back home one is likely soon to learn whether the ambition has any justification—and to reconcile oneself accordingly. Or, in the rare cases where the ambitions are justified, to "get out of the game"—as, for instance, did Hemingway. But in Paris men could delude themselves for a longer time—perhaps the pathos of distance, I don't know—and believe that soon recognition would come. In Paris, also, the American will (at least the American will-to-work) is enfeebled, and many a man, who, had he remained at home and worked hard with what special capacity he had, would have made a modest second-rate success, suffered just a sufficient sea-change to let the will, competent in the home environment to generate some activity, relapse into mere wishing and dreaming. It was tragedy, when you looked below the surface—sometimes the ageless tragedy of intrinsic imcompetence; sometimes the moral tragedy of failing to find any compelling incentive; sometimes both together.

There was something else, too, even more difficult to put one's finger on: The arrogance of being an American. This may seem a strange way of expressing it to the Cleveland or Detroit High School English teachers, who then were reading in their little and precious reviews about the "new" literary movements in Paris, which our own bright young expatriates were assimilating and even surpassing in originality, or—reading in their more conservative magazines—about the Da-daist, anti-intellectual, and violently revolutionary prose style experiments of these Parisian Columbuses of the dark continents of the co-conscious and sub-conscious—not to mention, unconscious. But the sad truth is that these great literary discoverers of new forms were only Americans after all, that is to say, belligerent when crossed—just as we are the easiest people in the world to get along with, when things are going our way. When first Cowley, then Macalmon, then others got into violent fisticuff encounters, or became screaming and loud, or, when ignored, even insulting to the French "bourgeois" who did not even know who they were or what they stood for, let alone had done them any harm—when all this happened, they were not fighting the great literary battle they imagined. They were trying, in a war-weary and cynical Paris, which already had had some experience with the run-of-the-mill kind of American soldier during the war, to impress upon a people, who didn't even care if it was true, that Americans were as up-to-date in literary fashions and absurdities as were the French themselves, if not more so. It was like the old paradox of the American riding around Paris for hours looking for something to compare with the home Flatiron Building or one of the latest gadgets that the French might happen to lack. In the old days, our youngsters used to come to Paris looking for culture; I suppose it was a mark of something or other in intellectual progress that at that time they came over looking for trouble. It was a strange form of New Nationalism, which I deliberately put in capitals just to annoy them—for afterwards, when they got home, they couldn't get on the Russian bandwagon fast enough. Impolite and aggressive Americans abroad, they became European and Russian yearners when they got back home—I wondered then, if there was not a certain connection between these two phenomena; if, in fact, they were not really two aspects of the same thing.

Remember as well that life really was pleasanter in France during many of those years—think of somebody so through-and-through American as Frank Ward O'Malley "retiring" to the Chateau Country in France, and, indeed, later on when I had arrived back home, dying there. There were not an inconsiderable number of those who, when they said they wanted freedom, would have hit a little closer to the truth, had they merely said they wanted a decent alcoholic drink that would not digestively kill, maim, or blind them. A lot of people need no encouragement to talk about the evils of oppressive stupidity and intolerance, when all they really want is the freedom to be irresponsible. (I know; I have done it myself, and I know the dangers.) The soft veil of the 19th century Murger "Bohemian" tradition had not been wholly rent by the shells of the war, and at times in Montparnasse you could have sworn you were only in a transplanted Greenwich Village of the 1912-16 pre-war epoch, except for the fact the some people still stubbornly persisted in talking French. Indeed, the measure of reality of this literary "revolt" was almost in exact proportion to the competent knowledge of the French language and history displayed by its standard-bearers—that is to say, nil. The people who really did know and care something about these last two subjects were in French universities and studying as exchange or scholarship students or Guggenheim fellows: They were interested in Montparnasse about as much, and for the same reason, as they might be interested in a brothel. (This was a mistake, but I for one found it a much more amiable one than the mistake of the idealizers, who saw a modern Villon in a cheap Quarter pimp or a literary "movement" in what was only untempered emotionalism overcoming weak judgment.)

In a chapter with this title I suppose some mention is naturally expected of a few magazines in the English language then, or a bit later, appearing in Paris—like Ford's *Transatlantic Review,* Titus's *This Quarter,* and William Bird's "The Three Mountains Press." (Not forgetting Mr. Macalmon's rather elaborately printed works, paid for by himself—or Mrs. Crosby's publications.) But a mention is all that is needed, for already these publications seem far away and remote—even the later "Story" (which was not Parisian at all) of Martha Foley and Whit Burnett. That James Joyce lived in Paris was, of course, more or less accidental (it was as remote as possible from Ezra Pound's highly self-conscious exile from Kansas)—at all events, it was so for American believers, so to speak, to whom he often has meant more as an influence than as an author in his own right. That Sinclair Lewis or Sherwood Anderson visited Paris meant very little, for they were visitors and nothing else. And many who did serious writing, like Glenway Wescott or Julian Green, for example, who *did* live in France for a time, were not part of this self-conscious and self-assured brotherhood of Montparnasse, except incidentally and *en passant*.

Hemingway, of course, got his start with the books he called "In Our Time" and "The Sun Also Rises," both of which were largely written in Paris—in fact, the first I sold for him myself, when I came to America, as I explain elsewhere. But Hemingway was no more Latin, basically, than was Ring Lardner. Nor was Gertrude Stein either, though she was a Paris institution . . . but as she has written an entire book about that herself, I see no need here to go into details about a career that has received a degree of attention not quite commensurate with its importance (in both the good and bad senses). Leo Stein, her brother, wrote an interesting, if somewhat difficult, book on aesthetics; however, I question that it has had much more influence, than it had slight attention.

For readers of a man I regard as possessing one of the keenest and most sensitive minds of our day—George Santayana—it is interesting to note that on his frequent trips to Paris in the old days he could more often be found at a plain commercial hotel in the Place de la Republique than at any of the cafés in the Quarter (if you are willing—as I am—to except the *Deux Magots*, which was conveniently near the home of an old Harvard philosophy friend of his, Professor Strong.) As far as the "literary" crowd went—the "literary" crowd with which this chapter is concerned—he was almost an unknown person, as most assuredly he was an un-read one, as their styles sometimes make one painfully aware. (Except for particular English authors, whom I knew and liked, such as Ronald Firbank and Ogden, of "The History of Civilization" fame, and Sullivan, the mathematician, I have kept to American writers arbitrarily in my generalizations in this chapter, just to avoid confusion. Paris is an old story to English writers from Lawrence Sterne down to Dickens and Arnold Bennett and the present day.)

During my first years in Paris I don't think I reflected much on the so-called expatriate problem, especially with respect to American writers. I was interested in what Van Wyck Brooks thought of the effect of England on Henry James, of course, and, too, the influence of Paris and France was unquestionable. But it always impressed me as an irrelevant thing. Simply, I am trying to say, an imaginative writer's problems (critical as well as "creative") are so essentially and forever internal that I for my part have never thought of outer circumstances—whether of color, race, time in history, or even language—as anything but incidental and accidental. It is the *spiritual* struggle every writer—every real writer, of course—has to go through: It does not much matter, when he comes to go through with that struggle, where he is or even what language he speaks—and certainly not terribly much what the economic system is under which he lives and writes at all.

This may be modern heresy. But I don't care. I am sick to death of hearing every explanation given of a writer except the true one: His genius as a master of expression; his imaginative sympathy and insight as a man.

XVII. WINNING DAYS

TO EVERYBODY who follows the races regularly for any length of time there come, I am certain, winning days—and I make it plural, for every gambler knows that there are inexplicable "runs" of good luck, exactly as there are those of bad luck. There is no way of telling—ah, if there only were!—when a "run" is going to begin, or, which is more disconcerting, when it is going to end. The successful gambler has a kind of intuition about this, and plays very strong or weak accordingly. It is not, I hasten to point out, a question either of his knowledge or of his judgment. You will hear a man say at the track, after you argue with him about a horse, "Yes, I know it's the form horse; he ought to win; I see nothing to beat him. His price is good, too. But I'm not going to play him. I'm laying off the race. My luck is 'out' right now."

Nor will it much matter to him whether the horse in question wins or not in fact. For if he wins, after all he did so without the gambler's support, and nothing will convince the true plunger that, *had* he bet on him, the horse would not have lost. His bet is what would have made the difference; his bet—don't laugh—would goad the horse to lose, and if no other way was possible, by accident. Hence it is not deception at all when a gambler will often advise *you* to go heavy on a horse—and not bet a cent himself. *Your* luck is in; *his* is out. And you will even hear him say, after the race, "Glad I laid off that, old man, and gave you a chance to win." And he believes it, too. Sometimes—almost—so do I.

"Winning Days" I have called this chapter—and so they were. But they were winning days in more than a gambling sense; they were days of what then seemed secure friendship and happy plans with Jim, as I have already mentioned towards the end of the racing and trotting chapter. For we had had our days of good luck, of judgment confirmed, of taking chances—and winning. My mood was one of confidence in the future, for almost the first time in years: To understand it, perhaps, a few episodes of previous smiling fortune will contribute. And most of these episodes are associated with Jim. For instance:

One day towards the end of March (in the spring before the Deauville trip) I came up to Jim's apartment for dinner late, after finishing my work at the office and duly giving my tips for the next day. Dolly had gone to a concert, and after the usual excellent dinner, Jim and I sat before the open fire talking horses and sipping—Jim, a brandy; myself, that "filthy sweetish liquor," as he used to call it, a *vieille cure*. Jim was busy studying Paris *Sport,* while I was reading an account of Fouchardière's inimitable and preposterous character, *Le Bouif,* at the snail races he had organized in Brittany.

Suddenly Jim looked up and asked, "Harold, do you remember that ancient mare we bet on in the handicap one of the last days of Longchamp in the fall?"

"Oh," I said, "you mean Belle of Zante? That name has stuck—and she ran a great race, too, for an old lady of her age, even if she only came in third. What about her? Is she dead? She was twelve or thirteen then."

"Dead, hell," said Jim. "Some owner I don't know has bought her and has evidently been training her all winter. By God, here she is down to run at Auteuil next week over the hurdles." He smiled; "Her *début en obstacles,* if you please."

I reflected a bit on this information, then said: "Why damn it all, that's like asking your grandmother to compete in a hundred-yard hurdle event. I never heard of such a thing."

Neither had I. Neither had Jim. But from that moment both of us knew that we were going to bet on Belle of Zante in that coming race. The conversation shifted then—as it often did when we reached a kind of unspoken agreement about our turf enterprises—to other topics, such as women and their duplicity, their unexpectedness, their (to us) reluctant charm. But it ended with no conclusion, either startling or pessimistic, except, possibly, Jim seemed a trifle harsh—in fact, so harsh that I almost suspected him of that curious male jealousy every man has towards the woman one of his close friends seems temporarily enamoured of—about Diana, my co-worker on the paper, or as the humorous sly Frenchman, M. Benoit, called her with a suggestion of other things than the word itself connoted—"*votre collaboratrice.*" And then Jim regaled me with a long account of the batting prowess of the Yankees, the skill of Cochet, the new (at that time) football invincibility of the Western colleges—and how to play squash, a game, to my horror, he was determined I should learn, for it would take off my "light beer and wine weight," as he called it. I countered feebly by saying I should learn squash, if he would study his damn psychology—he had bought, at my instigation, both the large two volumes of James's "Psychology" and Graham Wallas's "The Great Society," and was valiantly reading them. With pleasure, too, I ought to add.

About half-past ten or eleven the conversation lagged. We had talked everything over; there were no more secrets between us; there was no more mystery in the world. I had even heard enough of "Show Boat" on the phonograph for one evening.

"I'll take you home," said Jim as if it were an original idea, "and we can stop at the Select for a nightcap."

"Fine," I said.

For like every fundamentally lonely person—that is, perhaps, like every person who has had no genuine family life—I really hate being alone at any time. I should live in a club. Just as, even today, I like to write in a newspaper office with the rattle of typewriters and the comings and goings of different men of the staff and visitors a kind of obligato to composition. I don't really hear what is going on; I mean, I don't discriminate and pay attention—it is rather a soothing sense of being plunged into activity, which swirls all around me, yet leaves me miraculously free. And I sometimes think this is the reason old-fashioned newspaper men find it so difficult to do any "outside" work. They lack the stimulation, false or real, of the city room. Writing alone seems at times almost like what used to be called a "solitary vice."

We got on our coats and went over to the "Select" in a taxicab, for it was late and too much trouble to walk to the garage, where Jim's own car, the trick Talbot, was parked. Besides, even with double rates at night (after eleven in my day) taxicabs were still ridiculously cheap in Paris—the price of a single drink would get us to the café.

As usual, the "Select" was a seething mad-house of drunks, semi-drunks, quarter drunks, and sober maniacs (most of whom were "on the wagon" only temporarily, of course, because of unkind medical favors of the fickle goddess, Venus)—Scandinavians (the loudest, usually), Americans (second in volume of sound), English (men, women, and fairies, mostly the latter), a scattering of Russian men and German women—*émigrés* for different reasons—and quite a few French people, who were amused and looked almost out of place. Yet French or English were almost the only languages heard—when you could hear anything at all, for the hubub was tremendous.

Fernand made a place for us at the end of the bar. Jim was a good spender; I was one of the oldest clients. He was glad to see us both—and unaffectedly so, too, for at all events here were two customers who would neither start nor get into a fight. Fernand had worked in clubs and hotels in London after the war, and as a consequence spoke English almost perfectly.

But like all real Frenchmen who are bi-lingual, he conversed with you in French—unless you specifically asked him not to. And when you got "stuck" for an expression, he sometimes would give you the correct French phrase and its slang equivalent—even, on occasion, its *argot* equivalent, if it had any. That is to say, Fernand had what all Frenchmen of any dignity always have—pride in his own language. I hate those fawning, sycophantic waiters in many of the stylish French hotels and Casinos, who—after you ask them a question in French, with perhaps an accent or an inflection wrong, or with some slight hesitation—will answer you in English. Invariably it made me feel uncomfortable; I always imagined that somehow I had erred in the address and had got into a whore-house by mistake, where such lingual consideration is understandable—if not exactly flattering to Anglo-Saxon moralistic pretensions.

It is easy to tell a polite Frenchman, for when you speak with a noticeable accent, he will slow up his speech, enunciate very clearly, use the simplest and most direct expressions. In other words, he will cooperate with you in your attempt to speak his own language, quite aside from the elementary courtesy of trying to make you feel at your ease. Indeed, one reason Americans in Paris speak French so badly is that too many Frenchmen—and the better class they are, the more likely they are to do it—will hesitate to correct you outright, though often they will repeat your phrase with just the difference that makes it French, so that any American with a good ear who *wants* to learn French in Paris can hardly avoid doing so. I learned French—and correct French—but my accent was never good, though I avoided the most grotesque mistakes in inflection and vowel stresses, learning finally to give all of them relatively the same value; I practiced saying "Auteuil" and discriminating between the "r" sounds in *"couru,"* for instance, *"sur,"* and *"rue"* until I had lost my self-consciousness about them. But the truth is, though I spoke French fluently after a time, I never spoke it with a natural accent—race-track *argot* possibly aside. For I learned it—to speak, I mean—too late; one should learn to speak French before one's adolescence. German we learn much more quickly, despite its grammatical and other difficulties. The average American college sophomore, I think, *reads* French fluently, but speaks it abominably; he reads German with some trouble, but *speaks* it with comparatively little accent. This seems to me quite natural—we are more Anglo-Saxon—more Germanic, if you will—than we are Latin. And you don't really appreciate how much we are until you live—and work—a few years in Paris.

"A Scotch and soda for me, Fernand—Haig and Haig," said Jim. "And for you, Harold, I suppose one of your *coupes* of champagne. Shall we roll?"

I nodded, for this was a formality. Fernand brought us the box with the dice, and to my relief I went out on two straight rolls, for Scotch and soda was 15 francs, and with my drink, which was 6, there would have gone 21 francs, or practically a dollar. But when Jim won, he always insisted on rolling for the next, and the next—until, finally *you* won. In other words, he wanted you to feel the formality of equality. But when you won, all the drinks—and cigarettes and food, in case we became hungry, were "on" him from that time. In effect, this meant that practically all the bar parties were "on" Jim, willy-nilly, and when other people joined us, he would insist on buying, too, saying he had "no luck" with the dice. This generous consideration for the other fellow keeping his self-respect was an extraordinary trait in a young and wealthy man. The "sponge" never had much of a chance with Jim, but the honestly hard-up fellow was always made to feel at his ease and—something French people were quick to notice and to admire—on an equal footing.

"There are more of them here than usual," said Jim with an appraising look around the café, "the ladies with the lack of a certain virtue."

"Look at the calendar, Jim," I said cynically. "This is the

night of the 15th, or morning of the 16th, rather. This afternoon was pay-day in both senses. Salaried people are paid on this day, exactly as I got my joke 250 francs from the paper tonight—minus the 40 francs I borrowed on it last week, like all the other boys at the office. Some of them didn't get anything at all this afternoon; they already owed it all."

This was true, but it always surprised Jim. He couldn't seem to realize, any more than other people who always had had money, how some people live quite literally, in Mr. Strong's inelegant phrase, on the "skin of the wind."

"And bills are paid on this date, too," I went on. "Notice the relieved look on Madame Select's face—she probably has been paying out for bills since she got up at noon, and I saw Monsieur Select shelling out this morning before I went out to the track. Tonight is holiday. The agony of forking over good money—and it is agony to many Frenchmen of the small commercial class—is through with for another fortnight. No more *factures*."

"But what's that got to do with the girls?" asked Jim, almost naïvely.

"Simpleton," I replied. "When a lot of people have been paying out money, there are at least a few people who have been paid. This is the night of nights for many a petty tradesman and small landlord. They are relatively flush. And that's why the girls are here—not for any ulterior motive, you understand, they just like to see everybody enjoying themselves and having a good time."

"Oh, it's that kind of a horse, eh?"—Jim was in good humor. And he always enjoyed twitting me about my pathetic virtue. "You are the only person I know," he used to say, "who never brought any Bostonian sexual coals to Newcastle, that is, to Paris. You can't be a New Englander—where's your desire under the elms?"

"Speaking of horses, Jim, don't forget Belle of Zante."

"Forget her? Not likely. Haven't we been waiting for her

all winter?"

"Yes—without knowing it," I grinned.

"She's a fine horse, just the same," agreed Jim.

"A fine mare—a noble mare," I replied. "I hope to God she's learned how to jump. Of course it will only be a hurdle race, her *début,* but it's a long race for a starter in her new career. I wonder they have the nerve to do it. I should have thought they would have started her at Enghien."

"Maybe she's an Autueil horse, Harold."

"Perhaps. But how can they know in advance? It's odd, isn't it? Some horses simply can't stand Enghien—and some just make an exhibition of themselves at Auteuil. There's temperament for you."

Just then a plate crashed against the wall, back of us in the farther end of the café.

"And here's some more temperament," observed Jim.

Madame Select was up on the rungs of her chair. "Monsieur Paul, Monsieur Paul," imploringly (Mons. Paul was the director), *"Attention là-bas."*

Neither Jim nor I turned round. Fights were quite common in those days at the "Select" and we considered it bad form to get involved in them. Besides, Madame Select was an active, a courageous, and a determined woman; usually she herself could handle any situation that arose. (With Mons. Paul's assistance of a deprecatory *"Mais non, Monsieur,"* or *"Madame,"* or—if he wanted to be nasty and imply that a woman was no more than she should be—*"Mademoiselle."*)

Indeed, I recall seeing her once, unassisted, push out the door a tremendous six-foot four Russian, who had looked on the vodka when it was white and who had the amiable idea of killing all Bolshevist sympathizers at their first appearance. If things got bad, as occasionally they did (and by "bad" I mean something very closely resembling a riot), then Madame Select would send for the cops, *"les agents."* And, with their capes perfectly poised and their expressions those of grim politeness, the way they would hustle out an obstreperous client was a sight for sore eyes. What they did to the said client on the way to the *dépot* was something not so pleasant—but after all, I had lived in New York in the days before Gaynor was Mayor and had seen my fellow-citizens beaten up a-plenty. And I didn't need any explanation of what to *"passer au tabac"* at the station-house meant, either; no reporter of the old days who had to visit a morning Court, which disposed of the petty drunk and disorderly cases of the night before, needed a diagram to know how some of those precious "shiners" and bandaged noses were acquired. As Nina used to sing at the "Dingo":

"It's the same, the whole world over—
It's the poor what gets the bloime;
It's the rich what gets the honor—
Ain't it all a bleedin' shoime?"

But this time Madame Select did not have to descend from her throne and enter into the combat. Mons. Paul was escorting a pretty young lady to the door, while she was not at all reluctant to let the whole world know about her grievance—"Elle m'a insulté, suis pas une grue, moi!"

"I should hope not," I said to Jim. "There are over a hundred different words for 'whore' in French, and sometimes there are fine distinctions between what two of them mean. But *'grue'* is about the lowest term of all. Compared with *'grue'* what in my college days we called a 'two-dollar-whore' is a lady."

"Not a bad looking gal, though," said Jim gallantly. He was always gallant.

"But she doesn't look half so swell as Belle of Zante will look next week, if she gets across that finish line first," I reminded him.

"Well, here's to the old mare," said Jim lifting his glass. "I wish her luck."

And then we called it a night, Jim returning to his regal

apartment by taxi, and I walking up the few steps of the Rue Delambre to my narrow hotel room, which had just enough space in it to contain, besides the bed and a washstand, a small table with my old portable typewriter covering almost the whole top, and a couple of chairs on which were piled hundreds of back copies of *La Veine* and *Paris Sport*. A regular French-English dictionary, an *argot* dictionary, a few copies of my own paper, the Chicago *Tribune,* and of the *Daily Mail* and the New York *Herald,* as well as scores of *Le Figaro* and *Le Petit Parisien*—whose racing prognosticator I admired, and justly admired—completed the weird reading matter in my room.

I recall I was busy that week-end, and Jim had to go out of town for some reason or other. But the night before the scheduled race I called him up from the office. "It's all right, Jim," I said. "She's down to run tomorrow, according to the entries. There'll be a big field competing with her—just to make the price good, if she wins. And I notice none of the evening papers give her for tomorrow, not even as an outsider. I imagine I shall be the only one out of the bunch to have that honor."

"Fine," said Jim over the telephone. "I'll go down to the bank in the morning and get plenty of jack. Come up for lunch; Auteuil's just around the corner anyway. Bouboule can take us out, if you want. It's too much trouble to park my car at Auteuil anyway."

After work and a light dinner at Flo's with Strong, who was in an amiable mood of beer-drinking that evening, amusing me with tales of the moronic Freshmen he had had to teach at the University of Wisconsin—or rather, had had to try to teach—I wandered up to the Quarter and asked some of my scouts to keep a weather-eye out for Bouboule, who always had a few mysterious *"courses"* to perform every evening. He showed up about quarter past two in the morning, after my twelfth *coupe* of champagne—two of which I had won from Madame Select rolling dice with me. (This was a great honor, especially as her victories were dubious, even when she won, for I always charged my drinks from day to day—something quite against French law, too. I understand—and she would pile my saucers on a shelf at the end of the bar, sometimes until they almost touched the ceiling and represented 150 to 200 francs worth of credit—a painful visual reminder of my penury every time I came in. I "settled," of course, whenever fortune smiled at the track—as she was quite well aware.)

Bouboule bought me a nightcap, discussed the scandals of the day, swore he would have a little on Belle of Zante himself, and drove me home around the corner, saying he would come and wake me at *"Midi moins quart"* without fail.

Which he did. And there were more stories and more scandal while I was shaving and dressing. Then we drove out by the Avenue de la Bourdonnais, over the river, and to Jim's house just this side of the Trocadéro. Bouboule left me at the house and drove off for his own lunch, saying he would blow his horn outside the window promptly at 20 minutes to two o'clock so that we should arrive at the track in ample time "not to miss the first," which all French sportsmen, for some reason, regard as a great calamity—irrespective of whether or not they are going to bet on it, as in fact, they usually are not, since the first race at almost all French tracks is either a claiming-plate affair or a selling race—both notorious deceptions for the "form" follower. But it is a tradition, nevertheless, that you must arrive in time to see it. Otherwise your day is ruined, and everything will go wrong.

At lunch Dolly was so impressed at our confidence that she asked Jim to put a few hundred francs on Belle of Zante for her—something she rarely did. So rarely, in fact, that Jim was honestly surprised, even—not to forget old Dr. Johnson's distinction—astonished. Dolly had gone with us to the races two or three times on the "big" days, when it was obvious that her interest was chiefly on "who" was there, what they wore, and how much they bet—particularly if they lost, for Dolly, like so many American women of her class and position at that time, regarded big racing losses as just another form of what Mr. Veblen once called "conspicuous display," something like an ermine coat. I doubt if she ever looked—at least attentively—at any one single race, and she had no natural love for horses—something not true, I ought to add, of many sportswomen I have known. When Jim and I used to talk of Uranie and, in spite of ourselves, a note of affection would creep into our voices, Dolly would always look at us atonished, and I really believe that at times she thought we were talking about some girl, using a private code language to keep the facts to ourselves.

Right on the dot of 20 minutes to two o'clock Jim who had sharper ears than I said, "There's Bouboule now." Bouboule hadn't had to whistle at all; Jim had been able to distinguish the sound of Bouboule's famous little *torpédo,* coming up the hill from the Trocadéro "on high."

"Good luck to you low gamblers," said Dolly cheerfully, as we put on our coats."

"We'll be back for a cocktail, win or lose, right after the last race—about five-thirty or so," said Jim.

When we got on the street, I couldn't help laughing, for Bouboule had his noisy fox terrier (he must have gone way back to the Quarter for that wretched but lovable animal) on the front seat beside him—a dog that made a specialty of barking his head off at every *agent* he saw, and we always saw plenty, particularly right at the entrance to the track itself, so that anyone within a couple of hundred yards' earshot could always tell when Jim and I were entering the paddock.

In my day it was only 40 francs (around $2.00 then) to get into the paddock, but this was theoretical to me anyway, as I always had my racing press card—being France, with my photograph affixed—and usually, too, I had an invitation or two (the different French racing societies were very generous in this respect to accredited racing editors), so that for the most part Jim didn't have to pay to get in. Ridiculous as it may seem, he always took this like a sacred obligation he must repay—unmindful of the fact that he was always risking large amounts in betting for me, which by some generosity of Jesuitical reasoning he regarded as an operation quite independent of anything else—by buying the expensive drinks that the track furnished at either out-door bar, or the in-door bar and restaurant, inside the two grandstands.

Once within the gates, Jim bought his program, which at all French tracks is conventionally one franc—but here again he always was made to feel a curious sort of Freudian inferiority, for mine was given to me free, if I took the trouble to walk to the *salon de la press,* which I always did the first thing—partly out of courtesy, to say *Bon-jour* to my French colleagues, a few of whom I liked and all of whom I had known for at least three or four years, and partly to get my program, *gratuite.* I marked my card, as we call it, noting the scratches for the first race—a dull claiming-plate affair of the hurdle variety, with only 8 horses competing—and rejoined Jim outside.

"Let's have a drink at the suicides' bar"—as he called the rather dark, ill-lighted one in the grandstand at the extreme right of the paddock, next to the pavilion. "Maybe Rex and his housekeeper are there." (Rex was a charming Englishman, who went almost every day to the races—Enghien and Vincennes excepted—accompanied always by his housekeeper, a sturdy good-natured French woman, who seldom bet more than 30 or 40 francs on a race—which Rex gave her solemnly—and never by any chance on a horse that was not an outsider, the more an outsider the better. Favorites bored her.)

"Right you are," I said. "Besides, we're not betting on this fool's paradise curtain-raiser. We've done *our* duty, if we even look at the race."

Rex, immaculately dressed, as usual, but not flashily like a tout, was standing alone at the bar, having what he euphemistically called a "quick one" before the "old lady"—meaning his housekeeper—came back from buying her Pari-Mutuel tickets on the curtain-raiser, because she always made him cut down on his drinking. How many he had had before we joined him I don't know, but it must have been plenty, for he was clearly in a fog, though the soul of politeness, as usual.

"What will you have gentlemen?" he asked amiably. "The drinks here at Deauville are all rotten. Better stick to whisky."

"My God"—this to me from Jim sotto voce—"he's only about eight months off. He thinks he's still in Normandy."

My voice was clear and firm: "I'll take a glass of champagne anyway. But my friend Jim here will be glad to join you in a whisky. And by the way, Rex, I hate to mention it, but we are at Auteuil and this is March—we are *not* at Deauville, and this is *not* the month of August."

"Quite so, quite so," said Rex imperturbably. "Glad you reminded me. Here's luck."

Though ordinarily Jim and I asked Rex one or two questions about what he thought was good for the day—and Rex's judgment on horses, drunk or sober, was so fine that it was worth consideration—by tacit agreement, since Rex was this time so early in the afternoon already in the fourth dimension, we made the conversation as general, vague, and as Lewis Carroll-like as possible. Just before the bell rang, telling us the horses were off, the housekeeper come running up to us, and with a reproachful look at Rex (though it was brief, for of course she expected nothing else), showed us seven 10 franc tickets to win on horse number 14, which, according to the last yellow odds-sheet, which she also had in her hand, was the nearest approach to an outsider in the race—12 to 1 against.

After the bell rang, letting us know the horses were off, though the "old lady" dashed out to the front of the stand at once, for at least a full minute we continued our drinking, with a fine indifference to a cheap claiming-plate. The horses—seven of them, for one had fallen somewhere early in the race on the other side of the track—came swinging into the straight, with but two low hurdle jumps (yet how often I had seen tired horses fall at the last of these!) before the short run-in to the finish. All got over the first, but one horse went down at the second of them—the last jump of the race, and the bitterest fall of all—and as the six remaining on their feet came straggling up to the finish-line, it was easy to pick out the colors: *My* horse was winning easily (I always called the horse I gave to win in the paper "my" horse, irrespective of whether or not I bet on him, and for my racing honor I am glad to say that it was very, very seldom I bet against myself, that is, on some other horse, and then only when I found out something at the track I had not known the night before, when I gave my tips), and the "old lady's" outsider was a fair second, a couple of lengths behind, with the other five puffing and blowing in at different lengths.

"C'est dommage, Madame," I said politely to the housekeeper. *"Vous auriez dû gagner."*

"Alors, Monsieur," she came back smiling, *"mais je l'ai joué placé aussi"*—and triumphantly held up some "place" tickets on her outsider. As he was bound to pay at least even money for "place," though she hadn't won much—she hadn't lost either. She had, as the French express it, "defended" herself. I offered her *"mes felicitations"*—and with good grace, too, for the "old lady" was a remarkably shrewd picker of outsiders. I was always pleased when I found my own outsider coincided with hers—and Rex, too, I noticed, never made fun of her choices, no matter how wild they might appear. Experience had too often proved her mysteriously right."

So without any more ado, I asked her what she thought of Belle of Zante in the long hurdle race, and from the way her eyes brightened I knew at once that she regarded Belle as a specially succulent outsider. She was interested—because of the possible price—and dubious—because that is the only thing any normal turf follower can be regarding an old horse (and a mare at that) in a new and particularly difficult kind of race.

She said she had heard very favorable rumors from the training quarters regarding Belle's jumping ability and her liking for her new *métier;* about Belle's burst of speed—what the French call *pointe de vitessé*—there could be little doubt. Had we not seen it for ourselves at Longchamp that last fall. Anyway, Belle was an attractive *"tocard"* (outsider). We should see.

As a matter of fact, this was all the encouragement I needed; I had only wanted her not to say the choice was absurd —and she hadn't.

Jim and I left the bewildered Rex in her care, and went over to the outdoor bar, back of which the horses used to walk around when they had been saddled for the coming race.

"This," I remarked, "is a good race of its kind, but I regard it as an open-and-shut proposition. Barring accidents, the favorite will win."

"Will the 'old lady' be on it?" Jim asked smiling.

"No, she won't. But what's more important, she won't be betting on this race. She's waiting, like us, for Belle of Zante."

"My God, we're ruined, if *she* bets on her," Jim exclaimed.

"On the contrary, Jim, for once we stand a good chance from that point of view. It's been many a long week since she's had a big outsider to crow about to Rex. It's about time for her to crash through again. When she backed 'Les Rameaux' at those record odds at Maisons-Laffitte, it gave her something to talk about for months. She's about due for another 'I told you so.' Remember Rex, like most Englishmen, is rather conservative in his betting—that is, when he is sober enough to get a bet down."

"I s'pose so," said Jim. Then suddenly. "Look, Harold. *There's* a fine horse. Whose is it?" And we both looked at our cards. "Have A Drink"—and in English, too, just like that—proved to be his name; his owner was a well known French sportsman.

"We ought to bet on him, if only out of respect for his

name," said Jim.

"In spite of the fact I gave him as my first choice in the paper today for this race?"—This, of course, was that self-depreciation which Dr. Johnson called an oblique form of self-praise.

"Even with that against him," Jim agreed.

"All right," I said. "Give him a play. It's an odd name, but he's the favorite—and rightly so, I think. Not an overwhelming favorite, mind you. Oh, maybe 4 to 1."

So Jim marched over to the 500 franc booth and bought two tickets on "Have A Drink" to win. We both observed that only three other tickets had been bought on him before our purchase at that particular booth—"probably the trainer's own sentimental bet," observed Jim with a quizzical look at me.

"Stable connections seldom bet at the big booths in a race like this," I commented coldly. And as Jim was buying his two tickets I glanced at the yellow odds slip August had handed me, with some ribald remark to the effect that it was a grand day for the ladies of bent virtue to make money but a difficult one for honest sportsmen—by a complimentary grin including me in that rare category. I contented myself with saying that all days were like that, and August went off bellowing "Dernière côte jaune, dernière." As I suspected, the odds were 3½ to 1—evidently the stable connections were betting, or it was thought they would bet at the smaller booths at the last moment. And that was true. They did bet, and heavy. August was shrewd.

For "Have A Drink" won without the slightest difficulty, and, after a very short wait, the price went up 46 francs for every 10 bet to win. So "we"—for Jim and I always talked that way, and naturally, too, as old racetrack companions invariably will—had won 3,600 francs clear, or about $140.

"Now," remarked Jim, "we can go and buy Rex a drink, if he hasn't fallen down, and bet on Belle with a clear conscience—I mean, with their money as much as with our own.

'Have A Drink,' I feel sure, is the only favorite that is going to win today."

"Jim, there is just one thing at this moment of which I am certain in life. And that is that Belle will not go the post a favorite in the betting. She will be 'abandoned,' as our neighbors here so delicately put it. Mark my words. That is one delightful thing about working for the *Tribune*—the boys and girls who bet heavy don't take my tips seriously. And perhaps this time they will be sorry. They have been before." This was the only whistling I did to keep my courage up.

However, after we had performed our errand of mercy for Rex, when we saw Belle in the paddock, I needed to do considerable more. For the mare looked half asleep; she walked gingerly and rather haltingly, almost as if she had a game right hind leg. When the jockey got on her back, he looked the picture of despondency. Merely to see him was to know that he felt he couldn't win—a delicate bit of histrionics, which I had seen too often before to be impressed, that is, to be discouraged from betting, or "thrown off," as it is called. Yet it really was not easy to work up much enthusiasm for that ambling, almost downcast-looking animal, who might well have been thinking of her happier, sunnier days as a filly of promise and beauty.

Jim looked at me with world-weary languor.

"You have to be a Christian and believe in miracles to do this," he said.

And without another word—heedless of the odds, heedless of the curious looks from an interested group before the "big" booth—Jim went over, and said, *"Le numéro quatorze, dix fois gagnant,"* stressing the *"gagnant."* Quite obviously skeptical, the clerk was yet proud of his customer's order. And when Jim repeated it, again emphasizing the "to win" phrase in French, the clerk—almost with an admiring gesture—slowly, reverentially, tore off ten 500 franc tickets, stamped them, and handed them to Jim, who had put down the correct number of bank notes on the counter.

Interest in what we were doing had tricked us in our sense of time—hardly had Jim the tickets tucked away, when the bell rang. They were off already. We walked briskly to the front of the stands, and Jim remarked as we went along, hurrying and eager not to miss anything, "Come to think of it, Harold, probably we could buy the horse for not much more than our bet."

"Not after this race is over, we couldn't."

It is always curious what you will think of, when you are gambling heavily—even if by proxy, as I was. I recall that incidental things seemed important. I was delighted that we had just got our bet down in time, "They can't profit from our bet and go rushing to cover." I said this to myself almost triumphantly. I was so pleased at this protection of our long odds that for a moment I almost forgot that the really important thing, after all, was that Belle of Zante should win. Otherwise, our caution in betting at the last moment was pointless. Yet I felt glad we *had* been cautious in betting at the last moment. Belle could now run her own private race, urged on by no clear cheers—except ours. She could be disinterested; money meant nothing—no "big" money (except ours, too, but that I forgot for a second) was on her. She could win for the merit of it, "to show 'em."

Absurd thoughts? Of course—but have you ever gone racing?

When we reached the front of the nearest stand—and all of them at Auteuil are on fairly high ground, sloping up from the track, so that one can see all the way round and even across the crowded infield—the horses were wheeling and coming from left to right past the steeplechase water-jump in front of us. But they were turning aside a bit, on the flat turf, for this jump is not taken in a hurdle affair. They were fairly well bunched, and thus far not a horse had gone down—the fourteen that started (and Belle, being a débutante at this kind of race, had been given bottom weight, hence was number *"quatorze"* on the program) were still on their feet, all, seemingly, going easy and strong. But at the big hurdle jump way across the field, where some "bunching up" had already become noticeable and a few trailers were beginning to drag behind, two horses went down—and there were groans from the crowd, particularly from those who had bet on the unfortunate animals. Belle was neither of the two,—we could see the green-and-yellow stripes of her jockey's silks and the gray of his cap quite clearly "up with the bunch." So far, so good—and the race was almost half over. She was still in the race, still a danger to others.

It was right after this critical jump that Belle began to take a bit of a lead—just enough to see daylight (as racing men put it) between her and the nearest horse.

"What imbecile is that out in front?" roared a Frenchman beside me, and although it was not quite clear whether he was referring to the horse or the jockey, I somehow took umbrage at the remark, almost as if it were meant personally for me, and said in a quite unnecessarily strident tone, and in my best slang French, "There are more imbeciles watching this race than there are in it."

The Frenchman glared at me, but we were both too interested in what was going on before our eyes to bother getting into a fight. I knew this, and hence didn't care if I was courageous. Nor could I help smiling a bit, when Jim gave me an admiring glance.

Imbecile or not, Belle's jockey had chosen the right tactics—and at the right time. She had always been a horse, even on the flat, who liked to keep out ahead, what we term a "front runner." Over the jumps she liked the same thing; she didn't want any horse near her—and she wanted a clear field ahead of her. When she had negotiated the last hurdle, she was almost five lengths in the lead of her nearest competitor, and her jockey wisely eased her up on the short run-in to the finish, crossing the line almost at a walk and with the other horses straining at her heels, yet with plenty to spare. At the end the stands were curiously silent, for nobody had backed her and nobody had anything to cheer about. A few polite handclaps were all we heard. Fascinated, I watched while the number "14" went up over the judges' stand, and somehow my throat felt dry and strained.

Luckily the agony of waiting for the "All Clear" bell—and it is precisely that under such circumstances, when you have backed a big outsider—was really short, though it seemed to me interminable. At last the bell rang, clear and firm, and as we gulped our champagne and turned to the announcement board, that magic little thin line of red—from whence comes the expression, *"le rouge est mis,"* meaning the die is cast, or something equivalent—snapped into place over the "14." Belle had won; it was legal; we were "on" her! There is no glow like it in the world—all the other pleasures, even sensuous ones, are not to be compared with it.

Jim was quite obviously trying to moderate his excitement. "There are two thrills at the French races," he observed. "The first is when your horse wins; the second is when the odds go up—especially if it's an outsider."

"Also a third, Jim—when you drink your animal's health in champagne. Maybe some day we can do that in our own country."

As we solemnly pledged Belle, there was an audible murmur, growing into a chorus of *"Regarde-moi ça," "Incroyable,"* and *"Tiens, tiens."*

Jim turned to me—"Look at that *affichage*. Do you see what I see?"

"One thousand, two hundred and eighty-five francs, fifty centimes—that's what I see," I said, reading slowly, and yet not quite believing my own eyes.

"We have gone insane," announced Jim with conviction. "That means a little over $50 for every forty cents we put up—well over 100 to 1. Can such things be?"

"Can be—and are," I said, making a valiant effort to *act* indifferent, but I felt a trifle dizzy. I realized that never before had I seen, let alone bet upon, such a long-shot miracle as Belle—and that, probably, never should I do so (perhaps never have the chance to do so) again. That is the kind of bet which comes only once—if it comes at all—in a lifetime.

"Harold," said Jim looking at me with mock severity, "quite aside from what you won this time—for half of it is yours—I can't afford beeing seen at the races with anybody dressed the way you are. We are going to my tailor's, when we leave here, and I am going to buy you some clothes. You owe it to God, to Belle, and to me. Not to mention yourself."

And so, after the races and a few congratulatory glasses with August, Rex, his housekeeper, the barman himself (permissible on "great," i. e., big winning days), and some American schoolmate of Jim's, who had appeared miraculously from nowhere, we drove over to the stylish tailor that made Jim's and the King of England's clothing. Nor did we forget to stop off at a convenient café on the Champs Elysées and get Bouboule a drink too—though he was beaming already without it, for he, likewise, had had a glorious day and had bet on Belle himself—how much we could never get out of him—in the popular field, or *"pélouse."* At the tailor's I ordered a full dress suit, with dinner jacket, two sack suits, a heavy, formal overcoat, and a light one—the last, I have even to this day in America, and wear it to sporting events. Re-lined, and with the cuffs turned (for it rested on so many French bars that it became slightly worn and frayed there), it still looks—and is—superior to the most expensive of our ready-to-wear affairs. Both the dress and dinner suits—alas!—rest in the cellar of a Paris hotel (though long since worn by waiters, I feel morally sure), which later on I had had to leave before I had paid my entire bill—but those were my later, evil days. Coming back to town from Auteuil that afternoon, all the world seemed rose-colored.

There were many other days like that, though the winnings were not so dramatic. Yet some of the days were even more dramatic in other respects—the days at Enghien and at Le Tremblay, when I bet my last sou, quite literally, on a wild chance of my own liking—and the wild chances came through. I had so many ups and downs at the trotting races at Vincennes in the winter that it is not easy to remember them all—though never shall I forget when "Bébé Rose" won there at over 40 to 1 and I had exactly 30 francs on her, which was enough to make it a glorious evening; when I worked on the Baltimore *Sun* as a Paris correspondent and thought, consequently, I should bet on a trotter named "Baltimore," which I did out of sentiment—and he saved my week-end and my month's rent in the hotel; when Saint-André showed his stuff there, and later I bet on him at Enghien in the last harnessed trot of a disastrous day otherwise, and he turned the black clouds golden; when, above all at my first Grand Prix de Paris, I bet on the great grey, Filibert de Savoie, who did it easily—and then, years later, bet on his daughter (out of La Balladeuse), La Savoyarde, to repeat, and she did at Saint-Cloud, with Diana Swift out to see her do it and with her fortnight's pay on the outcome, at my urging; when Commanderie, a grey filly, won the Prix de Diane at Chantilly; when Ortie Pourpre—a handsome little filly, too—won at Deauville in the summer holidays, and Rex's housekeeper said to me (yes, she went to Deauville, too), *"alors, Monsieur Stearns, ca pique, eh?"* (And since *"ortie"* means nettle, that is about the closest I ever heard the housekeeper come to a deliberate pun.) There were the days of the wild big fields of starters—sometimes as many as 30 or more—at Maisons-Laffitte, when, if you could only win *one* race out of the seven, your day was saved, and better than saved, while if you won *two!*

I used to like the ride back from Maisons through the forest and to stop at Saint-Germain-en-Laye for a drink on the way home to Paris, after the races. There was a fine view from the terrace of the Pavillon Henri-Quatre, and I recall stopping there with Bill Bullitt once, after a fairish afternoon at Maisons, and his telling me what he thought the Soviets would do to encourage the breed of horses in Russia, and what he expected from America when there was a "new deal," and why he had adopted so many Turkish children, and of the novel he was writing. Bill was so unaffectedly nice a fellow that it was hard to take seriously anything about him—except his wealth, about which there was no joking. I liked to have Sunday lunch at his trick house in Passy, just outside Paris—where Eleanor Glyn is reputed to have written "Three Weeks"—and then walk over (for it was only a ten minute walk) to the Auteuil track, when the races were there. Bill had a keen eye for jumping horses, but gambling on the jumpers was only a secondary thing to him—gambling always is secondary, when you have plenty of money anyway. Bill was intelligent, friendly, rich—yet sometimes he made me uncomfortable, and I think it was what used to be called a curious "inferiority complex." I mean, Bill envied what he could not have been, even had he tried, for he had too much money—and something he would have despised really had he been forced to be it, that is, a Bohemian. He envied newspaper men, "free lance" writers, irresponsible artists, talented musicians, sometimes (I think rather childishly) even Casanova-like amorous sure-fire heroes —and the truth is, he would have been bored to death, had he been forced, consistently, to be any one of these things. Politics gave him more a sense of power; I am glad he is in the game now—I am sure he is happier. But I knew him as a horseman primarily; and he was a damn good judge of jumpers. Thoroughbreds on the flat fooled him exactly as they fool the wisest of us. However, I remember him with affection, for we shared winning days.

And Walter Duranty, too, who could hardly wait to get to the French track, whenever he had a holiday from Moscow, which he passed either in Paris or on the Riviera. Walter had backed horses, even when he was in school in England, and I am sure he would rather any day have seen a Grand Steeplechase de Paris than the finest ballet or opera the new Russian theatre ever produced in my time. After his accident, when he lost a leg in a railroad smash near Le Havre, he sometimes would not go to the track himself—and I still remember with horror the day he gave me a large sum to bet on what I considered a wild outsider (and a foolishly wild outsider) at Auteuil, and I put the money on the favorite—and the outsider won! I should have to work a year to make enough money to pay that debt, though I remember giving Walter all the money I had, when I returned from the track a sadder but wiser man.

If Walter found it difficult to forgive me for that bet I didn't make, there were many others who had occasion to bless me for bets I suggested—in the paper, or personally, or sometimes both. But towards the end I became reluctant to take bets for other people; I was always sailing too close to the wind myself. And I knew the dangers too well; I was tempted to take chances against myself, so to speak, that my horse would *not* win—and to keep the money in my pocket. And, of course, that was precisely the time he *would* come through it almost goes without saying, at odds that were ruinous to me, for it takes a braver man than I am to say, "I'm sorry, but I changed my mind when I got to the track and backed what I thought was a safer thing." Some people could say that—and get away with it, though not too often. But I could not. I had to tell the truth—and, when I couldn't pay, owe the money. Money which, whenever—if ever—I could, I paid somehow. If, as today, the Pari-Mutuel-en-Ville, by means of which one can lay a bet oneself at many a convenient tobacco store or café up to noon of the day of the race, had been functioning in my active racing career, I should have been spared many a temptation—and should have made a lot from grateful backers.

For my regular tips, played consistently and with the reservations I officially made in the paper (I mean, when I wrote "Go light on this race," or "Ignore this claiming plate as a betting proposition; it is a scramble"), were winning tips—rather remarkable winning tips, when I reflect on it now and look at what New York handicappers boast about in their racing form sheets the next day. All my betting troubles came primarily from not following my own tips, from being "thrown off" by some last-minute bit of information (false, too, nine times out of ten). There was, of course, a moral to this—and a moral much more pragmatic for action than that adorning the average sermon—but I refuse to draw it. What was worse, I refused to draw that moral for myself then. Like all people who believe in miracles, I regarded experience only as a series of annoying exceptions to a rule, of which I, above all, had complete understanding. That the rule didn't work was not *really* discouraging; regarded properly, this was but a challenge to one's faith. That the faith itself might not be correct or worth maintaining were possibilities not to be entertained—that would be weakness.

Perhaps, for the sake of gamblers, or of those pathetic people who are seeking for a system whereby they can beat the races—just as the number of tragic hundreds who have tried to beat Monte Carlo and the roulette wheel—I ought to say that in my opinion, which after all on this point is worth something anyway, there is no means by which to beat the horses successfully—except by luck. Knowledge, of course, helps; wide and extensive knowledge will ordinarily prevent one from making the worst kind of mistakes. But wide and extensive knowledge is impossible without a certain affection for the horses involved—and once you have affection for horses, which means in practice, for specific horses in specific situations, you are lost.

Put more simply, the rules are not, as they are, say, in chess, such and such, and the trick becomes only a matter of learning them—emotion enters into the compound, too. Breeders, trainers, and those who know most about horses, seldom die rich—at least from their gambling alone. Which is entirely to their human credit, for many and many a time they will make a bet, not as a man will make a move in chess, but because they *want* a horse to win. And there is enough of primitive-man magic left in all of us to make us believe that by the mere placing of a bet on a horse we somehow, in some mysterious way, help that horse to win. In fact the concept is involved in the very language of the race-track—Do we not speak of "supporting" a horse with our money, speaking naturally of "my" horse being out in front, or coming up, or "just making it" in a close finish? I often used to wonder, on the French race course, why the Freudians, who were then so popular in America and England and Germany and other lands of inhibition, bothered so much about formal (so to speak) dreams for their theories, when right at the French track, any day any month of any year, they could watch the psychopathology of everyday life—and have thousands of case histories at hand to study. The French track? Well, the French Casinos, also, particularly the hectic one during the short three-week season at Deauville in August, with which I was familiar—where sometimes a cool half-million of francs, on rare occasions even a million, was won and lost on the turn of a single card.

But Deauville meant much more to me from a racing point of view—there was a lovely "regular" track, i. e., on the green flat turf, and in later years there was also the curiously comic, but very pretty "mixed" track for both straight races and jumping affairs, at Clairefontaine, a short walk out of town—than it did as a resort, however chic and gay. For besides the races themselves—and some good polo matches, too—there were the yearling sales at Cheri's and Tattersall's at the end of the season, and all around Deauville in the rolling Normandy countryside, with its rich green grass and rich soil, were breeding establishments, such as the ones belonging to the Rothschilds and to R. B. Strassburger.

I used to like to watch the heavy gambling in the Casino at night, for there is always drama where there is gambling. I remember meeting one man there (an American from Colorado), who offered to roll me with the dice for a handsome brand new Voisin roadster against a bottle of champagne—that is, if I won, I got the car; if I lost, I bought him a bottle of champagne. (Need I add that I lost?—I suppose that is the nearest in my life I shall ever be to the ownership of an expensive car.) I met others who offered to stake me to as much as 15,000 francs, if I wanted to play baccarat. But I never accepted; I contented myself with a few modest plunges at that ridiculous game of "Boule," which intrigues Summer visitors at all small French watering places—where the percentage against the player is so high that only somebody divinely endowed with luck could ever beat it, even for a short run.

All this "extra" gambling interested me, as I have said, but I was on the whole personally indifferent to it. The gambling I was interested in was racetrack gambling—and at the track itself, where I could see the horses and get a run for my money in a genuine rather than metaphorical sense. I took no enjoyment or interest in "betting off the course"—I always wanted to see the race for myself. That was half the fun. I like poker; I like race-track gambling; I like rolling the dice with an individual opponent or two. But this impersonal, corporation-like, large-scale gambling, such as goes on at the Casinos—if my temperament had run that way, somehow I should early in life have contrived to follow a career in Wall Street, where such people really belong—and eventually get ruined, in much the same way.

Deauville—and Jim's company—that summer of 1929 prompted the above reflections on gambling in general. But the memory of that particular summer there has for me much more poignancy, as I look back now on those winning days. I had, of course, anticipated a happy winter—at the end of chapter 15 I speak of the plans Jim and I then had for founding a small stable. We were going to make money—he cared about that chiefly for my sake, since he had enough to live on in any event—and we were going to enjoy life.

But like so many anticipations in my life, those for a happy winter—that of 1929-30—proved to be tragically incorrect, as have so many of my other anticipations. For Jim took a trip to Italy, accompanied by his wife, Dolly, of whom I was so fond—and one night in Genoa, coming home to his hotel, he slipped on some rickety stairs and fell. That fall must have been about as bad as a fall can be, for Jim hurt his spine badly—so badly, in fact, that he died a few days after the accident without recovering consciousness. Heartbroken at this sudden tragedy, Dolly, his young wife, took an overdose of some strong sleeping potion, and she did not have many hours to wait before joining him. That *both* should have to be lost seemed to me then for a few days almost more than could be endured. Both were younger than I; both were my best friends—and among the very few loyal ones I have ever had. Both were attractive and charming, with so much in life before them.

Why should I always have to be the one left behind alone? I remember how gentle and decent and kindly Diana was that evening, when I got back from the races, and, finding on my desk a telegram from Italy, which I thought would be some message from Jim about a horse or about our plans, opened it and read the tragic news. She knew how I felt and how much I needed comfort; she was a woman first of all that evening; I think I felt closer to her then than I ever had before—or than ever I was going to again.

And all those winter weeks, even the spring weeks, too, until May, 1930, when I left the *Tribune* to go on the *Daily Mail* were a kind of torture to me: Every race-track I went to, as was inevitable, reminded me of Jim and happier days and the plans we had made. I turned for companionship to the men on the paper, to Strong particularly, who, whatever our temporary quarrels, had always been one of my friends—as, indeed, I think I can safely say he still is to this day, though, of course, one's mood and feelings are different after three years back "home." Though, really, I have no need to put "home" in quotation marks any longer.

After all, I am back in my own country.

XVIII. THE THREAT OF BLINDNESS —AND COLLIOURE

THOUGH I had a contract, by the terms of which I could not be discharged without a notice in writing giving me two months' advance warning, though I was changing from the perpetually "broke" class of people to the relatively secure type of citizen who could actually live on his 3,000 francs a month, though my prestige both with the racing authorities and with the reading public, whatever either might be worth, was considerably enhanced by over-night ceasing to be the rather flippant "Peter Pickem" of Chicago and becoming the dignified "Lutetius" of London—despite these obvious advantages in my new position in the world, I really didn't want to make the change.

First of all, I had had, notwithstanding the hard times, many many happy days on the *Tribune*—as Mr. Strong observed, with that delicacy for which he could not be praised too highly, to use his own phrase, we didn't make much money but we had lots of fun. What we did was not a job, according to him it was a joke—and I am certain that most of the readers of the paper were inclined to agree with him. But it was a happy, good-natured joke, and we might all have been mad, yet we were mad with the same accent, in an American manner that we could all, even when we could hardly approve, most certainly understand. A newspaper "gang," when there is not too much jealousy and backbiting, especially an American newspaper "gang" in a foreign country, can be the jolliest, most happy-go-lucky crowd in the world, an ideal human background for an even more amusing type of fantasy than Thorne Smith has ever written. Your morals will not be greatly improved; nor will your range of accurate information about either current or past events be greatly extended, in fact you may acquire masses of misinformation that it will afterwards take years to dislodge; your literary style, if you have or ever did have any, will not be made more subtle and more ingratiating. Finally, since most of the time a clean collar will represent the sacrifice of a possible meal and hence only be visible when you are prepared to go hungry for it, you will not move in any of the circles about which the Society Editor speaks with such glibness. Though you would like to be a frequenter of all the bars in Paris, you will in fact be welcomed only at a few—where you do not owe too much. But still, wherever you do move and whatever circles you do grace with your presence, it will be with a certain sophisticated ease of manner, an indifference to social criticism ordinarily characteristic only of the highest intellectual, instead of the most befuddled, ability. Literary pretence will be vacuum-cleaned out of you by the certain knowledge that very few people, if any at all, ever read your stuff, and by the sad conviction, when you break down and read it yourself, that it is just as well for your reputation for literacy that nobody does. Venomous gossip will fly far from you, because whatever modest murders or rapes your friends commit will seem tame, conventional, and uninteresting beside the deeds of the heroic thugs and criminals whose activities it is your daily duty to record. In Paris, moreover, all this will be touched with a bit of whimsy, delightful, irresponsible whimsy—for if everybody isn't intoxicated most of the time, it will be safe to assume that they are. Amorous details of life, about which people trouble themselves in our Anglo-Saxon world, will all blend in Paris, and assume their proper purely decorative function—for there, in such matters, there are no responsibilities and few consequences. And for the most part much more easy experience than you have the time for or can conveniently deal with, since the real problem becomes that of being able, at least once in a while, to go to bed alone. Though I didn't at the time fully realize it, working on the *Tribune* had been a one-way ticket to the Never-Never-Land of male irresponsibility, absurdity, and entertainment, of which all men in their hearts forever dream—and so seldom ever reach. But it had been my home town for years, and in this respect I was a home-town boy. I was afraid of the *Daily Mail.*

But on the first of May I made the change, and the Swan Song I wrote for the paper that last night was, I have been told, a classic of its kind. I gave only the necessary amount of space to the technical events and prognostics, saving a couple of longish paragraphs at the end for a brief expression of what association with the paper had meant to me. I said as a matter of courtesy that, of course, in my new position I should try to give at least as good a proportion of winners and occasional outsiders as I had done for the *Tribune.* But I also said—how truly I anticipated I did not then realize—that I should miss my old associations and memories, and that I left the paper with regret. If an imaginative and understanding owner had read that piece—I have often since wondered if McCormick ever saw it—he would have sent the following cable: "Whatever Daily Mail offers will outbid them stop stay with paper endall."

Of course that night after work each of the boys insisted upon getting me a drink at "Gillotte's"—it was pay-day, too, remember—and on twitting me a bit because I was going over to the "Limies." I think most of them—"The Once All Over," above all—if only selfishly, because it meant temporarily that horror of horrors, more work for him—quite sincerely; and, of course, Strong, too—were really sorry to see me go. I had become a sort of fixture for them; and few were those who had been on the paper longer than had I. I had seen them all come and go, while I, like the happy brook, had gone on forever. All knew that I got no pay to speak of, but all knew, too, that I had made money at the track—many of them had occasionally themselves profited by my knowledge. They may have envied, from time to time, my going out early at eight o'clock, my work all done while they were just getting down to the nightly grind, but on rainy cold days they thought with horror, as they turned over for another snooze in their cozy (sometimes too cozy, considering the other occupant) beds, of my actually getting up, dressing, taking a train or a bus, and physically going to wet Enghien, or to chilly Vincennes, or to wind and rain-swept Saint-Cloud—for everybody knew I really went to the track. I was not like poor old Bingham on the *Herald,* who most certainly, at his age, would have died of pneumonia, if he tried to leave the shelter of his bar, with its racing telegraph ticker, on the Rue du Louvre. His trips to the track were only on the pleasant, sunny days—otherwise, he stayed in town and studied the form sheets. Which is why he had such a high percentage of winners, for he never missed a favorite. And why, also, he practically never had an outsider. If you would look at the "Consensus of the Press," as it was called, in any of the sporting journals, you would find it almost identical with the *Herald's* selections—and that is the safe, conservative way to give racing selections in Paris. (Or anywhere else.) You will never make a fool of yourself—and hence seldom, either, will you get, or give, a thrill. It is suspiciously like life itself in that respect.

The first few weeks on the *Daily Mail* I was too busy to be miserable. The paper printed a ridiculously long "past performance" record of each horse entered in a race (the trotting races alone excepted, but then, the *Daily Mail* never regarded trotting seriously until I came on the paper); and it took me at least a fortnight to discover some method of keeping this form sheet accurate and up-to-date, without imposing upon myself too much technical work of looking up references and records. Besides, it was the height of the season—and we were going into the classic period of those three weeks in June which culminate, the last Sunday in the month, in the Grand Prix de Paris itself. Of all months in the year—October perhaps excepted, and naturally, too, the dead of winter, if you like trotting—May and June are the busiest and most exciting on the French turf. And that year was no exception.

The boys on the paper had different habits from those on the *Tribune*—that is to say, they patronized a bar and café near to their own office on the Rue de Sentier, as "Gillotte's" was the *Tribune* crowd's regular hang-out. I got along with them fairly well, but I never really felt, so to speak, "at home" with them. The English speak a quite different language from our own, and they look at things differently from what we do. If any American doubts my word, let him work with them on terms of equality—an equality they could hardly deny to me, since I was working as "their" expert on a matter all Englishmen rather plume themselves that they are expert about, that is, horses and horse-racing. That it was in France did, I suppose, excuse me to a certain extent. But there was always a touch of suspicion in their spontaneous attitude—how did it come about that an *American* knew anything at all, above all, that he knew anything about horses? I found that my instinctive habit of reserve with people—yet being an American, a habit easy enough to break down—here stood me in good use. In other words, I kept my mouth shut, made few criticisms, played for the drinks with the boys in their fashion rather than in the approved American fashion, even complimented them on their girls, when they had any—though they were terrible. Another thing, which it is just as well to be frank about, too. I didn't assume, as do far too many Americans that know a lot of things which aren't so, that any of them either were then or ever had been "fairies." Even though I hail from "the States," I can take most Englishmen, as other people, the way I find them—and let it go at that.

I found the *Daily Mail* crowd pretty decent and pretty hard working, all things considered. They didn't have the flair for strange fantasies, which made life so amusing on the *Tribune*, but for me just then that was something of a relief. I don't mind a holiday and I haven't any great terrors of the psychopathic ward—but I don't want to live in the latter all the time, nor enjoy the former otherwise than exceptionally. The *Daily Mail* crowd was a distinct—I had almost said wholesome, but perhaps healthy would be better—relief. Three or four of them actually lived respectable, hum-drum, bourgeois lives, even if they did work on a newspaper.

But most of us, whether we know it or not, are homesick for our own kind at least now and then, and if your own kind is slightly mad, that makes no difference either. It is all in the accent, the point of view, the curious assumptions that, naturally, we take for granted—until, of course, we go with an alien crowd and find that we cannot take *their* assumptions for granted, that in cold fact we often do not even know what those assumptions are. Most American expatriates in Paris, for instance, would not stay there ten weeks—unless there were other American expatriates with whom they could talk things over. And I believe I should have become a raving maniac on the *Daily Mail*, if I had not been able—any time I wanted—to walk over to the *Tribune* office and the boys' café, where I was always greeted like somebody who had been sojourning in a strange and foreign land, as indeed—from a real, that is, spiritual point of view—I had been. I was respected as a real adventurer.

As soon as I learned the ropes, things went along fairly well on my new job. My tips did well, too, which pleased the paper, for after all the only real excuse for a racing man—granted he can write a grammatical sentence—is that he can give you information and tips which are reliable up to the point of all fallible sporting advance knowledge. The *Daily*

Mail had a tradition of giving, outside the conventional first and second choices for each of the different races, a day's outsider—one horse believed to have possibilities, even though it was not the "form" horse. Right from the start I had remarkably good luck with these outsiders; in fact, it soon reached a point that sometimes I hesitated to give the most attractive one, from my own point of view, simply because the mere fact of my giving him in the paper automatically cut down his odds. It far too speedily became known that the *Daily Mail's* outsider really had no right to be an outsider at all—with consequences easy to foresee. And with certain other bad personal consequences for me. I mean, simply, people would inquire of me, "But what have you got really 'good' for today, Lutetius?" And when I replied, "You only have to look at the paper," they would give me a knowing wink and walk off, convinced that I was holding out some really hot inside stuff, when God knows, nine times out of ten, I had no more idea of who would be the winner than had they—if as much. And when the favorite—say a favorite which I myself had recommended in the paper that morning—won, these same people would look positively hurt, as if I had robbed them of their last five-franc note. And then, of course, to make it perfect, they would back the favorite in a race, where I had cautiously recommended a long-shot—and when the long-shot came prancing across the finish line first, as every now and then he did, you could tell from the way they looked at me that they regarded plain murder as much too kindly and considerate. I very soon learned, what every racing tipster sooner or later has to learn—that whatever you do, you are wrong, especially if you are right. If I am not becoming too involved.

The year I worked on the *Daily Mail* was the year, long to be remembered on the French turf, when the gray filly, Commanderie, won the Grand Prix de Paris itself—a feat so very rarely accomplished by a filly in this great classic event that you can count the number of times on the fingers of one hand. I gave her as my outsider for the big event, and was very proud of myself, too. I had written a story for the paper that would knock your eye-teeth out, actually having the nerve —nerve in an English paper, I mean—to begin the story with the words of a song very popular in America at that time, though I transposed it a trifle by starting off:

"And then they all stood still.

"At least that is the way it seemed yesterday in the great Grand Prix," etc.

For some reason I could never fathom, the boss thought it was a great story, and even took the trouble—which he did rarely—to compliment me upon it. I think he thought it was a new kind of subtlety; I don't know what he thought. Anyway, it was a vivid bit of reporting. But after all, as I told him, if a racing reporter couldn't write a good story on the Grand Prix de Paris—especially a dramatic Grand Prix—when, if ever, could he be expected to write a good one? But he was pleased, nevertheless.

So pleased, in fact, that a few weeks later, when the question of going down to Deauville arose (they always had three big weeks of flat racing there in August, when things—except for some summer trotting at Enghien—were quiet in Paris), he was quite affable. And not only did I go down, but for once I went down with something like an adequate expense account —and one needs plenty at Deauville, if you are, as the French put it, to "circulate" around at all and see people. I had dress clothes, too; I was privileged to enter the Casino—even to play myself, if I wished, though I rarely did—in the gambling rooms there. It was a dramatic contrast to my humble days in Deauville, when I represented the *Tribune,* and spent the last week of the season wondering whether or not I should have to walk back to Paris.

Unfortunately, it was almost too dramatic a contrast. The wife of the owner of the *Daily Mail* was a horsewoman herself and had a stable in France—a small stable, but an excellent one. R. B. Strassburger, who also had a stable in France, and in those days a big one it was, had known me the previous season. He was amused to find that I was on an English newspaper as the racing man, and nothing would do one afternoon at the track but that I should meet Mrs. Harmsworth, the wife of the owner of the paper. I didn't particularly want to, but there was hardly any way of avoiding it. She had bought that year, if I remember correctly, although in any event it was making its début that season at Deauville, a very handsome two-year-old filly, called "Mes Amours." We talked about that filly before its first race on the day of the race itself—and when the filly lost, in my opinion by poor riding on the part of the jockey (she won a great race at Maisons-Laffitte later in the autumn, fully redeeming herself), I wrote a stinging criticism of the whole thing, including Mrs. Harmsworth's poor judgment in allowing that particular jockey to ride her horse, which upset the Paris office terribly, when the telegram came in like any innocent news dispatch from one of their regular correspondents, until they began to read it. They printed it, naturally taking out my worst venom, but I got no satisfaction out of them. And when I got back to Paris a few days later, on the season's closing, it was gently explained to me that, after all, one did not call the wife of the owner of the paper for which one was working a jackass—even if it was only too true. Or imply it, either. I protested that I had only said she had showed bad judgment in racing; I had not said or implied that she herself was a jackass. But I observed that the subject was dropped, not to be re-opened, and later on I remembered that my real troubles on the paper began with that episode.

Yet now I am inclined to think that the thing would have blown over and been forgotten, had not something else—something much more serious and dangerous, something that changed the whole course of my life—arisen a few weeks later. What that was deserves a simple description.

The September month of racing had gone by; golden October—with the incomparable Prix De L'Arc De Triomphe at Longchamp, one of the finest races on any turf anywhere—had become a memory; the flat races were drawing to a close, and the last meeting of the year (before everything became either the jumping races at Auteuil or Enghien, or the trotting contests at Vincennes) was scheduled for a weekday afternoon at Saint-Cloud, up on the hill beyond Suresnes, just over the river outside Paris. It was a fine day for that season of the year. I remember going out with pleasure.

I think it was the fourth race of the afternoon, when it happened. I had had a rather "fair" day—I mean, one of moderate ups and downs, with nothing tremendously exciting happening either way—when the fifth event came around. The horses went to the post across the field; I had made a modest bet on my own choice; finally, the bell rang—they were off. They run anti-clockwise at Saint-Cloud, the run-in of the finish being from left to right, I should say possibly six or seven hundred yards straightaway, after they swing around the final bend. I remember "my" horse had a combination of blue and yellow colors, something like the Baron de Rothschild's colors but not quite. Anyway, he was not difficult to distinguish from the rest of the pack. As they began to get nearer to the finish, I could see "my" horse making a fine effort about in the middle of the front-runners—and I began to shout encouragement. But quite suddenly—so suddenly that afterwards I was told that all my confrères in the press box turned and looked at me curiously—I sat down and turned quite white.

Probably I had turned white—or green—or any other color. I shall never know. For what had taken place is something easy to write down in cold words, but the effect of which on anyone to whom it happens is likely to do more than merely change their color a bit. In a word, I went blind. Everything turned grey-black. I could not distinguish the track from the field, a person in front of me from anything else. All were jumbled in that oppressive sleeplike eyelid-closed nothingness of consciousness, with my eyes searching, as in a half-dream, to follow meaningless shapes flickering across the inner lids. And yet my eyes were wide open.

I closed them, and kept perfectly still. I hardly dared to breathe; I didn't dare to think. Slowly, ever so slowly—it seemed ages though it was only perhaps six or seven minutes—courage came back to me, and I opened them. Shapes were discernible; that is about all I could say. I closed them again, the tenseness of suspense hardly allowing for any feeling, either or fear or terror. And once more, after about the same length of time, I summoned up my courage and opened them. This time objects were fairly recognizable—but there was a blur over everything.

Slowly I stumbled down the stairs. The bell was ringing for the horses to go on the track for the next race; I remember asking myself, "Do some of these people really think it's important whether a horse wins or loses? Did I ever—ever—think anything like that?"

I reached the bar, and gulped down the largest whisky I had had for at least a month. I didn't dare to speak to anybody. I kept in the shadow back of the restaurant addition to the grandstand. Every now and then I would open my eyes to make sure that I could still see. And on each occasion I got a little more courage. For it was getting dark outside. "Really dark," I said to myself with a sense of relief, because the lights had been turned on in some of Pari-Mutuel betting-booth windows. Before the last race was run I left the track, walking very slowly down to the little electric train at the station called—iroically enough, it seemed to me then—"The Valley of Gold." Usually I talked with the first person beside me about the races (for practically everyone that got on at that time there had come, as had I, from the track). But on this trip in to Paris I didn't exchange a word with anyone. The races were far from my mind.

I think we are more terrified of possible blindness than of

almost anything else which may happen to us. We can, sometimes, "laugh off" losing a leg, as Walter Duranty had done after the train accident near Le Havre. It is not pleasant, I suppose; it is not agreeable, but one can do it. But the fear of going blind is something which makes all other things seem trivial—and you can try as much as you want to, yet you cannot take your mind off it.

I tried desperately that night after I finished my work—finished it so slowly that everybody in the office was astonished, for ordinarily I was quite speedy, and I tried to be out of the building by eight o'clock or half past at the worst. I went to the Café Namur for dinner, because that almost always made me feel more cheerful, and I was wise enough not to go alone—I called up Strong on the *Tribune,* but he was not there, so I invited Louis, who answered the telephone, to join me. I didn't say anything at that time about my real worry; Louis had sense enough to see that I was terribly concerned about something, but tactfully he didn't ask questions—I suppose he thought it was some money trouble, or some trouble on the paper. Newspaper men often have, Heaven knows, a full share of personal grief. And then they like to be with other newspaper men—though that doesn't mean that they like to talk about it. Usually, just the reverse; they want to talk about some general absurdity of the day's news; for there is always something absurd taking place in the world, even when news is, in the official phrase, "damn scarce." They want to get out of themselves.

Anyway, Louis was unusually amusing—gossip from the *Tribune* always had an extremely high quality of absurdity, and Louis had an excellent sense of humor. There was really nothing malicious or backbiting about this gossip, though I suppose, if anyone had over-heard us, they would have been at the least somewhat startled. And, as I have said, most of the talk was about things in general rather than about people in particular.

After that dinner I lingered long with Louis, finally persuading him to walk home with me. But when he had gone, the old nervousness returned—I couldn't stand my room. Over on the Rue Montmartre—or rather, the Rue Du Faubourg Montmartre, the distinction being made in the name after you crossed the main Boulevard—there were plenty of all-night restaurants and cafés, though of a rather dispiriting quality. I tried to forget what was worrying me. But it was difficult, because I didn't want to try to read any newspapers—I knew only too well how the type might blur. I even tried to find an all-night pool parlor, such as the one near the Namur, where I had often played with Shipman. But I reflected, almost as soon as the idea came to me, how absurd that was, too—was everything going to be absurd, if really I should go blind? What could one do? One, I meant, who had always had normal vision. Could one learn to be content in a world of shadows? Would anything ever again mean anything to me—anything except sight? And, I thought bitterly, here were people around me, worrying about trifles, damn them!

I can't remember today how release finally came. I suppose one simply cannot go on worrying the way I was without something snapping. Finally, I said to myself, "All right, damn it all, if I am going to go blind—why, then, I am going to go blind. But I'll not worry any more. I'll just pretend everything is all right—until something happens."

And almost as if by magic I felt better. I was able to go to my room and—probably exhausted by the inner emotional strain—go to sleep without too much tossing about. I tried to forget, to think of other things, not to weep at my ridiculous trembling and shaking. The strain, I suppose, is what did it. You can't keep up that degree of tension too long. The body simply won't stand it. Finally mine gave in. It was around four o'clock in the morning.

The next day I really thanked God for my job—simply because it kept me busy. And, as I went along the routine of the day, the only exception which I made (and how I tried to pretend that it was for *other* reasons!) was not too look at as many newspapers as was ordinarily my habit, my nerve finally returned to me. My vision *did* seem a bit off, but it wasn't anything serious—or so I kept confidently repeating to myself. And as the hours went by, with nothing happening, I became almost cheerful. By evening—able again to look at the fine type of the technical details printed in *Paris Sport*—I felt so elated because nothing untoward had in fact taken place, that, of course, I wanted to celebrate. And I did, too, rather quietly, but with a good dinner and a bottle of champagne—for I had won a bit of money at the track. Though for the life of me I couldn't today tell you what horse it was, or even why I bet on him.

For the next few days I took things quietly. The racing had now shifted entirely to jumping at Auteuil and Enghien, or to the trotting at Vincennes, which the *Daily Mail* did not consider any too seriously. The record part of past performances was only as much as I wanted to make it—for the paper's tradition was what one might expect an English paper's to be regarding trotting, that is, hardly as racing at all. Trotting was for halfbreeds—what Australians, I was informed, irreverently call the "Red Hots"—and hence suspect as a sporting proposition. The "Lutetius" before me, in fact, had regarded the trotting season as more or less an unofficial holiday, which he took in lieu of the fact that there were no days off during the rest of the year. But I felt strongly that the paper ought to deal more thoroughly with trotting. I wrote long pieces about the meetings, especially the holiday Saturday and Sunday ones, which attracted such big crowds; I tried hard to give winners, and I succeeded better than might have been expected; I even contributed one or two "feature" special articles on the subject, just to show my good-will.

It happened again—just before noon, as I was crossing the street near the office. I had meant to go across to the *"Tabac"* to buy some cigarettes before I took the autobus—there were many of them which cruised along the Boulevards from about noon on. The fare varied between 4 and 6 francs, depending upon the style of the autobus—new or old, glass-enclosed or open to the Parisian elements of rain or wind, driven by a smart-looking chauffeur or an obvious thug whose one idea was to get there in time to lay a bet himself on the first race. And, of course, the fare was a franc or two higher on the "big" days of Saturday and Sunday, when there was a crowd, following the old law of supply and demand. If you had the patience, you could take the *"Métro"* to the Porte de Vincennes, and pick up an automobile there—or, finally, you could go by train, once you had reached the Bastille railroad station, which was something of an adventure in itself. And even when you got off the train at Joinville-le-Pont—which is as far as it could take you—you had either a long, healthy walk to the track, or the choice, for two or three francs, of a ride with three others (and the driver), in an old-fashioned four-wheeler.

Despite the complications, I often went this way, because I could sleep in the train back to the Bastille station. But the conventional and simplest way, direct by autobus from the office itself right to the track, was the usual choice for me. I say the "Conventional and simplest," for so it was, provided you didn't mind the way the autobuses were driven. If you had any nerves at all, they would be shattered by the time you reached the track—as was the case, too, if you went by autobus to Enghien, or, for that matter, to almost any of the Parisian tracks. I had looked death in the face at least a half dozen times on my excursions to the race-track, and once I had actually been in an accident where two people in my car were killed. But, like most other things which become a matter of habit, the reckless driving—and the highly skillful driving, too, I ought to add, or otherwise there would have been accidents every day—soon seemed ordinary. Slow driving, cautious driving, got on your nerves, for—literally, not as a joke—your chances of being hurt were far less with a driver who followed the customary high-speed rhythm than with the driver who always played "safe."

But I was destined never to reach Vincennes that afternoon. I never took the autobus. I never even got across the Boulevard to buy my cigarettes. For, just as I started across, I went blind again—in the middle of one of the busiest main streets of Paris at one of the busiest hours of the day. Why I was not run over and all my troubles ended then and there, I shall never know. All I do know is that the traffic stopped and snarled, whistles blew, horns honked, a policeman came over and took my arm—somehow I found myself at a café table, with a sympathetic Frenchman asking me what was the matter. I explained as well as I could, but I found it difficult to tell him how everything had gone black—how, even as I talked with him, things were indistinct and uncertain. I tried to buy him a drink out of politeness, but it was no go—and after perhaps twenty minutes, during which time he had practically poured a *café-fine* down my throat, I found once again, as I had before, that my vision seemed almost normal.

"Mon vieux," the Frenchman said quite kindly, "I am not a doctor, and I can't tell you what is the trouble. But blindness is no joke, is it not? You had better go to a hospital and get a thorough examination."

He bowed and went his way, with only the admonition—"Don't neglect it. Go."

For a long time I sat at the café. Maybe I was reflecting; maybe I was getting up my courage; maybe I was coming to some really important decision. Who can say? I know I considered the idea of suicide—who of us hasn't? I considered many ideas. But certain vanities seemed to die within me forever—I realized that never again should I look at the world with the same naïve, confident, self-assured look that had once seemed the most natural thing in the world. For a moment I had just a glimmer—only a glimmer, I repeat, though I wonder how many of us ever even have had that much—of how a man feels when he is sentenced to be executed. I had, for the first time, that odd, terrible insight which tells us how we are—no matter what we do, nor to whom we turn, nor in what "imponderables" we pretend to believe—finally and fatally alone.

It was about half-past two. I got up, paid the bill, and went around the corner to the *Daily Mail* office. Luckily the chief was in his office. He looked curiously at me.

"I didn't go out to the races today," I said, though this was one of those foolish ways of breaking the ice, for it was quite obvious I wasn't there. "The truth is, I am having trouble with my eyes, and I don't know what's the matter. If it's all the same to you, I'll take my two weeks' vacation a little earlier than I planned—it's the short end of the season, as you call it, and this is as good a time as any from the paper's point of view. And I'm going to spend it out in the American hospital; a racing man, I think you'll agree, has got to take care of his eyes, almost above everything else."

"I'm sorry, Stearns," he said. "Go ahead, if you want to. It's all right with me. What's the matter with your eyes—been drinking too much?"

"No; I'm pretty sure it's not that—I only wish it were. I'd go on the wagon for life, if I knew for a certainty that that had anything to do with it. But that's just the trouble—I'm afraid it's more serious."

Even though he was the type of Englishman I don't like, I must say the boss was unexpectedly human about the thing.

"Stop worrying. Go out, and get fixed up. Your job will be here for you—and don't bother coming in tonight. Take it easy. By the way, go up to the cashier's and draw a month's salary in advance. You may need it. Cheer up. Everything will be all right."

And so I thought it would be, too. For Diana Swift took time off from her job to ride out with me—that heartbreaking ride beyond the Porte de Neuilly—to the hospital, where (like most every other American newspaperman and newspaperwoman, at some time or other, and for some reason or other, of which plain alcoholism was not the least infrequent) I was accepted without question. Yet being an American, and at the same time being on the one *English* newspaper in Paris, rather surprised the hospital authorities, despite Diana's simple explanation of the strange phenomenon. However, other Americans had worked for the *Daily Mail,* too, in particular those who got out the "News Of Americans In Paris" column, and I suppose I did not seem so unusual after all. But as a matter of fact in one respect I was more unusual than they thought: I have been one of the few Americans anywhere to do *racing* for an English newspaper. Anyway, Diana bade me goodnight; I was put to bed in a private room after a hot bath and a sleeping potion and a stiff drink; and for almost the first time for months I had twelve hours of dreamless sleep. I didn't want ever to wake up.

The next day the doctors were plainly puzzled. One test after another was given me. My "case" history for as far back as I could remember was duly put down. Every vital organ, as well as several that struck me as superfluous, were examined in shameless detail, as a Thorne Smith character might express it. My teeth were obviously in bad shape; I drank too much (that is, I confessed to drinking too much, though I never discovered just what was meant by "too" much—a gill or a gallon a day or an hour?); I smoked too much; my diet was not perfect even though I lived in France.

Despite the fact that for years I had walked in the open air, rain or shine, for at least three hours at the races, every single day of my life, I didn't take the proper exercise; I read too much fine print (or maybe I didn't read enough of it, I have forgotten); twice I had to repeat the simple fact that neither did I, nor ever had I, taken drugs—outside of alcohol of course. My love life was directly inquired into, and I could see that the darkest things were suspected of me. Talk about a Catholic confessional!—is there any secret, bodily or psychic, a modern doctor doesn't want to know? I marvelled. And when I jestingly asked why they didn't inquire as to whether I had ever subconsciously been armorous of my grandmother (whom, incidentally, I had never seen), they wrote something down, which I imagine was to the effect that I was an impossible and flippant patient.

Certainly I proved a difficult one. I had not a bit of confidence in their powers of diagnosis—for I have found it a melancholy fact that when you can question the general intellectual powers of a doctor, you oftenest end by questioning his specific professional ability as well. This is unfortunate, for there are many excellent doctors, who—take them on almost any subject outside their specialty—are none too bright. But my instinct is a sound one, nevertheless. For if a man is a fool in one subject, he is likely to be a fool in all subjects too. The quality of sound and logical thinking on evidence and drawing conclusions from the evidence is not a special faculty apart from specific aptitudes—it is a part of a man's whole way of thinking and acting. Beware of the doctor, who is not also an all-round cultivated man—beware of him, not because he is a dull fellow to talk with, but because he may in the end prove to be a bad doctor. Particularly, he may prove to be a bad diagnostician, who, more than anybody else, is subject to the temptations of faddism and of not seeing the forest of a human body because of the glandular trees.

When, finally, after two or three days of different tests, with no luck with any vital organs (and, as I told them, I had always been worried about my heart, but they laughed that one off), they went into a huddle, and announced that I had a blood disease, which—and this they were considerate enough to put in writing—was neither "contagious nor infectious," but which might be affecting my vision. They gave me a few injections, and told me I could go back to work, but that for a certain length of time I ought to return as an out-patient for treatment. There was no danger of my going blind; there was no danger of anything. I thanked them; and left the hospital with a light heart.

But not for long. For whether the *Daily Mail* chief didn't believe the hospital authorities, whether he didn't want to, or whether he was glad anyway of the chance to "take up" my contract (for though he tried hard, I know in his heart he couldn't forgive me for being an American), the result was the same. Shortly before Christmas I found myself in Paris without a job for the first time in several years. But at least I had a few thousand francs in my pocket. And I decided, remembering a letter I had received from Strong while I was in the hospital inviting me down there (he mailed in his five-days a week column, since he could—and did—write on any subject he chose) to Collioure and to take it easy for a few weeks. Phoebe Strong was an old friend of mine, too; finally, Diana Swift thought it would be a good idea, and said she had telephoned my doctor at the hospital, who approved.

Somehow I got down to Collioure—for I was really much more ill than I suspected. But I got off at the wrong station, and had the devil's own time before I finally found even Perpignan. That was near enough. I got out, and hired a car to take me over to Collioure—a good three hours' run skirting the foothills of the Pyrenées most of the way, until finally you climb up hundreds of feet above the Mediterranean, and then twist and fall down into that lovely little town, right on the sea. I sat down at the first café I met—the "Grand," it was called, of course—and sent a message over to the hotel, which as a matter of fact was only a stone's throw away. But I didn't know that, then.

Both Phoebe and Adolph came over at once. And I don't think I have ever been so glad to see any two people in my life. Many years have gone by since then, but I can still remember with what joy I saw, in a strange town and ill, two old and loyal friends, who spoke my own language and who—no matter about anything unpleasant in the past—had a real affection for me.

"We'll let nothing worry you down here, Harold," said Adolph. "This is a nice town, full of crazy people, but almost all of them are friendly. It's about the only small town in the world where there is not to be found any malicious peasant gossip. And there are a lot of dogs and cats, all of them just as crazy as the inhabitants."

I said I was glad to find that out. But the blood disease diagnosis, I confessed, got on my nerves.

"Those doctors up in Paris," Adolph continued scornfully, while Phoebe nodded her approval of his sentiments, "are so dumb that they couldn't distinguish between leprosy and just an ordinary hum-drum case of delirium tremens, such as you have. The real trouble with you, Harold, as I've always said, is simply that you don't drink enough."

And following precept with example, Adolph promptly ordered me one of the drinks of the country, a "Banyeuls"—a kind of port wine, but very strong. He said that after a half dozen or so of them you would feel able to, and might try to, swim to Africa. "And it's really a free country down here," he added. "Nobody would try to stop you."

I began to feel better already. Almost anybody would.

Our dinner at Madame Cantina's where Adolph and Polly lived and where they got me a room beside them (luckily, for there were only a few in the house, but it was the off season, even for belated traveling salesmen, who infest France exactly as they do our own fair land), was very gay. Madame Cantina herself was a handsome, big, goodnatured though strong-willed woman whose husband had disappeared (or been asked to leave) years before, and whose son was at Versailles, studying for the engineer corps of the army. She conducted the hotel herself, with the help of a part-time maid, and an all-time maid of all work, a child she had more or less adopted, but whom she treated very kindly. She was an excellent cook—in fact, an excellent manager, for she had installed modern plumbing. The lights, too, were modern electric—but that was not surprising, because all through this region of the Pyrenees there are power-conversion stations, depending, of course, on the water-flow from the mountains. And although Madame Cantina complained as a matter of principle about the bills, charges for current were very low, all things considered. For a good part of the year heating presented little of a problem, but when the "Tri-montagne" wind (something like the Mistral, only worse) came roaring down upon the valley, the stoves in each room, with the crackling brushwood snapping under the covers, were very welcome, even if the problem of making them burn without filling the house with smoke was apparently an insurmountable one.

I don't know, but I think a painter would have gone mad in Madame Cantina's dining room. For almost every inch of the four walls was covered with canvasses, good, bad, and just terrible. Not a few of them were gifts from former clients of the hotel—Collioure was very popular with painters, many of whom came from Germany and Italy in the summer months. The scenery was magnificent, and the light in the air, the colors, the *patina* on the walls of all the buildings, even the inhabitants themselves, were arresting to the eye, if you cared about things visual. Everything in Collioure was a provocation; even if you cared about nothing at all, there was no resisting the lure of that bright soft sunshine. The colored sails of the boats along the beach, as the old women gossiped and repaired rents in the torn blue, pink, green, even orange windjammers, were like a gay backdrop to a setting for one of the old Balkan operettas that used to be so popular when I was a young man. In fact the beauty of Collioure took my breath away that first morning walk the next day. I think I could have remained in the little café on the beach, only a small dog's dash from Madame Cantina's, every morning, with the sun pouring over you and the white and colored sails on the Mediterranean bringing out the extra deep blue of the water—and beside and back of you the towering, snow-capped Pyrenees.

Nor did I use the phrase "a small dog's dash" inadvisedly. There were thousands of dogs in Collioure—at least a half dozen for every human being in the town—and they ranged in size from the very small to the huge, with almost every known breed, or lack of it, in evidence. During my morning walks down and back to the beach I got to know scores of them, and it was less than a week before I had four that more or less considered they belonged to me, at least for the purposes of play, taking a walk, and begging for sugar, of which they were all inordinately fond. There was ridiculous Mascot (a lady, notwithstanding her name, as she gave evidence of with great regularity by becoming one of the most careless canine mothers in the world); sharp and keen and friendly little Togo (who could swim like a circus dog, when he wanted to, which was a little unusual for a Collioure dog, as most of the others seemed to have an almost sacred horror of water); the big, dignified "Squire" with the patient, greedy eyes; the pathetic Misery, who looked like her name, the poor little frightened, shivering wretch (I think the only unhappy dog in Collioure, though I ought to add in any other community on earth she would have been done away with by the health authorities on sight). And there were plenty of others, barking, gay, chasing their own tails when nothing better offered.

Rather oddly, cats were not one of the better things—though there were thousands of them, too, for the sardines brought in every morning by the boats made Collioure a cats' paradise. But there was a truce between the cats and the dogs in Collioure. That is to say, the dogs pretended not to see them. For the cats were enormous—and quite able to defend themselves stoutly when attacked, as all Collioure puppies early learned. The cats adopted different houses in which to live, as suited them—as I have said, it was their paradise, one of the few places on earth where there was plenty of food for all, warmth and sunlight, cool nights for love-making and vocal exercises, and no responsibilities. What more could any cat—even one of Don Marquis' famous felines—ask of life?

In many respects the citizens matched their menagerie. The sea was bountiful in sardines—the one real industry of the village—and wine and vegetables and sub-tropical fruits were abundant and cheap. Heating presented no problem. Except for the Christmas and spring festivals, when there was dancing and music for a week on end, and for church and courting, the problem of smart clothes did not arise—which from one point of view was a pity, since some of the younger women and girls were remarkably handsome, though the early bloom seemed to fade almost too quickly. (Madame Cantina—and I noticed the same thing with some of the older women on the beach repairing sails in the morning—was a striking and almost dramatic exception.) But the young women, at least a few of them, took your breath away with their beauty. I have never seen anything like it in any other small village in France—I only hope it is still true, when I go back to visit Collioure again in my old age. Perhaps canning factories, or some other industrial blight, will have turned the scales against beauty once more—as we have seen it do in so many otherwise idyllic spots. No place today, not even Collioure, seems to be able to resist at least one attack of the Manchester and Birmingham and Pittsburgh measles.

Collioure was just the place for me at the time I went there—I believe I should have gone morally and physically to pieces had I stayed on in Paris. Yet as my health improved, I began to miss Paris, the races, the cafés and people I knew, more than anything else, the newspapers and hum of things taking place, for after all the backwaters of life are—the backwaters. Collioure was lovely, but it was like stepping out of your own century into another. I won't make comparisons and say which is better or worse morally—I don't know. Though I do know which is the more charming. But unfortunately one cannot live with charm all one's life, and not have it turn sour.

That, I might add, is the mistake many young men seem to make in picking a wife—however, this has gone far enough. I say only—"Go to Collioure some day, if you can. But don't remain." For we confuse picture postcard sentiments too often with reality; our very uglinesses are things we should miss, if they were no longer there to be inveighed against. It is what we know and are accustomed to and can deal with—not what we can admire and look at—that counts for our lasting enjoyment, the real elation of being alive.

Yet I am terribly glad now I went to Collioure when I did. I think it saved my life.

XIX. BROKE AND BITTER

THERE was no staying on in Collioure forever—though I dreaded going back to Paris. Had Adolph been a millionaire, I believe he would have kept me on until at least my nerves had been quieted. But life was a bit "hectic" for him, too—he made it such. He quarreled with Phoebe unnecessarily, I thought, though I was myself in no position to judge; my own health and being out of a job absorbed what little energy I had, for with me at least there is nothing physically so exhausting and nerve-wracking as having literally nothing to do. Most of my life I have been busy at something; I like work, when it has any point to it at all—I believe most normal men do. "Loafing," as it is called—particularly when a man has money, like many men I have known—is not really loafing at all—it is fussing around, keeping oneself occupied with the semblance of activity. In all my life I have met only three or four of what might be called "natural born" loafers—and they were all gentlemen of a somewhat darker color persuasion than I can boast of. I haven't any moral objections to the loafer; in fact, I rather admire him, perhaps am a little envious of him, I'm not sure. But I'm not happy—most men of the temperate zone, so to speak, are not happy—doing nothing. It's a lost art, like the lost paradise of Eden.

To many people who saw me night after night at the "Select," piling up the saucers which represented so many *coupes* of champagne, it may seem odd for me to write in this manner—odd, until they remember that every day during that champagne period I was at the races professionally, that I worked from one o'clock in the afternoon until half-past eight in the evening with no let-up and at a high nervous tension: Not merely six days out of the week, but seven days, and for months on end without a "break." Watching the people—imbecilic or not—was my diversion and relaxation. Also I would read my newspapers and magazines. I have even—like a Frenchman—written articles in the café, as Scott Fitzgerald can testify. The paradox I am trying to explain is this: Paris is a wonderful place in which to loaf, if you also have a regular job. Your spare time is never long enough; whereas in America and England, too, far too many honest citizens have the fidgets, if they are not doing something—even such a low form of cerebral activity as attending moving pictures.

But I was going back to a new kind of Paris for me—a Paris of enforced idleness, of being a bum, whether I wanted to be one or not. I didn't realize it at first, of course. The train from the South got into the Gare d'Orsay about noon on a sunny Sunday, and I thought, the first thing, of the races that afternoon at Longchamp. I took my bag, with what few clothes I had in it, over to Harry's bar. I left it there, and borrowed a few francs from the barman, but I didn't see a soul I knew—though that is hardly surprising on a Sunday morning. Reluctantly, I decided not to go to the races. I couldn't bear to go and not go into the *pésage,* which meant 75 francs right off—and I would have to have a "sure" 10 to 1 shot to justify that. And I didn't even know what horses were starting.

Though Diana had seen me off on the train down to Collioure, and though she had even written me friendly and amusing letters, when I telephoned her that Sunday noon I knew at once that she didn't want to see me. That hurt. But at least she gave me one bit of cheering information. At Collioure, in a desperate mood, I had one day written to a friend and old classmate at Harvard, telling him of my plight and asking him, if he could and wanted to, to send me some money. Over the telephone Diana told me that my college friend had sent the money I had asked for to her, not being sure of where I was and knowing that she would see I got it. She had put it in Morgan's for me, and if I would go there in the morning, they would give it to me on identification. I thanked her for the good news—and that is the last time I have ever talked with her. I never saw her again . . . though, perhaps, some day here in America now that things have changed for me. Yet I am not even sure that I really want to see her—some things are too painful; some ashes can never be rekindled. Yet I know I shall always be fond of her, always be missing her. I should like again to hear her laugh, to listen to her comments on people and things. When I think of her, I sometimes say to myself: "I have spent years alienating people I love. Well, for the rest of my life I shall try to keep my friends. I shan't be afraid any more of being hurt by loving people. Only our foolish pride is hurt really."

The next morning that money seemed almost to burn me. I got myself a cheap room, paying a week's rent in advance. I bought a few sorely needed clothes. And then I went up to Montparnasse, just looking for trouble, though I didn't know it. Had the races on that Monday been anywhere except Saint-Cloud—which had then for me, as it has now, too much of evil memory of the day I went blind—I might have, I probably would have, gone out. And that might have changed everything; I might have been lucky at the track—you never can tell what you would have done, *had* you gone racing. You always think you would have backed the profitable long shots. But something seems to happen to your racing judgment when you need money, when you *must* win. I don't know why it is; it is always when you are "flush" that you can't make a mistake at the track. Anyway, I shall never know whether I should have won or lost, for I didn't go. I wish I had. Instead, I went up to the "Select" and tried to drink all the champagne in the house. And to make the score perfect, I ran into an American girl, who had been the mistress of a friend of mine, and insisted on taking her "up the hill" to Zelli's. I didn't want anything to do with her amorously—I was afraid to be alone.

Today I think I understand that fear of loneliness better than I did then, and, understanding it, the fear would largely disappear. But it was a fear which then cost me dear, for, when I woke up in my little room around noon the next day, I discovered I had left a package of "Yellow" cigarettes and 100 francs—or about the equivalent of five sizeable meals. I remember reflecting rather bitterly, "Why, I might just as well have gone to the races, after all. It would have cost me less, even had I not won—and I might have won." So I got dressed, went out to the nearest café, stopping at a newsstand long enough to purchase a copy of *La Veine* and of *L'Oeuvre* (which I usually read because of the column by Fouchardière, perhaps the cleverest daily column of comment in any newspaper in the world), and ordered a *croissant* and *café noir.* I dawdled over the papers and my *café* a long time, because I hadn't wanted to think. I didn't want to ask myself the question that I was going to be forced to ask myself so many times later on—that most hopeless of all questions:— "What shall I do now?"

Around two o'clock I decided I would go down to the *Tribune* office and see the boys. Perhaps there might be a letter for me—that had been my address for years, and sometimes I received letters from friends. Possibly, too, somebody I knew might be arriving on the boat that got in on Tuesday; there would be the list of passengers at the office. But in the back of my mind, of course, there was a different and more serious hope—a hope that there might be some kind of a job. I thought, with a pride that I hoped would somehow communicate itself to others, that I was a pretty good newspaperman after all, and that I could do about anything on a paper except set up the type. I took the *Métro* down to Notre Dame de Lorette, and walked over to the entrance on the Rue Trudaine, which I knew so well—where, so many times in the past when I returned from the races after a successful day, I had gone up the stairs with a light heart and a bulging purse.

As I expected, only one or two of the "day" men were fussing around the office, chiefly occupied in reading French newspapers in the hope of getting some kind of a human interest story that would have two attractive features—I mean, a story easy to read and translate, and, secondly, a story that would not involve the trouble of calling up anybody for verification or further information by telephone, for the *Tribune* boys were firm partisans of what the French call "the least effort." We exchanged greetings, and after some rummaging around they found two letters for me—one a bill from Tiffany's, stating that my stop-watch was repaired and asking me to call for it (with 175 francs, incidentally); the other a letter forwarded from New York, asking me to subscribe to a charitable fund being raised for former professional women, now in reduced circumstances. The S. S. "Olympic" got in the next day at Cherbourg, and I asked to look at the passenger list, which the publicity agents always sent around a day or so before the vessels arrive. But there wasn't anybody I knew on board—not even anybody I could remotely imagine I knew. On my way out I met Frankle, the new boss since my day on the paper (he had been a reporter in my time, and I knew him as one of the old gang). He was pleasant and friendly, but he pretty effectively dashed any hope I had of getting a job, for he said he was "full up" then and that his real problem at that moment was how to get rid of a couple of men rather than to put another man on the staff. My old racing job, as I knew, was done by somebody downstairs (by that, was always meant the copy-reading room) who doubled up his work for the extra pay. He was not brilliant, but he was good enough—and this arrangement cost the paper only a bit of extra money, "even less," Frankle added rather graciously, "than what we used to insult you with." Still, he would keep me in mind—and I went out, wishing to God he had not used that particular phrase, which in newspaper parlance means very simply "nothing doing."

For old times' sake—that is what I said to myself then, though probably for no other reason than I didn't know what to do—I went to the café of "The Three Doors" on the Rue Lafayette (like Gillotte's, one of the boys' hang-outs) and had a drink. No luck with the *Tribune*. The *Daily Mail*, naturally, was out of the question. If only the chief over at the *Herald* didn't dislike me so—why on earth had I gone out of my way to poke fun at him at that Anglo-American press dinner a couple of years before? He would be glad to see me in trouble now, I felt sure. (I never, as a matter of fact, found out how he felt.) Besides that, Diana was on the paper now, and although perhaps she wouldn't say anything directly against me, I knew perfectly well she wouldn't exactly espouse my cause. I was just plain out of luck, that was all there was to it. I had better recognize the fact. And to fortify myself sufficiently to face this unpleasant reality I took another drink—just as other men, just as foolishly, have done before me. In fact, I took several. But although vermouth-cassis is almost sickish sweet, they all tasted sour to me, sour and bitter. Finally, I paid the bill and left, as I counted my change saying to myself, "I won't have to worry about dinner anyway now—I can't afford any dinner."

There are periods in our life, I think—at least, I can only assume so, judging from my own experience—which stubbornly resist all efforts of our memory to recapture. The defensive mechanism of pride is terribly strong; it refuses to let us admit that such things could happen to *us*. *Those* are things we read about in books, that happen to characters in modern psychological novels, but never, never to us. I was starting on such a period right then, and it was to last for months. I imagine it lasted about as long as it can last without a man pretty definitely going out of his mind, that is to say, for about seven months. I think now, in fact I know now, that these were the most terrible months of my life, and that whatever happens to me in the future, *they* at least can never be repeated. There are some things none of us have the strength to endure twice over, though capacity for punishment is much greater than most people leading ordinary, conventional lives ever imagine. Yet when you are in such a *de profundis* period, so to speak, you are tricked in a strange way—as each new and more terrible thing happens, you say to yourself, "This is the last. I can't stand any more." But you do. You do and you do again and again. Sensibilities change. Happiness, which meant nothing less than security, friends, an amusing and interesting life, comes to mean much simpler things. Things like warmth, a full stomach, a decent pair of shoes, a clean bed in which to sleep even up to noon undisturbed, if you wish. When it gets down to about its lowest terms—as it actually did with me—you can look no further ahead than a glass of water, and you think of all the possible cafés where you might go and not be refused that sort of elementary animal courtesy.

Yet across this dark period there will be flashes of light—moments of relative peace, even charm. And those moments will be the ones that come back to you in after years, as they are the ones that recur most easily to me now. Of the other times—well, it is like the moments of pain in a hospital after you have been discharged cured. Try to think of them again, even remotely to feel them over once more. (What is most extraordinary, to learn the lesson of not repeating the same follies that caused the original trouble, is, seemingly, one of the lessons most light-heartedly and casually thrown out the window—I mean, the instant you feel strong enough to throw them out of the window.) You can pretend to do it, but you can't really do it—and I believe that what we think of as romantic literature, in the derogatory sense of that adjective, is the kind that has this faint, feeble echo of experience forever lost. There is a catch somewhere in the notion of "impassioned recollection" of things which you wish in your heart of hearts had never happened at all. Instinctively—at least normally, perhaps I should say—we all know there is sufficient pain in the world without our going to the trouble of trying to rebuild what has already become, as we say, an unpleasant memory. No, it is those moments when the ache in your heart lifted, if ever so slightly—those are the only moments when our vision is at all clear. The rest are moments like those of sleep, or perhaps of death. They are the moments of nothingness that enshroud our life; the moments we would passionately deny.

There were weeks at this time when, had you met me on the street and asked me where I had spent the night, I could not have answered you truthfully. I don't know myself. Sometimes it was on one of the low benches along the Boulevard Montparnasse near the church, where I would wait for early morning mass, and go in and sit quietly in the back pews—sometimes even stand in back—just for the little sense of warmth and change and human contacts. Sometimes it would be in a cheap room in one of those horrible little hotels for *"voyageurs"* that cluster around the streets leading to the Montparnasse railroad station—where, usually, you had to be out by eleven o'clock in the morning or else pay for an extra day. Sometimes I would run into a friend or an acquaintance who, oftenest shocked by my appearance, would "stake" me, as we say, to a night's rest and perhaps a meal. It may sound ridiculous, but many and many a time I have encountered somebody who would buy me 75 or 100 francs worth of drinks—which I didn't want—and then look pained, when I asked for 25 francs to get a cheap hotel room so that I might have a place to sleep.

Once or twice I had luck. I ran into a man on the Boulevard Montparnasse, who had met me but once before at Longchamp. "We're going to the races this afternoon," he said. "But you can't go in those rags you have on. We've just got time to go downtown and get you a new outfit, have lunch, and make the first race."

Almost in a dream, I went down with him to his bank. He bought me a new hat, a suit, shoes, shirts—a whole outfit. Then we had an expensive lunch, which I—damning my weak stomach all the time, for I wanted to eat and could hardly do more than nibble, of course—looked at rather than consumed, feeling also a little astonished and a little ashamed that the wine seemed to go to my head so easily. This strange gentleman—I honestly can't remember his name; I know only that he came from Texas, and hence had had considerable affection for all Texans ever since—actually had a car of his own (and a swank one, too), and we went out to the races in style. Rather ironically, I thought, the races that day were at Saint-Cloud, where I had not been since my misfortune—and there I was showing up, dapper and swell, as if I had suddenly come into a million dollars instead of actually having gone through months of hell. I don't remember much about the races that day, but my old instincts couldn't have entirely deserted me, for we did rather well, and my share—for he scrupulously divided the winnings in half—came to three or four thousand francs—enough to keep me going for a month, if I was careful.

Of course I wasn't careful. We had to celebrate our success that night, and I felt as a matter of honor I should at least pay half, since everything was due to him—and his idea of a celebration was a large and expansive one. But at that, I had something left. Furthermore, he decided I was such "good luck" at the races that we ought to go again a couple of days later to Maisons-Laffitte, which unfortunately is one of the tracks around Paris where finding winners is about as easy as finding a ten-dollar bill in a New York subway car. Yet I even managed to find a couple of miracles there, by some stroke of good luck or intuition or something. And that money—and my share again was about what it had been the previous day—I managed to keep my hands on more successfully. For at least a week or so my walking-the-street days were over. And I was fairly well dressed, too. My confidence began to come back to me. Perhaps I didn't need to work, anyway. Maybe I could get by without bothering.

I soon proved, of course, that I was in error. My Texas friend took himself and his expensive car to Biarritz, and I went out to Le Tremblay all by myself one fine day to repeat. I had studied the "form" sheets very carefully; I thought I knew at least three—or perhaps even four—winners of the six races of the day. Alas! it was the same old story—I knew exactly one winner, and he was an odds-on favorite. I left the track with exactly 50 francs—and I was due to pay another week's rent at the hotel in two days. Once again I began to think about getting a job, for of course during this strange interlude of prosperity I had forgotten that there ever was such a thing.

It was the day after this Le Tremblay disaster that I ran into "Hem," who had come back from America after his first success, and was then, if I recall correctly, on his way to Germany to see about some stage or translation rights of his book, "A Farewell To Arms." He did what he could—that is, he got my typewriter out of pawn, gave me some cash, paid for my hotel, and tried to suggest one or two possible markets for some articles. But by this time he was definitely out of the newspaper game—I think he was glad of it, too—and he had no leads to give me looking towards a regular newspaper job in Paris. He probably didn't realize the difficulties I was up against anyway in getting a job in Paris on a newspaper—how, by this time, the myth had grown that I could always make money "on my own" at the track and that I didn't need a job anyway, not to mention the fact, of course, that the whispering campaign about my health stood me in no good purpose either. However, this much I can say for Hemingway—and I am glad to say, too: He always has acted the way you would expect a friend to act in all the years I have known him; he has never "let me down;" and, what I think I like best of all, he has always been honest with me. As probably he would write it, he has never kidded me.

A few days later Shipman appeared unexpectedly on the scene, as he was in the habit of doing in those years. He had no particular plans, though vaguely he wanted to get some sort of a racing job in Paris, if there was one. He had a bit of money, and very kindly invited me to live with him at the Hotel Montana, in the Saint-Germain quarter, right around the corner from the Deux Magots, as a matter of fact. It was a nice hotel, full of fantastic people, but very comfortable and blessed with an agreeable *patronne*. Phoebe, for example, separated finally from Adolph and back in Paris to obtain a divorce and make it permanent, lived in a small but pleasant room on the floor below us. A couple of other Americans had rooms in the hotel—in a way, it was sort of a big family party. I don't know what *la patronne* thought of us; we must have outraged every French tradition of her class and education. But whatever she thought, she was tolerant in fact—and she had need of all her tolerance.

The weeks I passed there, though fairly happy because loneliness was one thing I don't believe anybody at that period ever experienced at the Hotel Montana, were weeks that brought me great disillusion in one respect. I had thought I was well enough to write articles, even a book possibly. But I wasn't. I couldn't concentrate; I couldn't seem to remember anything. I tried—tried with pathetic desperation—to write even as simple and straightforward an account of my stay in Collioure and the amusing people there as I have done in the previous chapter in this book. But I couldn't do it. I couldn't seem to remember anything, and what I did remember was as often as not wrong. I do remember applying for a Guggenheim scholarship to write a book on Rabelais—a book I intend to do anyway, if I live long enough—and feeling the victim of a conspiracy because I didn't even get a reply to my application. (No wonder I did not; Heaven only knows what address I sent with that application.) I even wrote one or two articles for the little magazines in English that were then being published in Paris—or rather, to be quite frank, promising to write the articles, and always somehow finding it impossible to get them done. The plain truth is I was in no condition to write anything; I was sick—really sick—but I didn't know it.

Finally, however, there was no disguising it. Shipman knew it; Phoebe knew it; everybody knew it apparently except myself. The weeks had turned into months at the Montana—it was getting near to the season I dreaded so in Paris because of the unhappy associations of the previous year, that is, the holiday season. But things were going from bad to worse. I hardly knew what was going on around me, and seemed to care even less—when I think back on it now, I must have been a terrible nuisance to my friends in that hotel. Perhaps it was a feeling of hopelessness, perhaps it was because I wanted to go back and once and for all get the American Hospital to go on record about me (as, of course, I had intended to do before, and had done nothing), chiefly, I think, it was because I was tired out, physically and mentally—anyway, I decided to go out once more to the Hospital, if they would have me.

My French friend, Pierre, who had a great deal of tact, spoke English perfectly, and was always loyal to me, at my request arranged the matter. And once more just before the New Year, exactly as the year before, though this time in a modest general ward rather than in a private room of my own, I found myself in bed when the churchbells announced that somehow, magically, 1931 had become 1932.

I stayed in the hospital until the 7th. As before, I thought I was better after a few days. But a few more days back in Paris were quite sufficient to convince me that I was wrong, as they did all my friends, too. Once more—it was to be the last time, though I didn't know it—I returned on the 14th. When careful diagnosis proved what I had always known—that I was being poisoned by my teeth, nothing else—they decided that, drastic as it might be, removal of all my teeth was the only thing that would bring me sure release. I consented, and one fine morning I tried to take the elevator from the ward up to the operating room with a cheerful countenance—coming back pretty weak and faint, my head covered with bandages, but free at last of the sources of infection that had been making a mess out of my life for years. I knew it instinctively then; I know it from the factual record since. Despite the pain, despite the dizziness and fever, despite the awful feeling of being, so to speak, forever mutilated, I knew, too, that I was free—that it was over with. Anyone, I reflected with what assumed cheerfulness most of us then try to exhibit, can get along with false teeth, but no one has yet invented a substitute for one's eyes. Indeed, after a long sleep of reaction, I woke up almost cheerful.

With no teeth, few friends, no job, and no money I naturally decided that all I could do was to return to my own country—and to try to start all over. Everything about Paris had suddenly become distasteful to me; I suppose because I felt so alien and alone. Something deep in me, however, kept saying, "Go home, go home, that is the place for you. Go home to America." But how?

Well, I don't know exactly how I did it. First, I had to obtain a passport, more to prove that I was I instead of somebody else. The American Consulate testified to that, and gave me a passport without much difficulty, as they had a record, I believe, of my previous one, and in any event there was no real question—except, I ought to add, the slight difficulty of a $5.00 Consular stamp, which meant 125 francs in those days. Pierre got me the passport. In those days, too, there was an "American Aid Society" in Paris, which made it a business to send home Americans in my situation. They got me passage on a half freighter, half passenger boat, as well as a ticket to Le Havre. Pierre gave me a few simple things I might need on the voyage; Phoebe, too, did what she could; Shipman gave me a little extra cash for the boat. It was all "set," as we express it. And thus on the next to the last day in January, 1932, I found myself on the train for Le Havre, bound for home. It was not quite the sort of parting with France I had ever anticipated.

The freighter did not go from the conventional docks of the big liners, and I had considerable difficulty finding where the boat was. I got there late, but not too late by about a quarter of an hour, thank God, for I should never have had the courage to go back to Paris, had I missed the sailing. It was a pleasant enough freighter, and although the food was nothing to boast about, and although there were two other people in the small cabin with me, I didn't care. I felt safe, at least for the few days that the boat made the crossing. Nothing would, nothing could, hurt me now. For after all, I was going home.

We sailed rather late in the evening, going by docks and through ship canals before we reached the Channel, and even after we had, for an hour or two one could see the lights on the shore. It was quite late before we reached the open sea and darkness all outside. But we were going directly Westward; we were on our course. I fell asleep late, wondering vaguely what this new adventure of returning home could mean at my age. And in the condition I was in, too, I thought sleepily. Also, there was a depression on at home—and with that final thought I lost consciousness.

Like most North Atlantic crossings, there was nothing special to record about the trip—a few fine days, despite the season of the year, several nasty ones, but fine or nasty always steadily plugging Westward. The Captain was not a bad sort —an old-timer with lots of tall stories, but an American, after all, who spoke a familiar accent—and there was a very agreeable fellow from Saint Louis or Cincinnati, who somehow made me realize that, when all was said and done, genuine human beings still lived in America,—I had been away a long time, but there was nothing to be frightened about. Things were bad, yes; but they would get better. And it was lucky I was coming home to America to get my false teeth; that, I gathered, was one of the great accomplishments of our age and our country—i. e., our marvellous dentistry. He was a likeable chap, and one of the things I liked about him was that he said quite frankly he preferred the American girl to the French girl—though I gathered, too, that he had been a bit luckier with the former than with the latter. However, I felt even at the time that henceforth my interest in girls would be largely academic—as most certainly it has proved to be, at least up to the time of the writing of this book. Indeed, I find myself losing patience with chaps who get into emotional tangles about love, or near-love, affairs—and I am not wholly convinced that it is just the advancing years, for even at the age of 44 men have been known to cut quite a figure.

As we got nearer home, the weather seemed to improve. Certainly there was more sun, and it was curiously warm for that season of the year. I was glad of that, for I knew that the only kind of warm welcome—or any welcome, for that matter—which I had to look forward to was one given by Mother Nature. There would be nobody at the dock to meet me; I hadn't had time, in the confusion and strangeness of my leaving, to write to anybody in advance. Besides, to whom should I write? To my mother? Yes, but she lived in Boston. And at her age she would hardly feel able to come down to New York to greet me—moreover, I didn't want her to come down. I was a returning prodigal with too much of a vengeance. I wanted to wait until at least I had teeth and looked respectable, until I had a job or work of some kind and *felt* respectable. She had waited now eight years to see me again, since that time I had left her in New York to go back to France—a few more weeks would not make much difference. Little did I then realize that I should, to be sure, talk to her again over the telephone from New York, but that never again should I see her. I had yet to learn that the losses of life are inevitable; that you must be prepared for whatever happens—simply because anything may.

Not only did the weather get better, as we neared New York, my excitement grew. When I came to reflect seriously about it, I realized that this was in reality a voyage of rediscovery for me—after all, nobody can stay away as long as I had from home, and then expect to step right into the new rhythm of things, especially in America.

We passed Ambrose Channel lightship rather early in the morning, and we finally got into port before noon—a radiant, sunny day, with the skyline of Manhattan as clear as you could ever want to see it. And I found myself wanting to see it, as if I had never seen it before, which, in its first impact and arrogance, almost seemed to me true. I kept looking at it, as if I expected a sort of sign of recognition, though I didn't know what it was. But the deepest impression I have not yet forgotten: There were new buildings, there were unfamiliar spires, plenty of them; yet somehow everything seemed at once something I had always known and been an unconscionably long time away from. I couldn't understand this lack of any feeling of strangeness, a kind of vague wonder and doubt as to whether or not you really have ever been away at all. What was happening to me, however, was really the simplest thing in the world, though I didn't know it until I experienced it—I was coming home. And when, slowly, the realization came to me of what it was, I smiled a bit though there was a lump in my throat, too, and I asked myself with what I tried to make an inward sardonic voice, "Home to what?"

Anyway, I knew one thing then right away, and knew it clearly. One part of my life was over—forever. I had landed at home once more. What was the immediate future to be like? How was I going to live? Were any of my old friends in New York?—and if they were, would they want to see me or would they regard me as a sort of renegade? Well, I meditated further, as the boat slowly warped into her pier on the Jersey side, other men before me have returned to their own country, too, and many of them much later in life than I am doing. I am not going to be intimidated; why, even some immigrants I have known have come to America as late in life as I am doing, and sometimes with but the feeblest command of English. If they can do it, why cannot I? If they are not afraid, why should I be afraid?

But I know now in my heart that it took all the moral courage I had left to keep a stiff upper lip. There would be nobody to see me when we landed—that was the worst of it. If only I didn't have to do everything in the world alone. And yet that wasn't true either—most people, when all is said and done, do the really important things of life, such as getting born and dying, all alone. What was I complaining about? I tried to joke with the customs officials—and I managed one or two feeble ones when they discovered, quite obviously regarding me as a curiosity, that I had no clothes, no trunks, not even a package of cigarettes. I said that I had only brought back my own sweet self, at which remark they looked frankly dubious, though one of them made a jesting comment to the effect that that was plenty, with which I heartily—or I thought it was heartily—agreed. Anyway, I was glad to get away, and I accepted with alacrity the invitation of my Middle Western boat friend to ride over with him in a taxi, through the new traffic tunnel under the river which was not there in my day, to New York—for he hardly assumed that I was going to stay in Hoboken.

When he learned that I was landing literally without a dime, he generously asked me to stay a couple of days with him at his hotel. It would be that long before he went West, and it would give me a chance to look around and find some of my friends.

"Yes, sure," I said—adding to myself the reflection, "If I have any left."

XX. HOME ONCE MORE

HAD I had any kind of assurance of anything—a home, money, friends, my health, or a job—I should very much have enjoyed that two days' stay in that new New York hotel, with all the modern gadgets—I mean, radio as well as telephone, the latest of bath and toilet fixtures, closets that lighted up mechanically when you opened the door, over-night laundry service, and almost anything you wanted to eat (but still, at that time, not to drink, which at first seemed strange to me)—anything, what is more, served any time of the day or night, and in five or ten minutes after you had ordered. Memories of cheap Paris hotels, along with other memories of little hostelries on my trip through Southern France, combined again—much as they had done that first night in the Rice Hotel in Houston, Texas, on my trip home after five years abroad—to underscore the fact that once more I was in the land of mechanical efficiency. I liked that; I revelled in it—there was sufficient vestigial memory of the engineer-adoration era of childhood: I *like* mechanical things; I *like* to survey the blueprints of new inventions filed in the Patent Office; I *like* to read publications, such as the *Scientific American* of my boyhood, which are dedicated to the new machine-age marvels.

My Missouri boat-companion noticed this—and went out of his way to buy me a new trick form of safety-razor, with which I was delighted, as I was, too, with the "brushless" soap for lather (another novelty since my day). But pleasant as he tried to be—and was—he had to leave me pretty much to my own devices, for he had only two days in New York before his business called him on to Kansas City. So I telephoned Vyvyan again—just as I had done years before on my return to New York from Chicago—and she came over to see me, relating to me the wonders of the new "talkies," in which she was commercially interested, doing fashion "shots," I think she called them, for the news-reels. I was embarrassed at my lack of teeth, of course, and did very little talking. After she had gone, I tried to find some of my old friends in the telephone book. Fortunately, two or three were there still, including A. B. Kuttner, who evidently had kept the old house on Washington Place, where I had written "Liberalism" and had learned of my wife's death that terrible morning; Thorne Smith, who answered the call himself and invited me down to his home in "the Village;" and a couple of others, who did not answer, either because they were out of the house, when I called, or out of town. But even getting in touch with *anybody* gave me a little assurance. On the docks in Jersey I had felt, for a few moments, almost like an immigrant—and it wasn't true! There were still quite a few who remembered me; perhaps, like Thorne, they would even be glad to see me "home" again.

It was pleasant to go down to "the Village" after so many years; even more pleasant to see Thorne and Celia, his wife, who had known me well in the old days too, and to meet the children, who had come into the world and begun to grow up enough to want their "Amos 'n Andy" on the radio—during the time I had been dilly-dallying in France. We called up Felicia, who lived not far away in "the Village" likewise, and she came over, looking very much the same as ever, much to my astonishment, for the women in Europe simply do *not* keep their youth and good looks and vitality the way our girls seem to be able to do. "Bootleg" booze, chiefly gin—to partake of which I was immediately invited—had not had the disastrous effects on her, at all events, I had seen it have on others I had met, shaky and broken-down, when they visited Paris to, as they ironically would term it, "recuperate." Of course I asked about prohibition and the economic situation (the depression was cutting down American tourists to France at an alarming rate, even before I left): On the first point I was informed that one might get "the stuff" almost anywhere in New York and at a low rate, but that most of it was pretty poor, when not downright rotten; on the second, that things were very bad, but that there seemed a faint chance of their getting better, simply because the bottom had been reached. The only consoling thing in the economic set-up was that prices for everything, except rents, were very low—and if I could beg, borrow, or steal any money, right then was the time to buy. The "crime wave"—it was only a short time after this that the Lindbergh baby was killed—was a real thing, too, and seemed to be getting worse. Everybody was tired of Hoover, but the Democrats had no real candidate with whom to oppose him, for "Al" Smith was "all washed up." To all these opinions I made little comment or retort. I just listened, pleased to hear the old accents I had once known so well. It was not so bad after all—being home again.

My Missouri friend had to continue on to the West. Thorne suggested that for a few days, while I looked around, I go to the Albert Hotel, on University Place, since it was in "the Village," was comfortable, and not too expensive. He and Celia would stake me there for a week, during which time I might get on my feet. Thorne found me an extra shirt or two, and a few pieces of clean underwear—the little things that give a man self-respect. It seemed a strange home-coming, but after all, less strange than the different ones I had in imagination pictured on the boat coming over.

With a curious confidence (I say curious now, after the fact, for right then I had no real notion of how tough things were in my own country), I went up the next day to see the editor of *Scribner's* to try to sell an article in advance, that is, simply, before I had written it. I picked out *Scribner's* for the natural reason that I had already had an article printed by them—the one that Scott Fitzgerald sold for me from Paris—and I thought my stock with them might be high enough to justify their taking a small chance on my writing something they could use. It was, too,—and I was given part payment of $50 to rent a typewriter and to do the article, the balance to be paid me when I completed it. I know it seems a little thing to relate, but I came down in the elevator from that office and stepped onto Fifth Avenue a new man. "One couldn't do that in France, if you were God Almighty," I remember saying to myself, as I headed over to the typewriter rental shop.

Well, I finished the article—which was correctly titled "A Prodigal Returns"—in a couple of days, working hard and sticking close to my room. With the balance of the money coming to me in my pocket, I paid up my hotel bill, and moved to the Hotel Marlton on 8th Street, where the weekly rate for a very comfortable little room adjoining a bath, was a bit cheaper, since the Marlton was more of a family hotel. And when I think of my first weeks back home, I think always of that hotel, of the old man on night duty, of the Irish elevator boy, and of Washington Square at night with the "bums" huddled on benches.

Out of courtesy, I rang up Shipman's mother to let her know that I had left Evan in good health and spirits back in Paris. She very kindly invited me to come up to her home on Beekman Place, overlooking the East River, where—from five in the evening, when her own work was finished (she is a landscape architect of considerable distinction)—I might use her office facilities, including a typewriter, of course, and the telephone. She also said that dinner would be served me there, too, so that the rather peculiar hours ought to prove no barrier—a graceful way of doing something nice for somebody without "rubbing in," as our phrase has it, their temporary hard luck. And suddenly, too, I realized that whatever the depression had done, it had called forth a latent fund of good-will and neighborliness and decency—that the score had not been all one-sided, despite the bread-line I saw in Columbus Circle, the beggars who made the walk of a few blocks a lesson in how to stifle one's generous impulses, and the misery and heart-ache I could see only too plainly behind so many pinched and intense countenances that tried to don the mask of proud reserve.

Never in Paris in the worst days of the falling franc had I seen anything to match what I was seeing in New York that spring of 1932—and every now and then I couldn't help making to myself certain generalizations. I was astonished again—as I had been astonished before—at the way we swallowed, first the war propaganda, and then endured the prohibition tyranny which followed it. Perhaps it was because we were so big and sprawling, for in this land of rugged individualism the single person fighting for existence, alone without a family and with only a few friends, felt impotent and lost. Even had he wanted to, the average person couldn't revolt. Revolt against what? against whom? and who should be his comrades—if any? Joining a "radical" or Socialist party makes the ordinary American deeply uncomfortable, if only because this act is in itself a tacit acknowledgment that he has been a fool, that all he has hitherto implicitly believed about equality of opporunity is but a sham and a delusion, that, in brief, the cards are stacked against him as an individual. Furthermore, it makes him uncomfortable for another reason—"radicalism" had for too long a time previous to the depression been regarded as something alien, imported, and foreign, oftenest it spoke with a German or a Russian accent. To become an out-and-out, simon-pure Communist, for instance, you had to ask the average American not only to give up the political and social ideals he had acquired almost at his mother's breast (a renunciation which might have been possible after long months of semi-starvation and suffering), but also to give up the friends with whom he played Kelly-pool, went with to the ball games and the movies, and with whom and with "the missus and kids" of whom he now and then had dinner—something which was quite impossible. The average man simply isn't born (nor do I see any reason why he should be) to play that kind of heroic rôle. Literary "guys," to used a Hemingway for the moment, may do that sort of thing, but it is more the itch for publicity than the urge of conviction that animates them, and I have observed the "martyr" complex to take strange and unexpected forms in those who felt that not sufficient attention was being given their transcendent genius through the ordinary channels of literary criticism.

This is not merely cheap cynicism on my part, either: There is something in the very air of America which excites the exhibitionist tendency dormant in all of us; our social history is a long succession of what we amiably call "crackpots." One could hardly expect anything so searing and unpleasant as the depression not to have provoked such phenomena as technocracy, Communist yearnings, political and economic cure-alls, a new religion or two, even nudism. Also in most Americans, as in most healthy animals, there is, beneath the surface, a powerful streak of belligerency—and we haven't had a good bang-up, first-class war recently enough to drain off that streak, so to speak, normally. But if we can't fight the Japs just yet, we can fight "the cops"—and that is almost as good. Where tradition is weak and there is no ancient, historical enemy, we have to do the best we can. It would be amiable and childlike, if we also did not have temperaments that, to put it mildly, are not exactly averse to violence—which is why, if ever it does come to anything like a general and serious social revolution in this country, the bitterness with which it will be conducted will be ghastly. We have a sense of humor, admittedly, but there is also a dark and murderous side to it—we can laugh at corpses. Like all peoples prodigal in life, you need only to change the direction, alter but a little the focus of the picture—and we can be prodigal in death, too.

Perhaps it was reflections like the above which bothered me; perhaps it was worry about my mother's health and whether I should ever see her again:—I did speak to her over the telephone, for the last time, though I didn't then know it was to be the last time, in that room overlooking the East River, as, ironically and bitterly enough it seemed to me afterwards, the evening boat to Boston passed by up towards Hell Gate and the Sound. Perhaps it was a kind of inarticulate bewilderment; I don't know, even today, what it was—but I found it almost impossible to do any writing in that room. For the hours I was there I would oftenest sit quietly at the typewriter looking out over the river and watching the afternoon shadows deepening into the New York electric-light studded night.

Soon after I had started what I had hoped to be work, but was in fact mostly dreaming, at Mrs. Shipman's, I began, one by one, to see the people I had known in Paris. First was Viola Brothers Shore, who had gone with me to the trotting race I had seen last at Vincennes. She seemed to be making good as a scenario writer in Hollywood; she stopped at Delmonico's during her New York visit, and with her I had my first really luxurious meal since returning home. I had always liked her for her wit and ability, but I liked her even more now for her common sense and kindliness. Louise Bryant, John Reed's wife and then Bullitt's, was in New York then, too, having just returned from Washington, where she had attended some political expedition—it seemed strange to be having dinner with her in the Grand Central restaurant after those luxurious days in Auteuil.

Walter Duranty, who had won a Pulitzer Prize for his Moscow correspondence in the *Times,* came to New York about this time, too—and he told me that only forgiveness was in his heart for my *not* betting on that horse in the Grand Steeplechase de Paris. Not merely did Duranty get me a typewriter of my own—the one I had rented with so much trouble had long since been returned to the shop—but he did me a great and really important service. He rang up a good dentist, made an appointment for me, and sent him a sizeable check—so that I might have false teeth made for me and be again presentable. I was frankly amazed at the excellent and naturalistic job that dentist did; I felt a new man. And whatever Duranty may do to me or say about me later on, I shall always be grateful to him for that good turn. No longer was I ashamed to meet people—gone were the slinking and hiding days, which, with a start, I realized had been my life for far too many months.

Meanwhile Evan Shipman had returned from France. He was pleased that I was working at his mother's house—I think he was glad, too, that besides my article in *Scribner's* I had managed to get some work doing book reviews for W. Soskin, then on the *Evening Post,* and a bit later for the Sunday edition of the *Herald-Tribune*. I had also written an article on the French—and whether or not they are naturally militaristic, which I for one don't believe—for my old paper, the Baltimore *Sun*. Evan, whom I had taken to his first trotting race years before in Paris, wanted me to see the American trotters in action. So he arranged that I go up to Avon, Connecticut, and following that, to Sturbridge, Massachusetts, where I could see the Bay State Circuit. I met him at Hartford, and we motored out to the old Charter Oak track, where training was going on, but no races, for a few days—and where I slept in a stall, with horses in the next stall snoring (did you know horses sometimes snore?), and where the stable cat chased rats across the floor most of the night.

The trotting crowd I like enormously; after all, it was like getting really back home, for they were New England through and through. After Avon, we went over to the Cedar Lake Park at Sturbridge for the meeting of June 21, 22, and 23, this time stopping at a good hotel near the town, for Evan felt he was going to be "lucky" at the meeting—as in fact he was, though of course somewhat more modestly than he had hoped. I enjoyed our method of trotting in "heats," the crowds, the "pool" selling and betting in "the tent," the blaring band that played between the different events, the humor of the old-timers, like Harry Brusie, the gossip and crap-shooting of the grooms at dusk, when the races for the day were over and the crowd had melted away. Somehow it seemed very familiar and homelike to me; I wondered at times why I had so long been away, for now—for the first time in over ten years—I was speaking my own language exclusively at the races. It seemed odd, but delightfully odd, and memories of County Fair days, like the Brockton Fair, came back to me with a rush from my childhood. I remember, too, that one day we drove the car as far as Springfield, and I debated whether or not it was worth while going on to Boston to see my mother. Had I, too, been "lucky," I should have gone. But I was not betting those racing days for a change; I was merely a spectator.

Right after Sturbridge I returned to New York; Evan went on to New Hampshire and his mother's summer home. Of course I was still worrying about how I was going to live, as always, but at least I was doing a little reviewing work, which paid me something. Nor were old friends lacking. My first publisher, Horace Liveright, had returned from Hollywood and had a stylish pent-house apartment in the East Forties, where I was made welcome. Horace, who as usual was up to some promotion plan—this time for another new play, as I recall it—could not do much for me financially; he himself was skating pretty close to the wind, he told me—and I knew it was true. Also he had been in some automobile accident, or something of the kind, and was laid up with an injured hand —which, he laughingly assured me, was painful but not serious. I recall this now because he seemed in such good health and spirits then, despite his temporary business troubles (something not unknown to Horace before); his death from pneumonia but a few months later came as a genuine shock. Yet I cannot help but think he would have preferred it that way himself—suddenly and without any lingering on. He was too full of vitality to be an invalid; it had to be either life or death with him. Right at that time, however, death was the furthest thing from his thoughts—I can see him yet, smiling amiably and consoling me, saying, "Harold, have another drink and forget your troubles," when I learned by calling up the cable editor that Sunday evening, that A. J. Duggan's Strip-The-Willow had won the Grand Prix de Paris—and I hadn't been able to have a bet on him. (For of course, when we *don't* bet, we always fondly imagine that we *would* have backed the winner.)

Like most men without a home or a family circle, holidays depress me. Evan was in the country; Duranty had gone out of town. It was hot, too; I wanted desperately to go up to Boston both for the trip and to see my mother. But on that Fourth of July, 1932, the very best I could manage was a trip down to Coney Island, which I think depressed me even more than if I had remained quietly in the little room I kept so precariously at the Marlton. I couldn't help but notice how few people spoke English—or rather, not to exaggerate, how many people spoke a foreign tongue. I remember feeling that I was more alien at Coney Island than on the beach at Deauville, where, in the old pre-depression days when I had been there, one might run into Americans from Denver, Boston, Baltimore, New York, Chicago, or even the small towns of the Middle West. I remember I kept asking myself, "Do I have to come back to my own country to feel an alien from America? That is a pretty state of affairs." I looked at the free fireworks like a dumb yokel of one of the old comic strips—what was all the celebration about? Our "freedom"? I laughed at that to myself—freedom to starve, I said bitterly. And I imagine I was not alone in that sentiment. On that day I obtained some vivid sense of what it means, when smart editorial writers refer so glibly to "being disinherited." I realized how thousands and thousands of my fellow-countrymen, without jobs and without hope, were feeling, too—that they didn't belong. They were "free," yes, but what did it mean in terms of human happiness? Yet this was "the land of promise." All the old phrases kept ringing in my head that hot, stuffy day—and they were all touched with acid, the acid of homelessness, of being without a job, of not belonging.

That mood couldn't last, of course. What broke the spell of discouragement I cannot quite remember—I know only it was a dangerous, close to suicidal spell but I think it was calling up my old Paris friend, Lorimer Hammond—a Connecticut Yankee, if ever there was one in spirit. He invited me up to his home near Central Park West; there was his wife, too, whom I had known in the old days in Paris. Lorimer was full of his new-found Americanism (or, perhaps, his old Americanism; I recalled that in Paris I had accused him once of being almost sentimentally chauvinistic, but he didn't seem to mind), and his wife, who was doing a series of fashion notes for some newspaper syndicate, was enthusiastic, too, about everything American. It was the one country to work in; you could make real money here; prohibition was not going to last; people were more amusing, too. Oh, it was a rosy picture—and I wanted to believe it then; wanted desperately to believe it. Perhaps it was true. Perhaps all these difficulties were just a temporary trial. They both assured me that such was the case—and I must say, in fairness, they turned out to be nearer the truth in their contentions than at that time I should ever have thought possible.

A day or so later I met another Paris American friend—Bill The Connolly. He was about to go on his vacation—we met by chance in the Grand Central Station—but he did put the notion in my head of going out to Newark and living with him, when he returned. He was working for the Public Service Corporation of New Jersey—which ran the buses, streetcars, electric lights (as far as I could see, the whole State)—and had taken a little flat on Bleeker Street in Newark.

Gradually, it seemed to me, I was getting back into circulation. For I had gone down to the *Nation* office and seen Villard; I had seen Spingarn, too, though he was no longer connected with Harcourt, Brace, And Company, and I had gone to see Harcourt himself also, but all I had received from him was a little gratuitous advice about how good the country would be for my health. (My experience is:—Pay no attention to people who advise you to solve your problems by "getting off into the country" or "joining the navy," or something similar. They are not trying to advise you—they are trying to get rid of you.) Even Mr. Bing—whom I had helped in the writing of his book on the War Labor Board in the old days—had received a call from me at his imposing real estate office. And he was pleasant and agreeable, very little changed in looks after thirteen years or more; evidently, too, still not ruined by the depression, even with the difficulties in collecting rent and mortgages, and the shrinkage in values of New York apartment buildings.

Furthermore, I did a bit of exploring around at the newspaper and magazine offices—I remember selling George Soule some French books, which I am sure he didn't want, for a couple of dollars. And while I was up at the *New Republic* office I met Malcolm Cowley again, who did *not* invite me to review books again, as I had in the old days, but instead loaned me a few dollars to "get along on until something turned up." Charlie Merz—who had been on the *New Republic* when I had worked for it, too—was a "feature" editor for the Sunday *Times;* he advised me to go over to see Hartmann, editor of *Harper's*—which, as will later appear, turned out to be a good tip. Both Soskin, then on the *Evening Post,* and Gannett (a classmate of mine at Harvard) on the *Tribune,* who introduced me to Mrs. Van Doren, succeeded in getting me some book-review work. Some time later on I met John Chamberlain, shortly after he had taken over his work as daily book columnist for the New York *Times:* He had spoken very highly of "Liberalism In America" in his own first book, also published by Liveright, curiously enough, which he had called "Farewell To Reform." Of course he had no reviewing to offer me, but he really was helpful in suggestions. And two or three times later, when dinners would otherwise have been lacking, he went out of his way to give me a bit in cash, which he did, as he politely put it, "as one newspaper man to another." I thought of this coming down in the elevator in the *Times* office one day, when I met "Jimmie" James, whom I had known quite well in Paris—but at least I have a distinction in the newspaper world: I am one newspaper man who came back from Paris broke, and did *not* ask James for a job. I figured it might be, to use an old backwoods expression, "sorta crowding the mourners."

When that first awful summer "back home" was beginning to come to a close—early in September, I mean—Bill The Connolly was as good as his word. Better, in fact, for he paid out what I still owed at the Marlton Hotel so that I could get "clear" to come out to live with him in Newark. I can still recall going down to the "Tube" at 8th Street, sweating and swearing, with the heavy old-fashioned typewriter that Duranty had bought for me; then transferring at Journal Square, after the train had gone under the Hudson, and arriving at Newark, the end of the line. There I actually took a taxicab—I think for almost the first time since I had been back home—over to Bleeker Street. It was only a short distance, back of Kresge's Department Store, but what I was carrying (for I had brought along what books I possessed still) made that extravagance imperative. Bill, of course, was at work, so—after I had taken one depressed look at that awful suburban small flat interior—I walked out to look at the town.

The park before the "Tube" Station, with the old Colonial Church, was pleasant—as was another one in front of the public library—for it had about it something of the quality of an old New England town. Around this main park was the business, financial, movie, and shopping center of the city, such as one sees today in scores of other second-string cities in the United States (the old Colonial Church excepted, though there may even be an imitation of that): You felt at once, I mean, that you were looking not so much at Newark as at middle-class, fairly prosperous, industrialized—but not too aggressively industrialized, like Pittsburgh, America. Prohibition still was in effect, hence there were no saloons; instead, you saw gaudy candy "shoppes" and the ubiquitous "drug store," which served also as a clearing house for publishers' "remainders." The new books could be rented at one of the two or three libraries I saw in the side streets, while in Kreske's Department Store itself there was quite a bit of floor space given over to books—next, as was inevitable, to children's toys, cosmetics, the lunch bar for women shoppers who came in from the outlying suburbs in their own cars, and "novelties"—a descriptive noun, to understand the full implications of which you have to be an American.

Somehow, the whole "layout" of the store, together with what I saw when I went outside—the central park surrounded by its bank and "Terminal" buildings, its hotel, its radio and cigar stores, the many lunch "bars," the movie theatres, and the other department and "specialty" shoe shops—filled me full of gloom. I like mechanical things; everywhere there were cars, and I knew that almost every side and back street had a trick garage, while in one of the show windows of the Terminal Building was an electrical display—refrigerators, model kitchens, toasters, sweepers, lights, curling irons, and electric razors. I gave full vent to the boyish toy instinct, and thought how, when some day again I had money and perhaps a home, I should have all these marvels of the machine age. But in spite of that temporary titillation, the gloom persisted—I could not help reflecting, "What good are all these gadgets, if the life you live with them is mean and unimaginative?" I wished there had been a dark and dingy Paris *"bistrot"* on a back street, where I could have gone and got drunk on Pernot. After an hour of aimless walking and window-shopping around that central square, I should gladly have thrown the whole of modern civilization into the muddy river and kissed it a happy goodbye forever—for just an afternoon and evening at Maisons-Laffitte, where people still acted like human beings that were part of a long tradition and a history, and a history and tradition they enjoyed and were proud of.

To get the full flavor of where I was, I then walked out to see Bill where he worked, at the bus terminal on Springfield Avenue—a good four or five miles out. We were to come back to Newark together and have dinner at the flat (cooking it ourselves, too, which became a regular routine.) And never shall I forget that walk—which I was to repeat several times. The appalling dreariness of semi-industrial American suburbia—remember there were still no corner saloons then, as now, to lighten the burden of ugliness—came upon me as a revelation of what, in France, I had so carefully tried to forget. It was like the bad dreams of my boyhood days in places like Attleboro and Taunton and Brockton coming mercilessly true. I had seen dirt and ugliness in industrial Paris, too, but somehow there had always been a "lift" to it—whereas this was just unmitigated and impossible. It seemed hardly credible to me then—nor does it still—that men could have struggled and worked, dreamed dreams, had wars and revolutions for centuries just to produce this. Bad as it was, I was glad to get back to our little flat, where I could shove a table next to a window, with the sunlight coming in—and work. Work, blessed and healing work, which took my mind off my surroundings.

In Newark I realized suddenly the whole psychological intensity back of our early wall-motto incitements of young men to industrious habits. For if you did not work, you might look around and reflect; and the results of that might be just too awful. In the kind of America which Newark represented—and it was in microcosm a good example of suburban America, neither rural nor wholly industrial, but half and half, a sort of satellite to a great city (as are all other small cities and towns in America)—your one salvation was activity. That is why the "leisure" of unemployment there, and in the many towns and cities throughout the United States that are similar to it, was proving a curse. In France, even if you are poor, there is something to amuse you when you loaf; in America, if you are rich, there may be some ways of amusing yourself with conspicuous display and plain idling and philandering, but if you are poor, there is nothing—you are just poor, that is all, just a bum. You can sit in the park of course, as I saw so many doing in Newark. If it is early October, there are some afternoons when you can watch the scoreboard—put up as an advertising stunt by the local newspaper—and get a vicarious thrill, I suppose, out of seeing the results of the World's Series (again my boyhood came back to me), or you can listen to some radio, near a filling-station, say, and on Saturday afternoons hear the play-by-play account of the college football games.

To lighten the burden of my first evening in Newark, Bill came back with me himself from the bus terminal. He had invited his friend, Mary—a New York stenographer, and a good sport, too—to come out to prepare dinner for us and to enjoy our scintillating company; a flagon or two of bootleg gin of the era was likewise purchased. After all, unless we went "in" to New York, there was nothing to do in Newark except work—or get drunk.

Or, on Sundays, take walks. Those were Bill's free days, as they were also those of Mary, whose first action on arriving from "town" was almost inspectorial—she made sure that our quarters were tolerably clean. (Although, in self-defense, I want to state that I am a stickler for cleanliness myself, once I can get moving—I mean, I will endure dust and dirt and soiled clothes and unwashed dishes for just so long, and then will have an almost hysterical outburst of neatness; out will go the clothes to a laundry, the floors will be scrubbed and swept, and the dishes washed, even at the cost of breaking a third of them. Then again will come the relapse and indifference, for days at a time—until, of course, the place finally looks like a pig-sty.) Mary's second action was to prepare and serve Sunday's combined breakfast and lunch. Then, the weather permitting (and that is the fine season of the year, usually), we all three went out for the weekly walk—sometimes just around Newark, sometimes to Jersey parks far enough away to require our using a bus, at least for coming home. Suburbia forever, I thought on these walks—a wilderness of homes!

Bill's favorite walk, however, was down to the Newark air-port, for he was not only interested in flying (and particularly in internal combustion engines) but had also at one time taken the regulation number of training "hours" in the air and had himself flown planes alone as far as to Boston and back. I liked that walk, too, for the towers of Manhattan stood up imposing and clear across the flatlands, when you reached the air-port; and you knew it was only a matter of a few minutes and you could return, as it were, to civilization. The planes themselves, with the improvement in the models even when only a year distinguished the date of manufacture of one from another, were something real and modern and exciting. As you looked at them, you knew instinctively that in a generation or two the conventional way of crossing the ocean for those on important business would be by plane—and I was rather glad that I should not be here to see it, I remember feeling, because I like a boat and at least a few days for savoring the mystery of the sea.

Encouraged by Hartmann's friendly reception at *Harper's*, and with my days free except for some book reviews I had to finish up both for the *Evening Post* and the *Tribune*, I set myself to the job of writing an article on my racing experiences in Paris. But I didn't like the old second-hand typewriter I had got through Duranty's kindness: Absurd as it may appear (but it is not absurd in fact; after all, I am a writer, and any mechanical annoyance to one who has always used the "touch" system of typewriting and has never written by hand is fatal—he will not write at all), I went to the Smith-Corona people and exchanged my old machine for the new standard portable model (substituting French accents, like the ç and ù for characters I did not use, on the side—but keeping the English keyboard, of course, on which I had learned to "touch" typewrite—so that I might write *both* English and French). This may seem a little thing to anybody not a writer: To me it was a crucial thing. Keeping and paying for that typewriter became a curious symbol of success or failure—but a real symbol to me. If I lost that, I lost my reason for living at all. With a deeper pride than many fathers have in their offspring, I want to point out to my reader that this autobiography has been written on that typewriter—I am, whatever else, that much of a success.

The racing article was not easy; it took me weeks of writing and re-writing to get what I wanted. The trouble was slightly different from the one most writers would have had with a similar bit of exposition—I knew my subject too well. Literally and simply, I knew too much about it. The problem became in essence one of how to compress, without being unnatural or forced. Finally, I hit on the simple expedient of describing *one* actual day at the races—of course at one single track—using each episode of that day, as it arose naturally in my narrative, as illustrative of other days and other tracks, either by similarity or by contrast. And when you were through reading the article, you had a good picture not only of what that day was like, but what most other days were like, too. It was an excellent piece of exposition; "Copey," my first Harvard English teacher, would have been, I think, proud of me for its workmanlike quality—its clearness and its interest—

had he read it.

But I worked so slowly on this article that it was somehow the first of November before I sat down to do the "definitive" copy—after so many rewritings, corrections, modifications, looking up of records, and I don't recall what else. And before I had quite finished it (on November 15th, to be exact), I received a bit of news that, for several days, made any serious work out of the question—the news of my mother's death in Boston. My brother's son, whom I had not seen since he was the "little Roger" of a small snapshot sent to Alice and myself during the early days of our marriage, came out to Newark and told me the news. I remember sending a telegram to my brother—he had gone at once to Boston—asking him to do what he could in my behalf, since it was obviously impossible for me to go to Boston myself. Nor did I want to go—then.

Had I been able to see and talk with my mother for even a moment before she died (had I in fact even known that she was dangerously ill), I think I should have stolen the money needed to get there, if I had had to. But I could do nothing for her now—or ever again. I think it was that which seemed bitterest, this feeling of never-ending impotence. Fortune might smile on me, some time in the future (as we all dream it is sure to do, some day), but it would now smile too late for me ever to give her even the littlest and the least of the many things I had hoped and believed I should eventually bring to her surprised and pleased old age. I had lost all chance now to show how much I had cared. And again, as when Alice died, everything seemed empty, blank, meaningless. Now I could disguise it no longer—I really *was* alone in the world. With painful vividness I realized as well that I, too, might die then, perhaps that same night—and that it would only be a "stick" in a newspaper account; that somehow, say what I wanted or delude myself as I liked, there were not above a half dozen people in the world to whom it would mean much more than a passing item of news, and that even to that half dozen it would not mean very *much* more. Here I had reached my forty-second year (when one is supposed to be in the "prime" of life, I thought ironically), with the result that spiritually—and actually too—I was as much the center of a social life, with all its normal ramifications, as is a casual in a "flop" house. And for those long, interminable, sleepless hours of that endless night, I knew that I had reached the ultimate humility, —I did not care whether I lived or died. It was not important. Not even to me.

But the elasticity of life is miraculous. Though I was in no mood to do it—perhaps just as a relief from my own thoughts—I finished up my racing article and sent it to *Harper's* the night before Thanksgiving. Bill had received some special dainties from an aunt, and we took them into town to Shipman's on Charles Street, where I now live. It was a strange, unhappy holiday for me, despite the comforting assurance that at least I had a few friends left.

During the fortnight that had followed my mother's death I had been, I suppose, too preoccupied to pay much attention to what was going on around me. But soon I began to notice that Bill—as I had known him to do before in Paris in the old days—was getting restless. And when he got restless, he always wanted to move. Besides, he thought the Bleeker Street flat was too expensive, even when I was able to pay my half of the cost of upkeep, and he decided that he wanted to move to the local Newark Y. M. C. A. because of its cheapness. This meant, of course, that there was nothing left for me to do but to return to New York. Living in Newark with an old friend was exasperating enough; without one, it was plain impossible —at least for me. I should have preferred to take my chances on park benches in New York. which, after all, were not entirely unknown to me.

But I was less terrified of New York this time than I should otherwise have been. For all I knew to the contrary I had sold my article—that gave me a little confidence. Shipman was in

New York, too; I should not be entirely alone—and besides, one is always meeting people in New York (or one thinks one is, until one goes broke, when it miraculously becomes a very empty city, where people are always "out" and telephone messages never seem to arrive). In any event, one thing was certain: Whatever I sold of my writings would be sold in New York, whatever chance there was of my getting any kind of a newspaper job, that chance was in New York.

Thus I returned to Manhattan—disillusioned, unhappy, without a cent, as I had done when I landed from France. But at least now I had my health, and, notwithstanding all the immediate difficulties, a new belief in myself. I was no longer bewildered, as I had been when I stepped off the boat from France. *This* time I would stay in New York; *this* time I would succeed. I would *not* be submerged. I swore it.

My first step was to take a small room on 11th Street in a house owned by the same man who owns the house where Evan lived on Charles Street. And I was only there a few days, fortunately, when I found out that *Harper's* would take my article (with a little suggested rewriting)—and that they would give me $200 for it, $100 immediately, the other $100, when I turned in the slightly rewritten manuscript. When I came out of that office with the first check, went over to the bank and cashed it, and then came down in the subway to my room—well, all the world had changed again. I had so much confidence that, when the landlord told me there was at last a vacancy at 10 Charles Street (a very pleasant big room, overlooking a garden in back, with plenty of sunlight—just the room I had always wanted, for I had seen it when I visited Evan), I decided, come what might, I should take it. And I would stay there—that would be the symbol of my success. It was, to make the symbol complete, necessary also for me to keep my typewriter—to pay it "up" in full.

Well, I *have* remained here, and I *have* bought my typewriter, as I said before. Also I wrote "Rediscovering America" in this room—and I have written here, too, every line of the book you are now reading. It is not much, I know—a poor thing, but my own, if you wish to be cynical. When I think back, however, to some of those nights on the benches of the Boulevard Montparnasse, I am not wholly ashamed of what I have done. It is, say what you want, quite a distance to have come in so short a time.

It is easy enough to write that *now,* after the event. Remember there have been plenty of nervous, anxious moments during that period—moments when I have thought, in spite of everything, that I simply could *not,* as the English put it, "carry on." But when I moved to Charles Street my faith in life was again restored. I had, I thought, done the impossible.

Not even Evan's going away for the Christmas holidays—nor, later, his going South to visit Ernest Hemingway in Florida—could make *that* Christmas, my first Christmas back home after so many years, wholly discouraging, even if I was alone—as always. It was sad in a way: I wished intensely that my mother had lived just a few more months, now that I *could* go up to Boston to see her. It was not fair, always to have death just a little ahead of me, as it had been so often before.

My quiet holidays over, and my second $100 now fast vanishing—for my typewriter had taken some of it, while several of the petty but exasperating bills, which accumulate so fast when you are broke, had taken some more—I cast about for ways to keep going. I made two or three stabs at trying to find some newspaper work, but I didn't force these attempts because of two reasons: The first, that jobs were scarce anyway on account of the depression (most newspapers seemed to be cutting down on their staffs rather than expanding); the second, that I hoped to be able to make the grade by independent writing—which feat, unless you have a more or less assured market for your "stuff," is a heart-breaking gamble, especially if, moreover, you are not—as I am not—a writer of fiction. For even fair short stories there is always a demand, while really excellent general articles will often go begging. That seems preposterous, but it is true. Magazines usually have a policy, avowed or unavowed, and what does not support or flatter or further that policy (unless it is plain humor—sometimes, perhaps, when one considers such a magazine as, say *The New Yorker,* even subtle humor; or unless it is pure description, like my horse-racing piece)—what does not, I repeat, help towards any one of these three ends will not be greeted with much favor by the editors.

Which explains, I might add without meaning to be sarcastic but only purely descriptive, why so many "little" magazines, even in depression days, are born, seemingly flourish for a certain length of time, and then suddenly, for no overt reason, go out like a light. There are still some people—a few of them with the money to do it—who want to say something so badly that, when the regular contributors' channel is closed to them, neatly solve the problem of expressing themselves (as did Scofield Thayer, my classmate who bought *The Dial*). It is a "house organ" in a rather peculiar sense—and everybody will know of examples without my here bringing them up and drawing down upon myself an irrelevant critical barrage. As Plato says of certain venomous snakes to be encountered when you walk through savage countries, it is not necessary to know what each one is—it is sufficient to know that it is there.

Not having any luck in looking for a newspaper job, I determined to do what I could do after all—write a book. Just as other people, in hard times, turn to their real profession, why should not a writer do the same thing? But writing a book (unless you have capital, which I have never had, always living, in my Paris confrère's elegant phrase, "on the skin of the wind") involved finding a publisher who wanted to bring my book out sufficiently to stake me while I was doing it. The depression had hit the publishing business harder than many others I might cite, but at least I was not an unknown quantity. I thought . . . there might be a chance.

It is not worth while going into the discouragements of that quest now; instead of the gambling spirit I had known in the old days, most publishers were too frightened to have much confidence even in their authors who had always previously sold well. It was cold refusal after cold refusal "to listen." And then one day I remembered—when I saw a copy of Henry L. Stuart's "Weeping Cross" in a new reprint edition in a book store, bearing the imprint of "The Dial Press" —that my old classmate at Harvard, Lincoln Macveagh, was now a publisher. Surely he, if anybody, would "take a chance."

And he did—giving me a small sum each week to "keep going on" while I finished the book. It was my salvation just at that time. Quite happily, I remember, I set to work on "Rediscovering America." I felt sure everything was going to be all right now.

It wasn't, however. Macveagh, even in college, had been interested in Greece, usually spending his vacations there; he was a friend, I believe, of the Roosevelt family. And Macveagh's own family, I recalled from my Harvard days, had always been mixed up in politics. Hence it was no surprise to me, when, shortly after Roosevelt's election, he was appointed to either a consular or some other official position, representing our country, in Athens. I knew he would enjoy his new work, and I had a suspicion that he had become tired of the publishing business, having brought out many of the books he had always wanted to and having seen the whole business from the inside. But unfortunately—for me, I mean—Macveagh had an assistant in his publishing business, an Englishman of the type I had learned to dislike so thoroughly on the *Daily Mail* in Paris, and I think the dislike was reciprocal. Anyway, the sum and substance of the whole thing was that after I had done considerable on my book—and Macveagh was about to leave for Greece—we cancelled the contract by mutual agreement. (Incidentally, I don't know anything more discouraging than—whatever the reason—to have a publishing contract for a book cancelled in the middle of the book's composition. It does not exactly confirm you in any pride of opinion about your own merits.)

After all this work (seemingly for nothing)—it was now August, 1933—Shipman came back to town. But not from Florida. He came from France. While he had been South in Florida with Hemingway, his father had been taken seriously ill in Paris, and Evan had sailed directly from Havana. After his father's death abroad, he had not wanted to remain long in France, but had come home. Partly to take his mind off the nerve-wracking months he had just gone through; partly out of old habit and an idea about a job (which idea turned out to be a good one), Shipman wanted to go up to Goshen, New York, for the Grand Circuit Meet staged there during the middle of the month. And as we had gone to Sturbridge together, he wanted me to go with him also to Goshen. I did—and I am glad I did, too. When I returned to New York, I put a supplement to my chapter on "The Horses" in "Rediscovering America"—a supplement, by the way, which received high praise in many of the several favorable reviews of "Rediscovering America," when it came out later. This addition, fairly long, was mostly a description of the trotting races at Goshen; but my heart was in it, and I did a good job.

Because luckily, on my return to New York from Goshen, I was able to sell my book to the publishing firm that still bore the name of Liveright, though poor Horace had been gone these many months. There was still plenty of work to do on it, but my confidence was restored—and again, by a miracle, I had saved the situation. I had a little money to work with and to carry on. Consequently those autumn months of 1933 passed quickly and fairly happily for me, and just before the holidays I turned in the completed and rewritten manuscript. (For I had worked on it still more, when Macveagh had decided not to publish it.) Shipman had taken a house on Horatio Street, and was negotiating for a regular job with, and was already doing work for, the *Morning Telegraph*. Hence the Christmas celebration of 1933 in the Horatio Street house, over near the docks, was a gay and happy one for both of us. Perhaps especially so for me, since, in addition to having finished "Rediscovering America," I had begun to work on this autobiography—the book you are now reading.

And when, in March of last year, 1934, "Rediscovering America" appeared on the bookstands, I was already well along with this work. The reviews I received for that book would have encouraged anybody. For example, in the *Times* John Chamberlain concluded his review of March 21 with these words: "It is rumored that Mr. Stearns is to follow up 'Rediscovering America' with an autobiography. One hopes he will not falter on the job."

Well, I don't know. It is now March, 1935, a year later—and just a few weeks before my 44th birthday this coming May. I have finished the book. I have tried to tell the truth, and to tell it interestingly. As far as I can, I have avoided heroics, and I have tried not to sentimentalize about myself.

How fast has come and gone the year now that has elapsed since "Rediscovering America" came out! I know that its actual appearance on the bookstands was to me a kind of talisman, a sign that I had once more picked up the threads of my real, my American, life again. I was uncertain and bewildered the first two years, from February 12, 1932, to February 12, 1934. I couldn't seem to become adjusted to the change, though everything was deeply familiar, too. But this last year to March 1st, 1935 (when this book, as far as I am concerned, is finished) has fitted into the pattern of my old American life and ambitions more naturally—sometimes, it is not easy for me to realize I have ever been away at all. It seems quite a matter of course, too, that old Paris friends, like Sammy Dashiel, are back in New York and working in the newspaper game—was all our Paris experience just a gay and tragic and sometimes funny dream? It must be; why even my Wild Irish Rose, as Jim used to call her, is back home, too—and lives around the corner from me. Of course there have been inevitable losses—I speak of some of them in Chapter 12, "Civilization Finished"—but the continuity of life is astounding nevertheless. Even the depression, even the outward changes, even the new emotional attitudes are not sufficient to break it. That is, not here, while I am home, while I am in America.

My health is better than it has been for years. It must be, for I even believed I had fallen in love again, after all these years, with the fair Dora. But she proved herself a sensible girl; I had forgotten that American young women—especially if they are independent and have a good job of their own—resent a man's economic insecurity much more than the old-fashioned "sheltered" girl of a generation ago, chiefly because they have no romantic notions about "earning one's own living." How could they have? They have tried, and they are trying, economic independence; and it is not so sweet in fact as it had looked in theory—the Victorian "love in a garret" idea evokes only their mirth, if not their contempt. The consequence is that the 1935 American girl is the most demanding on earth. She wants (still being a woman) the romantic trimmings, but she wants security, too. Maybe the depression left a scar—but she will not gamble with possible poverty. (And I can't really, in my heart, blame her.) Unfortunately, however, when the gamble is taken out of love and marriage, some of the charm is, too. It is like betting on a "sure thing" at the races—and even if the "sure thing" *does* win, the price will be so low that you might almost as well have kept your money in your pocket. If a girl won't take even a small chance on your possibly getting across the economic finish line first, then you might, for all the real happiness you will get out of it, almost as well, similarly, stay single. Marriage should mean sharing the early struggles together as much as enjoying the later success.

Of course I want to visit Paris and France again—I want

especially, before I have my final rendezvous, to do a proper guide-book on the French races; and I have always harbored the notion that, with a year or so of leisure for browsing in the libraries of Montpelier and for dawdling in Touraine, I might do the kind of book on Rabelais that I can give to my son (now fifteen and soon, I hope, to go to college) for purposes of introduction to a writer who has kept sanity alive for all of us through the ages. Modest ambitions are not lacking in this full flood of life and experience.

I said "full flood." The reader who has followed my inner experiences with anything like sympathy will, however, understand why I can now feel that the real period of maturity, and the real period of the work I have always wanted to do, has just begun. Correctly, I put the title of my last chapter in the form of a question.

But you know the answer.

XXI. CAN LIFE BEGIN AGAIN AT 44?

WHEN I was staying with Strong at Collioure in France often I would walk back by myself from Port Vendres—along the high road, chiseled from the side of the mountain range which jutted out over the blue Mediterranean. Not infrequently it would be dusk, when I left Port Vendres; a few electric lamps gleamed in one or two of the outlying houses I passed, and sometimes I might catch the twinkle of lights from a small boat on the darkened and quiet sea below me. Now and then an automobile, its flare flashing around one corner and then its tail-light disappearing around the next, would go by on the winding highway, and even more rarely, a pedestrian. Usually, however, it was a solitary walk, with only the sea and the sharply rising hill on either side of the almost dangerously narrow road. My own footsteps and the faint barking of a dog in one of the distant small houses in the sloping vineyards were oftenest the only sounds I heard.

Though it was beautiful country—intriguing and caressingly warm and romantic—my heart was full of a bitterness that at times touched almost on despair. I was worried about my eyes; I couldn't clearly determine how (or why, it then seemed so pointless) I was going to live; at times, "getting back" to my own country took on the proportions of a feat almost as impossible as my getting to Tibet or Siberia. And even if I did get back "home," who would remember me? Who would want to see me? Boston was no longer home to me; it had not been for years. Perhaps New York—yet I had vague forebodings about that, too, a kind of yearning for what was familiar, yet a dread that in those familiar surroundings there would no longer be anybody I knew. My mother? Probably—but I felt so helpless and so ashamed of feeling helpless; I should have to wait until I was "on my feet." I couldn't bear it, nor did I want her to bear it either—the thought that I was a failure. My son? But he was a young boy of thirteen then to whom I was just a name and a vague memory, if that much. His affections and interests would be elswhere. My brother? He would not want particularly to see me; he never had that I could remember. A girl?—but I had to smile at that, remembering only vague memories of happier days, when one had confidence in oneself, belief in one's attractiveness, certainty of one's talent and of one's ability to get on in the world. I wondered at my former arrogance, my former self-assurance. The delusions of propinquity—the cloak under which we all hide our loneliness—could not be summoned up on that solitary French road. I felt defenseless—even had Togo, the bright little dog, been with me then, it would not have helped much; he was not, after all, my dog. I merely borrowed him: Just as, I reflected with that searing kind of self-punishment from which there is sometimes no escape, I had borrowed almost everything I had ever—and always so fugitively—possessed.

Possessions? I had to smile at that. Why, even the shoes I had on my feet were borrowed from Strong because I had none of my own. Perhaps that was also true of the shirt on my back—I couldn't remember. How many of my own had I brought down with me from Paris? Even in the little things, always and forever this vicarious sort of life—nothing of my own, no dignity, no security, no convictions, no happiness. What had availed the fact that I had at least tried to make my thought honest? Indeed, what did we mean by honesty of thought? Was not that, too, vainglory and pride and delusion? What man—or, indeed, what beast—cared about such a bloodless abstraction, when he was warm in his bed, well fed, with his well-beloved close to him, comforting him and transforming existence from its original emptiness to an eternal triumph of comradeship and love? Why had we been created at all, if this agony of isolation could be our lot? How cheap seemed the agnosticism of youth, and yet how hopeless *now* to try to repudiate its skepticism. I could not say—I tried and tried again—"Our Father, who art in Heaven." That was weakness and a desire to return to the warm protective womb. I knew that—or felt that I knew it, which came to the same thing. I had tasted of the fruit of the tree of knowledge, and now, when so passionately I wanted to sink back into a kind of animal faith, I could not. I could do nothing; thought availed not at all, except to sharpen and intensify the sense of impotence and helplessness and de-personalization. Things—even the rocks and the sea—and myself were in the same blind, senseless category of non-being, of eternal death—made all the more piercing to us by the transient illusion of existence, like the evanescent colors in the spray of a wave against the sunny rocks of Collioure.

Yet if existence is only an illusion, perhaps no reality is stronger than it seems to be; its validity lies in that seeming. For where else could it lie? In an external world, the very awareness of which is necessarily a part of our limitations?

There was no clear answer. I was caught in the old solipsistic net. Nor could I extricate myself from it—that is, so long as the pain of knowing I was aware (or the burden of consciousness, if you wish) could not be assuaged. Primitive peoples, children, and animals identify themselves with the objects of their perception; and what we call their personality is—for them, I mean, and in fact—only a kind of broken segment of the original pattern. What we flatter ourselves is our ego *is*, in reality, but the organization of our little broken segment into something which can set itself off in dramatic contrast to that of which it is merely a minor part, like the reverberation of an original melody. The reverberation is due to the echo; but the melody itself must first exist—for we revolt at the notion of something being created out of nothing. The pitiful collection of atoms, the composite bit of animated lard we call our body—do we not *survey* this rather than identify *ourselves* with it? Naturalistic theory can use as pretty terms, when put to it, as can even a frankly anthropocentric, or anthropomorphic, philosopher—and in trying to escape from the puzzle of the ego we plunge even more deeply into the paradoxical waters of individual and selective response.

And I gave it up—I was content to use the ordinary language of discourse. To be sure, I hate views which are obscurantist, and I hate even more views which are undisciplined and capricious—simply because discipline of this kind is so severe. Also so thankless, in the deepest sense; they are not consoling. But it seemed to me then—in a sort of strange, sudden flash of conviction, perhaps the deepest belief in me—that true dignity in life consists in an acceptance of this dilemma—not, of course, a blind acceptance, but that of the alert, the responsive, and the generous mind, as a man may commit the most odious of crimes, yet rise to a certain measure of heroism, when he comes to be executed. I was learning this small measure of wisdom: That there are many things in one's life a man can no more control than the color of his eyes, and that certain things will as infallibly happen to him as will the sun rise in the East, for all his yearning to have the power to make it, if only for a single day, rise in the West. Yes, that there *is* the prison of circumstance. But that there is also—and without it, we might ourselves be as the rocks and the sea with which your true romanticist wants always to identify himself—the freedom of opinion, which is not an idle and jejune freedom at all, but a flexible and responsive one with all kinds of moral implications. We cannot help dying, perhaps, but we *can* help lying about it—we *can* consciously choose between the dignity of facing facts frankly, or of shrinking from them and calling them by false, pretty names. We may be conscripted for any army and fight with courage, but we do not have to believe that the cause for which we are fighting is *therefore* necessarily just. And like most terrors, most facts—when faced—lose their power of mastery over us. *They* can merely happen; but what attitude we take towards them is a matter of our own choice. We cannot deny them and retain sanity, but we do not have to say that they are all there is to existence any more than we have to say our reflection in a mirror is all there is to our individual body—merely because it is all we can see. Men like simple clear explanations of complicated processes, but children, too, want toys that will "run" and will break them in a rage when they do not. Many men do the same sort of thing, too. Only they call the toys ideals.

Most arguments from origins are as fallacious as trying to define a house in terms of the thought that existed in the mind of the architect before the house was built. Because loneliness is what causes men to become intrigued in things outside themselves, or because animal urgencies lead to attitudes towards the opposite sex, the realities of those things and those attitudes is not impugned. What causes an automobile to move does not invalidate the fact that it does—and because love may arise from and be prompted by appetite is not to destroy love's existence. We do not worry particularly about the sun and air, if we are free to enjoy them; it is when they are denied us that we become conscious of their necessity. Some people are cursed with my kind of temperament—those for whom only when love is taken from them can they be aware it ever existed at all.

And the irony, of course, is that it is precisely the people so cursed—the people who need it most—for whom love always is being lost. It is the tragedy of finally—even if reluctantly—coming to the determination to apologize to a man you have thoughtlessly maligned, only to arrive at his home to discover that an hour before he had been killed in a street accident. Though I am by profession—as far as I have any—a writer, and hence ostensibly somebody skilled to a certain degree in expressing myself, I pay for it almost too dearly. For as a result I am always leaving the overt and immediate statement of a regret (which I may deeply feel) or the acknowledgment of a mistake (of which I may be fully conscious) until such a statement or acknowledgment has lost its meaning for the person concerned. It is like trying to lend a man money after he has starved to death because of the lack of it. Sorrow changes its accent with the passage of time much more quickly than joy, and an apology too long delayed becomes only a further insult. The social curse of the possession of too much self-control is almost as severe as the lack of it—because not merely must you be sure of yourself before you give way to an emotion you have in fact already long felt—you will be so slow in exhibiting a genuine grief that the person for whom that exhibition might earlier have been a comfort will find its tardy formulation only a reminder of something he has already wished to forget.

Sometimes—above all when I think of the awful misery and loneliness of those walks back to Collioure from Port-Vendres—I feel humiliated at any temporary misfortune causing me unhappiness; I feel the same even at any misunderstanding arising with those you would love, if only you were permitted to do so. For in your own country whatever misfortunes happen, or whatever misunderstandings arise, at least they are recognizable and familiar, and they have a homelike emphasis. While happiness shared, says the old proverb, is multiplied, misfortune shared is divided. But abroad, where the background is not the same and where tradition takes subtly different channels, it seems sometimes easy enough to share the happiness (when it exists) but it becomes next to impossible to divide the misfortune; for in sorrow and grief men feel their differences and their isolation—their distinctions of language and custom—much more than they do in the common experience of laughter, of physical pleasure, and of sheer joy. Men are united by misfortune as much as they are separated by it—as many a man does not discover that he is really a patriot until his own country is invaded. And as, partly in a similar manner, I myself discovered that I was an American after all—only when I was brought by misfortune, ill-health, and no work to a realization that all this might or might not be inevitable in America, but that in any event it was unnatural to experience it abroad. When we leave our own country, it should be only for a pleasure trip or a relatively brief voyage of study—otherwise we shall not find even a fraction of what we have left behind. Prosperity and money may give us temporarily the illusion of not caring about being uprooted—but it *is* an illusion, nevertheless. We cannot escape a dim feeling of uneasiness and insecurity, just as we never are really certain how people, basically not like ourselves, will act in the emergencies of life—whatever the civilized veneer. I mean, simply, we are homeless enough in this world under the best of circumstances without going to any special effort to test our capacity to be more so. I think I have the right to say that—I have tried being homeless more than most people. And if one man's testimony counts for anything, I am ready to depose that it simply doesn't work. At least, that it doesn't work very well—that the returns in happiness or in a boost to your pride are pretty slim. If it is only the mirror of your vanity that you want rubbed, there are certainly more expeditious ways of having that done than by trying to find distinction in the mere fact of running away.

Yet if you do—as I did—can you retrieve that mistake? I think so, for when everything is said and done the most you have lost is time, and you have not even lost all of that. All experience, even what seems painfully unnecessary experience, has some disciplinary and some educative value, provided you have a mind and a sensibility at all. And time—up to the last drop of that wine which seems, when we are young, so inexhaustible—has the great virtue of always being new in fact; it is really your own choice and nobody else's whether it shall be new for you.

Thus the title of this chapter is not meant to be merely a rhetorical question; I mean it for a real and vital one. And I think the answer is clearly "Yes"—not, of course, because that title says "44" (which is merely accidentally the age at which I am) any more than if it said "54" (and when that is my age, my answer will be the same), but because it is a fact. Life is always re-beginning in each moment of our experience; it is this desperate clinging to past experiences (especially, I believe, sensuous experiences) as if we could carry them around with us and never feel them as a burden but only as the delights they originally were—it is this foolish and wilful act, prompted, we can only suppose, by fear of losing what we have and by a sense of insecurity about the future, which destroys and withers life as locusts destroy crops. It is this which is the ultimate fear and the ultimate resignation.

If a man is courageous and logical, I think he will understand this paradox—that death can hardly be an experience until we embrace it; and that when we embrace it, we shall have no experience thereof. It is idle folly to be fearful of it before it arrives, but it shows a lack of sense and of proportion about life not to realize that it is even worse folly not to envisage it as inevitable. But the most inevitable things of our experience, like growing up and becoming disillusioned, and holding ideals or not holding them after bitter experiences, have a way of taking care of themselves, when they arrive, and of settling their own problems. Death is not to be feared—lingering pain, never-ending impotence, perpetual disillusion: Those are the things to be feared because they make of our life, even though it be short, something less than our instinctive demand and reward—reward, that is, for the process of living at all.

But whatever our demand—whatever our final reward or our final punishment—there can be no substitute for the feeling of release and serenity that comes to any man when he makes an honest attempt to see things as they are rather than as he would like them to be. Life may not have many satisfactions and the pessimist may be right, but it does give us the opportunity, even if brief, to experience the profound peace of shunning illusion, scorning sham, and taking to our hearts and our minds the experiences which, whether they be painful or joyous, could not be understood or felt whenever we cheated, or pretended, or lied. For even what in moments of our weakness we think of as this highly desirable life, would in fact become intolerable, if there were not death to crown it—or at least to make an interlude. That it should go on forever, as we know it even in its best moments, would not satisfy the heart of man—and it is perhaps in that dissatisfaction in the heart of man, a dissatisfaction so deep that on occasion even the ordinary man is not unwilling to forego life itself for a better idea of living,—it is perhaps here that we have the only valid intimations of immortality and never-ending existence.

THE END